I0606359

To the Ends of the Earth

A Grand Tour for the 21st Century

Layout and Typesetting
Oliver Atwood, Philadelphia
Richard Weller, Philadelphia

Cover Design
Bureau Est, Leipzig
Lisa Petersen & Alexandra Vögtle

Illustrations
Oliver Atwood, Philadelphia
© Richard Weller, Philadelphia

Project Management
Henriette Mueller-Stahl, Berlin

Copy Editing
Tatum L. Hands, Philadelphia

Production
Anja Haering, Berlin

Lithography
Repromayer GmbH, Reutlingen

Paper
Fly 06, 115 g/m²

Printing
Beltz Grafische Betriebe, Bad Langensalza

Library of Congress Control Number: 2023937012

Bibliographic information published by the German National Library.
The German National Library lists this publication in the Deutsche Nationalbibliografie; detailed bibliographic data are available at http://dnb.dnb.de.

ISBN 978-3-0356-2793-0
e-ISBN (PDF) 978-3-0356-2794-7

Im Westfeld 8
4055 Basel
Switzerland

9 8 7 6 5 4 3 2 1 www.birkhauser.com

To the Ends of the Earth

A Grand Tour for the 21st Century

Richard Weller

Birkhäuser
Basel

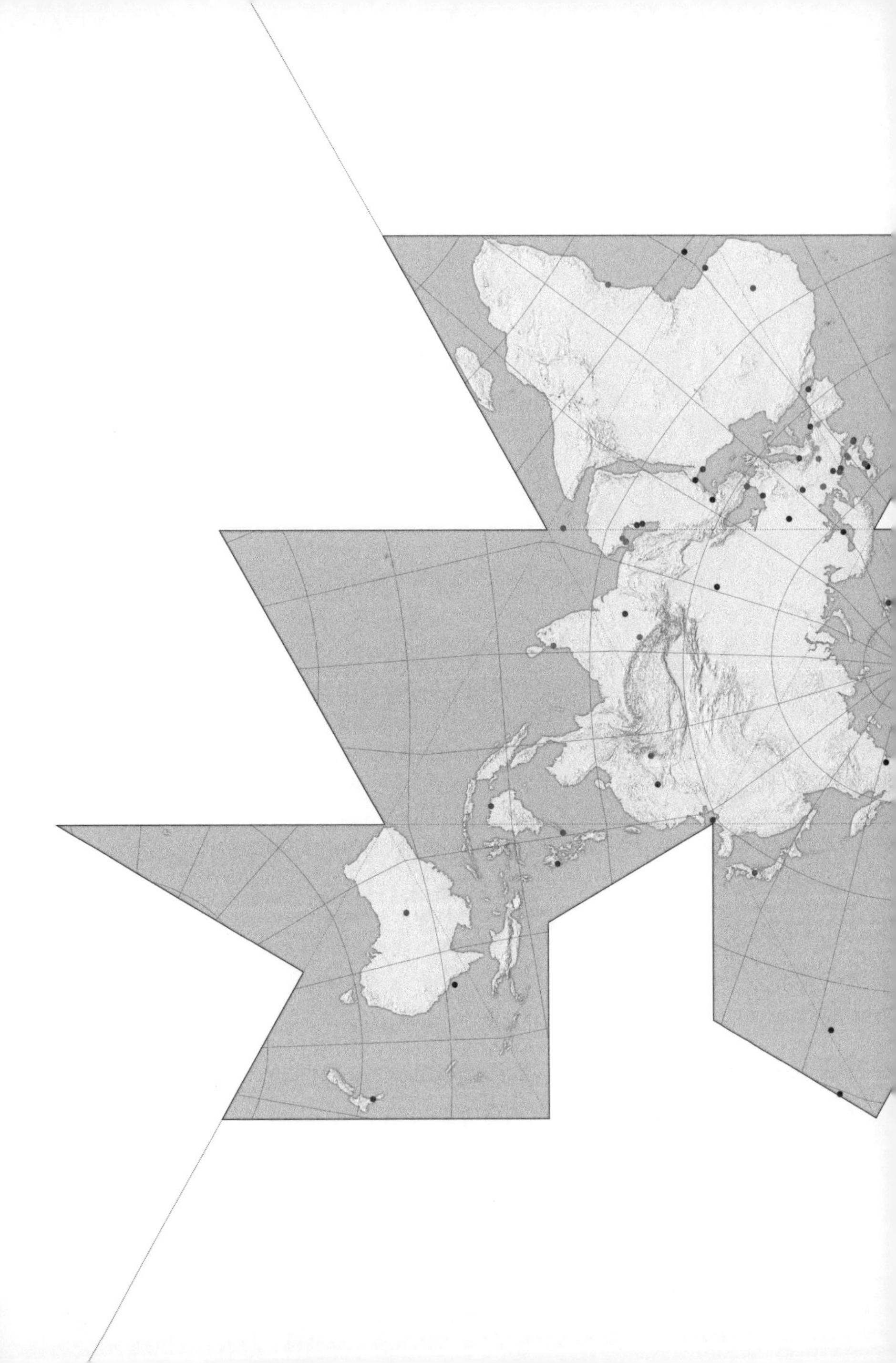

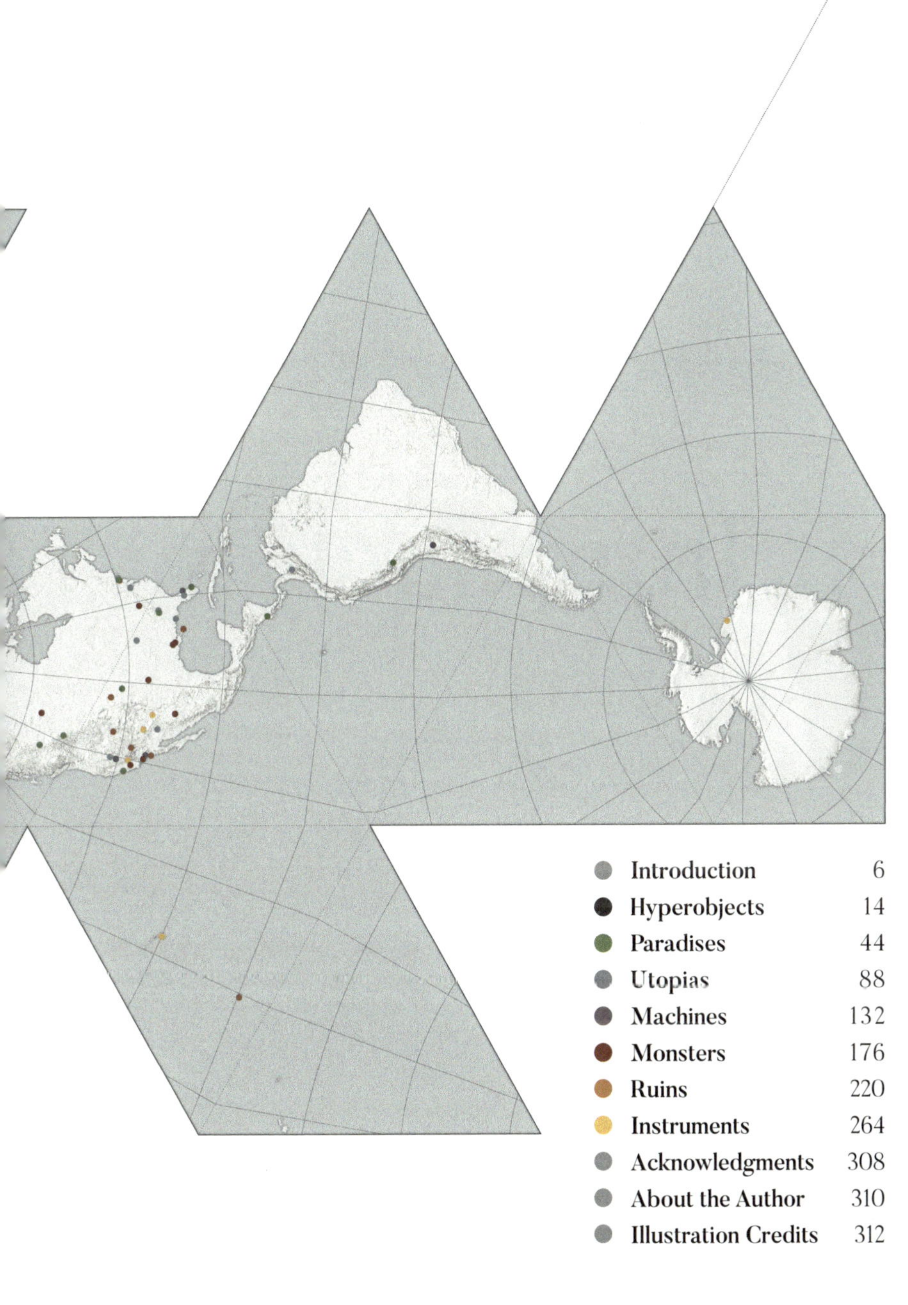

Introduction

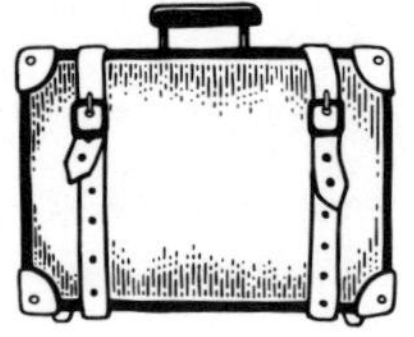

In the 17th and 18th centuries it was considered a rite of passage and an educational necessity for northern European and British gentry to travel south to Italy and Greece to study firsthand the art, architecture, and landscapes of classical antiquity and the Renaissance. This was called the Grand Tour and it could last for months, if not years. While it was intended to instill virtue and connoisseurship in the hearts and minds of young aristocrats, it could also, of course, lead them astray. Indeed, this was part of the tour's allure, as it is in one way or another for every tourist seeking adventure to this day.

While the Grand Tourists were fossicking about in the Roman Forum, buying art in Florence, or peering into the volcanic abyss of Mount Vesuvius, more practical men back home were cutting open coal seams and firing up the new-fangled machinery of the Industrial Revolution. Little did they know they were also igniting the insidious process of what we now know to be global warming: the central dilemma of the so-called Anthropocene, a new geological epoch defined by the fact that human activity has reached such a scale that it is now altering the fundamental workings of the planet.

So where in this new world of the Anthropocene should today's student of culture travel for an education? If not the Pantheon and the Parthenon, which places are most pertinent to the human condition today? This book is a field guide offering an answer to this question, and it comes with two caveats—the first is temporal and the second is spatial. With all of history at our doorstep, the choice of destinations is vast, but for the purposes of being as contemporaneously relevant as possible, this grand tour is restricted to places and things created in the 20th and 21st centuries. Second, for a destination to qualify for inclusion in the tour it had to be considered relevant to the tour's main purpose of elucidating and questioning what the Anthropocene is, and what we, the *anthropos*, have now become. Put simply, the premise of this book is that by undertaking the tour you should learn something about both the world and yourself.

In order to do that, this grand tour is not about escaping reality, it is about confronting it. Accordingly, whereas the destinations the Grand Tourists sought out were predominantly couched in terms of consolidating and mythologizing their Eurocentric pedigrees, this tour's destinations are necessarily somewhat less ennobling. Indeed, many of the sites we will visit could be taken as indictments of modernity and the human exceptionalism that underpins it. To be clear, this is not a field guide to great monuments of great empires, great men, or great deeds—if anything, it is a collection of anti-monuments that become meaningful as metaphors for, and measures of, contemporary culture.

In this sense the greatness of contemporary 'civilization'—if one can still put it that way—is not that it has so thoroughly colonized and transformed the world, but that it can now take responsibility for the consequences of its own historical process. Per Mary Shelley's Frankenstein, we must confront and take responsibility for our monsters.

There is a fine line, however, between wanting to confront the truth in this way and overindulging in the aesthetics of ruination, and so this field guide attempts to walk a line between the two. While the majority of this tour's destinations are certainly not as picturesque as those of the original Grand Tour, they do invoke aspects of the original's search for something called the sublime. As developed by German philosopher Immanuel Kant and English political theorist Edmund Burke in the 18th century, to experience the sublime is to feel an acute sense of being overawed by nature, a combination of terror on the one hand and attraction on the other. As well as visiting art galleries and ruins, to feel the sublime the Grand Tourists would visit specific landscapes that were reputed to inspire it. The difference between the sublime then and now, however, is that whereas for the Grand Tourists nature was something God-given, awesome, and seemingly inviolable, for us post-moderns it is something polluted and irrevocably altered by technology. Today's scholars refer to this as 'the technological sublime' and, as we will see, it is arguably even more frightening than its natural precursor.

Whereas going weak at the knees as you teetered over the edge of Mount Vesuvius was authentic proof that the sublime was within reach, since our experience of our world is now so technologically mediated it leaves us somewhat uncertain of our feelings. Rather than reject these feelings as inauthentic, the grand tour set out in these pages asks today's tourist to stay a while with them, for it is in this uncanniness that we might get closer to what it means to be human today. On a more practical level, traveling in mind instead of body not only has the advantage of avoiding all the inconveniences and indignities that mass travel now entails, it also has the added benefit of lowering your carbon footprint!

Turning the pages at your leisure, dipping in and out, you can take this tour any way you wish. But to give it some logic and legibility, the destinations have been organized into a taxonomy of seven chapters: Hyperobjects, Paradises, Utopias, Machines, Monsters, Ruins, and Instruments. Each is briefly explained below and then fleshed out a little further in each respective chapter introduction.

In preparation for traveling to all, or any of the destinations it is recommended that the introductory chapter: **Hyperobjects**, be first taken into consideration. A term coined by contemporary ecological philosopher Timothy Morton, hyperobjects are entities that powerfully shape both the cultural and material nature of things, but that can't so easily be grasped as discrete things unto themselves—at least not in their totality.

Think of things like climate change or the internet: on the one hand they are very real things, but their extension through space and time and their cultural and material complexity makes them impossible to apprehend in the same way as one can, say, a cup or a rock. By way of introduction, the hyperobjects serve to provide an overarching context for the paradises, utopias, machines, monsters, ruins, and instruments to follow.

So, let's begin with **Paradises**. These are contemporary landscapes, which in one way or another manifest archetypal themes of transgression, hubris, and loss. These are places that raise theological, ecological, and ethical questions concerning humanity's role in relation to both the planet and all the other forms of life with which we share it.

Whereas the crucible of paradise is of course the garden, for the following chapter—**Utopias**—the key frame of reference is the city. Unlike paradise, which is God given and unchanging, utopias are, by definition, attempts at creating ideal societies through human ingenuity, on human terms. As such, utopias almost invariably go wrong and become dystopias. In addition to visiting some prominent examples of this tendency, we also visit other utopian derivatives, such as cornucopia and ecotopia.

The **Machines** chapter focuses on utopia's engine room, places where the application of technology to the problem of work is concentrated with particular intensity.

Generally, the machines we encounter are not freestanding mechanical objects as their name implies—they are landscapes that have, for better or worse, been turned into forms of infrastructure in a Herculean effort to extract and distribute resources. These are the working landscapes of modernity and through their disfigurations of the land, they often create monstrosities.

The **Monsters** tend, then, to be places where humans and their machines have created, and continue to create, horrific socio-ecological consequences. And yet, in some cases these badlands are not simply repugnant. Like the character of the monster in literature and cinema, that which is on one level aberrant and abhorrent can also, upon reflection, beguile us with its own strange form of beauty. Though not always easy to find, there are glimmers of redemption in the monstrous.

Over time, irrespective of whether they are monstrous or beautiful, all things become **Ruins**. Indeed, it was primarily the ruins of classical antiquity that inspired the romance of the original Grand Tour in the first place. Some ruins we encounter on this new tour are architectural, but, reflecting our current cultural condition, many are environmental, for it is in this new manifestation of ruination that we find the most confronting images of the Anthropocene. If there is to be hope for some kind of reconciliation between humans and their environment, then inspiration for it will likely grow out of these types of places and our efforts at ecological restoration will be measured against them.

We conclude the tour with a set of **Instruments.** The instruments we are primarily concerned with are those that measure environmental change—instruments that produce knowledge about how the material world works, how our bodies work, and how the planet is changing due to human activity. These are the tools with which we, the *anthropos*, will better understand our contemporary circumstance and determine our future.

And it is to that end that I now wish you *bon voyage*!

Richard J. Weller

October 2023

Hyperobjects

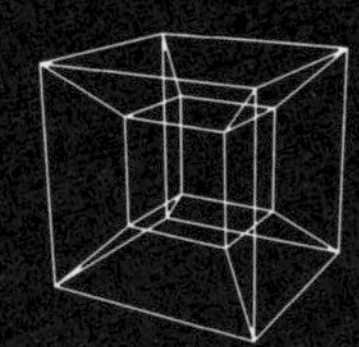

The term 'hyperobjects' was coined by ecological philosopher Timothy Morton. Using the example of a polystyrene cup, Morton explained that the hyperobject version of the cup is all the polystyrene in the world. While you can hold a single cup in your hand, you cannot hold all the polystyrene in the world. Indeed, we can barely imagine it. Morton's point is that, despite its difficulty, we must try to think of objects *and* their hyperobjects, because to do so approximates a more ecological way of understanding the world. And if, as is routinely reported, we are amid an ecological crisis, then it follows that this way of thinking should, in theory, be helpful to our predicament.

As well as thinking spatially—linking the single cup in your hand with all the polystyrene on earth—the hyperobject also asks us to think of things temporally; that is, to take the cup and run it both backward and forward in time. Among other things, running it backward considers the industrial processes necessary to the cup's creation, while running it forward encompasses its use, disposal, and eventual breakdown in the environment. In this way the hyperobject concerns all the interactions with other things and other places that an object has as it moves through time. Thinking this way leads to a greater appreciation of the true scale and nature of the object's life cycle, which in turn heightens our awareness of ecological relationships and opens the possibility of forming more ethical relationships with the world beyond just those things in our immediate grasp.

In addition to objects like cups, which become hyperobjects through their multiplication in space and dissolution through time, some things—such as, say, the universe—automatically qualify as hyperobjects because of their sheer complexity and scale. Even though they are named as if they are simple objects, this class of hyperobject can't be reduced to the sort of comprehensible form that most objects can. Take climate change, for example—while it has a relatively simple name, it is an infinitely complex and amorphous phenomenon that cannot be reduced to a single object. A key characteristic of this class of hyperobjects is the way they shape-shift between popular culture and highly specialized discourses, moving in and out of politics, science, and philosophy to profoundly influence the way we perceive the world and our role within it. These hyperobjects have tremendous power to attract different values and divide societies in terms of their various meanings.

It is this type of hyperobject that is presented in this first chapter to provide an overarching set of contexts for all the destinations we visit on the tour in the subsequent chapters. They can be used as lenses through which to interpret the destinations, and vice versa. Either way, if the purpose of travel is to broaden the mind, then the hyperobjects gathered here should help set the scene.

The Universe

Because we can only perceive things in four dimensions (objects in time), when physicists tell us that the universe began 13.8 billion years ago and has been expanding ever since, we tend to imagine something like a swelling balloon. But the universe—the hyperobject *par excellence*—is probably nothing like a simple three-dimensional object in space. Indeed, almost all of its fundamental characteristics, insofar as we know them, defy representation. First, something from nothing is impossible. Second, it is not expanding into empty space, it is expanding into more of the nothing from whence it came! Third, it is thought to have at least ten dimensions, most of which we cannot perceive. And finally, just to complicate matters, quantum physics suggests there isn't just one universe, there could well be a gazillion of them.

There are other versions. For example, in many indigenous cultures the universe was created by spirit beings who live on in the natural world. In the Abrahamic religions, a single entity, God (Yahweh) created the whole thing in six days. While in Greek mythology, cosmos (order) emerged from chaos in the form of Ouranos (sky) and Gaia (earth). By the 6th century BCE, however, the Greeks started to question their capricious gods and conceive of the universe as a phenomenon that could be mathematically decoded, geometrically represented, and materially explained. We now call this science.

Aristotle imagined a cosmos in which the planets move in perfect concentric circles around a stationary earth at its center. Later this translated into Christianity and held firm in the Western imagination until Nicolaus Copernicus (1473–1543) declared, correctly, that the sun, not the earth, is the true center. Galileo Galilei (1564–1642) then found evidence of a universe with multiple centers and Johannes Kepler (1571–1630) worked out that the planets move elliptically, not in perfect circles as the Greeks had believed.

But it is Isaac Newton (1642–1727) who really opened up the *horror vaccui* of modern cosmology by describing space and time as infinite, albeit mechanistically lawful. Newton's model worked very well until the 20th century when, in the mind of Albert Einstein the universe became a blob of silly putty. Einstein found that the energy of a thing equals its mass multiplied by the speed of light squared ($E=mc^2$), but struggled to apply this at the subatomic level, which quantum physics now accepts as fundamentally unpredictable. The number on the opposite page is the split second of time after the big bang—as far back as our scientific understanding of the universe reliably goes.

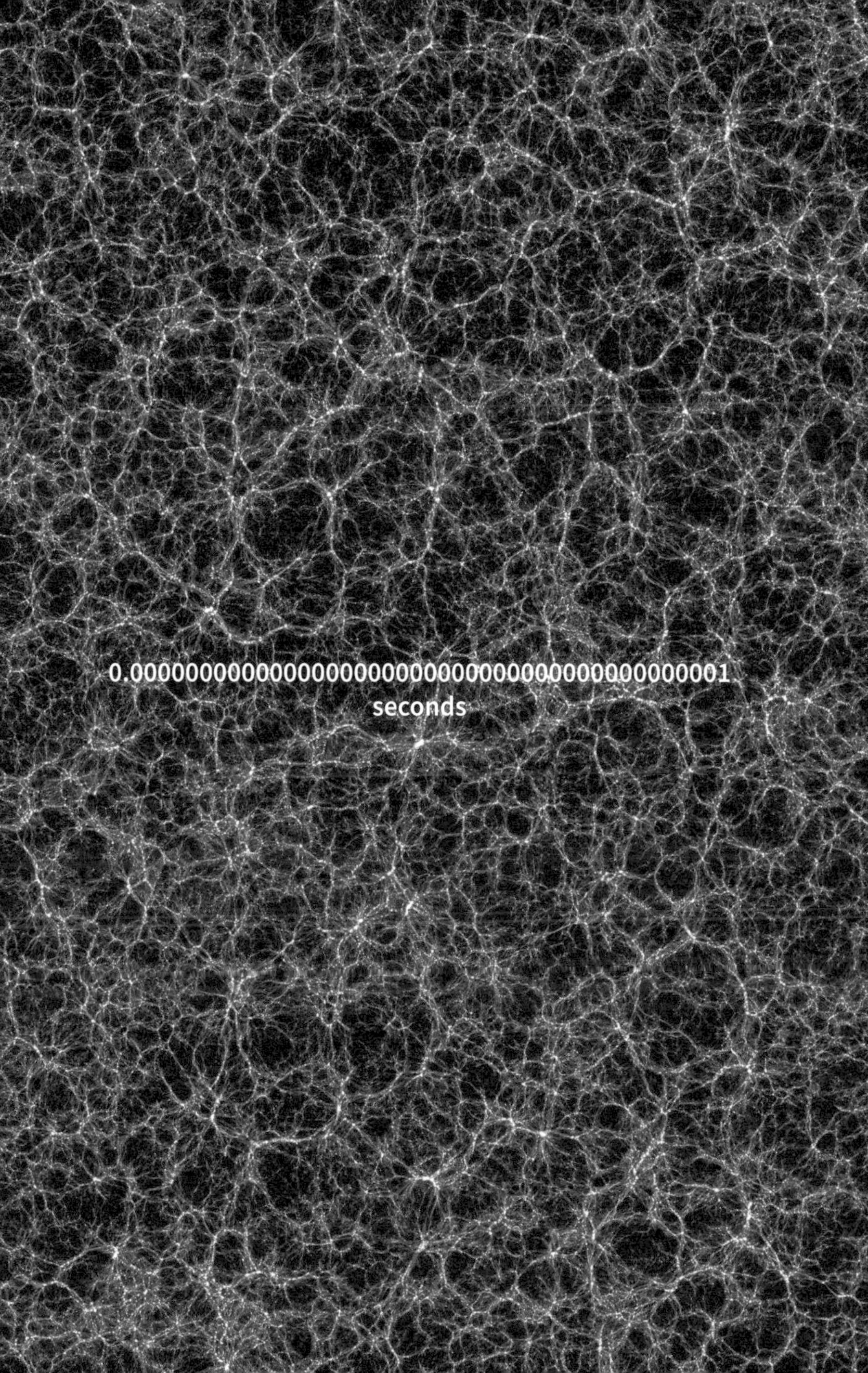

0.0000000000000000000000000000000000000000001
seconds

Evolution

Until the 19th century it was commonly thought that life on earth was a form of divine creation. God personally designed and placed each species in an immutable hierarchy with humanity, made in his image, on the top. This providential Ponzi scheme began its fall from grace in 1830 when geologist Charles Lyell speculated, correctly, that the earth was much older than scripture suggested. Echoing the Reverend Thomas Malthus, Lyell also concluded that at its core, life is a "struggle for existence." These two maxims—a geological timeframe and competition for limited resources—provided the naturalist Charles Darwin (1809–1882) with both the scope and the source that his incipient theory of evolution needed.

Darwin reached three fundamental principles of life: first; organisms vary randomly within a species; second, more offspring are produced than can ever survive; and third, over time, variations best suited to the environment are reproduced and others are eliminated. Setting aside the question of life's original source, taken together these principles mean that life self-generates over time without any attendant 'designer.' They also infer that 'man' was not miraculously made on day six, but instead descended serendipitously from the process of evolution itself. For his part, Darwin avoided the question of life's meaning, writing only that there is grandeur in the evolutionary scheme of things. Translated into popular culture as the mean idea of survival of the fittest, Darwin's theory of evolution has been variously appropriated to speciously justify sexism, racism, nationalism, and capitalism. The ongoing study of life reveals, however, that in addition to being selfish and competitive, life is also cooperative and, in many cases, altruistically so. Whether the evolution of life is as much a story of symbiosis as it is one of mortal combat, and the degree to which such sweeping aspersions can be used as models for culture, is moot.

Though we may well be hairless apes, what has been most preciously guarded as the unique, crowning glory of humanity is our level of consciousness as manifested in and accelerated through the collective intelligence of culture. Today, however, it is hard to think of this level of intelligence as ennobling when it is also the hallmark of a species actively perpetuating the sixth extinction and serving as nature's executioner. Contrary to this, new forms of consciousness are emerging that seek greater empathy with *all* species as different to, but no less than, human. This is reinforced by the new tree of life diagram (opposite) by evolutionary biologist David Hillis, showing humans no longer on top of the tree, but just one of many branches.

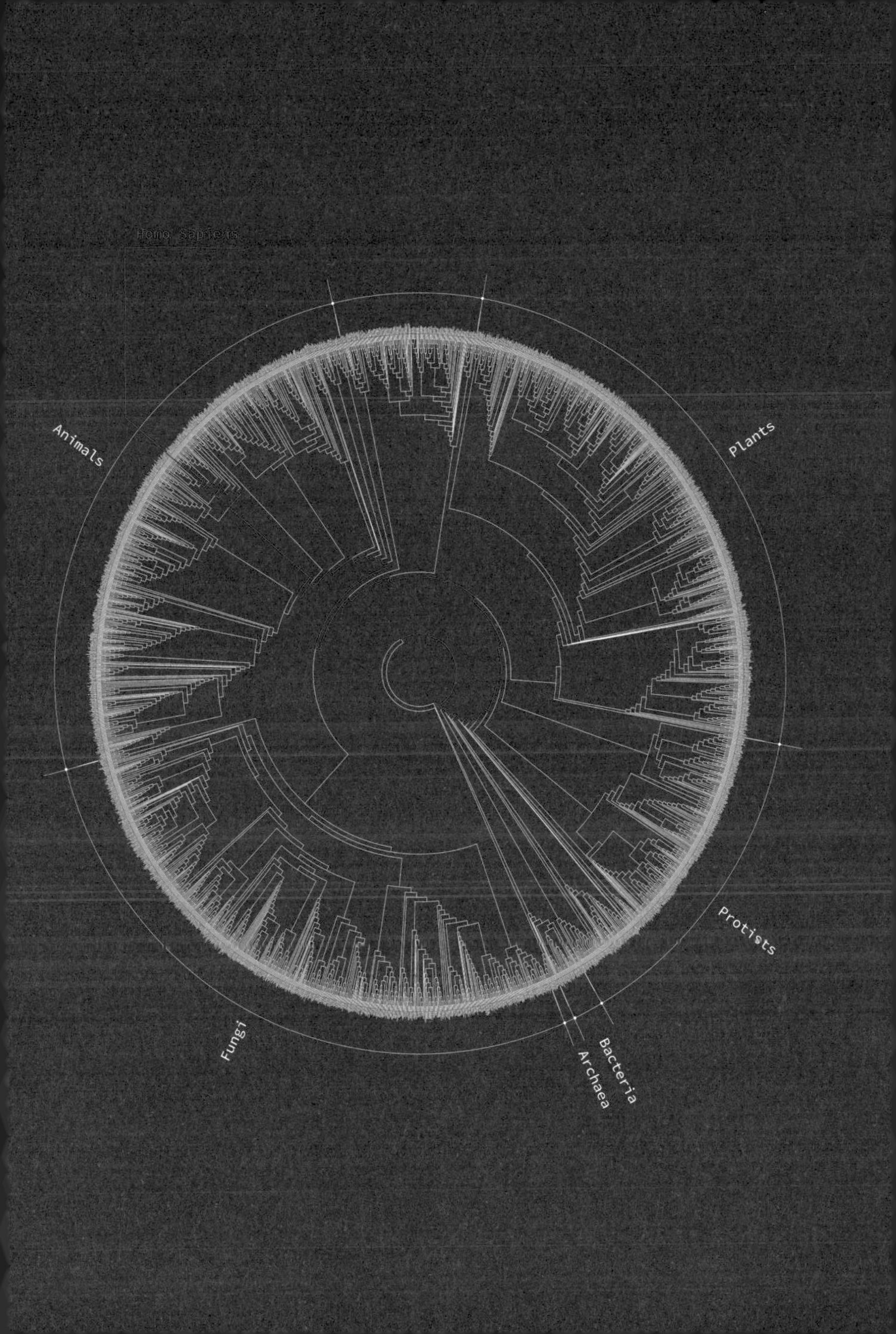

Homo Sapiens
Animals
Plants
Protists
Bacteria
Archaea
Fungi

The Critical Zone

The critical zone sounds like an expression that would come from the arts, but it is a term coined by earth system scientists and pertains to the thin planetary bandwidth in which all life exists. The study of the critical zone—from lava below to ozone above—seeks to build an integrated model of how the earth system works as a whole, not just as a collection of mechanistic parts. In other words, the critical zone is about how the biosphere (life on earth) is produced by and in turn produces the lithosphere (rock and soil), the hydrosphere (water), and the atmosphere (air). This is an ecological approach to studying the world, one with its own history and its own heroes including, but not limited to, Alexander von Humboldt in the 19th century, Vladimir Vernadsky, James Lovelock, and Lynn Margulis in the 20th century, and Paul Crutzen and Jan Zalasiewicz in the 21st century. It should also be acknowledged that many indigenous people have long understood the earth in this integrated manner.

Today, the scientific project of understanding the critical zone as an integrated system is in part monitored through an orchestrated planetary network of 46 so-called Critical Zone Observatories. These are field stations where customized sensors collect data in relation to specific research questions and where interdisciplinary teams of scientists come together and share knowledge to piece together the puzzle of how life self-regulates. Crucially, in addition to studying how its four natural spheres work together, the conception of the critical zone includes studying how the actions of humans—the technosphere—are also now involved in the workings of the earth system. In this schema, humans are not situated as outside nature or merely as (negative) disturbances to it, but as active ecological agents, just as trees, water, and microorganisms are.

The modern history of the critical zone is dominated by the fact that (some) humans have violently colonized and exploited its land and water, not so as to honor its awesome beauty and respectfully find their ecological niche within it, but to plunder its riches, oppress its indigenous people, and vaingloriously try to transcend its earthly limitations. Because this has now culminated in the calamity of climate change, we find that the critical zone is not only a project of scientific analysis, but also a powerful metaphor for what French philosopher Bruno Latour speaks of as a return to earth—not a return to a pristine, maternal nature, but to the emergent, novel ecology of the Anthropocene.

The Body

Born prematurely with big heads, weak limbs, and fuzzy perception, we cling desperately to our mothers like the hapless little monkeys we are. The long duration of the bond between child and parents makes the human an exceptionally cultured and socially dependent animal. Through learned behaviors and language, the child's identity is shaped by the mother, the family, the tribe, the village, and eventually larger more abstract entities such as the city, the nation, and ultimately certain constructs of 'the world.' As one graduates through these expanding envelopes of identity, each individual has to constantly navigate the intimate reciprocity between the environment outside their skins, and what French philosopher Rene Descartes referred to as "the thinking thing" within.

For animists, individual identity is largely constructed through connections with the world of other living creatures outside the body, whereas in the course of Western philosophy and theology it is constructed through forms of clear differentiation between inner and outer realms. For the ancient Greeks the idea of the soul (psyche) permeated both the body and the world at large, but over time this once ubiquitous spirit retreated exclusively into the human mind where it is secreted away as a ghost in the machine. In most religious conceptions, the body's purpose is then reduced to the mechanistic job of carrying the ghost (spirit) through this life on its ultimate quest for reunification with the Creator in a heavenly realm unencumbered by flesh.

No matter what otherworldly fantasies we might conjure, our bodies are deeply of the earth. They are ecologies, not machines or ghosts. The human brain itself is a matryoshka doll of other species, and the rest is a maze of microbes interacting with trillions of cells: each cell featuring a DNA archive reaching back to the very origins of life. In the 21st century the human body is entering a new post-human evolutionary phase where technology can splice parts of humans, animals, and machines into new assemblages and rewrite genetic codes that took billions of years to compose. Not only is the internal nature of the human body radically changing, but so too, through the infrastructure of the internet, its neurology is expanding such that it is not fanciful to think that the whole planet is now the thinking thing and our human bodies its microbes.

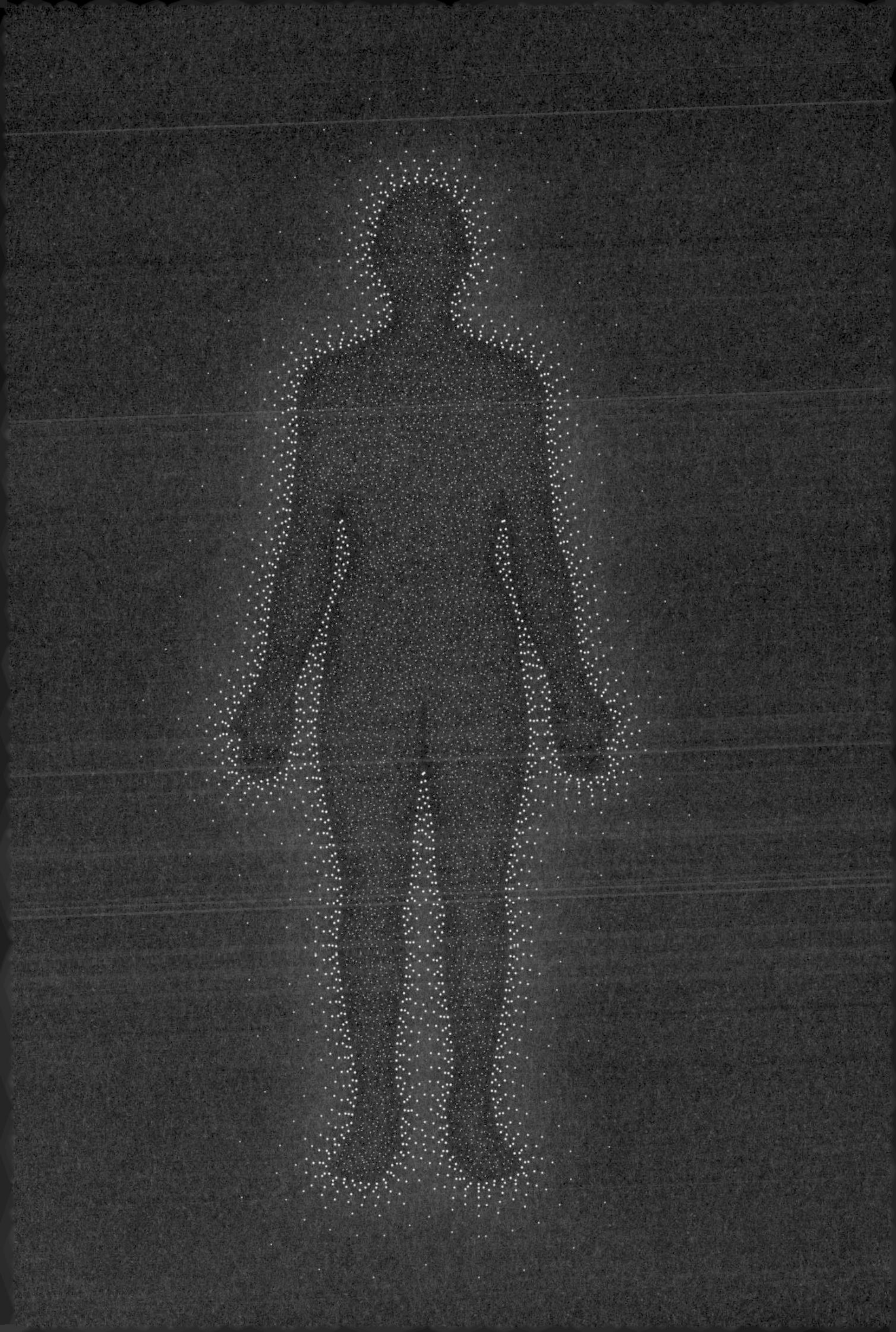

The City

With its roots in the ideals of the Greek polis and Roman *civitas*, veneration of the city has historically been synonymous with Western civilization as if it were a progression from simpler forms of social organization to something superior. This self-serving teleology is questionable in three related ways: first, urbanization is not a Western achievement—it is an anthropological phenomenon that emerged independently more or less simultaneously in the fertile river deltas of the Nile, the Tigris, the Euphrates, the Indus, and the Huang He (Yellow River), as well as in numerous agriculturally viable parts of the Americas. Second, unlike nomads who travel light and can adjust accordingly, settled peoples find themselves rooted in a vicious cycle of exhausting the very land that made permanent settlement viable in the first place. And third, it cannot be said that peoples who didn't urbanize are in some way inferior—they simply had no material or existential need to settle and build armies and monuments to oppress an agrarian and industrial underclass on which the urban elite have always depended.

It is estimated that the first big cities in Mesopotamia had around 50,000 inhabitants; Rome then peaked at a million and now megacities of more than ten million citizens are commonplace. The world's cities now contain over 3.5 billion people—a figure likely to double as global population approaches ten or more billion sometime this century. As implied in the image opposite, the city is no longer just a local or regional entity, it is a planetary phenomenon.

Despite the fact that citizens of the city typically have larger ecological footprints than nomads or peasants, urban living does tend to have the net environmental benefit of reducing rates of childbirth. Extrapolating from this, it is possible to project a global urban future with a stable or even decreasing population, which at some point in the future could alleviate pressure on the ecosystem. The question for the planetary city will be, as ever, whether it can feed and fuel itself within the limitations of the land's capacity while maintaining peaceful and productive geopolitical relationships.

In addition to its socioeconomic and ecological challenges, the more subtle question for the city of the future is how it will edify the human spirit. How will the city impress upon its citizenry that a sense of civic virtue is something still worth working for? This is a matter of how cities are designed and governed—a question of how they can enshrine democracy, opportunity, and well-being without becoming either authoritarian utopias or anarchic dystopias.

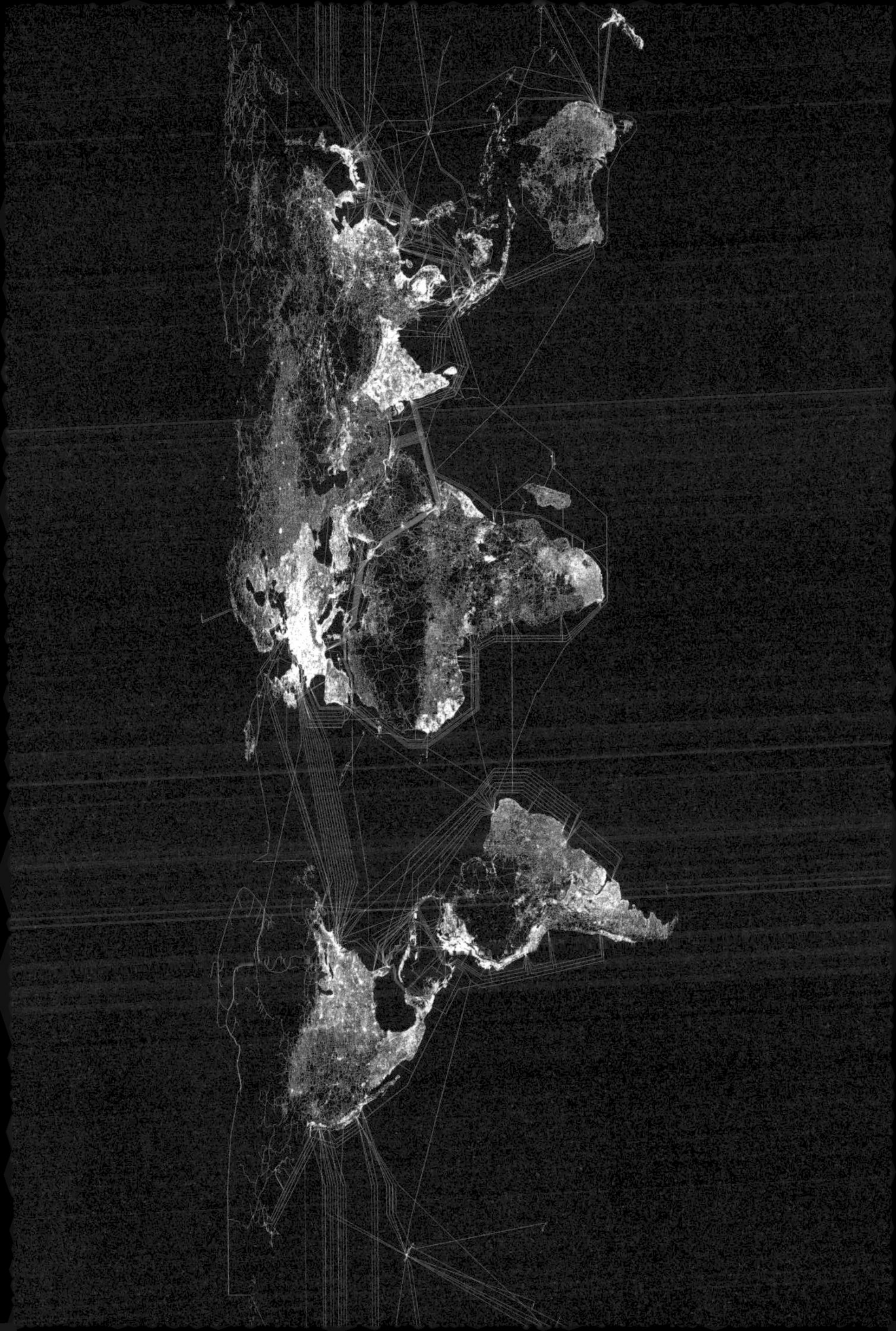

The Environment

The environment refers to the physical context in which an organism exists and with which it interacts. The environment creates the conditions of natural selection, shaping the evolution of all living things over time. Reciprocally, organisms also shape their environments.

The idea of the environment was popularized in the late 20th century by the global conservation movement as something humans have exploited and damaged and something now requiring preservation and restoration. Accordingly, an environmentalist is someone locked in a Manichean struggle against industries, which have a reputation for seeing the environment as only a resource to exploit or a place to dump waste. The environmental movement as such has its roots in the counterculture of the 1960s and consciousness of its plight is traced to, among others, the writings of American marine biologist Rachel Carson.

The environment is now both an economic and aesthetic construct. Economically, it provides societies with so-called 'ecosystem services' such as food, air, water, and raw materials, ostensibly in perpetuity and for free. Environmental scientists and activists now argue, however, that none of this is free, and that its value can be quantified to draw attention to the real cost of its despoliation.

Aesthetically, the environment is associated with imagery of wilderness and national parks and venerated as something of not just biological value but also immense spiritual value. This is problematic for established religions, not only because orthodox scripture has little to say on the matter, but also because it implicitly threatens the privileged position of the human in the hierarchical scheme of things that montheistic religions enshrine. There are, however, significant signs of late that the valuation of the environment in both economic and theological terms is changing. President Xi of China, for example, has said China must become an "ecological civilization" and the aptly named Pope Francis has passionately argued that we must care for the environment as the expression of God's munificence. And for its part, the chameleon of capitalism will happily turn a shade of green and champion the environment, so long as it returns a profit.

Ecological Footprint

A concept credited to Mathis Wackernagel and William Rees of the University of British Columbia, ecological footprinting is a total calculation of all the resources (food, energy, water, materials, and waste) required to sustain an individual. It can also be applied to a city, a nation, or indeed the entire human race. While your spatial footprint is, say, the size of your apartment, your ecological footprint includes all the so-called 'ghost acres' from which you derive all the resources necessary to maintaining your standard of living. So, while your apartment may be only 200 square meters, if you are an average American your ecological footprint is around 8.2 hectares (think 16 football fields). On the other hand, if you are an average Eritrean, then your ecological footprint is only 0.5 hectares or 1 football field. While it is not technically possible for ecological footprint calculations to be absolutely correct, they do purport to provide a reasonable approximation. What matters is not the numbers themselves but the way they are used to support powerful polemics about how we live, or, rather, how we should live.

For example, you can extrapolate that if the entire global population lived as Americans now do, we would need approximately four earths to sustain everyone. Or you can run the numbers in reverse and divide the ecological capacity of the earth by global population to show that, all things being equal, everyone should have an ecological footprint of around 2 hectares. Whichever way one looks at it, the inference is that as a matter of global environmental equity the average American should consume about a quarter of what they currently consume, whereas the Eritrean is entitled to consume about four times more. Put another way, one can argue that it is only because the Eritrean is consuming so little that the American can consume so much.

Footprinting data can also be used to compare a nation's global ecological footprint with the biological capacity of its actual land mass. For example, in the case of the island of Singapore, its 5.6 million people are living at a level of resource consumption that is around 80 times that which the island can by itself provide, whereas the people of the Solomon Islands live well within the biological capacity of theirs. Ecological footprinting implies, then, that a truly sustainable nation should live either within the limits of what its own territory can provide, or within its relative proportion of what one earth can provide.

Carbon

Cropland

Forest

Livestock

Urban

United States of America

8.2 Global Hectares (gHa)

Eritrea

0.5 Global Hectares (gHa)

100 m

Climate Change

As a paleontological and cultural phenomenon, climate change was known in the 1960s but did not gain popular currency until 1979 when a US National Academy of Sciences committee forecasted temperature rise, and in 1988 when the United Nations Intergovernmental Panel on Climate Change (IPCC) was formed. Since its inception the IPCC's research reports, resulting from the volunteer work of thousands of scientists, have become increasingly shrill in their warnings that human-induced climate change is real, and its consequences will be devastating.

Climate change portends that our exploitation of the earth's resources has now created a biophysical catch-22 that could in fact lead to our demise and much else with it. It is little wonder then that the expression 'existential crisis' increasingly prefaces the otherwise relatively innocuous term 'climate change.' That this crisis has been met by panic, denial, misinformation, blame, and geopolitical wrangling over liability, only adds to the sense that this is now modern civilization's slow-motion crash landing. If anything beneficial is to come from the advent of climate change it is that it redefines our interpretation of and relationship to nature. Nature can no longer be naively thought of as a mere resource we can exploit without consequence. We can also no longer venerate nature as something inviolable. Nature in the era of human-induced climate change is not some endlessly fecund thing 'out there,' it is now what we make it.

What we make of a climate changed world this century will slide along a scale that has 'adaptation' at one end and 'mitigation' at the other. Adaptation means learning to live (and die) with the consequences: rising seas, wilder weather, shifting biomes, species extinction, mass migration, and related sociopolitical tensions. In extremis, adaptation could mean attempting to geoengineer the earth's climate by creating a stratospheric veil or messing with the chemistry of the oceans. Mitigation on the other hand means shutting down fossil fuels as the root cause of the problem and transitioning to clean, renewable energy, asap. The positive version of climate change is that through this crisis humanity will reorganize its settlement patterns, redesign its infrastructure, reform agribusiness, rewrite its theologies, revalue its economy, restore ecosystems, and generally learn its lesson.

In news just in, humans pumped 36 billion tons of carbon into the atmosphere in 2021, more than in any previous year in history and many countries plan to increase, not decrease fossil fuel extraction out to 2030. On the upside, countries responsible for most of the world's emissions have made net-zero emissions pledges.

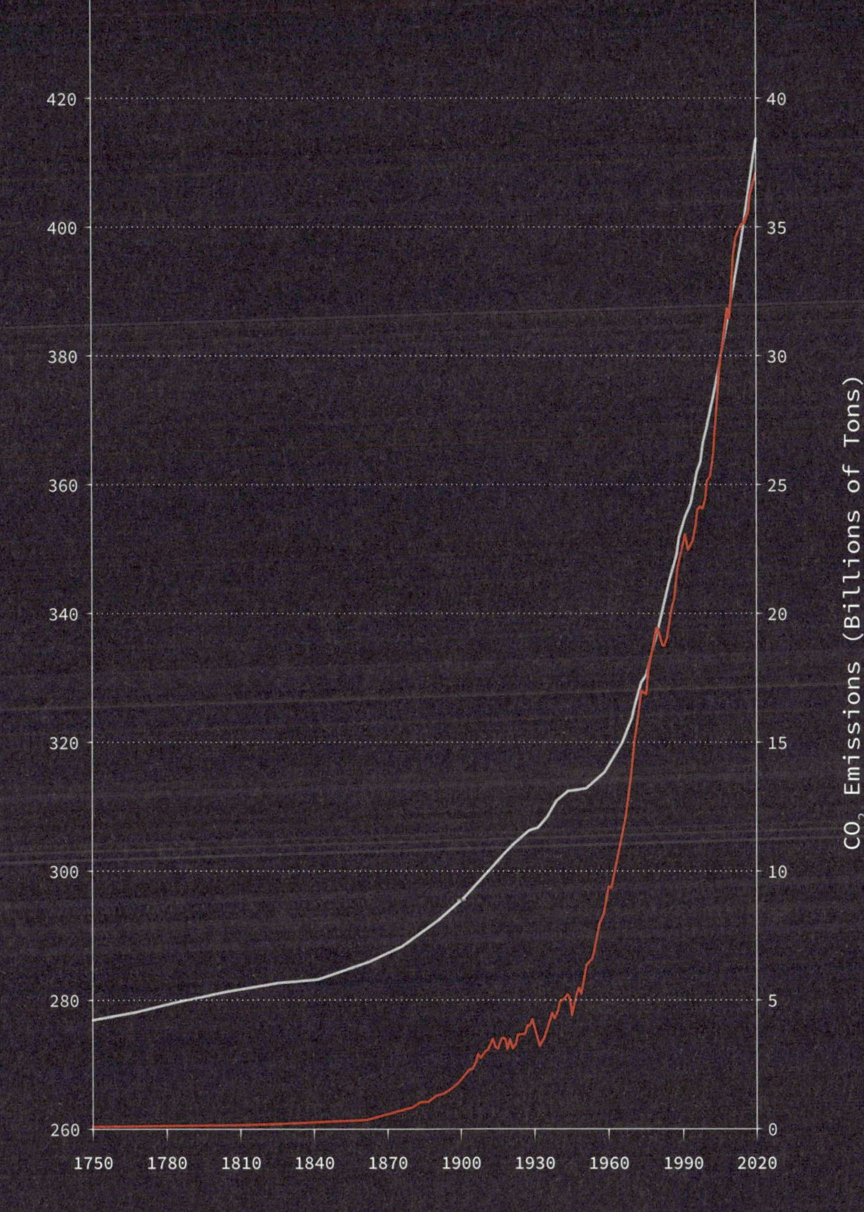

Atmospheric CO_2 (Parts per Million)
CO_2 Emissions (Billions of Tons)
420
400
380
360
340
320
300
280
260
40
35
30
25
20
15
10
5
0
1750
1780
1810
1840
1870
1900
1930
1960
1990
2020
Year

Carbon Cloud

The earth system is constantly processing around 550 gigatons of carbon through the natural carbon cycle. Some of this carbon moves through daily and seasonal cycles of photosynthesis and respiration, and some of it is sequestered through a much slower geological cycle as it forms the building blocks of life on the land and in the oceans. As animals and plants die, the carbon in their bodies is enfolded into the earth's crust via soil and the ocean floor, which, in turn, is uplifted through tectonic activity to form new landscapes. As these landscapes weather and corrode they re-release the carbon into the atmosphere, where plants and animals will again absorb it.

Cycling through geological periods of freeze and thaw, the earth ultimately self-regulates its weather to maintain conditions conducive to life. Should an external force—such as humans pumping almost 42 billion tons of excess carbon into the atmosphere per year—disrupt this system then the fear is that it could shift into positive feedback. In that event, instead of cycling through ice ages and interglacial periods, the planet would continue to overheat, life would be extinguished, and the carbon cycle would shut down. The other planets in our solar system show you what this looks like.

Even in the unlikely scenario that carbon emissions were halted tomorrow, because there is already so much extra carbon in the system global temperatures will increase, sea levels will rise, and storm events and droughts will continue to intensify. The question is just how much extra carbon humans will emit and how long it will take for the earth system to stabilize. Because we are entrenched in cities and dependent on agricultural ways of life and globalized supply chains, climate change amounts to the greatest challenge humanity has ever faced. We need to adjust our crops to keep pace with shifting seasons, cool our cities to cope with heat islands, withdraw our settlements from rising seas to prevent flooding, and ensure biodiversity can survive rapid environmental change. Most difficult of all, we need to decarbonize our economies without reducing peoples' right to security and prosperity. An invisible cloud of excess carbon hangs over us, growing by 42 billion tons every year. We moderns in the so-called First World made this frightening hyperobject, and now we must unmake it.

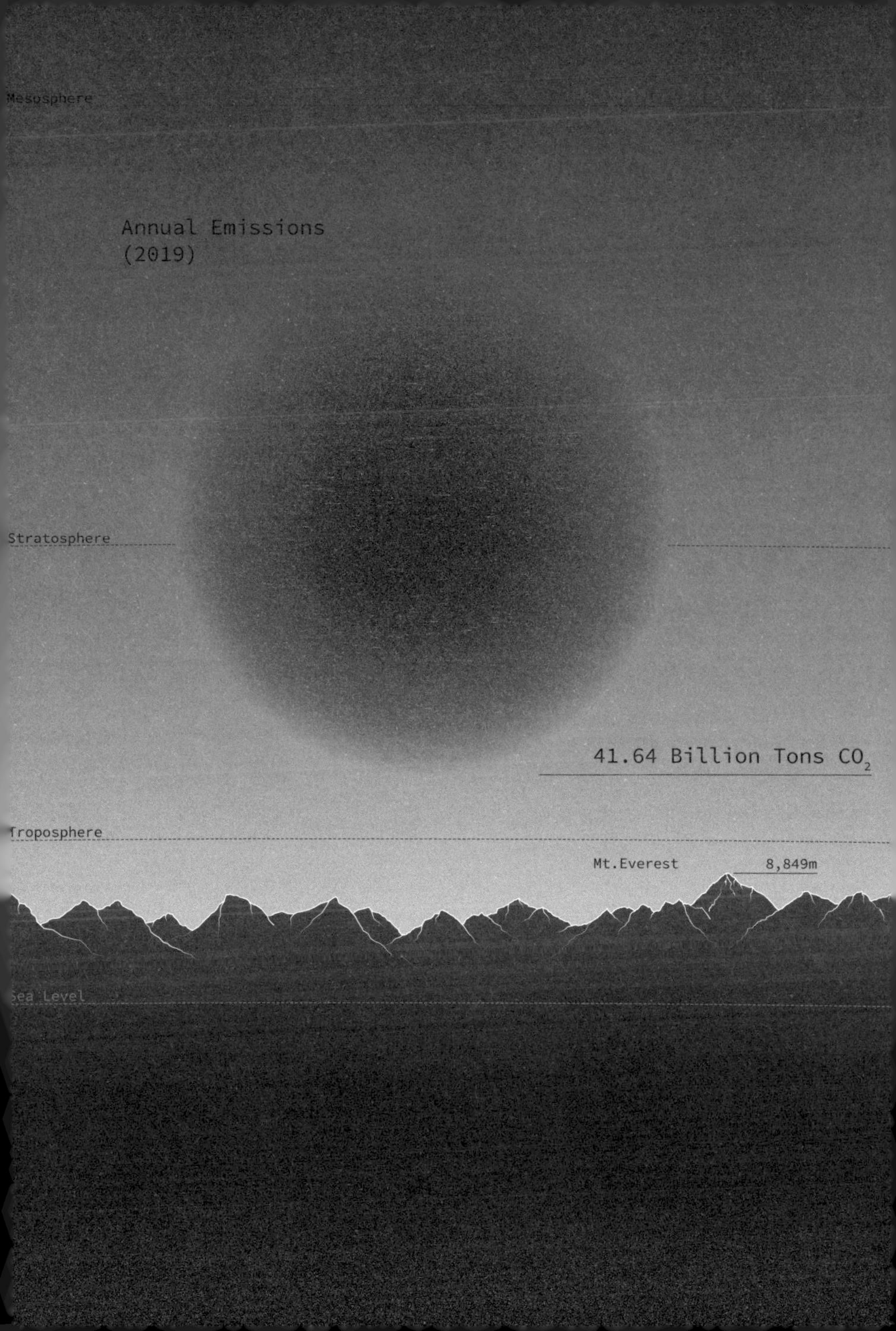

Mesosphere

Annual Emissions
(2019)

Stratosphere

41.64 Billion Tons CO_2

Troposphere

Mt.Everest 8,849m

Sea Level

The Economy

For most of human history people have bartered things, and, as a matter of both ritual and survival, shared whatever they had at hand. With the agricultural revolution, however, came the need to administer the subdivision of land and labor and the opportunity for elites to accrue wealth and power through taxation and trade. As trading networks between cities developed and the quantities and diversity of things being traded grew, money (silver and gold) emerged as an abstraction of value and a practical convenience, radically expanding the time and space of exchange. This inculcated the generation of debt, profit, competition, and innovation, as well as reinvestment in production—the fundamental elements of what would later become the global system we refer to as capitalism. It also unleashed the seemingly unlimited human desire to own and accumulate things, even just money itself.

As commerce sought evermore raw materials and new markets through colonial exploitation, banks, companies, corporations, the stock exchange, and government regulators all emerged as essential institutions to manage the semi-deterministic chaos of a global economy. So too, economics itself emerged in the late 18th century as a specialized discipline of study, one characterized by a wide range of ideological and theoretical constructs as to what an economy is and how it works, and above all, how it should work.

From the 19th century onward a theory of socialism, leading to self-regulating communism, emerged as the utopian alternative to free markets and the exploitation of labor and nature that bedevil capitalism. In this not-for-profit, communitarian approach to collective well-being—based on Karl Marx's critique of capital—the government guarantees an even distribution of goods and cradle-to-grave welfare. To date, however, neither communism nor capitalism have proven to be able to successfully guarantee a dignified, equitable, and desirable economic existence for all citizens.

Comprising a mosaic of national economies—each in their own way trying to balance the social values of communism with the economic effectiveness of competitive capitalism— the global economy is now a hyperobject worth something in the order of $85 trillion. Immensely powerful yet at the same time highly vulnerable to perturbation, the global economy has three key problems: first, the vast discrepancy between a wealthy elite and the billions who toil in conditions of degrading labor and live in grinding poverty. Second, no economic theory has yet proven capable of securing the sustainability of the natural resources that ultimately sustain the entire system. And third, no one knows how to correct the disparity in the former, without exacerbating the problem of the latter.

ANNUIT COEPTIS
MDCCLXXVI
NOVUS ORDO SECLORUM

The Internet

The progenitor of today's internet known as the ARPANET emerged in the 1960s from the Pentagon's desire to create a decentered communications network that could not be 'taken out' by a single strike. By the 1990s the system had moved from the military to academia and then to the public. The information conveyed by the infrastructure of the internet is known as the World Wide Web, a system of 'hyperlinks' created by Timothy Berners-Lee in 1991 that allows users to connect from one document to any other with a single click.

In just over three decades the amount of information on the web has grown to 59 zetabytes (one zettabyte = 10^{21} (1,000,000,000,000,000,000,000) bytes. Data centers around the world process over ten exabytes (ten billion gigabytes) of internet traffic per day. That's the equivalent of 360 years of nonstop, high-quality video streaming. There are now almost five billion internet users around the world (62% of the world's population) and on average users consume almost seven hours of internet content per day. The number of new users is increasing at a rate of more than one million every single day.

How to make sense of this unprecedented phenomenon? For starters, the internet can be understood as the outcome of a historical process of human's self-organizing into ever-larger networks of relations—from tribe to city to nation to planet—and communications systems changing accordingly. These communications systems contribute significantly to shaping both individual and collective identity. They are the conduits for power relations, affecting the politics, economics, and aesthetics of their societies. The internet, for example, began with the dream of the democratization of information; a new encyclopedia of enlightenment, but just as quickly as it made the world's great libraries available to all, it also loaded up with misinformation, porn, violence, trivia, and not least of all, advertising.

We can also think of the internet in terms of natural history and speculate that it represents an evolutionary phase shift whereby the earth has evolved its own neurology with each human user a synapse in a new form of planetary superintelligence. In this telling the planet has evolved from a dumb rock to one now bristling with digital intelligence. Or to put it less teleologically, perhaps the planet was always bristling with 'intelligence' (broadly defined as the sensory capacities of organisms) and this is just the latest iteration. Either way, the internet is the most interesting thing to have emerged since the origins of language itself. Indeed, its codes are a new form of language spoken both by humans and machines.

The Sixth Extinction

There have been five major extinction events in the earth's history, the fifth being the case of the dinosaurs eliminated by an asteroid crashing into the Yucatan peninsula some 65 million years ago. While horrendous for the dinosaurs, their sudden absence gave small marsupials an ecological opportunity, and an evolutionary pathway that ultimately led to humans opened up. Able to outrun and outwit animals, humans chewed their way through the megafauna of most continents and now, by grinding down their habitats for farms and cities, we seem intent on extinguishing the rest. This is known as the sixth extinction and its grim ledger is the IUCN Red List of Threatened Species.

Resistance to this biological holocaust has underpinned the global conservation movement, which, since the mid-20th century, has focused on creating protected areas—large patches of land from which destructive and extractive human activities are excluded. In 1962 there were 9,214 protected areas globally, today there are over 266,000, amounting to a grand total of 15.6% of the earth's terrestrial area and almost 6.5% of the world's oceans.

In terms of helping to mitigate the sixth extinction by creating safe havens for threatened animals and plants, the future of protected areas faces two major challenges. The first is that protected areas do not map accurately onto the world's most threatened biodiversity and the second is that where they do the land areas are not large enough to facilitate the movement of species as they now seek to adapt to global warming. Seriously addressing these two challenges means reorganizing land use in a coordinated manner, on a planetary scale. To that end, at the 2022 United Nations Biodiversity Conference (COP15), 188 nations agreed to a new target of placing 30% of the earth's terrestrial area under protection.

Evolution waits for no species. Over the course of a few million years or so, every species effectively becomes extinct—either they naturally evolve into something else, or, as fate would have it, they are eliminated by competitors, disease, or some other form of environmental calamity. For many species today, humans are now the greatest threat to their survival. Human activity is the equivalent of a slow-motion asteroid. And yet, it is only the human who has the capacity to prevent a real asteroid hitting the earth.

STENELLA ATTENUATA ° BALAENOPTERA BOREALIS ° KOGIA SIMA ° ANTILOCAPRA AMERICANA ° FERESA ATTENUATA ° NEOMONACHUS SCHAUINSLANDI ° BALAENOPTERA EDENI ° BALAENOPTERA PHYSALUS
RHINELLA MARINA ° ELEUTHERODACTYLUS COQUI ° ELEUTHERODACTYLUS PLANIROSTRIS ° GLANDIRANA RUGOSA ° LITHOBATES CATESBEIANUS ° DENDROBATES AURATUS ° OSTEOPILUS SEPTENTRIONALIS
MESOPLODON GINKGODENS ° TADARIDA BRASILIENSIS ° EUMETOPIAS JUBATUS ° PEROMYSCUS BOYLII ° MESOPLODON CARLHUBBSI ° MYOTIS EVOTIS ° URSUS ARCTOS ° GLAUCOMYS SABRINUS
ZALOPHUS CALIFORNIANUS ° URSUS AMERICANUS ° MARMOTA FLAVIVENTRIS ° NEOTAMIAS SPECIOSUS ° DIPODOMYS MICROPS ° DIPODOMYS PANAMINTINUS ° NEOTAMIAS MERRIAMI ° NYCTINOMOPS MACROTIS
CHAETODIPUS RUDINORIS ° THOMOMYS BOTTAE ° CHAETODIPUS FALLAX ° CHAETODIPUS FORMOSUS ° MESOPLODON PERRINI ° DIPODOMYS MERRIAMI ° DIPODOMYS SIMULANS
ANTROZOUS PALLIDUS ° ONYCHOMYS TORRIDUS ° CHAETODIPUS CALIFORNICUS ° DIPODOMYS STEPHENSI ° LEPUS CALIFORNICUS ° UROCYON CINEREOARGENTEUS ° MEPHITIS MEPHITIS ° CERVUS CANADENSIS
MESOPLODON STEJNEGERI ° TAXIDEA TAXUS ° MYOTIS YUMANENSIS ° PHOCOENOIDES DALLI ° MICROTUS LONGICAUDUS ° PUMA CONCOLOR ° ARCTOCEPHALUS TOWNSENDI ° LYNX RUFUS ° SOREX ORNATUS
XEROSPERMOPHILUS TERETICAUDUS ° XEROSPERMOPHILUS MOHAVENSIS ° SCIURUS NIGER ° BASSARISCUS ASTUTUS ° DIDELPHIS VIRGINIANA ° CALLOSPERMOPHILUS LATERALIS ° SCAPANUS LATIMANUS
DIPODOMYS AGILIS ° CHAETODIPUS PENICILLATUS ° NEOTOMA BRYANTI ° PEROMYSCUS CALIFORNICUS ° OTOSPERMOPHILUS BEECHEYI ° NEOTOMA LEPIDA ° NATALUS MEXICANUS
SYLVILAGUS AUDUBONII ° SYLVILAGUS BACHMANI ° VULPES VULPES ° DELPHINUS CAPENSIS ° OVIS CANADENSIS ° NOTIOSOREX CRAWFORDI ° AMMOSPERMOPHILUS LEUCURUS ° NEOTAMIAS MINIMUS
CANIS LATRANS ° NEOTOMA MACROTIS ° LASIURUS BLOSSEVILLII ° PEROMYSCUS CRINITUS ° MYOTIS CALIFORNICUS ° PEROGNATHUS ALTICOLA ° NEOTOMA FUSCIPES ° PHOCA VITULINA
CHAETODIPUS SPINATUS ° CHOERONYCTERIS MEXICANA ° DIPODOMYS DESERTI ° ESCHRICHTIUS ROBUSTUS ° EPTESICUS FUSCUS ° EUMOPS PEROTIS ° LISSODELPHIS BOREALIS ° MACROTUS CALIFORNICUS
MYOTIS LUCIFUGUS ° MYOTIS THYSANODES ° NYCTINOMOPS FEMOROSACCUS ° PEROGNATHUS LONGIMEMBRIS ° PEROMYSCUS MANICULATUS ° PEROMYSCUS TRUEI
AMMOSPERMOPHILUS NELSONI ° PEROMYSCUS EREMICUS ° NEOTOMA ALBIGULA ° REITHRODONTOMYS MEGALOTIS ° CORYNORHINUS TOWNSENDII ° SOREX MONTICOLUS ° MUSTELA FRENATA
SYLVILAGUS FLORIDANUS ° EUMOPS UNDERWOODI ° MYOTIS AURICULUS ° MYOTIS FORTIDENS ° NELSONIA GOLDMANI ° PTERONOTUS DAVYI ° NYCTINOMOPS LATICAUDATUS ° PEROMYSCUS PECTORALIS
PEROMYSCUS MELANOTIS ° PEROMYSCUS DIFFICILIS ° PEROMYSCUS LEVIPES ° REITHRODONTOMYS FULVESCENS ° MOLOSSUS SINALOAE ° REITHRODONTOMYS ZACATECAE
REITHRODONTOMYS SUMICHRASTI ° ZYGOGEOMYS TRICHOPUS ° BAEODON ALLENI ° BAEODON GRACILIS ° SOREX SAUSSUREI ° OSGOODOMYS BANDERANUS ° CONEPATUS LEUCONOTUS ° SPILOGALE PYGMAEA
SOREX VERAECRUCIS ° SOREX EMARGINATUS ° SOREX ORIZABAE ° STURNIRA PARVIDENS ° STURNIRA HONDURENSIS ° HODOMYS ALLENI ° SOREX MEDIOPUA ° LEPTONYCTERIS YERBABUENAE ° EUMOPS FEROX
NOTIOSOREX EVOTIS ° MICRONYCTERIS MICROTIS ° CYNOMOPS MEXICANUS ° NEOTOMA LEUCODON ° SPILOGALE ANGUSTIFRONS ° BAIOMYS MUSCULUS ° PEROMYSCUS GRATUS
HETEROMYS PICTUS ° HETEROMYS SPECTABILIS ° TLACUATZIN CANESCENS ° GLOSSOPHAGA MORENOI ° NEOTOMA MEXICANA ° CRYPTOTIS ALTICOLA ° PEROMYSCUS SAGAX ° PECARI TAJACU ° NASUA NARICA
SACCOPTERYX BILINEATA ° MORMOOPS MEGALOPHYLLA ° CHAETODIPUS HISPIDUS ° DICLIDURUS ALBUS ° THOMOMYS UMBRINUS ° LEPTONYCTERIS NIVALIS ° PEROGNATHUS FLAVUS
LASIURUS INTERMEDIUS ° DASYPUS NOVEMCINCTUS ° HERPAILURUS YAGOUAROUNDI ° HANDLEYOMYS MELANOTIS ° IDIONYCTERIS PHYLLOTIS ° MEPHITIS MACROURA ° GLOSSOPHAGA COMMISSARISI
NOTOCITELLUS ANNULATUS ° SCIURUS AUREOGASTER ° DERMANURA AZTECA ° EIRA BARBARA ° SIGMODON MASCOTENSIS ° GLYPHONYCTERIS SYLVESTRIS ° SIGMODON FULVIVENTER ° SIGMODON LEUCOTIS
PEROMYSCUS PERFULVUS ° NOCTILIO LEPORINUS ° DIPODOMYS ORDII ° REITHRODONTOMYS CHRYSOPSIS ° ANOURA GEOFFROYI ° ICTIDOMYS MEXICANUS ° MOLOSSUS RUFUS
ORTHOGEOMYS GRANDIS ° CHOERONISCUS GODMANI ° GLAUCOMYS VOLANS ° ARTIBEUS HIRSUTUS ° NYCTINOMOPS AURISPINOSUS ° TAMANDUA MEXICANA ° EPTESICUS FURINALIS
XENOMYS NELSONI ° LEPUS CALLOTIS ° BAUERUS DUBIAQUERCUS ° ENCHISTHENES HARTII ° ARTIBEUS LITURATUS ° BAIOMYS TAYLORI ° CHAETODIPUS NELSONI ° OLIGORYZOMYS FULVESCENS ° DESMODUS ROTUNDUS
LONTRA LONGICAUDIS ° MACROTUS WATERHOUSII ° PTERONOTUS PERSONATUS ° MOLOSSUS MOLOSSUS ° DERMANURA TOLTECA ° NYCTOMYS SUMICHRASTI ° DERMANURA PHAEOTIS ° PAPPOGEOMYS
SIGMODON ALLENI ° ARTIBEUS JAMAICENSIS ° SOREX OREOPOLUS ° SYLVILAGUS CUNICULARIUS ° CHIRODERMA SALVINI ° GLOSSOPHAGA SORICINA ° PEROMYSCUS MELANOPHRYS ° CENTURIO SENEX
RHOGEESSA PARVULA ° SOREX MACRODON ° BASSARISCUS SUMICHRASTI ° ORTHOGEOMYS HISPIDUS ° MEGADONTOMYS NELSONI ° PEROMYSCUS MEXICANUS ° PEROMYSCUS AZTECUS ° PEROMYSCUS
RHOGEESSA TUMIDA ° SYLVILAGUS GABBI ° DIAEMUS YOUNGI ° MYOTIS ELEGANS ° CRYPTOTIS MEXICANA ° GALICTIS VITTATA ° PLATYRRHINUS HELLERI ° MARMOSA MEXICANA ° CRATOGEOMYS PEROTENSIS
CRATOGEOMYS FULVESCENS ° PEROMYSCUS BEATAE ° CRYPTOTIS OBSCURA ° HABROMYS SCHMIDLYI ° HABROMYS DELICATULUS ° HANDLEYOMYS ROSTRATUS ° MYOTIS KEAYSI ° LASIURUS EGA
EUDERMA MACULATUM ° PEROMYSCUS FURVUS ° MICROTUS QUASIATER ° MAZAMA TEMAMA ° HANDLEYOMYS CHAPMANI ° OTOTYLOMYS PHYLLOTIS ° CAROLLIA SOWELLI ° DIPODOMYS PHILLIPSII
COENDOU MEXICANUS ° URODERMA MAGNIROSTRUM ° TAPIRUS BAIRDII ° DASYPROCTA MEXICANA ° SOREX VENTRALIS ° SCIURUS OCULATUS ° GLOSSOPHAGA LEACHII ° PHILANDER OPOSSUM
MYOTIS NIGRICANS ° HABROMYS SIMULATUS ° MIMON COZUMELAE ° PEROMYSCUS LEUCOPUS ° CAROLLIA PERSPICILLATA ° CUNICULUS PACA ° DIDELPHIS MARSUPIALIS ° SCIURUS DEPPEI ° PERIMYOTIS SUBFLAVUS
HANDLEYOMYS ALFAROI ° CRATOGEOMYS MERRIAMI ° ATELES GEOFFROYI ° CALUROMYS DERBIANUS ° DIPHYLLA ECAUDATA ° SIGMODON TOLTECUS ° SIGMODON HISPIDUS
SPILOGALE PUTORIUS ° LASIURUS BOREALIS ° EUBALAENA GLACIALIS ° GEOMYS ATTWATERI ° GEOMYS BREVICEPS ° ONDATRA ZIBETHICUS ° SCIURUS CAROLINENSIS ° STENELLA CLYMENE
LASIURUS SEMINOLUS ° ORYZOMYS PALUSTRIS ° MICROTUS OCHROGASTER ° PEROMYSCUS GOSSYPINUS ° REITHRODONTOMYS HUMULIS ° STENELLA FRONTALIS ° NYCTICEIUS HUMERALIS
BLARINA CAROLINENSIS ° MICROTUS PINETORUM ° ICTIDOMYS TRIDECEMLINEATUS ° SCALOPUS AQUATICUS ° CASTOR CANADENSIS ° CORYNORHINUS RAFINESQUII ° CHROTOPTERUS AURITUS
MICRORYZOMYS ALTISSIMUS ° MICRORYZOMYS MINUTUS ° MICROSCIURUS FLAVIVENTER ° LEOPARDUS COLOCOLO ° MOLOSSOPS AEQUATORIANUS ° NEUSTICOMYS MONTICOLUS ° PTERONOTUS GYMNONOTUS
TRANSANDINOMYS TALAMANCAE ° PROECHIMYS SIMONSI ° VAMPYRESSA THYONE ° SCIURUS GRANATENSIS ° PHYLLOTIS ANDIUM ° PHYLLOTIS GERBILLUS ° PHYLLOTIS HAGGARDI
OECOMYS BICOLOR ° MELANOMYS CALIGINOSUS ° PATTONOMYS OCCASIUS ° SAGUINUS FUSCICOLLIS ° MARMOSOPS NOCTIVAGUS ° MARMOSA REGINA ° PHILANDER ANDERSONI
ATELES FUSCICEPS ° ZALOPHUS WOLLEBAEKI ° RHOGEESSA IO ° RHOGEESSA VELILLA ° VAMPYRODES CARACCIOLI ° STURNIRA KOOPMANHILLI ° STURNIRA LUDOVICI ° PLATYRRHINUS DORSALIS
PLATYRRHINUS ISMAELI ° MYOPROCTA PRATTI ° TAYASSU PECARI ° CENTRONYCTERIS CENTRALIS ° EUMOPS WILSONI ° THOMASOMYS CAUDIVARIUS ° MARMOSA PHAEA ° ANOURA FISTULATA ° HETEROMYS TELEUS
STURNIRA OPORAPHILUM ° CAENOLESTES CONDORENSIS ° THOMASOMYS HUDSONI ° RHYNCHONYCTERIS NASO ° MELANOMYS ROBUSTULUS ° ALOUATTA JUARA ° ARTIBEUS AEQUATORIALIS
LOPHOSTOMA SILVICOLUM ° AEGIALOMYS XANTHAEOLUS ° ICHTHYOMYS HYDROBATES ° MACROPHYLLUM MACROPHYLLUM ° NEPHELOMYS AURIVENTER ° STURNIRA MAGNA ° OREORYZOMYS BALNEATOR
VICUGNA VICUGNA ° VAMPYRISCUS BIDENS ° CRYPTOTIS EQUATORIS ° EPTESICUS CHIRIQUINUS ° MICRONYCTERIS HIRSUTA ° THOMASOMYS FUMEUS ° CHILOMYS INSTANS ° CERDOCYON THOUS
CAENOLESTES FULIGINOSUS ° RHINOPHYLLA PUMILIO ° SACCOPTERYX LEPTURA ° STURNIRA TILDAE ° GLIRONIA VENUSTA ° GARDNERYCTERIS CRENULATUM ° ICHTHYOMYS STOLZMANNI
HYLAEAMYS TATEI ° THOMASOMYS BAEOPS ° PROECHIMYS DECUMANUS ° THOMASOMYS PARAMORUM ° THOMASOMYS PYRRHONOTUS ° PITHECIA NAPENSIS ° LYCALOPEX SECHURAE
SCIURUS SPADICEUS ° STURNIRA BAKERI ° MYOTIS OXYOTUS ° STURNIRA NANA ° SAIMIRI SCIUREUS ° AOTUS VOCIFERANS ° PLECTUROCEBUS DISCOLOR ° THOMASOMYS CINNAMEUS ° SIGMODON INOPINATUS
DINOMYS BRANICKII ° CAROLLIA CASTANEA ° PRIODONTES MAXIMUS ° PLATYRRHINUS MATAPALENSIS ° THOMASOMYS AUREUS ° CEBUS ALBIFRONS ° CYCLOPES DIDACTYLUS ° MICRONYCTERIS MINUTA
THOMASOMYS TACZANOWSKII ° MAKALATA MACRURA ° BASSARICYON ALLENI ° ICHTHYOMYS TWEEDII ° RHINOPHYLLA ALETHINA ° RHIPIDOMYS LATIMANUS ° COENDOU RUFESCENS
MESOPLODON HOTAULA ° LAGIDIUM AHUACAENSE ° CHOERONISCUS MINOR ° SACCOPTERYX CANESCENS ° SIGMODONTOMYS ALFARI ° STURNIRA BIDENS ° STURNIRA BOGOTENSIS
MARMOSA RUBRA ° METACHIRUS NUDICAUDATUS ° CRYPTOTIS MONTIVAGA ° MOLOSSUS BONDAE ° DIDELPHIS PERNIGRA ° CHIBCHANOMYS ORCESI ° COENDOU QUICHUA
ANOURA CAUDIFER ° ANOURA AEQUATORIS ° ANOURA PERUANA ° LOPHOSTOMA OCCIDENTALIS ° PROMOPS DAVISONI ° BASSARICYON MEDIUS ° PROMOPS NASUTUS ° SPEOTHOS VENATICUS
LYCALOPEX CULPAEUS ° CYNOMOPS ABRASUS ° SIGMODON PERUANUS ° CAROLLIA BREVICAUDA ° AMORPHOCHILUS SCHNABLII ° MAZAMA AMERICANA ° ANOURA CULTRATA ° ARTIBEUS FRATERCULUS
CHIRONECTES MINIMUS ° DASYPROCTA PUNCTATA ° THOMASOMYS AURICULARIS ° SCIURUS STRAMINEUS ° EUMOPS AURIPENDULUS ° CONEPATUS SEMISTRIATUS ° EPTESICUS ANDINUS ° MARMOSA MURINA
MESOPHYLLA MACCONNELLI ° PLATALINA GENOVENSIUM ° LICHONYCTERIS OBSCURA ° PROECHIMYS SEMISPINOSUS ° MICRONYCTERIS MEGALOTIS ° MYOTIS ALBESCENS ° NEACOMYS SPINOSUS
PEROPTERYX KAPPLERI ° PHYLLOSTOMUS HASTATUS ° CUNICULUS TACZANOWSKII ° AKODON AEROSUS ° NEOMICROXUS LATEBRICOLA ° AKODON MOLLIS ° NECROMYS PUNCTULATUS ° AOTUS LEMURINUS
PEROPTERYX MACROTIS ° MESOPLODON PERUVIANUS ° PROECHIMYS CUVIERI ° URODERMA BILOBATUM ° DERMANURA RAVA ° CAVIA PATZELTI ° TAPIRUS PINCHAQUE ° TAPIRUS TERRESTRIS ° MAZAMA RUFINA
LONCHOPHYLLA HESPERIA ° LONCHOPHYLLA ROBUSTA ° LONCHOPHYLLA THOMASI ° LONCHORHINA ORINOCENSIS ° COENDOU VESTITUS ° VAMPYRESSA MELISSA ° MICROSCIURUS ALFARI
MYRMECOPHAGA TRIDACTYLA ° OLALLAMYS ALBICAUDA ° OLIGORYZOMYS GRISEOLUS ° PEROPTERYX PALLIDOPTERA ° PLATYRRHINUS VITTATUS ° VAMPYRISCUS NYMPHAEA
RHIPIDOMYS FULVIVENTER ° DASYPROCTA FULIGINOSA ° CYNOMOPS PARANUS ° LAGOTHRIX LUGENS ° ATELES HYBRIDUS ° TONATIA SAUROPHILA ° MOLOSSOPS NEGLECTUS ° SAPAJUS MACROCEPHALUS
EUMOPS GLAUCINUS ° HYDROCHOERUS ISTHMIUS ° SACCOPTERYX ANTIOQUENSIS ° HETEROMYS AUSTRALIS ° MAZAMA BRICENII ° MOLOSSUS COIBENSIS ° CRYPTOTIS THOMASI ° SCIURILLUS PUSILLUS
CAVIA APEREA ° MAZAMA NEMORIVAGA ° LIONYCTERIS SPURRELLI ° LUTREOLINA CRASSICAUDATA ° NASUA NASUA ° HANDLEYOMYS INTECTUS ° GRACILINANUS DRYAS ° CABASSOUS UNICINCTUS
GLOSSOPHAGA LONGIROSTRIS ° COENDOU PREHENSILIS ° EUMOPS DABBENEI ° NECTOMYS GRANDIS ° PLATYRRHINUS UMBRATUS ° CRYPTOTIS MEDELLINIA ° NECTOMYS RATTUS
INIA GEOFFRENSIS ° THOMASOMYS BOMBYCINUS ° THOMASOMYS NIVEIPES ° RHINOPHYLLA FISCHERAE ° SIGMODON HIRSUTUS ° PROCYON CANCRIVORUS ° PLATYRRHINUS ALBERICOI
LASIURUS EGREGIUS ° DASYPUS KAPPLERI ° HISTIOTUS HUMBOLDTI ° EUMOPS HANSAE ° THYROPTERA DISCIFERA ° CORMURA BREVIROSTRIS ° LOPHOSTOMA BRASILIENSE ° GRACILINANUS MARICA
NEACOMYS TENUIPES ° DERMANURA GLAUCA ° CYNOMOPS GREENHALLI ° OECOMYS CONCOLOR ° BASSARICYON NEBLINA ° SPHAERONYCTERIS TOXOPHYLLUM ° RHIPIDOMYS CAUCENSIS
MOLOSSUS PRETIOSUS ° ZYGODONTOMYS BREVICAUDA ° SIGMODON ALSTONI ° STURNIRA ARATATHOMASI ° AOTUS BRUMBACKI ° PLECTUROCEBUS ORNATUS ° PHILANDER MONDOLFII ° COENDOU PRUINOSUS
EUMOPS TRUMBULLI ° PLATYRRHINUS ANGUSTIROSTRIS ° THOMASOMYS PRINCEPS ° LONCHOPHYLLA CADENAI ° LONCHOPHYLLA ORIENTICOLLINA ° NOCTILIO ALBIVENTRIS ° AOTUS GRISEIMEMBRA
NECROMYS URICHI ° ANOTOMYS LEANDER ° MARMOSA ROBINSONI ° ZYGODONTOMYS BRUNNEUS ° HOLOCHILUS SCIUREUS ° AMETRIDA CENTURIO ° DERMANURA GNOMA ° ARTIBEUS OBSCURUS
THOMASOMYS CONTRADICTUS ° THOMASOMYS LANIGER ° THOMASOMYS NICEFORI ° DASYPUS SABANICOLA ° FURIPTERUS HORRENS ° HETEROMYS ANOMALUS
PLATYRRHINUS BRACHYCEPHALUS ° LICHONYCTERIS DEGENER ° GLYPHONYCTERIS DAVIESI ° MICRONYCTERIS SCHMIDTORUM ° MICROSCIURUS MIMULUS ° DERMANURA BOGOTENSIS ° PHYLLOSTOMUS ELONGATUS
NEOMICROXUS BOGOTENSIS ° ANOURA LUISMANUELI ° ARTIBEUS AMPLUS ° CABASSOUS CENTRALIS ° MOLOSSOPS TEMMINCKII ° MIMON BENNETTII ° CHILONATALUS MACER ° MORMOOPS BLAINVILLEI
PHYLLONYCTERIS POEYI ° PHYLLOPS FALCATUS ° PLAGIODONTIA AEDIUM ° CAPROMYS PILORIDES ° PTERONOTUS PARNELLII ° EROPHYLLA BOMBIFRONS ° LASIURUS PFEIFFERI ° PTERONOTUS MACLEAYII
MONOPHYLLUS REDMANI ° MYSATELES PREHENSILIS ° PTERONOTUS QUADRIDENS ° LASIURUS INSULARIS ° SOLENODON PARADOXUS ° NATALUS MAJOR ° BRACHYPHYLLA NANA ° LASIURUS MINOR
TASMACETUS SHEPHERDI ° TYMPANOCTOMYS BARRERAE ° MESOPLODON GRAYI ° MICROCAVIA AUSTRALIS ° LEOPARDUS GEOFFROYI ° LEOPARDUS GUIGNA ° PHOCOENA SPINIPINNIS
ARCTOCEPHALUS PHILIPPII ° BALAENOPTERA BONAERENSIS ° OLIGORYZOMYS LONGICAUDATUS ° PHYLLOTIS XANTHOPYGUS ° CTENOMYS JOHANNIS ° CTENOMYS VALIDUS ° LYCALOPEX GRISEUS
LAGENORHYNCHUS OBSCURUS ° LOXODONTOMYS MICROPUS ° ABROTHRIX ANDINUS ° SPALACOPUS CYANUS ° LONTRA FELINA ° LEPUS EUROPAEUS ° CHELEMYS MEGALONYX ° LAGIDIUM VISCACIA
GALICTIS CUJA ° HISTIOTUS MACROTUS ° MESOPLODON TRAVERSII ° EUNEOMYS PETERSONI ° ABROCOMA BENNETTII ° ELIGMODONTIA MORGANI ° AKODON SPEGAZZINII ° ZAEDYUS PICHIY
MYOTIS DINELLII ° PHYLLOTIS DARWINI ° CHAETOPHRACTUS VILLOSUS ° LOXODONTOMYS PIKUMCHE ° OCTODON BRIDGESI ° OCTODON LUNATUS ° ABROTHRIX LONGIPILIS ° CAPEREA MARGINATA
MYOCASTOR COYPUS ° MYOTIS CHILOENSIS ° OCTODON DEGUS ° CHELEMYS MACRONYX ° THYLAMYS PALLIDIOR ° EUNEOMYS MORDAX ° CTENOMYS PONTIFEX ° GLOBICEPHALA MELAS
LAGENORHYNCHUS CRUCIGER ° OTARIA BYRONIA ° RHIPIDOMYS MACRURUS ° THALPOMYS LASIOTIS ° NECTOMYS SQUAMIPES ° OLIGORYZOMYS NIGRIPES ° EURYORYZOMYS LAMIA
THYLAMYS VELUTINUS ° CALLITHRIX PENICILLATA ° ALOUATTA CARAYA ° CRYPTONANUS AGRICOLAI ° PYGODERMA BILABIATUM ° THYLAMYS KARIMII ° EUMOPS DELTICUS ° OLIGORYZOMYS MOOJENI
OLIGORYZOMYS ELIURUS ° SAPAJUS LIBIDINOSUS ° OXYMYCTERUS ROBERTI ° JUSCELINOMYS CANDANGO ° THALPOMYS CERRADENSIS ° MICROAKODONTOMYS TRANSITORIUS ° CALOMYS CALLOSUS
CERRADOMYS SCOTTI ° CHIRODERMA DORIAE ° GRACILINANUS AGILIS ° PROECHIMYS ROBERTI ° MARMOSOPS BISHOPI ° LEOPARDUS GUTTULUS ° STURNIRA LILIUM ° THRICHOMYS APEREOIDES
HYLAEAMYS MEGACEPHALUS ° LYCALOPEX VETULUS ° DIDELPHIS ALBIVENTRIS ° CALOMYS EXPULSUS ° CABASSOUS TATOUAY ° HISTIOTUS VELATUS ° MAZAMA GOUAZOUBIRA ° OLIGORYZOMYS STRAMINEUS
DASYPUS SEPTEMCINCTUS ° MOLOSSOPS MATTOGROSSENSIS ° CARTERODON SULCIDENS ° AKODON LINDBERGHI ° OECOMYS CLEBERI ° CALOMYS TENER ° MONODELPHIS AMERICANA
MONODELPHIS DOMESTICA ° SCIURUS AESTUANS ° LONCHOPHYLLA DEKEYSERI ° CLYOMYS LATICEPS ° OLIGORYZOMYS FLAVESCENS ° CERRADOMYS SUBFLAVUS ° BRUCEPATTERSONIUS SORICINUS
MAZAMA NANA ° SOORETAMYS ANGOUYA ° MARMOSA PARAGUAYANA ° RHIPIDOMYS MASTACALIS ° MAZAMA BORORO ° AKODON MONTENSIS ° TRINOMYS GRATIOSUS ° DELOMYS COLLINUS
PHYLLOMYS KERRI ° OXYMYCTERUS CAPAROAE ° MARMOSOPS PAULENSIS ° OXYMYCTERUS HISPIDUS ° OXYMYCTERUS QUAESTOR ° MYOTIS RUBER ° SAPAJUS NIGRITUS ° CALLITHRIX AURITA
GRACILINANUS MICROTARSUS ° MYOTIS LEVIS ° CAVIA FULGIDA ° PONTOPORIA BLAINVILLEI ° BRUCEPATTERSONIUS GRISERUFESCENS ° VAMPYRESSA PUSILLA ° KANNABATEOMYS AMBLYONYX
EUMOPS MAURUS ° DELOMYS SUBLINEATUS ° MONODELPHIS SCALOPS ° PHAENOMYS FERRUGINEUS ° TONATIA BIDENS ° DIDELPHIS AURITA ° LEONTOPITHECUS CHRYSOPYGUS ° PHILANDER FRENATUS
COENDOU SPINOSUS ° WILFREDOMYS OENAX ° EURYZYGOMATOMYS SPINOSUS ° RHAGOMYS RUFESCENS ° BRUCEPATTERSONIUS IGNIVENTRIS ° CALLICEBUS NIGRIFRONS
SOTALIA GUIANENSIS ° LONCHOPHYLLA PERACCHII ° EPTESICUS TADDEII ° RHIPIDOMYS ITOAN ° BIBIMYS LABIOSUS ° DASYPROCTA AZARAE ° PHYLLOMYS SULINUS ° JULIOMYS PICTIPES ° AKODON CURSOR
ARTIBEUS FIMBRIATUS ° ARTIBEUS PLANIROSTRIS ° BLARINOMYS BREVICEPS ° CALUROMYS PHILANDER ° EURYORYZOMYS RUSSATUS ° DELOMYS DORSALIS ° DICLIDURUS SCUTATUS ° PHYLLOMYS NIGRISPINUS
TRINOMYS IHERINGI ° PHYLLOMYS MEDIUS ° MONODELPHIS DIMIDIATA ° MARMOSOPS INCANUS ° THAPTOMYS NIGRITA ° AKODON SERRENSIS ° OXYMYCTERUS DASYTRICHUS ° HOLOCHILUS BRASILIENSIS
STEATOMYS CAURINUS ° MYONYCTERIS LEPTODON ° HYBOMYS TRIVIRGATUS ° SCOTONYCTERIS ZENKERI ° ICHNEUMIA ALBICAUDA ° MOPS CONDYLURUS ° MUNGOS GAMBIANUS
PAN TROGLODYTES ° OUREBIA OUREBI ° OTOMOPS MARTIENSSENI ° CROCIDURA DOLICHURA ° PROCOLOBUS VERUS ° LEMNISCOMYS STRIATUS ° GENETTA CRISTATA ° MUNGOS MUNGO ° HERPESTES ICHNEUMON
CROSSARCHUS PLATYCEPHALUS ° ATILAX PALUDINOSUS ° MELLIVORA CAPENSIS ° MYOPTERUS WHITLEYI ° NYCTERIS MACROTIS ° PRAOMYS DALTONI ° PRAOMYS DEROOI ° ARVICANTHIS NILOTICUS
NEOROMICIA GUINEENSIS ° PHILANTOMBA WALTERI ° FELIS SILVESTRIS ° MASTOMYS NATALENSIS ° MUS MUSCULOIDES ° CHLOROCEBUS TANTALUS ° EPOMOPS FRANQUETI ° CEPHALOPHUS RUFILATUS
PHACOCHOERUS AFRICANUS ° PANTHERA PARDUS ° SCOTOPHILUS NIGRITA ° EPTESICUS PLATYOPS ° MEGALOGLOSSUS WOERMANNI ° CEPHALOPHUS SILVICULTOR ° CERCOPITHECUS ERYTHROGASTER
GERBILLISCUS KEMPI ° GLAUCONYCTERIS POENSIS ° CERCOCEBUS TORQUATUS ° LEPTAILURUS SERVAL ° PHATAGINUS TETRADACTYLA ° PHATAGINUS TRICUSPIS ° GALAGO SENEGALENSIS ° GALAGOIDES DEMIDOFF
CERCOPITHECUS NICTITANS ° SCOTOECUS ALBOFUSCUS ° COLOBUS VELLEROSUS ° CHAEREPHON PUMILUS ° TRICHECHUS SENEGALENSIS ° SYNCERUS CAFFER ° CRICETOMYS EMINI
GRAMMOMYS KURU ° CARACAL CARACAL ° CHAEREPHON ANSORGEI ° CHAEREPHON NIGERIAE ° CHAEREPHON MAJOR ° DASYMYS RUFULUS ° HYDRICTIS MACULICOLLIS ° HELIOSCIURUS RUFOBRACHIUM
KOB ° LOPHUROMYS SIKAPUSI ° FUNISCIURUS LEUCOGENYS ° CROCIDURA CROSSEI ° PERODICTICUS POTTO ° ALCELAPHUS BUSELAPHUS ° THRYONOMYS SWINDERIANUS ° KERIVOULA LANOSA
EPOMOPS BUETTIKOFERI ° CROCIDURA VIARIA ° NANDINIA BINOTATA ° CIVETTICTIS CIVETTA ° CROCIDURA GRANDICEPS ° CROCIDURA LAMOTTEI ° CERCOPITHECUS MONA ° ANOMALURUS BEECROFTI ° GRAPHIURUS

The Anthropocene

According to geologists the history of the earth is divided into eons. These are then subdivided into the consecutively smaller time frames of eras, periods, epochs, and ages. Beginning some 11,700 years ago, the current epoch is the Holocene, an interglacial period known for its good weather and the global expansion of human settlements. New phases in the geological record are formally recognized by the International Commission on Stratigraphy (headquartered in London) when there is empirical evidence of a fundamental change in the biophysical nature of the earth system and this evidence can be definitively identified in geological strata. So-called 'golden spikes' are hammered into rock faces to mark these phase transitions.

Because of human-induced climate change and other environmental impacts, many are now arguing we have entered a new epoch and are calling this epoch the Anthropocene, meaning the age of the human. The expression stems from the Greek *anthropos*, meaning those who are beneath the gods. To invoke the Anthropocene is to assert that humanity has itself become a force of nature that has irrevocably changed the earth system. The scientific and more broadly cultural argument for the arrival of the Anthropocene comes in three main forms: exhibit A is climate change, exhibit B is the sixth extinction, and both are consequences of C, the 'hockey stick' graphs depicting what is known as the historical period of the Great Acceleration. As its title suggests, the Great Acceleration refers to the rapid increase in the consumption of resources and concomitant destruction of the environment that has occurred from the mid-20th century to today.

Contenders for evidence in the geological record of the new epoch of the Anthropocene include radionuclides (fallout from mid-20th-century nuclear detonations), the prevalence of microplastics from around the same period, and heavy metals and carbon dioxide dating back to the Industrial Revolution. Some suggest that even chicken bones, now spread liberally over much of the world, could also serve as the hallmark of the human in the strata. While the geologists squabble over what will be the best empirical evidence, critics worry that the concept of the Anthropocene sweeps everyone up into a new form of 'natural' history, when in fact the state of the world that it headlines is a result of specific historical forces such as colonization, patriarchy, and above all, neoliberal capitalism, all of which have been perpetuated by particular groups of people who now need to be held accountable.

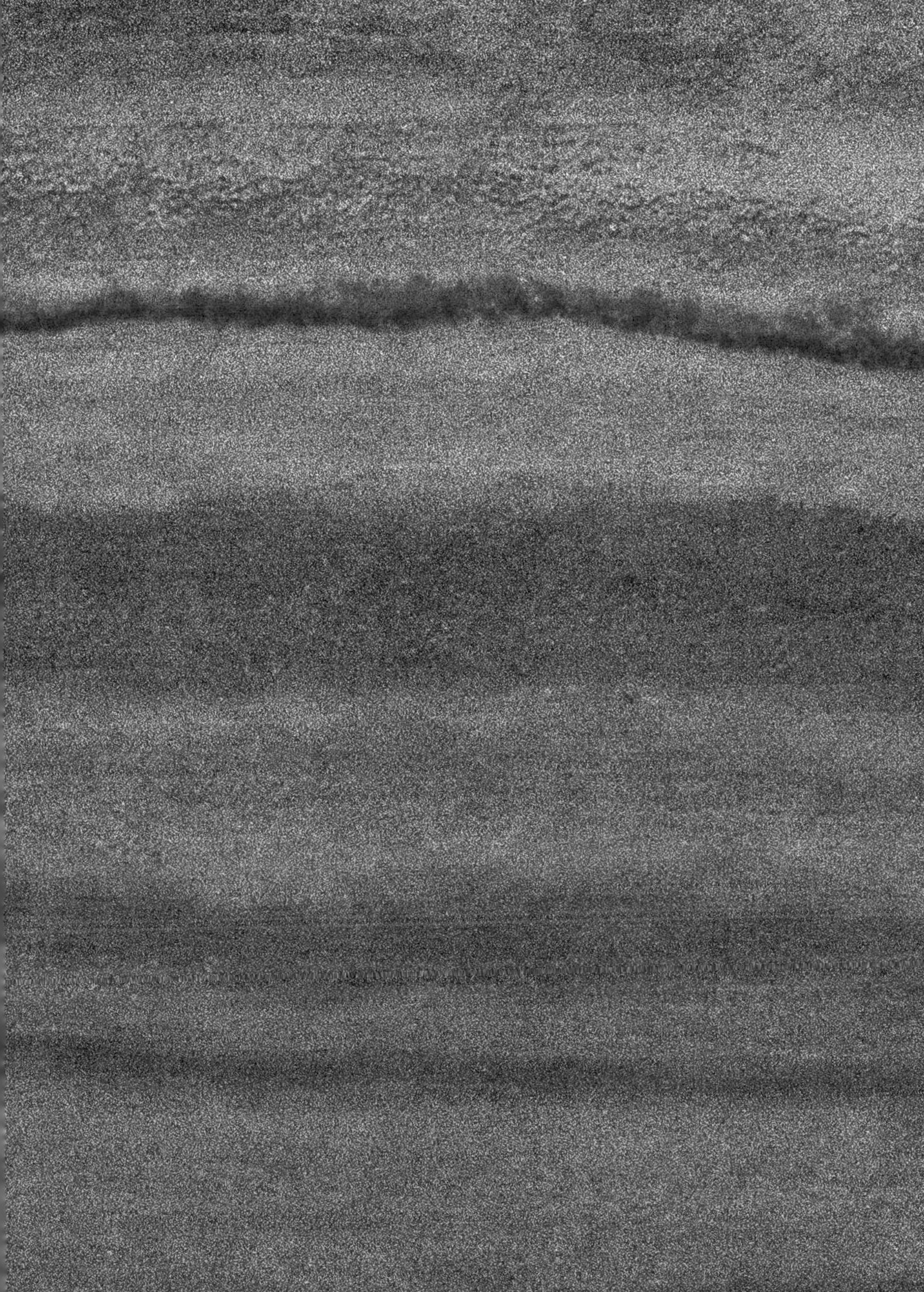

Paradises

Recurring in many cultures, the idea of paradise as a state of bliss set in the past, the future, or perhaps just over the horizon, would seem to be hardwired into human psychology. In the case of the Abrahamic religions—Judaism, Christianity, and Islam—paradise is figured as a Garden of Eden, a place of innocence and immortality. It is, however, also the setting for the original sin wherein the parents of humanity, Adam and Eve, transgress God's authority by eating the forbidden fruit to gain self-consciousness and knowledge of good and evil. For this sin, they are evicted from the garden and sentenced to a life of agricultural toil, clearing the stage for their son Cain to murder his brother Abel, and then construct Enoch, the first city.

Taken anthropologically instead of theologically, this narrative signifies the agricultural revolution and interrelated phenomena of city building, writing, and monotheism. Caught in a positive feedback of population growth and food production, the history of the city is one of territorial expansion tensioned against environmental limitations. As well as incubating the arts and sciences and increasing economic opportunity, cities also lead to famine, pestilence, political struggle, and war. Amid all this, a peaceful garden in a city has always served to symbolically recall a paradisical state prior to the city or point toward a heavenly paradise that lies ahead.

The question of whether the original Garden of Eden was a metaphor for the whole world or an actual garden within it has troubled theologians, explorers, and mapmakers for centuries. According to scripture, Eden's epicenter was the wellspring of the four great rivers of the known world—the Tigris, the Euphrates, the Ganges, and the Nile.

This special place was often thought to be somewhere in the vicinity of the Persian Gulf, a notion that probably grew out of even older stories related to the once-rich biodiversity of the region.

Theologically and philosophically, paradise functions as an allegorical setting for ethical and moral questions concerning humanity's role in relation to the other forms of life with which we share the planet. For example, from variations of Genesis it is possible to infer that with God's imprimatur humans were granted dominion over nature and can therefore make of it what we will. The alternative narrative is that we were placed in the garden as its stewards and instructed by God to "dress and keep it." Either way, now that the city has reached the ends of the earth there is scant garden left. And while its original state of bliss required us to literally do and think nothing, if paradise on earth is to be more than a mirage it now requires us to do the exact opposite.

Apple Park
California, United States

Referred to as a campus and opened in 2017, Apple Park is the headquarters of the multinational technology company Apple Inc. Famous for its former CEO Steve Jobs, its forbidden fruit logo, and its super-sleek products designed by Jony Ives, Apple is synonymous with the digital revolution that now infiltrates every aspect of contemporary culture.

At Apple Park, the company's local workforce of around 12,000 is contained within a single circular building equal in size to the Pentagon. Designed by British architect Norman Foster, the building is a homage to the Platonic ideal of geometric perfection set deep within 60 hectares of faux Californian landscape created by landscape architect, Laurie Olin. The juxtaposition of this massive silver disc to a naturalistic landscape has earned the building the moniker of 'the spaceship.'

But if one stays with the apple metaphor, it is less a spaceship and more a monastery. Like monasteries, the building defines a threshold between an interior garden and the exterior world. Typically, in monasteries the interior was a paradise garden (*hortus conclusus*) protected from a threatening and fallen world beyond. The monks would perambulate around the cloister at the garden's edge, meditating on the tension between their physical proximity to and spiritual distance from the material world. At the center of these monastic paradise gardens was invariably a small water feature symbolizing the Edenic source of the four rivers (Nile, Tigris, Euphrates, and Ganges). Aligned north, south, east, and west, four paths from the center to the edge of these paradise gardens signified the cardinal virtues of temperance, fortitude, justice, and prudence.

The garden inside the Apple building is also anchored by a symbolic water feature, in this case a large, dark, circular pond. The pond has a small mechanism at its center that creates a consistent, radiating ripple, a symbol perhaps for the electromagnetism that now fills our universe with information. If so, then along with the spaceship, the garden inside Apple Park is a monument to Steve Jobs—the first nerd to ever become a god.

See Also: Data Center (164), Agbogbloshie E-Waste Site (242), Microchip (268), Smartphone (270)

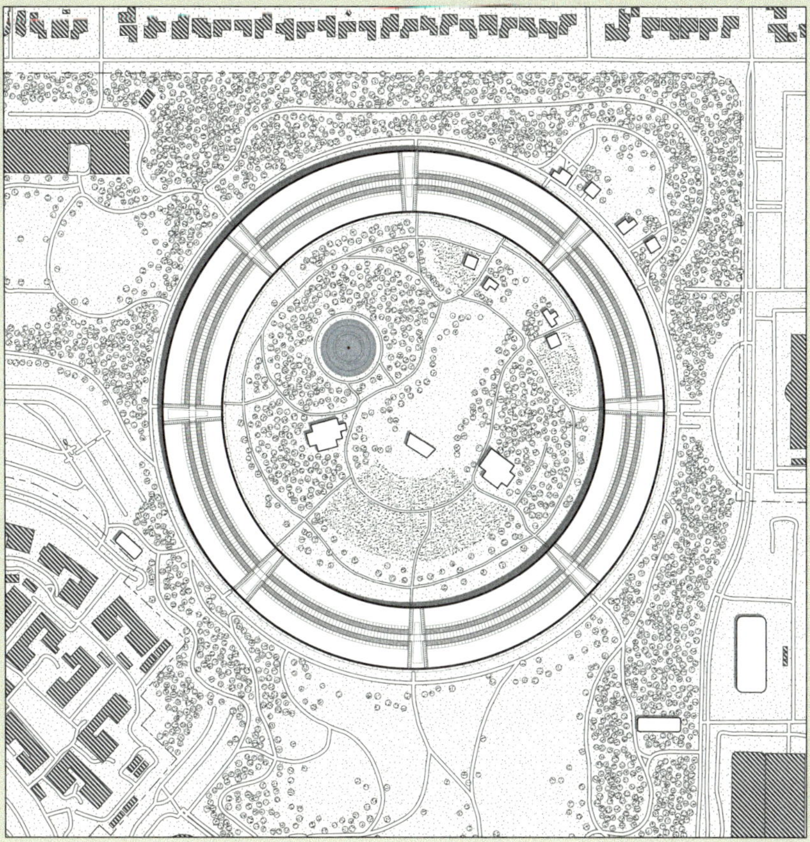

37°20’05.8”N 122°00’32.8”W

400 m

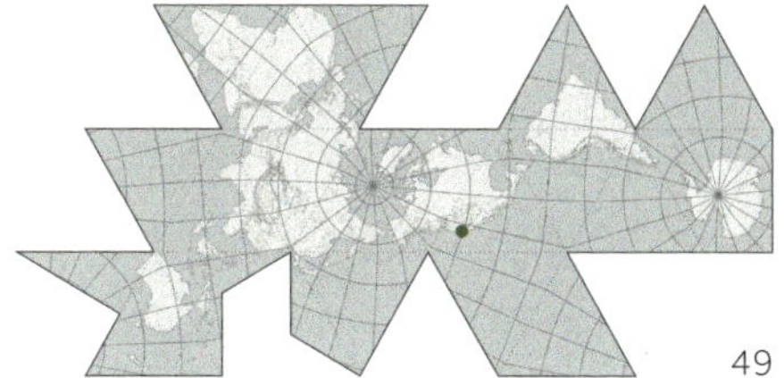

The Eden Project

Cornwall, England

Opened in 2001, the Eden Project is a botanic garden set partially inside a cluster of geodesic (ethylene-tetrafluoroethylene) domes in a former clay pit. The stated mission of the project is "to promote the understanding and responsible management of the vital relationship between plants and people and resources leading to a sustainable future for all." Floating in the landscape, the Eden Project appears as a kind of high-tech botanical ark, setting out to correct the fact that in the case of the original, Noah forgot about including plants altogether.

Unlike historical zoological and botanical gardens, which aimed to gather one of each of God's creations to venerate his creative munificence, the Eden Project presents simulations of tropical and Mediterranean biomes. As an institution, the Eden Project has ambitious global outreach and educational goals in areas such as climate change and energy; humanity, community and social recovery; food nutrition, health and well-being; and biodiversity and natural resources. Built on monies from the British national lottery and donations by the mining giant Rio Tinto, the project emerges from the seemingly contradictory, yet increasingly common, nexus between capital and conservation. As Eden's organizational project developer Howard Jones explains it, not only does the Eden Project seek to increase awareness of sustainability, it also tries to show that there isn't a conflict between environmental ethics and profitability. Despite criticism that attracting visitors who all arrive by car only adds to the world's environmental problems, the Eden Project is a tourism success story. Buoyed by this, Eden Project International Ltd is currently working on franchising the concept in the United Kingdom, Australia, Chad, China, and Costa Rica.

Whereas in the original narrative, Eve's acquisition of knowledge was the reason for the Fall, in this new Eden it is the union of science, technology, and education that will enhance humanity's otherwise slim chances of environmental redemption. Where the original and this new Eden are similar, however, is that both claim the moral high ground built around narratives of salvation.

See Also: Biosphere II (126), Svalbard Global Seed Vault (260), Frozen Zoo (262)

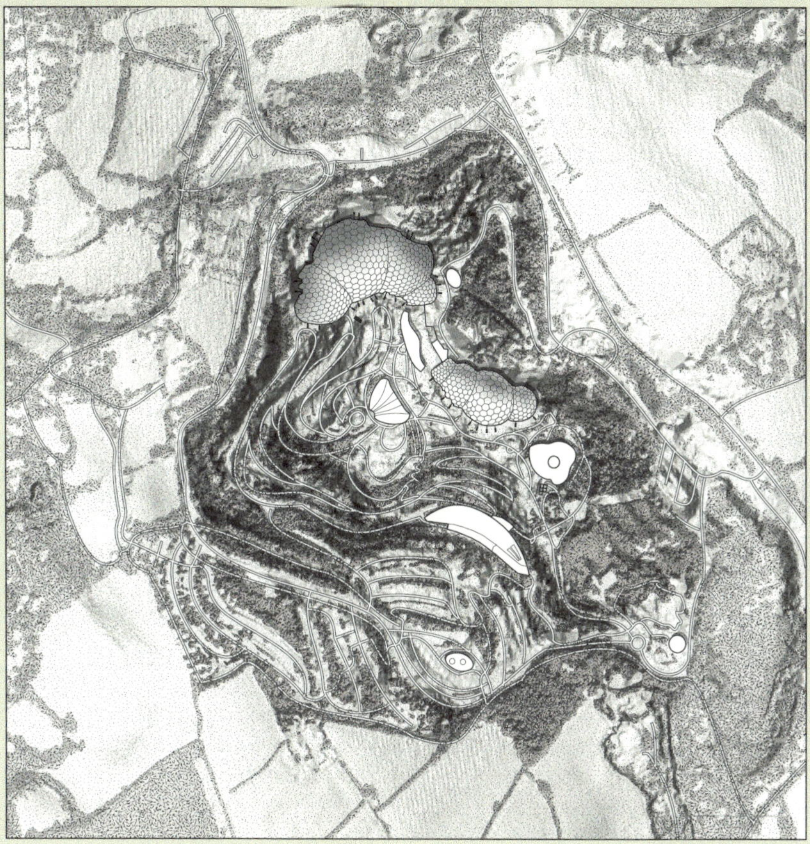

50°21’37.5”N 4°44’41.3”W

300 m

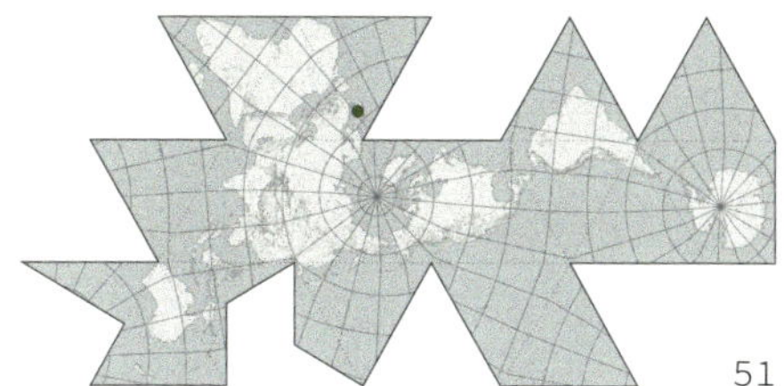

The Four Rivers of Paradise

International

Though geographically improbable, according to Genesis the Gihon (Nile), the Pishon (Ganges), the Hiddekel (Tigris), and the Prath (Euphrates) rivers all flow from the center of the Garden of Eden. Although it is historically uncertain whether the Gihon is what we now refer to as the Nile, and the Pishon is today's Ganges, the metaphor of the world once being a garden and the question of our role within it, is what really matters. One way to reflect on this question is to test the actual water that now flows through these mythic rivers.

The Nile is still Egypt's lifeline. However, since the river has been dammed by the Ethiopians in the south and the Egyptians in the north, the rich, fresh silts from the river's annual inundation no longer arrive. Agricultural fertility is instead now achieved by the constant application of industrial fertilizers to the thin band of arable land adjacent to the river. The chemicals leach out through the soil into the river causing hypoxia (a lack of oxygen) and killing aquatic life. The Nile is now also Egypt's main drain, flushing much of the nation's raw sewerage and industrial effluent out into the Mediterranean. Tourists who cruise the river to see the ruins of ancient Egypt are instructed to avoid any contact with the water.

The Tigris and Euphrates start in Turkey and pick up additional waters coming in from Syria, Iran, and Iraq as they head toward the Mesopotamian marshes at the Persian Gulf. Due to damming, water flow in the two rivers has been reduced by 80% over the past 50 years causing the loss of arable land and the decimation of the marshes. Like the Nile, the Tigris and Euphrates also serve to flush human, industrial, and agricultural waste, all of which has been exacerbated by the years of war in Iraq. Saddam Hussein notoriously tried to drain the marshes to flush out political opponents.

As for the fourth and last river of Paradise, the Ganges is now one of, if not the world's most, polluted rivers. It is sacred to Hindus and used to convey the ashes of the dead to moksha, liberating the deceased's soul from the eternal cycle of reincarnation. Water is being diverted from the main river faster than it can be recharged. This reduction causes farmers to dig wells, reducing the amount of available groundwater, which in turn further reduces the level of the river, and so on in a vicious cycle of depletion.

See Also: Ogallala Aquifer (54), Fertilizer Production Plant (140), Water Desalination Plant (148), Three Gorges Dam (150)

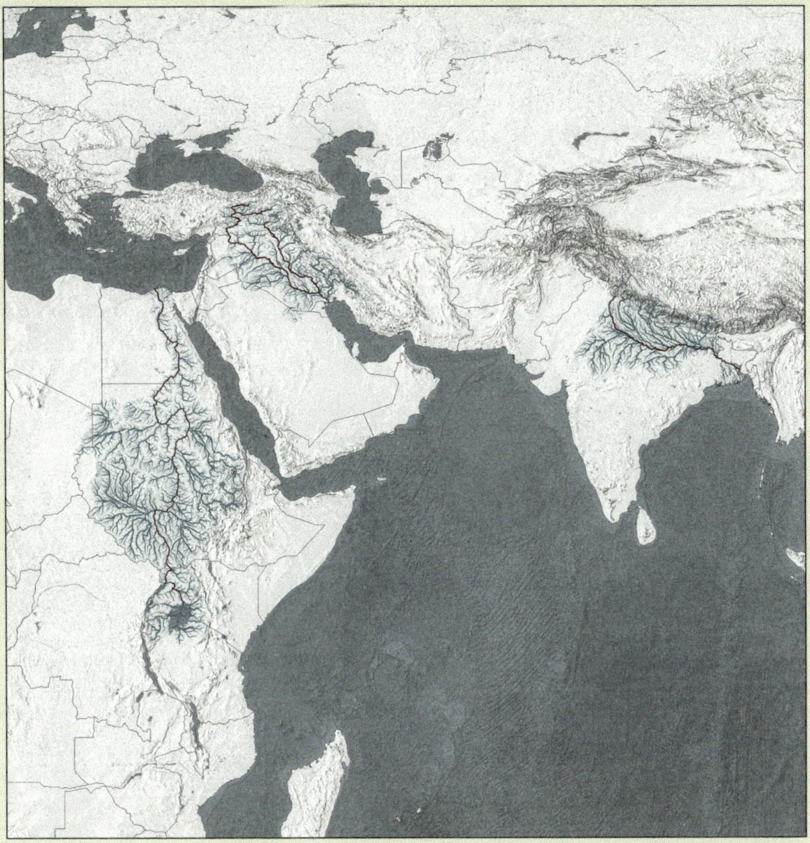

13°12'51.5"N 56°47'05.2"E

3,000 km 

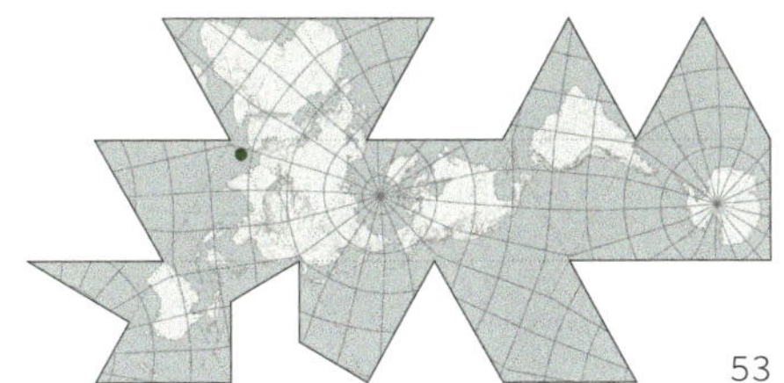

Ogallala Aquifer
High Plains, United States

In symbolic renditions of paradise, water rises from the ground as the font of life and spills over with abundance. The image of water as limitless is, however, an illusion. Apart from a negligible amount of mist that falls down to earth from outer space, the world's water supply is limited to the 326 million trillion tons that was mostly delivered by an icy asteroid some 3.6 billion years ago. Metamorphosing through solid, liquid, and gaseous states, this water moves endlessly through the hydrological cycle of the earth system, most of it held at any given time in the oceans and the polar ice sheets. The relatively small amount of water that falls on land collects in rivers and lakes and seeps down into underground aquifers from where it is tapped by wells, and qanats powered by windmills and mechanical pumps.

Recently, however, the level of ground water extraction has exceeded nature's supply. A case in point is the Ogallala Aquifer. Stretching from North Dakota to the Texas panhandle the Ogallala Aquifer is the largest in the United States. One-fifth of all wheat, corn, cotton, and cattle produced in the United States comes from farmlands that use the Ogallala Aquifer's water.

The aquifer was created over 15,000 years ago as ice melted and percolated into the ground, and has been topped up by seasonal rains ever since. Since the advent of pivot irrigation systems (think big crop circles), the Ogallala Aquifer's water is now being extracted at a much higher rate than it is being recharged. In some areas (western Kansas and the Texas panhandle, for example) the depletion rate is as much as four feet a year, while the average recharge rate is a mere three inches. This imbalance has amounted to hundreds of feet of depletion in some areas, in others, total depletion. An aquifer that took 15,000 years of organic processes to create may be bone dry within 150 years of its discovery. As droughts exacerbated by climate change become more frequent, the depletion rate of this aquifer will only increase. This problem is repeated wherever aquifers are tapped for agricultural production: the same dilemma exists in India, Australia, and the Middle East.

It's hard to imagine a massive, amorphous, underground entity like an aquifer. Like many aspects of modern infrastructure its invisibility aids and abets its exploitation. The map opposite shows the extent of the great Ogallala Aquifer. In gradated tones of red it also shows the location and the rates of depletion.

See Also: The Four Rivers of Paradise (52), Fertilizer Production Plant (140), GIS Crop Harvester (142), Water Desalination Plant (148)

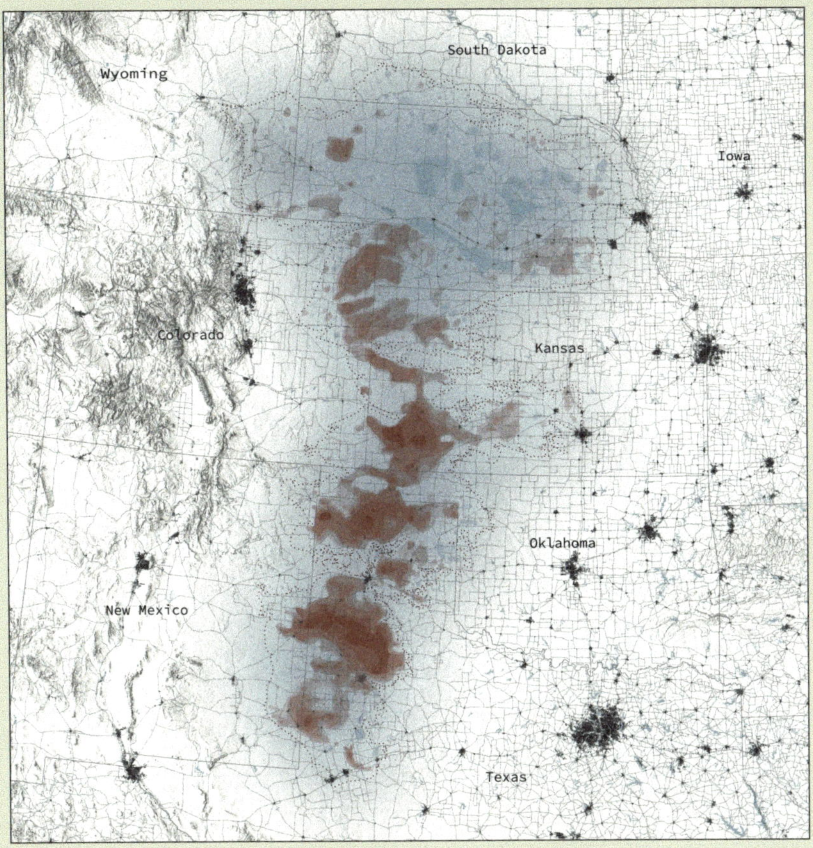

South Dakota
Wyoming
Iowa
Colorado
Kansas
Oklahoma
New Mexico
Texas

41°06'39.3"N 101°44'03.0"W

4,000 km

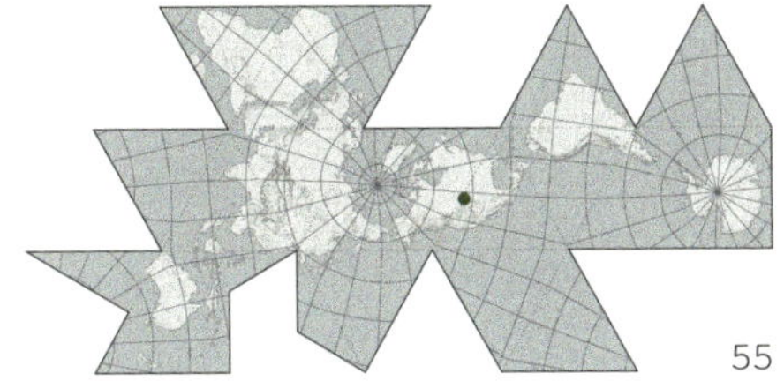

Yedikule Bostan

Istanbul, Turkey

Some of the world's oldest continually used market gardens are in Istanbul, a megacity of over 14 million people. There is evidence that small-scale agriculture has existed in the city from as far back as the 4th century, when the (UNESCO designated) city walls were built. Up until the mid-19th century, *bostan* (market gardens) were common throughout the city and produced enough food to feed large numbers of people. The bostan helped sustain the city, particularly during long running sieges.

A 10th-century Byzantine agricultural manual lists many of the same vegetables as are still planted in Istanbul today—cabbage, beets, carrots, onions, and turnips. Additionally, many plants no longer cultivated, such as mallow and orach, are still growing as edible weeds in the city. The 1,500-year-old Yedikule bostan, indicated opposite as a thin strip of land, even has its own variety of lettuce, the *Yedikule marul.*

The Yedikule bostan is one of Istanbul's last market gardens and is under constant pressure to be developed. Part of the garden has recently been converted into a park design associated with surrounding residential development. Some local residents welcomed its conversion to a park, however, many historians, environmentalists, and urban designers disapprove of the project because it doesn't address or attempt to conserve the site's rich agrarian heritage. Nor does it concern itself with the loss of space for low-income food gardeners. These gardeners will not only lose their food gardens, they will also eventually lose their homes as gentrification is triggered by the upmarket park design.

Istanbul's fading community gardens are sacrificial symbols of the contested and contradictory nature of urban development. On the one hand, the pressure to remove the food gardens is driven by the growth of the city, which is itself driven by the influx of people leaving rural, food-producing landscapes. On the other, in addition to those who feed themselves from the bostan, the heritage of Istanbul's food gardens is valued perhaps most highly by urban citizens who have never had to work the land for their food. Either way, good urban design should be able to reconcile the binary divide and antipathy between heritage and development. Through careful design, if not strict preservation policy, the rich cultural history and practical value of the bostan can be extended into the future of the city.

See Also: Parque de la Papa (74), GIS Crop Harvester (142), Greenhouse Agriculture (144), Space Garden (302)

40°59’47.5”N 28°55’15.9”E

1 km

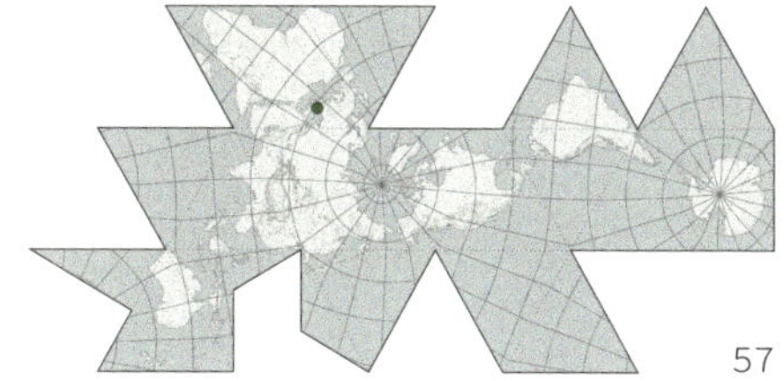

Yellowstone to Yukon Initiative

United States & Canada

In 1991 on the Kananaskis research station in Alberta, Canada, a wolf was captured and fitted with a transmitter so as to track and better understand her seasonal movements. In two years 'Pluie' (rain) ranged over an astonishing 100,000-square-kilometer area, crossing through 30 different jurisdictions, most of them hostile to wild animals. She was found four years later, along with a male partner and three pups, all shot dead.

Legend has it that Pluie's movements gave rise to the idea of amalgamating and conserving large tracts of land in the region so animals like her could conduct their wide-ranging lives in greater safety. The ongoing effort to achieve this is known as the Yellowstone to Yukon Conservation Initiative or 'Y2Y' for short. The Y2Y involves 1.3 million square kilometers of land stretching from Yellowstone National Park in the United States to the Yukon Territory in Canada. Working with the region's diverse constituents of retirees, ranchers, hunters, and indigenous people—all of whom have different legal rights and different attitudes in relation to the landscape—the Y2Y and its many partner organizations have achieved a doubling of the region's protected areas.

The aim of the Y2Y is not to just secure more ad hoc fragments of protected area, but to combine land parcels in strategic locations to maximize large-scale habitat connectivity. Achieving such connectivity is widely endorsed by landscape ecologists and conservationists as a key factor in building more resilient and biodiverse landscapes because it creates migration pathways for animals and plants to extend their gene pools and adapt to a changing climate.

Creating large-scale networks of connected habitat means educating, compensating, and negotiating with many different landowners. It also means recreating viable habitat in regions where it has been degraded or erased entirely. Inspired by Y2Y, there are now hundreds of similar large-scale connectivity projects being planned around the world. At the dawn of the United Nation's Decade of Ecological Restoration (2020–2030) these projects represent the profound hope that humanity can become a constructive force of nature and create a world in which humans and other species can live more respectfully alongside one another.

See Also: The Great Green Wall (60), Banff Wildlife Crossings Project (64), Griffith Park (182), Terrestrial Metatron (292), Wildlife Tags (294)

CANADA
UNITED STATES

55°36'14.2"N 121°36'13.7"W

1,500 km

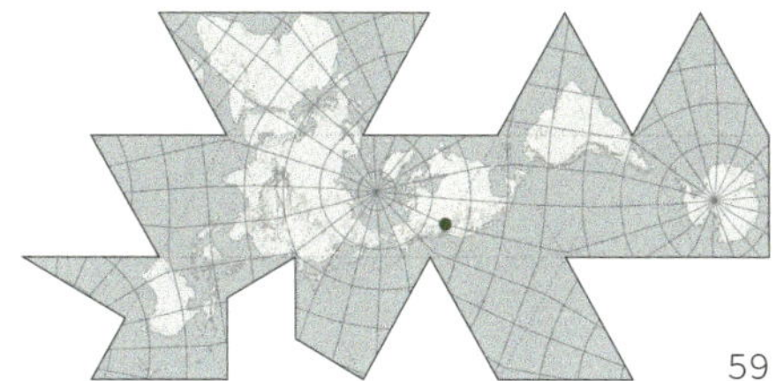

The Great Green Wall

Central Africa

As an idea, the Great Green Wall spans approximately 8,000 kilometers from Senegal to Djibouti to combat desertification by greening degraded lands on the front lines of the encroaching Sahara Desert. This involves the restoration of 100 million hectares of degraded land, sequestering 250 million tons of carbon and creating 10 million green jobs, all by 2030. When it is complete—if that day ever comes—it will be the largest human-made, living structure in the world.

The idea of a wall of trees at the edge of the Sahara and the semiarid belt of the Sahel is not a new one; it was originally proposed in the 1950s, revisited in the 1980s, and considered again in 2002 by President Olusegun Obasanjo of Nigeria. However, it was not until 2007 with $14.3 billion of funding through the World Bank and France that the governments of the eleven nations whose territory is involved, endorsed the idea and began to undertake the project.

Since 2007, the original idea of a monolithic greenbelt of trees has evolved into a mosaic of different approaches and micro-projects that are more closely attuned to local ecological and cultural conditions on the ground. Instead of a monoculture of trees—which would in any case be unlikely to survive—the wall now comprises the use of native trees, bushes, and grasses, and incorporates local agricultural techniques such as farmer-managed natural regeneration, agroforestry, and zai pits (small holes dug to retain runoff and manure). Incorporating local farming, animal grazing, and food production into the project has also created new jobs and opportunities for communities. Scientific monitoring of the project has aided the Great Green Wall's growth by determining which techniques are most successful in these harsh circumstances.

Some of those who live along the Great Green Wall's proposed path are considered the world's most multidimensionally poor, and many of the countries involved in the initiative have faced or are currently facing extreme challenges, including food shortages, drought, out-migration, conflict, and in some cases, civil war. More politically stable countries such as Senegal and Ethiopia have therefore led the restoration works and provided strong governmental support. Niger, Nigeria, and Burkina Faso have also made headway. Around 15% complete, like many other large landscape conservation and planning projects around the world, the Great Green Wall is an important and optimistic work in progress.

See Also: Yellowstone to Yukon Initiative (58), Parque de la Papa (74), Terrestrial Metatron (292)

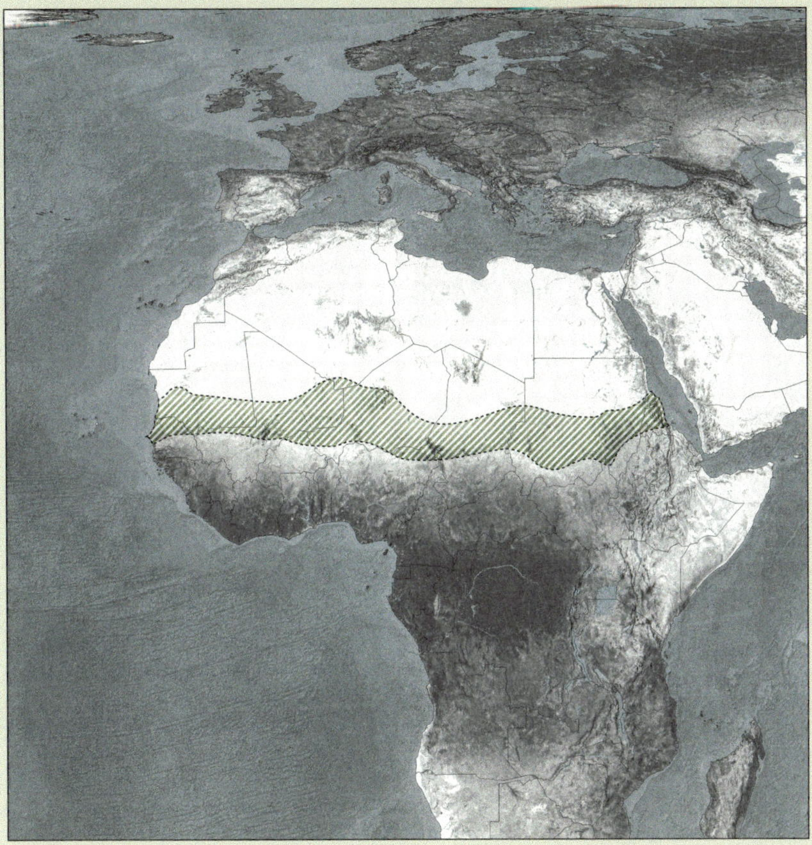

14°55’02.1”N 5°58’00.2”W

3,000 km

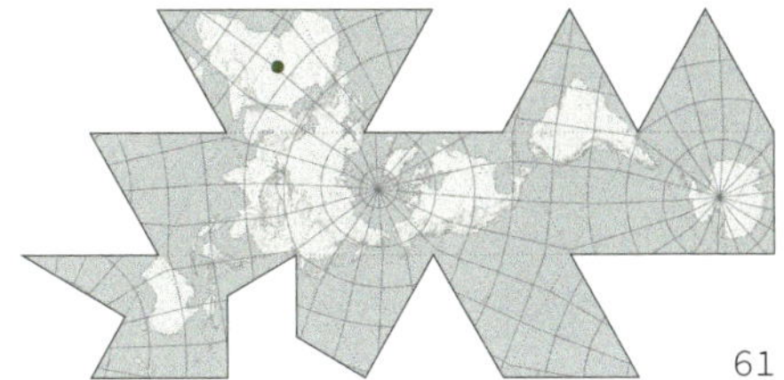

Oostvaardersplassen
Flevoland, the Netherlands

The Oostvaardersplassen is a fenced-off 56-square-kilometer nature reserve just outside Amsterdam. As a wetland ecosystem, the Oostvaardersplassen emerged from the reclamation of the South Flevoland polder (low-lying land reclaimed from the sea) in 1968. Though originally intended for industrial use, a group of biologists persuaded the Dutch government to designate the area as a testing ground for 'rewilding.'

The key to the ecological process of rewilding is the reintroduction of species, which through their behavior create niches for others, setting in motion a chain of ecological relationships, which over time can restore biodiversity and create a resilient, self-sustaining ecology. In the case of the Oostvaadersplassen this meant first introducing heck cattle, descendants of aurochs, which were rendered extinct in Europe in 1627. In addition, red deer were brought in from Scotland and wild horses imported from Poland. With these species in place, it was a case of sit back and see what happens.

As it did happen, these initial species thrived and their alteration of the landscape had the desired effect of creating opportunities for a variety of both native and invasive species to also move in. To the delight of ecologists, foxes, muskrats, buzzards, goshawks, gray herons, kingfishers, kestrels, white-tailed eagles, and a rare black vulture have all participated by their own volition in the Oostvaardersplassen rewilding experiment. But with life comes death, especially when populations exceed the limited resources of a certain land area. While scientists saw it simply as nature at work, the optics of large animals dying off due to starvation was unacceptable to much of the general public. Consequently, Oostvaardersplassen soon became a battle ground for different ideas of nature. On the one hand, the experiment was accused of animal cruelty; on the other, its defendants argued that nature shouldn't be anthropomorphized or seen through the lens of human values. As a result of public and scientific debate Oostvaardersplassen is now a more conscientiously managed landscape and no longer left to completely self-organize as was originally intended.

Rewilding is fascinating because it situates humans as active agents in designing ecosystems by manipulating their genetic stock. Landscape design in this sense is no longer solely the province of the landscape architect, the gardener, or the farmer—it is rapidly becoming the province of the scientist, playing God.

See Also: Guanacaste National Park (66), Camp Leakey (68), Giant Panda National Park (70), Pleistocene Park (184), Frozen Zoo (262)

52°26’25.3”N 5°20’53.4”E

4 km

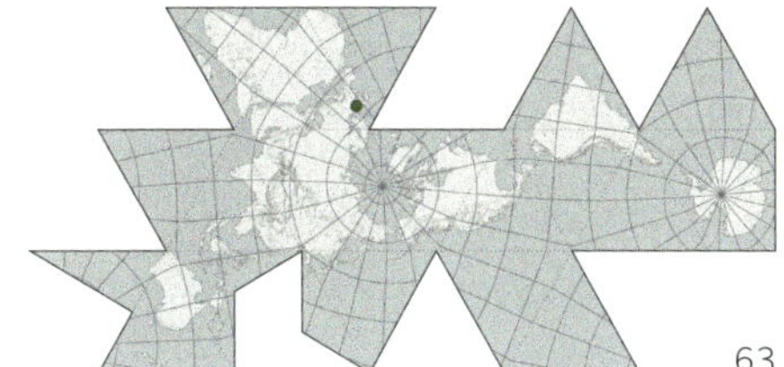

Banff Wildlife Crossings Project

Alberta, Canada

Created in 1887 in the Rocky Mountains, Banff was Canada's first national park. It is also one of the only two protected areas in North America that has a four-lane highway, the Trans-Canada, bisecting it. The Banff Wildlife Crossings Project—a bridge for wildlife to cross the highway—began in the mid-1980s when the Canadian government started the first phase of expanding the width of the highway. The main goal of the project was to decrease roadkill and restore critical migration routes that had been severed by the highway, preventing wildlife from accessing food, shelter, and mates.

The Banff Wildlife Crossings Project is world-renowned as one of the first successful large-scale highway mitigation projects for wildlife. Today, there are 38 underpasses and six overpasses, making Banff National Park a global leader in road ecology. The combination of fencing and crossing structures in Banff have reduced collisions with wildlife by over 80%. From continued monitoring, Parks Canada has also learned that different species prefer different types of crossing structures. For example, grizzly bears, wolves, and ungulates prefer larger open structures, while cougars and black bears are more likely to use narrower passages and even underground passages.

Humans have successfully created a world for themselves where goods, services, and information move almost seamlessly across the global landscape. However, this has been achieved at the expense of other species whose habitats have been sliced and diced by human infrastructure, presenting them with life-or-death thresholds every day. Designing safe passages such as the Banff wildlife crossings can assist some animals, but to better mitigate roadkill a more holistic understanding of species movement in relation to changing ecosystems needs to inform road design in the first place. So, too, driver behavior can be modified through technology that detects animal movement and sends warnings to vehicles.

It is estimated that there are over 64 million kilometers of roads and over 421,000 kilometers of railways in the world today, with more being added every day. And it's not just roads and rail that interrupt animal movement—almost everything humans make requires the eviction of other species and presents obstacles to the movement of species large and small. If our buildings, infrastructure, and land uses were planned and designed with multiple species in mind, then the world might not exactly be paradise, but it would be a far richer and more biodiverse place.

See Also: Yellowstone to Yukon Initiative (58), Guanacaste National Park (66), Wildlife Tags (294)

51°22’25.1”N 116°06’38.0”W

300 m

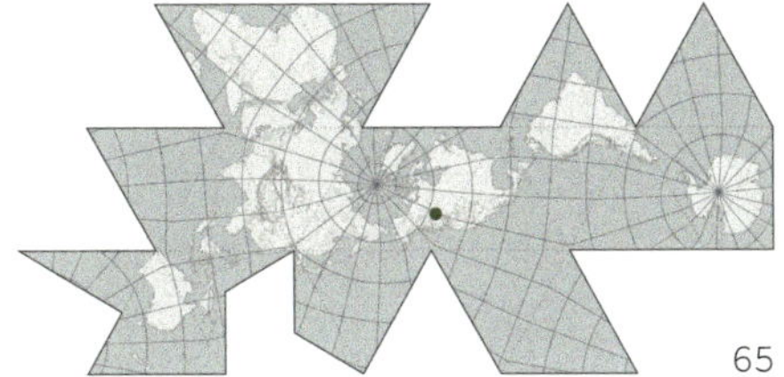

Guanacaste National Park

Costa Rica

The Guanacaste National Park in northeastern Costa Rica was officially formed by executive decree in 1989. The creation of the park is due to the American biologists Daniel Janzen and Winnie Hallwachs, who have devoted their lives to documenting and conserving the biodiversity of the region. In addition to their scientific work, through a combination of local partnerships, lobbying, and philanthropy, Janzen and Hallwachs have been able to strategically amass parcels of degraded agricultural land and undertake experiments in ecological restoration to form the backbone of the park.

The park now serves as the vital link between the existing Santa Rosa National Park on the coast and the volcanic heights of the Rincón de la Vieja National Park further inland. By forging a land bridge between the two existing parks, Guanacaste enables species to expand their ranges and make seasonal migrations between the dry forest and evergreen cloud and rain forests. In this way the overall resilience of the region's biodiversity is enhanced.

For Janzen and Hallwachs, wilderness is not something simply to be fenced off and set aside from people. Nor is it something that can be decreed from an NGO office in Washington or Geneva. For them it is something that has to be actively cultivated by human hands in a process of what Janzen and Hallwachs refer to as 'gardenification.' For them, as well as their students and their local team of coworkers, Guanacaste is a constant work in progress. This involves the negotiation of the legal, political, and financial frameworks for conservation, as well as the hard physical labor of bioremediation, reforestation, afforestation, maintenance, and monitoring. It is a process of engaging with local communities to learn the lore of the land, and to inculcate an ethos of scientific curiosity and stewardship to engender an ethic of care for the land. It is also about creating jobs that can lead to careers in conservation.

Janzen and Hallwachs's 32,512-hectare 'garden' epitomizes the end of a certain scientific and romantic idealization of ecosystems as inherently inclined toward equilibrium and best kept free of humans. In this way it is a model for actively managing existing protected areas, as well as for how we might create new conservation areas in lands that have been degraded from previous uses. If the story of paradise was to be rewritten so that it now celebrates science, compassion for all living things, and lots of hard work, then Janzen and Hallwachs would be its Adam and Eve.

See Also: Yellowstone to Yukon Initiative (58), Oostvaardersplassen (62), Camp Leakey (68), Tree Planting Drones (172)

Guanacaste

Santa Rosa

Rincón de la Vieja

Liberia

10°57'16.7"N 85°30'50 7"W

30 km

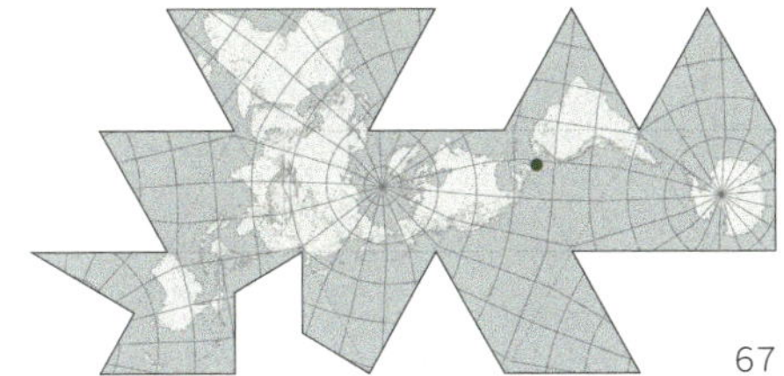

Camp Leakey
Kalimantan, Indonesia

Established in 1971 in the heart of the Tanjung Puting National Park in central Kalimantan (Borneo) by primatologist and conservationist Birutė Galdikas, Camp Leakey is a small field station for the research and rehabilitation of wild orangutans. Named after famed paleoanthropologist Louis Leakey (1903–1972) who mentored Jane Goodall, Diane Fossey, and Galdikas, Camp Leakey takes in and gradually rewilds orangutans that have formerly been captive or injured and displaced.

The camp is a remote, working research station, not a tourist attraction. Local operators do, however, offer day trips and when a tourist arrives, they are briefed about the camp's research agenda and its mission to resist the further destruction of Kalimantan's incredible rainforest. Some orangutans are on site in the Camp's nursery, but the real action begins when a cart of food scraps is wheeled out along a small boardwalk jutting into a wetland in the midst of the forest.

As the clang of a pot rings out through the forest, without either haste or aggression, the local band of orangutans, some of whom may have spent time in the camp's nursery or its rehabilitation center, come swinging through the forest toward the boardwalk. Of course, food is their primary objective, and they know the drill, but the orangutans are highly curious animals and as such they like to frisk the tourists for whatever else they may have in their possession. Mortified and enthralled in equal measure, the humans are instructed to stay calm and submit to the incessant prying and probing of their captors. Here on this little boardwalk in a remote camp in Kalimantan, the normal order of things is turned on its head and it is the animals who briefly have the upper hand. In this encounter, the cultural divide between the human and the ape that is otherwise so heavily policed, is transgressed. It is a beautiful and unforgettable experience.

Zooming out from Camp Leakey, however, the situation is anything but in favor of the animals. Tanjung Puting is surrounded by gold and zircon mines and palm oil plantations hungry for more territory. This and other human activity in the region, such as illegal logging and clearing for agriculture, not to mention a new Indonesian capital city, are eroding one of the earth's last great forest ecosystems. If left to continue unabated, these activities will soon kill off the forest's most charismatic denizen—the gentle, intelligent orangutan.

See Also: Giant Panda National Park (70), Frozen Zoo (262)

Teloekmadon

Pembuang

Kumai

Camp Leakey

3°05'14.0"S 111°55'11.3"E

50 km

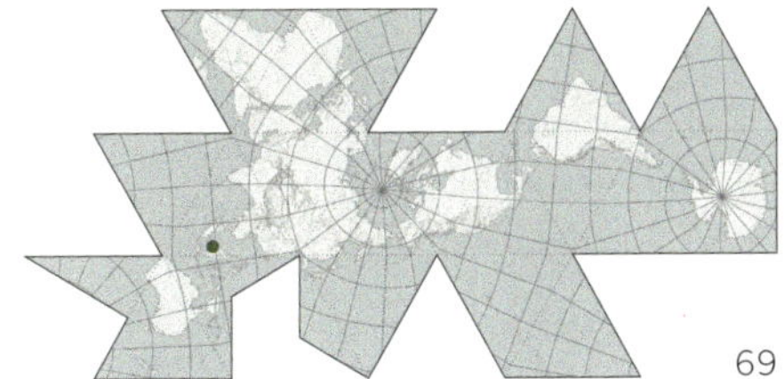

Giant Panda National Park

Chengdu, China

Paradise for a panda (*Ailuropoda melanoleuca*) is a bamboo forest high in the mountains of central China. Pandas are found nowhere else on earth and in this region there are only about 1,800 left. To secure their future and increase their numbers, the Chinese government is evicting around 1,700 people from a 27,134-square-kilometer zone in the foothills of the Tibetan plateau outside Chengdu. The Giant Panda National Park (GPNP) amalgamates many existing smaller panda reserves into one larger landscape and includes the development of a Panda Research Hub. Along with the creation of the GPNP, the establishment of a Panda Park and a Panda Village offer a range of tourist experiences close to the city and the airport. The whole ensemble is expected to attract 20 million visitors per year—more than Disneyland.

Like Disneyland's charismatic cartoon mouse, the panda also serves as the logo of one of the world's most successful conservation NGOs, the World Wildlife Fund (WWF). In terms of brand recognition, the WWF's panda logo is up there with Coca-Cola and the Rolling Stones' mouth. But more than anything, people want to see the real thing. Given the global demand for pandas as star attractions in zoos, in 1984 China's then president Deng Xiaoping began an international program of renting pandas to other countries. This is sometimes referred to as 'Panda Diplomacy,' since the pandas have often been used as bargaining chips in connection with China's geopolitical machinations.

Typically, pandas are leased to zoos for $1,000,000 a year for a ten-year period, though in the case of the Moscow zoo, two pandas have had their lease extended to 15 years. Per the loan agreements, any cubs born during the loan period are automatically the property of the People's Republic of China. Since pandas are notoriously difficult to breed, especially in captivity, this caveat is generally not an issue. Indeed, at their wits end, zookeepers have been known to show pandas videos of 'panda porn' to try and raise their interest in the task. A major aspect of the new Giant Panda National Park therefore is a high-tech panda breeding facility designed to help boost their numbers in the wild, but no doubt also to increase the number of active diplomats working their magic in the field.

See Also: Yellowstone to Yukon Initiative (58), Oostvaardersplassen (62), Camp Leakey (68), Griffith Park (182)

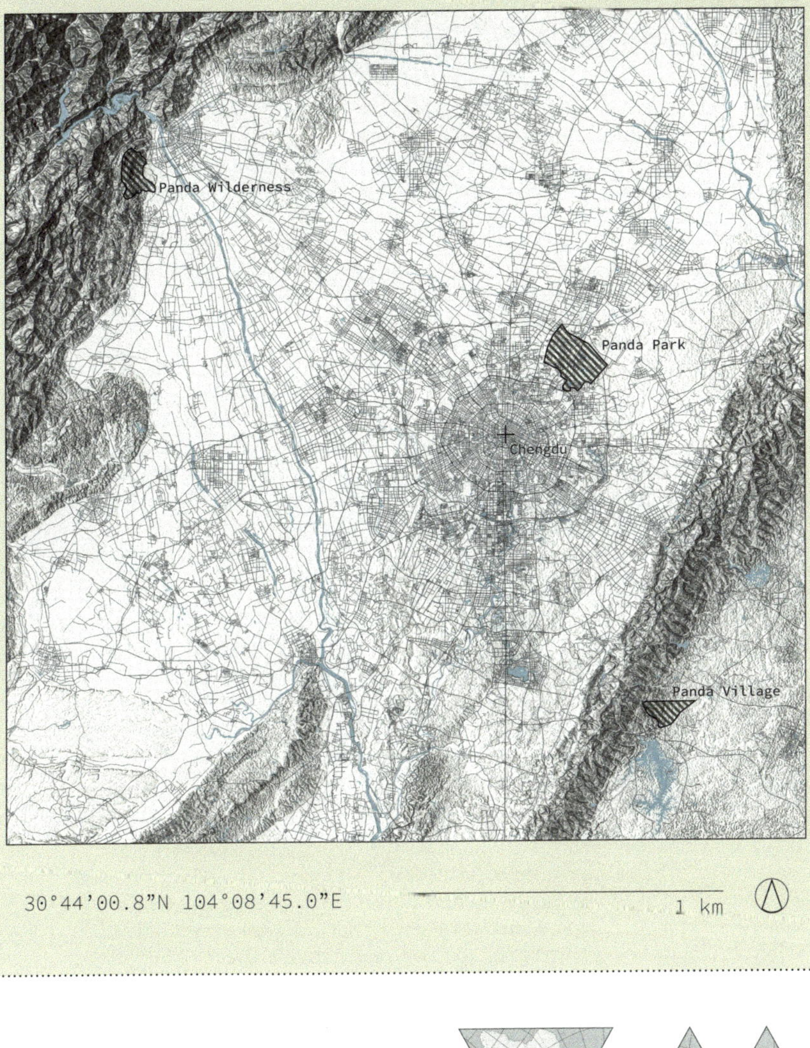

Panda Wilderness

Panda Park

Chengdu

Panda Village

30°44'00.8"N 104°08'45.0"E

1 km

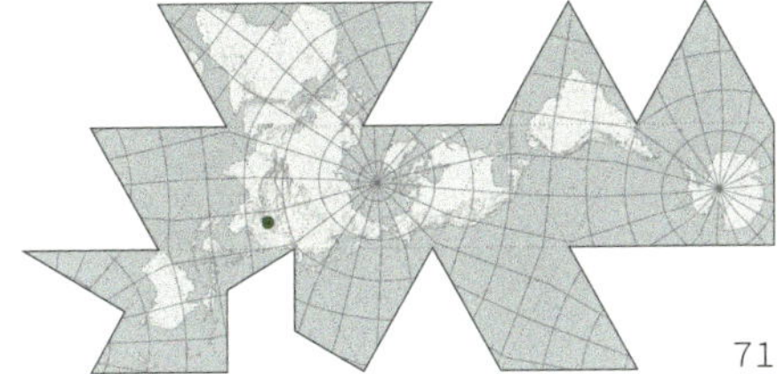

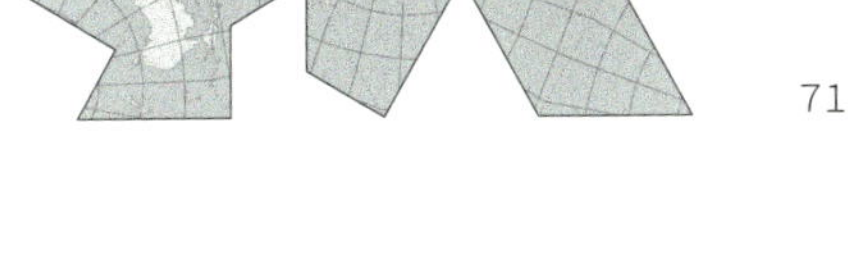

Mutijulu

Northern Territory, Australia

Mutitjulu is a small Aboriginal settlement next to Uluru, a 550-million-year-old rock formation in the center of Australia. Set in a vast desert plain, the massive rock outcrop is in fact just the top of an eroded mountain that continues for 6 kilometers below ground level. For the Anangu people—who have probably lived in the lands around the rock for 30,000 years or more—this landscape was formed by spirit beings in the Dreamtime. Knowledge of this creation and how to care for it is passed from generation to generation through storytelling, painting, and ritual.

Motivated by a combination of desire to find the original Garden of Eden, scientific curiosity, capitalist greed, and England's need for an offshore penal colony, the British invaded and annexed Australia in 1788. This massive land grab was based on the legal fiction that Australia was *terra nullius*—a land devoid of people. At the time of this conquest there were well over 300 different Aboriginal 'nations' spread across the Australian continent in a tightly knit mosaic. As the colonizers fanned out across the nation the Aboriginals were displaced from their lands, or as happened in Tasmania, exterminated. Many adults were placed in Christian missions and many children were forcibly removed from their parents for reeducation and assimilation into white Australian culture.

In a national effort to confront this shameful history and repair the damage, since the 1970s Australia has engaged in a sincere, yet painfully slow process of reconciliation. A big part of this process has been awarding land rights to Aboriginal people and providing government support for people to return to their ancestral lands. While this policy enabled Aboriginals to live again in their spiritual homelands, the remote and inhospitable landscape renders these communities dependent on welfare. Living conditions in Mutitjulu, as in most other government-issued housing for Aboriginals, are appalling.

Uluru is a world-renowned tourist destination and the navel of a nation. Until recently (2019) when the request of the Anangu that tourists not walk on the rock was taken seriously, white Australians have considered clambering up Uluru's slopes a rite of passage. Most Australians and many international tourists still list Uluru as a 'must see,' but what they don't see, or don't want to see, is Mutitjulu in its shadow. In 2017, representatives of Aboriginal Australia gathered in Mutitjulu to craft the Uluru Statement from the Heart—a declaration demanding justice and wide-ranging reform. The current Labor government, led by Prime Minister Anthony Albanese, has pledged to engage with Aboriginal Australia in good faith.

See Also: Parque de la Papa (74), Black Lives Matter Plaza (94)

25°20’42.5”S 131°02’18.4”E

2 km

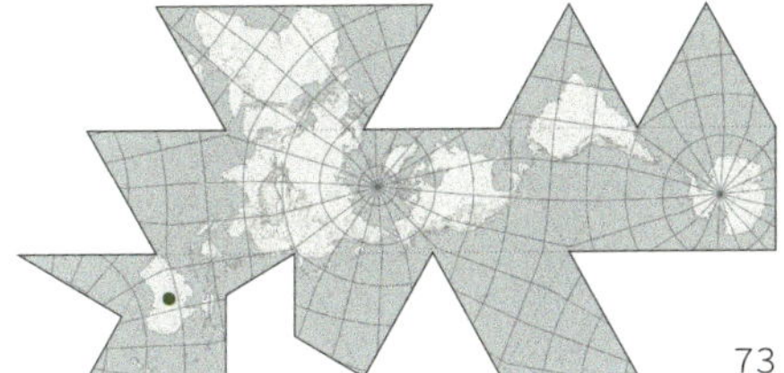

Parque de la Papa

Cusco, Peru

As well as expulsion from the Garden of Eden, one of the punishments for the original sin was a life of agricultural toil. And yet, while working the land is hard, it is arguably far more rewarding than lolling about in Eden for an eternity with nothing to do. Cultivating and collecting food binds people to a community, and a community to its landscape. Working the land can be a strong and simple way for communities to maintain traditions, alleviate poverty, and give people a sense of place and purpose. This is the case with the Quechua people of Peru who have farmed a diverse array of potatoes in the Andes for millennia and are responsible for the Parque de la Papa (Potato Park) initiative.

Located near Cusco in the Sacred Valley of the Incas, Parque de la Papa is over 9,000 hectares of farmland and habitat that supports a self-governing and self-sufficient community of nearly 4,000 people from five Quechua communities; the Amaru, Chawaytire, Pampallacta, Paru-Paru, and Sacaca. Parque de la Papa is based on the practice of *ayllu* or *Sumaq Qausay*, meaning the formation of harmonious relationships between humans, their social environments, and the land. Parque de la Papa was the first Indigenous Biocultural Heritage Area (IBCHA) established by the Asociacion ANDES, which links communities to their agricultural heritage and aims to secure it in perpetuity as a form of intellectual property. For example, one of the most important factors in the establishment of Parque de la Papa was securing the intellectual property rights to the genetic traits of endemic potatoes so that they cannot be grown by companies or corporations other than the Quechua.

By demonstrating an alternative to private property, extractive industry, cash cropping, and large-scale agribusiness, Parque de la Papa presents a sustainable future for its community. It also presents a counternarrative to indigenous people being cast as victims of colonialism and globalization, whose only choice is to leave their land and assimilate, or be tempted into the criminal world of cocaine production. By symbolically retrieving the humble potato from its status as a monocultural global fast food, the Parque de la Papa points to a world where the authenticity of local culture and local biodiversity can rival the global gods of consumerism.

See Also: Yedikule Bostan (56), GIS Crop Harvester (142), Greenhouse Agriculture (144)

Market

Parque

Pisac

13°24'03.6"S 71°50'13.4"W

1 km

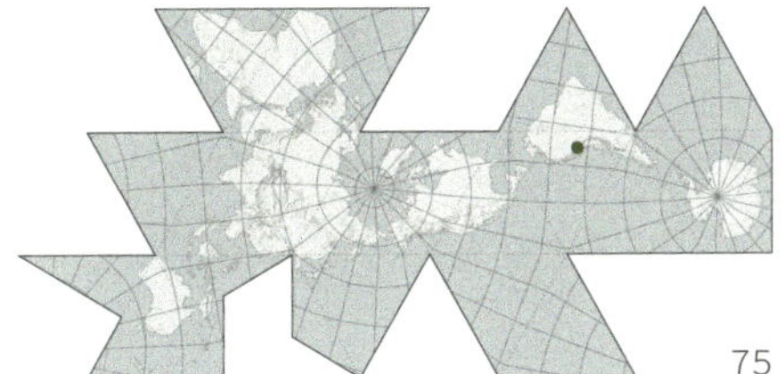

Suburban Backyard

International

Whether it be escaping the disease and decay of the ancient city or the crime and congestion of the modern city, a place in the country has always been romanticized as an antidote to the ills of urban living. And what the Italian villa, French chateau, or English mansion is to the aristocracy, the mass-produced 20th-century suburban home—replete with a front yard, a back yard and a carport—is to the modern middle class.

In suburbia, the front yard is about projecting a public image whereas the backyard is about private activity. The front provides a picturesque setting for the house and its fastidiously maintained verdure signifies conformity with a touch of competitive pride. On the other hand, the backyard is familial and informal—a space in which all the paraphernalia of quotidian family life can spill out. Amid an eclectic array of plants and maybe a vegetable garden, it is common to find in backyards a cubby house, a dog kennel, a clothes line, an assortment of sporting equipment, toys, a shed, a BBQ, and, in warmer climes, ideally, a pool. Through all this stuff the backyard tells the story of the family's fads and phases.

The one thing both the front and back yards share is a swath of green grass. Keeping up appearances, the front will be primed with fertilizer, well-watered, and neatly cropped, whereas the back will show the wear and tear of its various overlapping uses. It is said that in the United States alone, the amount of grass in suburban yards is now more than twice the entire surface area of England—the place largely responsible for creating the idyllic image of landscape as a green swath in the first place.

Once the norm in suburbia, a big front yard and a big backyard is becoming less and less common. As planners increase the density of suburban development in an effort to contain suburban sprawl, or parents 'cash in' when the kids grow up by selling off the backyard for another house, suburbia is losing the open space that was always its *raison d'etre*. Despite this, a suburban house and garden—no matter how small—remains the property of choice for the majority of consumers. For them it's as close as one can get to paradise in this life.

See Also: Welwyn Garden City (98), Levittown (100), Walmart Supercenter (102)

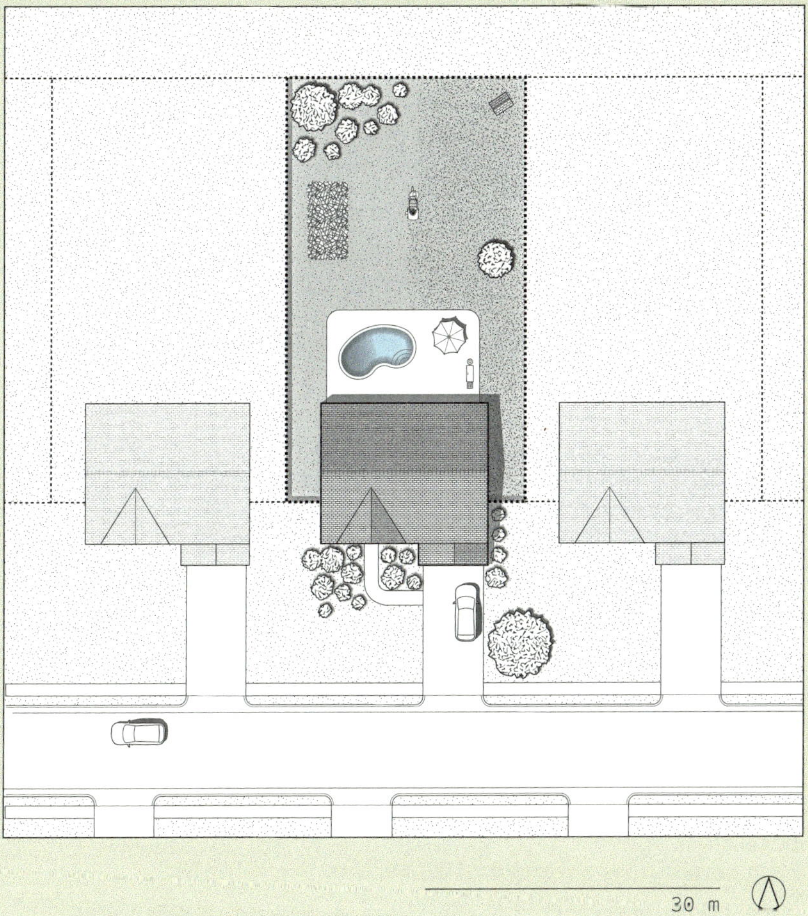

30 m

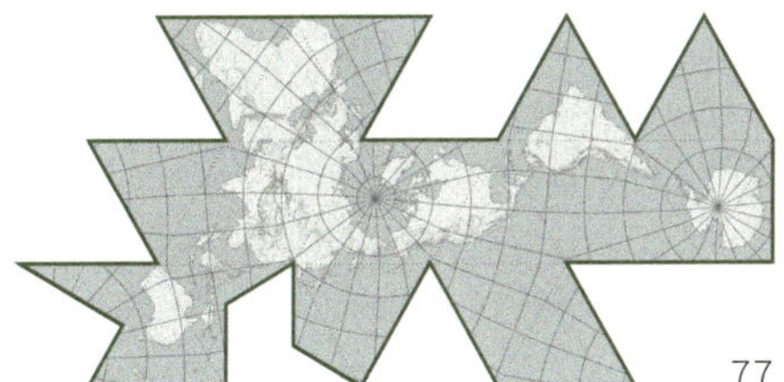

Mar-a-Lago

Florida, United States

Mar-a-Lago is a United States national historic landmark, a private resort, and the current residence of former US president Donald J. Trump and his wife, Melania Trump. The name Mar-a-Lago (Spanish for sea-to-lake) stems from its location between Florida's Intracoastal Waterway and the Atlantic Ocean. It is one of the wealthiest enclaves in America, where the rich enjoy tax breaks.

Mar-a-Lago was originally built by the owner of General Foods Corporation, Marjorie Merriweather Post, between 1924 and 1927. The mansion was designed by Marion Sims Wyeth in the style of a 'Mediterranean villa'—whatever that exactly means—and the interior and exterior decorated with an abundance of gold accents by the architect and set designer Joseph Urban. The mansion has 58 bedrooms, 33 bathrooms, a 9-meter-long marble-top dining table, twelve fireplaces, and three bomb shelters.

Upon Post's death in 1973, the property was bequeathed by the eponymous foundation to the National Park Service as a Winter White House for sitting presidents. Due to high maintenance costs, however, the National Park Service turned over the property rights to the Post Foundation, which sold it to Donald Trump in 1985 for $10 million. New additions to the property have since included a massive ballroom, five tennis courts, and a waterfront pool. Now a members-only club as well as Trump's private residence, the current value of the estate is around $160 million.

Mar-a-Lago has become synonymous with the former president as his 'southern White House' and throughout his presidency he used the resort to conduct business, host foreign leaders, and generally stay away from Washington, which he frequently referred to as a 'swamp.' The private nature of the resort also allowed Trump and his cronies to conduct their business outside of the reach of White House protocols. Ongoing tensions between authorities and Trump spilled over in August 2022 when the FBI searched the property for stashes of classified documents that Trump had refused to hand over to the National Archives.

Mar-a-Lago is a fine example of American kitsch, but for some it is also a symbol of the nepotism and corruption that is corroding America's venerable institutions. Certainly, it unashamedly extends a long tradition of politicians living lifestyles that are the very opposite of those they claim to represent. With its swaying palms and faux Mediterranean villa, Mar-a-Lago represents the cliché of paradise as a place of pleasure and taboo. In the case of the Trumps, however, it is perhaps Adam who has tempted Eve.

See Also: Banwa Resort (80), Black Lives Matter Plaza (94), USA-Mexico Border Wall (210)

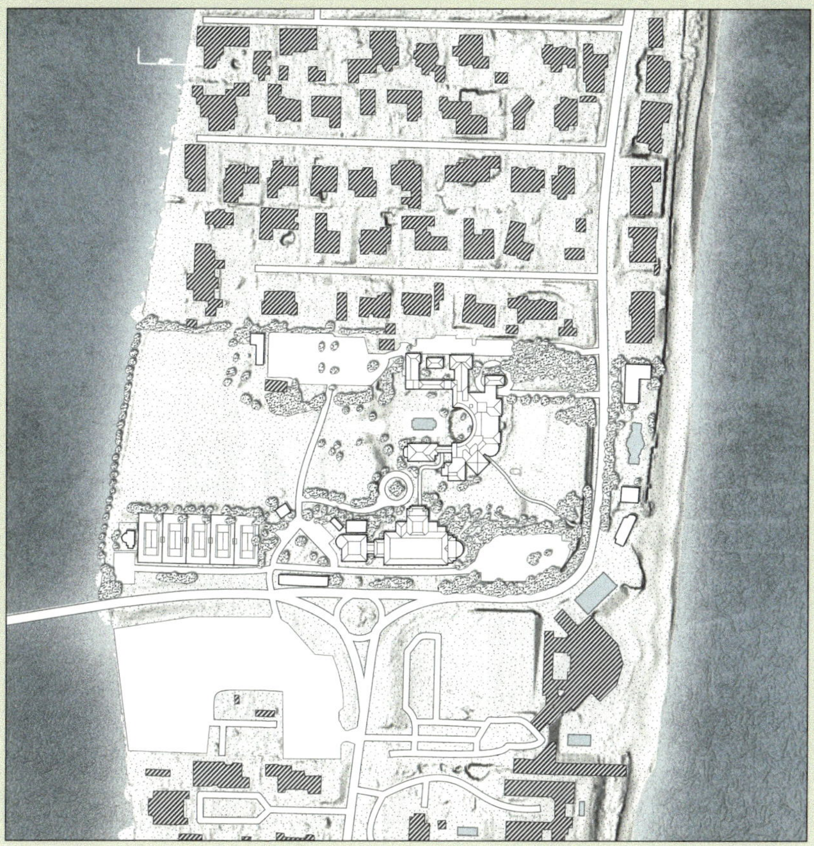

26°40'37.3"N 80°02'13.6"W

200 m

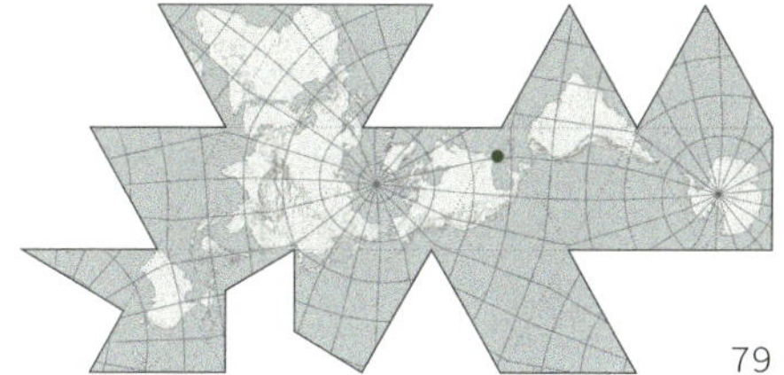

Banwa Resort

Palawan, Philippines

Despite the many bad things that have taken place on tropical islands both in fiction and reality, the image of the palm-fringed isle as paradisiacal remains firmly entrenched in the popular imagination. The trope of a tropical paradise—azure horizons, lithe bodies, and exotic fruits—finds its way into the advertising of almost every resort on earth. The best of these, or certainly the most expensive, is Banwa, a sandy speck in the Palawan archipelago, some 500 kilometers south of Manila.

Chosen by the resort's developers, the name Banwa means community in the Palawan dialect. No doubt this was considered more commercially viable than the island's actual name of 'Puerco,' or pig. Even so, it's a strange choice for a resort where the whole idea is to be more or less alone in paradise and not do any of the things normally associated with being a member of a community.

Boasting great care of the environment in its construction, as well as working off its own supply of pure food and water, Banwa presents itself as an elite ecotourism destination. Taken seriously, ecotourism entails minimizing not just the aesthetic impacts of development on a particular piece of land, but also reducing the development's entire ecological footprint. This means minimizing the environmental costs of its food, water, energy, materials, transportation, and waste. Applying this accountancy to the case of Banwa, just the flights visitors must make to get there would blow any ecological benefits the island itself achieves out of the water. This glaring contradiction at the core of ecotourism is compounded when we also consider the ways in which Banwa's mega-rich guests might have made their money and how they live their lives when not on the island.

Ecotourist destinations worthy of the moniker are also expected to tangibly contribute to local conservation efforts and the local community above and beyond simply providing jobs in the tourism industry. Banwa does support local conservation efforts—in particular, reef regeneration—but it is unclear what it does for the real community from which it draws its local labor. Given that guests pay $100,000 per day to rent the resort's six villas, and the average income of a Filipino worker is around $20 a day, one imagines there is plenty of money sloshing about with which it could do so.

See Also: Nauru Island (188), The World (216)

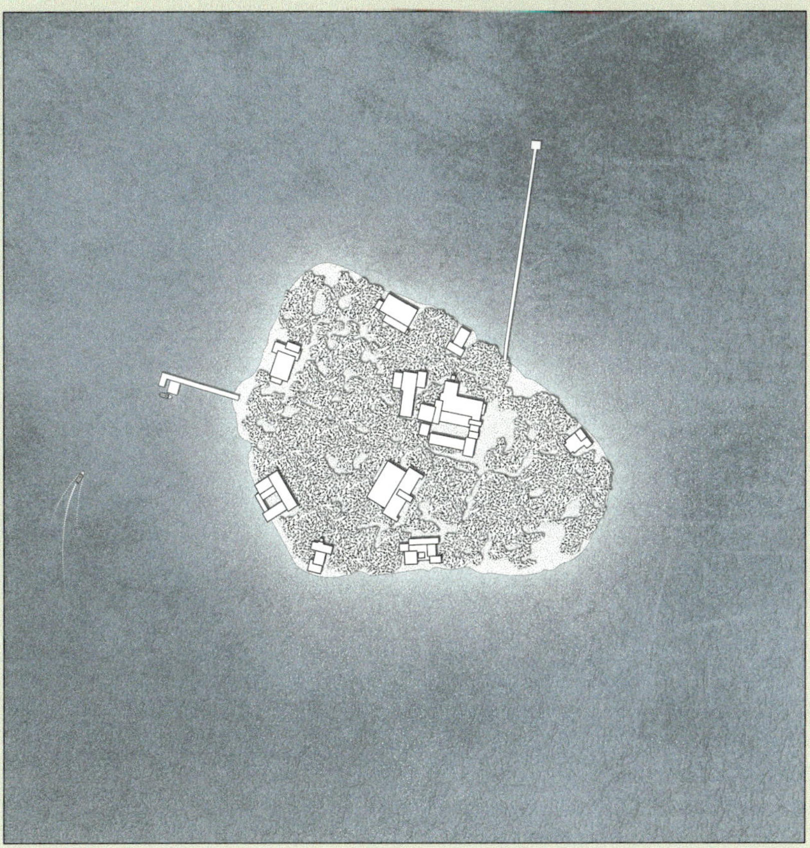

10°19'07.6"N 119°28'53.1"E

200 m

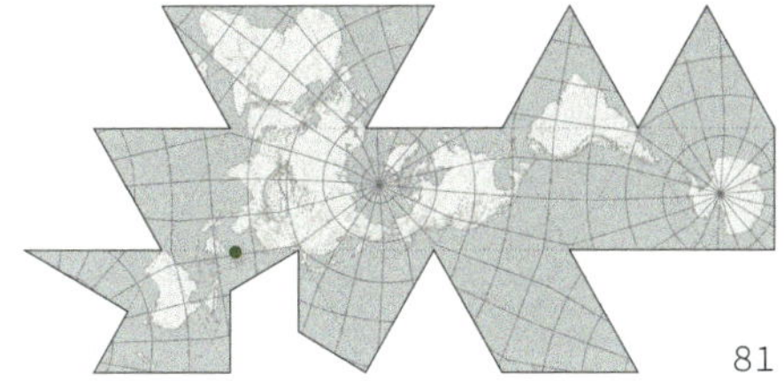

Time Landscape
New York, United States

Time Landscape is the title of a 1978 work of art by artist Alan Sonfist on a small plot of land at the intersection of LaGuardia Place and Houston Street in Manhattan. The project was one of many that Sonfist hoped to distribute throughout the city, each in some way intended to recall the landscape character of 'Manahatta,' the name given to the island by the Lenapehoking Native Americans prior to the arrival of Dutch colonists in the 17th century.

Originally, *Time Landscape* comprised indigenous plants laid out to represent the process of forest succession from moss to grasses, shrubs, saplings, and eventually mature trees. In this way the garden charts a convoluted temporal arc—it represents growth forward in time while simultaneously taking us back in time to when such a forest preceded the city. From its inception, *Time Landscape* raised tricky curatorial questions. For example, should its representation of wilderness be carefully maintained or left to chance? And once the forest microcosm had been achieved, was its clock to be stopped and its image of landscape freeze-framed or again left open to chance? And what of those pesky local animals, the New Yorkers? Should they be allowed into the work's rarified timezone or banished? All this rasies the question of whether the primary subject of the work is landscape and human agency, or time itself? Or perhaps, as the title suggests, it's both.

One can only wonder what creative rights the artist has over his art in this situation, but the Department of Parks and Recreation seems to have answered some of these questions by maintaining it so that it leans toward a permament representation of (faux) wilderness. On the one hand this is akin to the original Garden of Eden in so far as time is stopped, and yet, on the other, it is unlike the original Eden because there, wilderness was exluded. In a further twist of paradisiacal symbology, while there are no cherubs with swords of fire, Parks and Recreation has built a fence around *Time Landscape*. That the fence was originally built by the authorities for security reasons seems paranoid in today's Manhattan, but it serves now to reify the work of art in the context of the city in the same way a frame does a painting in a gallery.

See Also: Site of Reversible Destiny (84), Spiral Jetty (258), Roden Crater (296)

40°43'37.45"N 73°59'58.3"W

100 m

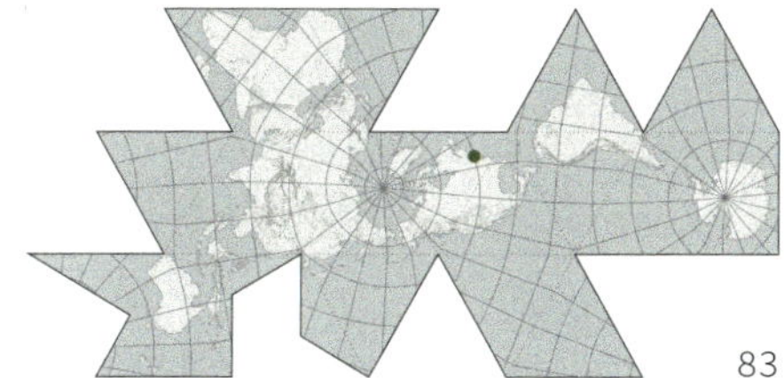

Site of Reversible Destiny

Gifu Prefecture, Japan

The conceptual art and built environments of Madeline Gins and Shusaku Arakawa aim to disorient and destabilize the viewer so as to induce a heightened level of self-awareness. Gins and Arakawa believed that a door to immortality (paradise) could be opened by jolting human perception from its habituation in routine and comfort. Whether for the artists this was metaphor or fact, is moot.

Over the course of their careers, Gins and Arakawa moved from presenting work in galleries to designing rooms, buildings, gardens, and, hypothetically at least, whole cities. Their largest built work came a year later with the commission for a 2-hectare garden, the Site of Reversible Destiny in the semi-rural setting of Yoro, in Gifu prefecture near Nagoya. Roughly the size of two football fields, the Site of Reversible Destiny is a colorful crater—a sort of sunken garden in the shape of an ellipse. At the entrance to the garden the visitor receives a map, a set of instructions, a helmet and an especially grippy pair of sneakers. You then make your way through a maze-like building to a large area of concrete patterned with maps of cities at the edge of the crater. Cast in silver-colored concrete, the shape of Japan appears to be oozing down the slope. Cantilevered out from a massive wall defining the crater's edge are a series of large green UFO-like discs.

The crater itself is a cacophony of colorful shapes, undulating planes, follies, random bits of furniture, plants, and other strange objects. The map identifies certain zones with names like the Exactitude Ridge, the Imaging Navel, and the Geographical Ghost. As you try to make sense of all this, your body simultaneously struggles to navigate the steep topography and the labyrinth of pathways. Falling over is therefore not uncommon, indeed, that's the idea.

One also notices that when visitors are not stumbling about, they appear to be intermittently moving their bodies in unusual yet quite specific ways. In fact, they are performing a set of choreographed moves at certain locations as per the artists' instructions set out on the back of the map. They are, according to the artists, attempting to 'reverse their destiny' by breaking themselves free of normal behavior. This is serious fun, and interesting art, but if it really is meant to forestall the inevitable, then it failed: Arakawa died in 2010 and Gins followed him four years later.

See Also: Time Landscape (82), Garden of Cosmic Speculation (86), Roden Crater (296)

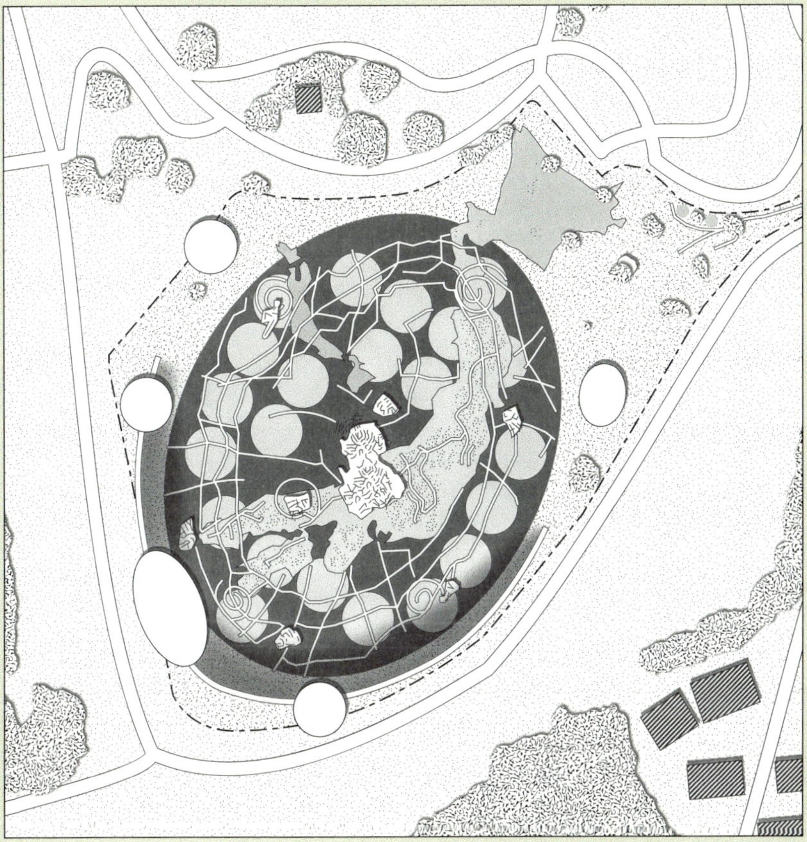

35°16’55.0”N 136°33’01.4”E

80 m

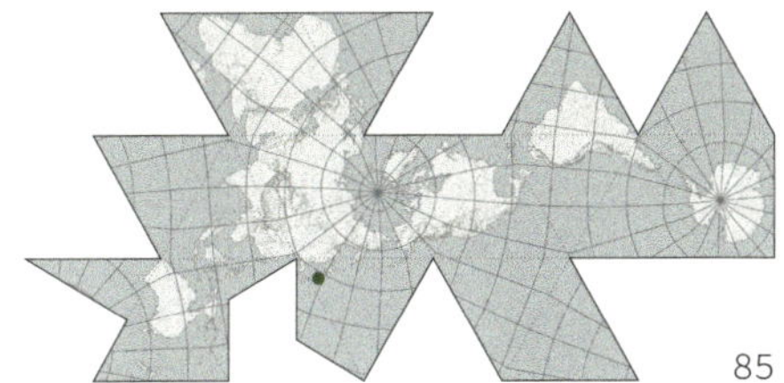

Garden of Cosmic Speculation
Dumfriesshire, Scotland

Throughout history great gardens have symbolized the relationship between culture and nature. Gardens representing Western conceptions of paradise originated in Persia then spread throughout Christendom and along the lines of Islamic expansion into India, Spain, and parts of Africa. Typically, these gardens are organized around two intersecting, cardinal axes with water demarcating the point where they intersect. This geometry symbolizes an ordered cosmos. For example, at the Taj Mahal in Agra where Shah Jahan (1592–1666) entombed his wife, Mumtaz Mahal, the quartered garden symbolizes heaven. Around the same time, though in the West, this geometry finds its most grandiose expression at the court of Versailles. There, landscape architect André Le Nôtre directed the garden's central axis toward the sunrise so that his client, Louis XIV (the Sun King), could play Apollo riding his chariot across the skies.

While also signifying ideal worlds, Chinese and Japanese gardens do not use such geometry. In these gardens, the structure, order, and beauty of nature is found in miniature concentrations of the organic forms one finds in the natural world. In the 18th century, reports of this approach contributed to the invention of the picturesque English garden. Instead of superimposing abstract geometry on the land, English gardens were stylized expressions—or as they liked to say, 'improvements'—of natural beauty.

A contemporary design that endeavors to extend the venerable tradition of gardens as symbols of nature and microcosms of the cosmos is the so-called Garden of Cosmic Speculation, created by renowned architecture critic Charles Jenks. The Garden of Cosmic Speculation derives its forms from contemporary physics, not the observation of nature per se. Instead of orthogonal geometry or picturesque scenery, Jenks's design is formed with explicit reference to computer-generated patterns associated with fractal geometry and chaos theory. To walk through the Garden of Cosmic Speculation is thus to walk through a three-dimensional representation of contemporary mathematics, which in turn represents current thinking on the deep structure and behavior of matter. What distinguishes this new geometry of nature from historical precedents is that it incorporates the fourth dimension of time in its modeling to show that behind the scenes of what might appear to the naked eye as something inchoate, there is in fact a high degree of order. The question for Jenks then, as it is for all gardeners, is the degree to which the garden is just an image of an idea of nature, or the thing itself.

See Also: Roden Crater (296), Very Large Array (298)

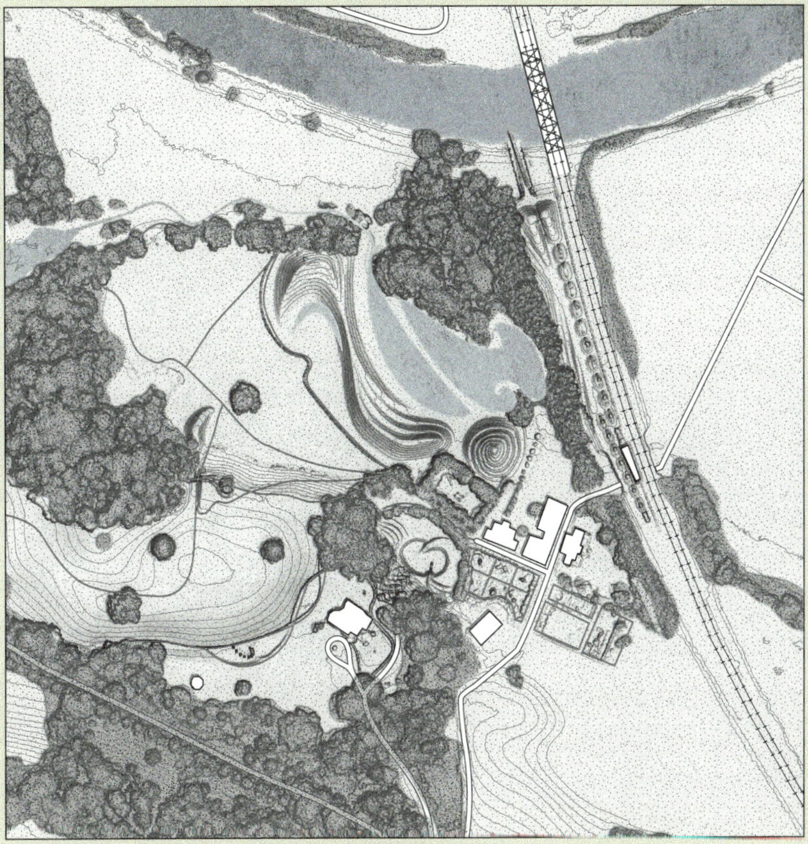

55°07’47.2”N 3°39’57.0”W

200 m

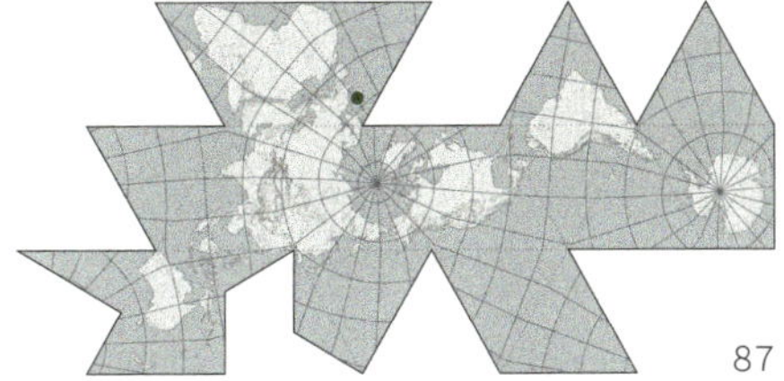

Utopias

The literary genre of imagining and describing a better society has its roots in Plato's *Republic* of 380 BCE. Reflecting its author's scorn for democracy at one end of the political spectrum and tyranny at the other, the Republic was ruled by an elite caste of specially educated "philosopher kings." Society was conceived militarily, the family unit was outlawed, the weak and infirm were ostracized and artists were treated with suspicion, if not outright contempt.

The neologism 'utopia' was invented by Sir Thomas More in 1516 when he spliced the Greek *eutopos* (the place where things are well) with *outopos* (no place) and attempted to do for England what Plato had done for Athens. Set on an island, More's utopia was less cold-hearted than Plato's but no less organized. The plan was for 54 self-same cities, each with 80,000 people evenly distributed in neighborhoods of 30 houses around a communal hall. It was socialist, agrarian, and, when compared to the religiosity of the times, rational. More's medieval vision of utopia could not, however meet the challenges of industrialization. As the Industrial Revolution violently and rapidly transformed Europe's landscapes and cities in the 18th and 19th centuries, it was the political theorist and philosopher John Stuart Mill who, in 1868, coined the term 'dystopia' to signify utopia's antithesis. Mill's dystopian perspective became real in the 20th century when fascism showed that utopia's ideal of perfection can only be maintained by authoritarianism.

In addition to utopia and dystopia there is also cornucopia, a state of abundance. Rather than plans for building a better society, cornucopia aims only to satisfy individual desires. Cornucopia finds its apotheosis in the consumer culture of mid-20th-century suburban America, nested within the broader utopian project of achieving unlimited progress, while simultaneously guaranteeing individual liberty through the rule of law. Motivated by the realization that there are environmental limits to consumerism—not to mention the fact that shopping and gluttony don't necessarily make you happy—the counterculture of the 1960s and 1970s rejected cornucopia for a place called 'ecotopia.'

In Ernest Callenbach's 1975 novel of the same name, Ecotopia is a society built on the three pillars of environmental care, democracy, and spiritual enlightenment. Ecotopia manifested the principles of what we now routinely refer to as sustainability—the reorganization of industrial society to be symbiotic with, rather than parasitical upon, the ecosystem. Under the rubric of a Green New Deal, ecotopian thought today confronts the imminent catastrophe of climate change with plans and policies to make contemporary cities and their related agricultural and industrial landscapes not only more sustainable, but more equitable. This too is a good place, no place.

Potsdamer Platz

Berlin, Germany

By the 1920s, Potsdamer Platz in the center of Berlin had a reputation as Europe's most vibrant and hedonistic urban hub. Potsdamer Platz was the eye of Berlin's cyclonic modernity, which, with the rise of Nazism, would soon collapse in on itself. In 1938, just one block north of the platz (indicated with red cross), Albert Speer erected the massive Reich Chancellery where, deep in its bunker on April 30th, 1945, Hitler shot himself as the city lay smoldering in ruins above.

In 1961, the newly formed German Democratic Republic, a puppet of the Soviet Union that controlled the eastern sector of the city, constructed the Berlin Wall to isolate and starve the population living in West Berlin—the area of the city under French, English and American administration. The wall ran directly through the Potsdamer Platz and for the next 28 years the platz was a ghost, its former streets and buildings nothing but faint outlines etched into the ground of 'no-man's land'—the militarized zone between the communist east and the capitalist west that encircled West Berlin.

Soon after the fall of the Berlin Wall in 1989, the 155-kilometer-long tract of no-man's-land was suddenly *everyone's* land. Despite being merely a field of rubble, Berliners quickly self-organized myriad events to celebrate the new public space. It became an impromptu people's park, Berlin style. In 1991, however, a major redevelopment master plan for the platz and its surrounds was unveiled by the government with the Mercedes Benz Group appointed as its landlord. From an urban design perspective, most controversial was the way the master plan proposed to reconstruct Potsdamer Platz essentially as it was before World War II. For some this seemed not only to lack innovation, but also to be an intentional act of amnesia. Apologists for the design argued that the city's form needn't change just because shameful historical events had previously taken place there.

As it happened, Potsdamer Platz was indeed reconstructed according to its prewar form, but if it was the halcyon days of the 1920s that its planners sought to selectively channel from its fraught history, they soon learned that the resurrection of the form of a city and the resurrection of its spirit are two very different things. Today Potsdamer Platz is a soulless corporate enclave, and while Berlin's propensity for hedonism certainly lives on, you won't find it here.

See Also: Heavy Loadbearing Body (224), Teufelsberg (226), Auschwitz (228)

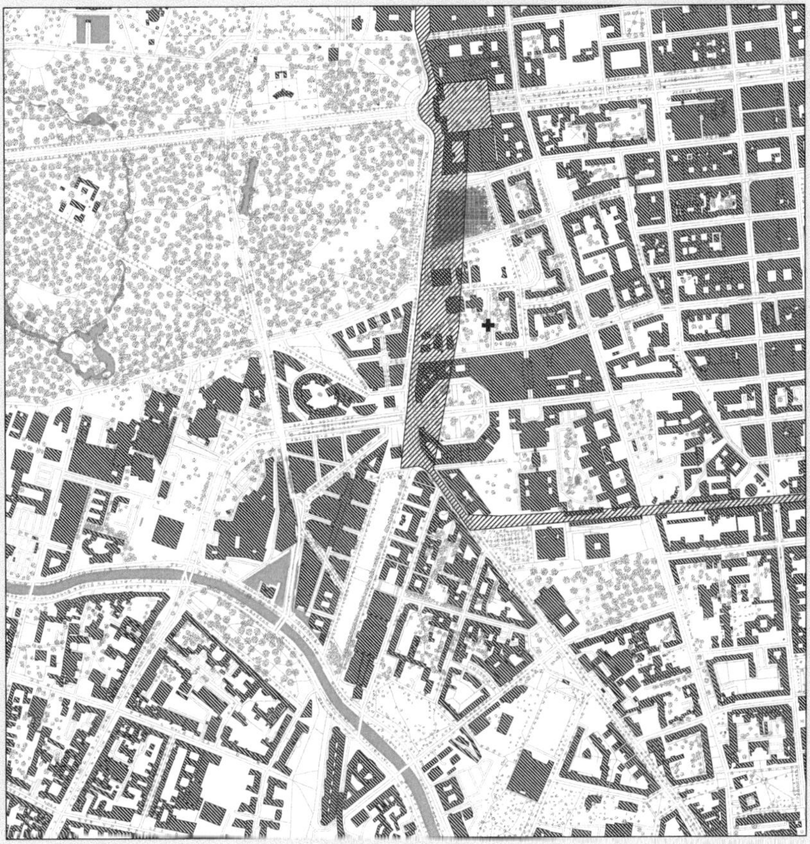

52°30'33.8"N 13°22'35.4"E

500 m

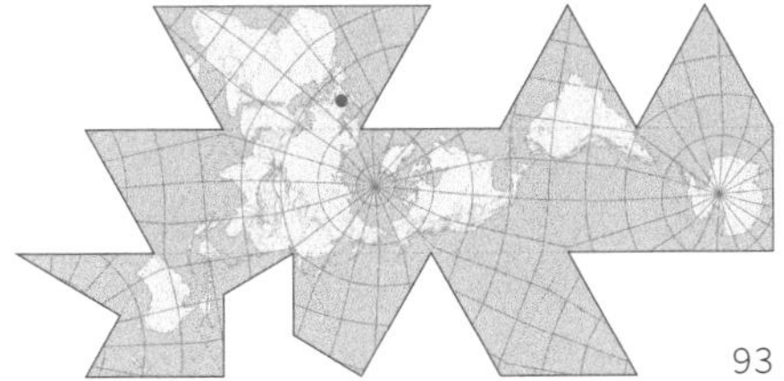

Black Lives Matter Plaza

Washington, DC, United States

In the wake of the murder of George Floyd on May 25th, 2020 by police officer Derek Chauvin, "BLACK LIVES MATTER" was painted in massive yellow letters along a two-block stretch of 16th Street leading to the White House in Washington, DC. This was one of over 2,700 similar public art installations across the United States in the wake of the murder.

The work of art was conceived by DCMurals, a division of the DC Department of Public Works Graffiti Prevention Initiative, and implemented by the department's staff and volunteers by stealth in the early hours of June 5th, 2020. Later that same day, DC Mayor Muriel Bowser officially renamed the area taken up by the text as 'Black Lives Matter Plaza.' This is now marked by a street sign at the intersection near St. John's Church, the backdrop to then-President Donald Trump's notorious photo-op in which he held aloft a bible after he'd instructed police to clear protesters from the area (indicated with red cross). In an interesting twist, the DC chapter of Black Lives Matter Global Network Foundation, Inc. has rejected the plaza as a distraction from more substantive policy change.

Exacerbated by social media and journalism not worthy of the name, American politics at this moment in time is extremely partisan. The right provokes the left with draconian policies and gun-toting bigotry, and the left provokes the right with hyper-sensitive identity politics and political idealism that is seen as disconnected from the daily life of many citizens. The right clings to an America that is white, Christian, capitalist, and exceptional. The left seeks an ecosocialist Green New Deal that prioritizes mitigating climate change and advancing social justice in the wake of colonialism, slavery, and neoliberalism.

Through these different lenses, monuments and memorials across the nation are being attacked or defended, and in some cases removed altogether. For some, the fact that the identity of a prominent public space in the nation's capital can be remade in the name of anti-racism is inspirational. For others it signals a threat to the very fabric of traditional American society. This rift threatens to now undermine the entire utopian experiment of the United States as it struggles to cohere internally and command respect externally.

See Also: Mar-a-Lago (78), Louisiana State Penitentiary (206), Vietnam Veterans Memorial (236)

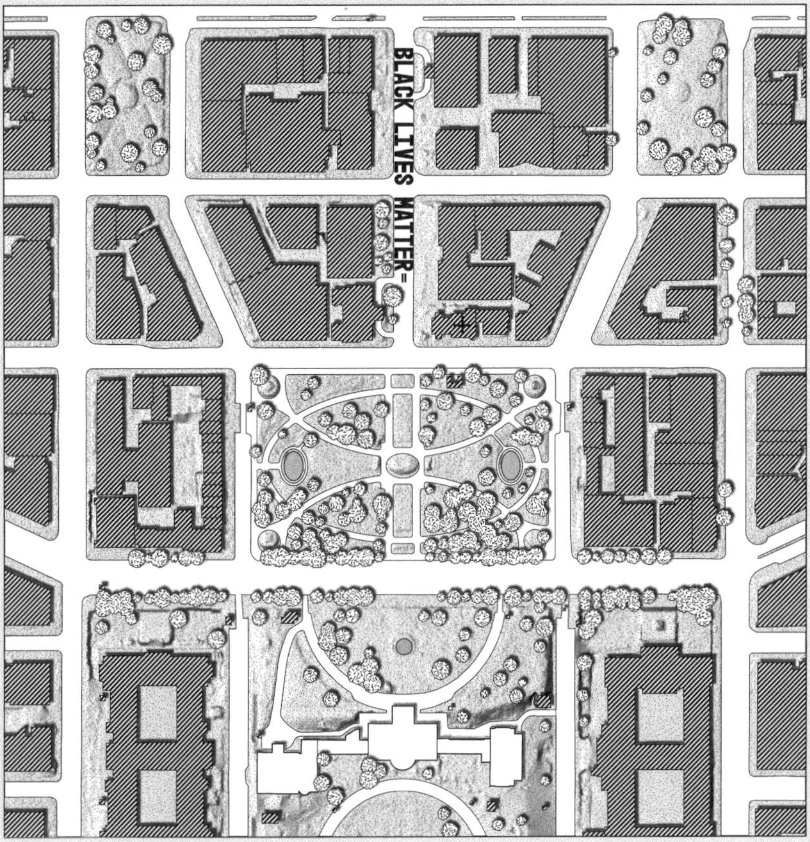

BLACK LIVES MATTER=

38°54'04.1"N 77°02'11.6"W

200 m

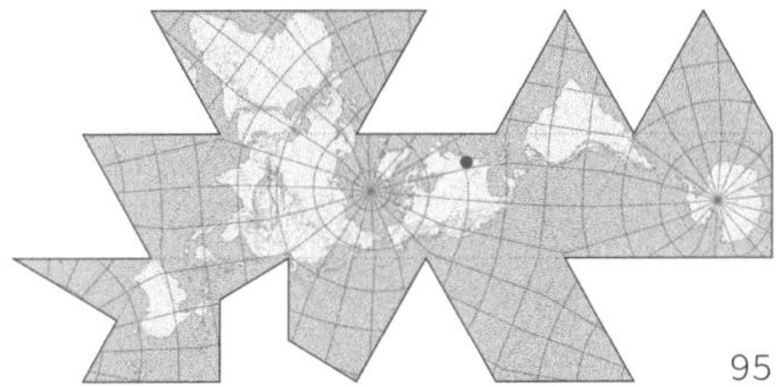

The United Nations

New York, United States

World government was a key theme in H.G Wells's 1905 book *A Modern Utopia*. While many of his other ideas as to the perfect society—eugenics for one—are repugnant to us now, a step toward world government was made with the creation of the League of Nations in 1919 and lives on today in the form of the United Nations. In fact, Wells helped draft one of the UN's first milestones—the Declaration of Human Rights—formally adopted by the assembly in 1948.

Every year, over 5,000 delegates from the UN's 195 member states convene at its (extraterritorial) precinct on Manhattan's east side. Though far from governing the world, in its 77 years of existence the UN has made several major contributions to a better world. It created the International Convention on the Elimination of All Forms of Racial Discrimination in 1969, held the first World Conference on the Human Environment in 1972, and drafted the Universal Declaration of the Eradication of Hunger and Malnutrition in 1974. This was followed by the World Conference of the International Women's Year in 1975, the Convention on the Law of the Sea in 1982, the Convention Against Torture in 1984, and the Montreal Protocol in 1987, which effectively saved the earth's fragile ozone layer. This was followed with the momentous Earth Summit in Rio and the creation of the Convention on Biological Diversity in 1992, and more recently, in 2015, the adoption of the Sustainable Development Goals and the formulation of the Paris Climate Agreement.

Like everything the UN does, the design of its New York headquarters was intended to be reached, however imperfectly, through consensus and collaboration. A board of ten (male) architects developed 50 possible designs, from which the preferred scheme by mid-career Brazilian architect Oscar Niemeyer was eventually selected as the winner. Legend has it, however, that the most senior and most famous of the ten architects, Le Corbusier, manipulated the outcome to the extent that he could claim the project as his own. Le Corbusier had until then not built anything in New York and so by all reports he bullied his way into sharing the project with Niemeyer in order to secure his first big New York commission.

Symbolizing a united world, the UN complex is today a montage of materials and works of art gathered from many nations, but the thing that really holds it all together is the building's cornerstone. Inside that cornerstone is a small metal box containing the UN's Charter and a copy of the Declaration of Human Rights.

See Also: Chandigarh (108), The World (216)

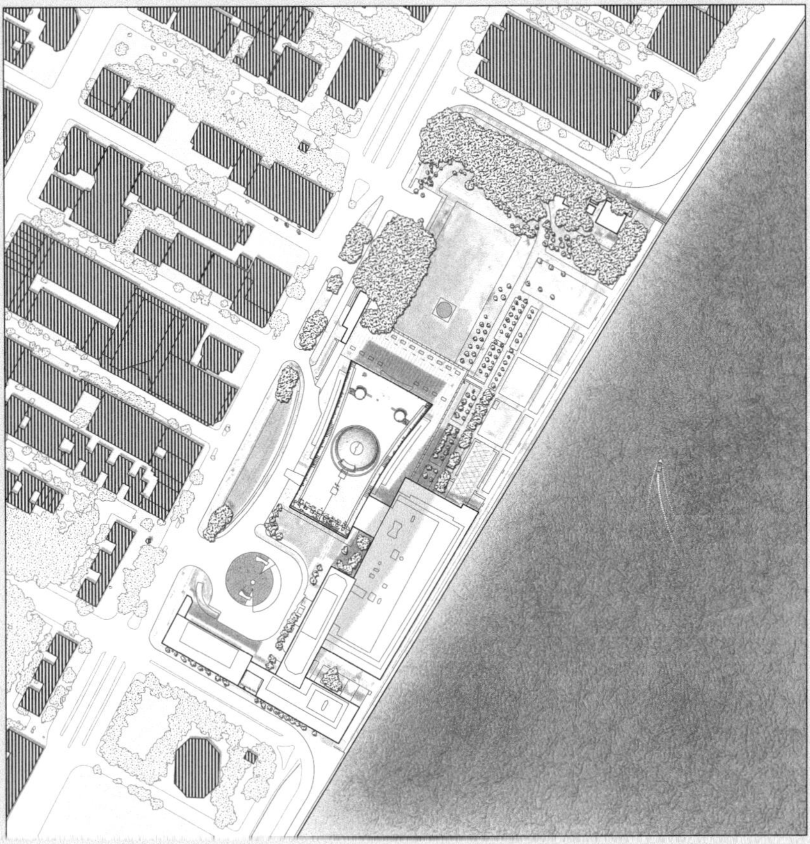

40°44’55.8”N 73°58’05.3”W

200 m

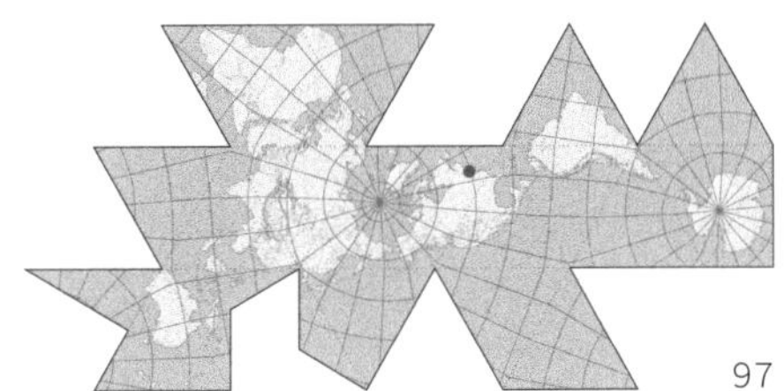

Welwyn Garden City
Hertfordshire, England

In the late 18th and 19th centuries, rapid industrialization caused chaotic urban restructuring and led to social problems as the new proletariat crowded into urban slums. As an alternative, utopian thinkers such as Charles Fourier (1772–1837) in France and Robert Owen (1771–1858) in England proposed that housing be connected to industry and developed in rural settings. While rejecting as fantasy the idea of any utopian reconciliation between capitalists and workers, Karl Marx also wrote of the need to spatially integrate the city and the country.

As a stenographer recording the debates of the English parliament at the turn of the century, Ebenezer Howard (1850–1928) was familiar with these ideas and the issues motivating them. Though untrained in town planning, Howard developed the personal conviction that new towns built in rural settings could be rationally planned in such a way that they would offer their citizens the best of the country and the best of the city, without the drawbacks of either. He referred to this as the 'Garden City' and devoted his life to figuring it out in both financial and spatial detail. As if to rebuke Marx's preference for violent revolution as the only way to really change the world, Howard published his vision under the title *To-morrow: A Peaceful Path to Real Reform* in 1898. This was subsequently reissued in 1902 as *Garden Cities of Tomorrow*.

As Howard conceived it, a network of small Garden Cities of 32,000 people radiating around larger ones of 58,000 people would fan out across the landscape. At the center of each Garden City would be all the major civic amenities (the best of the city) and at their edges forests, farms, industry, and philanthropic institutions (the best of the country).

Not only did he publish his ideas, most importantly, Howard put them into practice. The first Garden City was built at Letchworth, just outside London, in 1904. Then, in 1919, Howard established Welwyn Garden City 20 kilometers away. Neither Letchworth nor Welwyn succeeded exactly in providing the best of the city and the best of the country, and nor did they provide affordable housing and jobs for the proletariat as Howard had originally intended. Instead, they became far flung, middle-class suburban towns struggling to maintain the critical mass necessary to provide jobs, services, and cultural amenity. With his life's work complete, Howard died in Welwyn in 1928 as the specter of London's expansion appeared on the horizon.

See Also: Suburban Backyard (76), Levittown (100), Pruitt-Igoe (106), Seaside (110), Auroville (114)

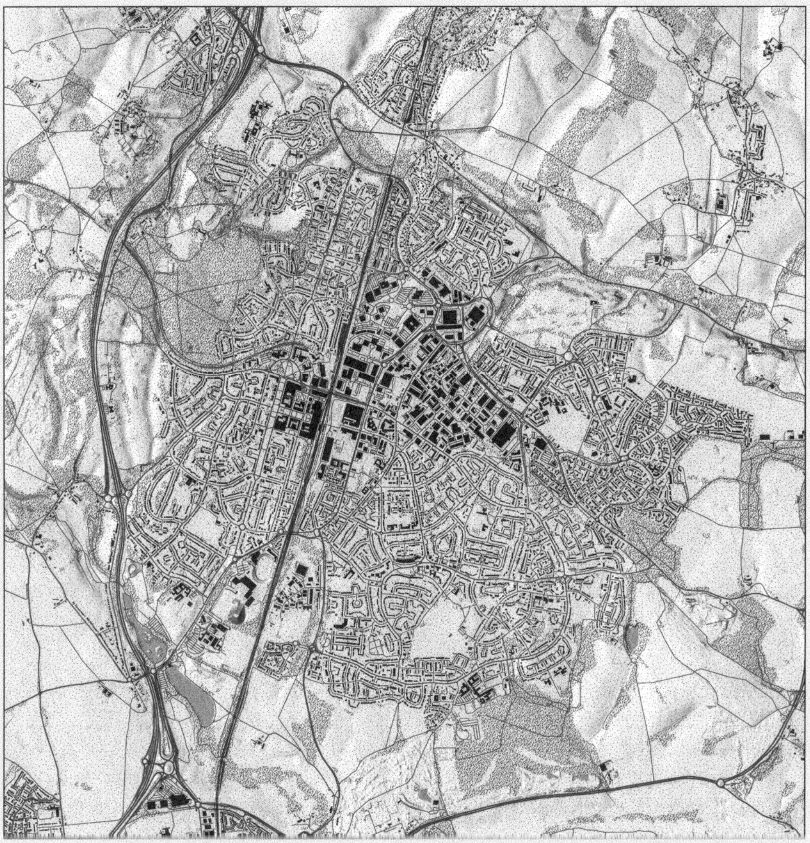

51°48’16.3”N 0°12’27.0”W

2 km

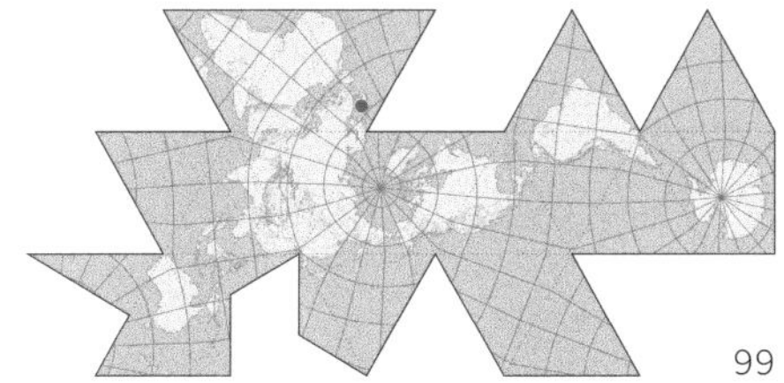

Levittown

New York, United States

Frederick Law Olmsted and his partner Calvert Vaux planned America's first suburban community at Riverside in Chicago in 1869, but it was not until the development of Levittown in 1947 that the modern phenomenon of mass-produced suburbia really appeared. Planned and built over a four-year period by William J. Levitt (1907–1994), the eponymous town had 17,000 homes for 84,000 people. What Ford did for the car, Levitt did for housing: in just 27 mechanistic steps a Levitt home, replete with appliances, could be assembled in a matter of hours and sold for around $90,000 in today's money. As a modular system of affordable housing—complete with roads, parks, schools, and shops—Levittown became the prototype for postwar suburbia the world over.

As the Levittown prototype proliferated, it became synonymous with the American dream known pejoratively today as 'suburban sprawl.' While no one could deny its success in terms of providing much-needed postwar housing, from the 1960s onwards suburban development was routinely criticized as racist, sexist, conformist, ugly, and environmentally destructive. The counterargument is that suburbia is affordable, capacious, functional, clean, safe, friendly, and individualistic.

In 1967, sociologist Herbert Gans published *The Levittowners*, a book documenting his experience of living in Levittown for two years. Gans reported that the actual lives of residents were significantly more complex—not to say better—than critics had imagined. A little later the celebrated architect Robert Venturi also came to suburbia's defense, summarized by his tongue-in-cheek quip that "Americans don't need piazzas; they should be home washing their cars." In any event, the fact is that to this day suburbia is the preferred form of living for a majority of people in the developed world.

Despite being nominated as one of the most important 100 people of the 20th century by *Time Magazine* in 1998, what bedeviled Levitt's achievements was the fact that all his developments explicitly excluded people of color. He argued this was just what his customers wanted. Statistically, suburbia has now largely transcended its original whiteness, but in the 21st century it faces new challenges related to reining in its massive ecological footprint. If it is to endure, the next phase of suburbia's evolution will need to embrace new forms of mobility, energy, and materials, and, to Levitt's retort, zero tolerance for racism.

See Also: Suburban Backyard (76), Welwyn Garden City (98), Pruitt-Igoe (106), Seaside (110), Auroville (114)

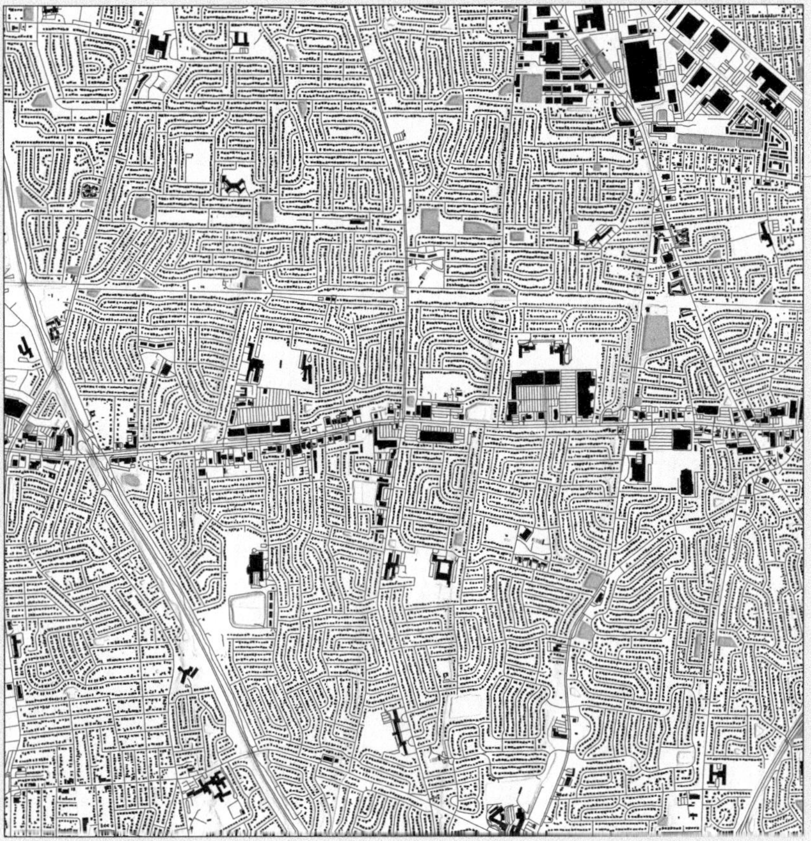

40°43’33.4”N 73°30’52.2”W

2 km

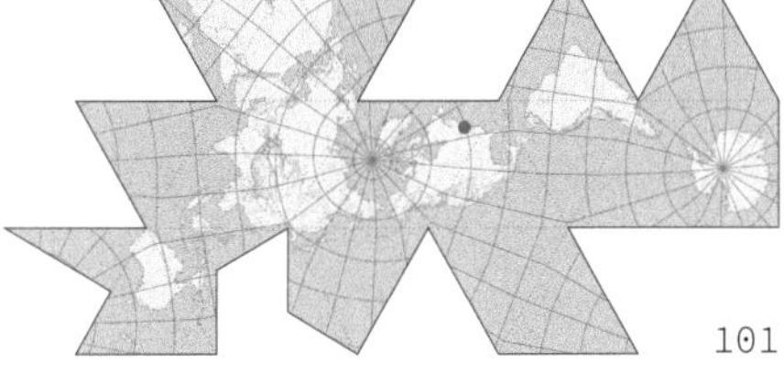

Walmart Supercenter
Georgia, United States

In case you hadn't noticed, Walmart is the largest retail chain and the largest company in the world. It has over 10,500 stores in 24 countries, with 2.2 million employees and an annual revenue of around $550 billion. In the United States, 90% of the population resides within a 15-minute drive of a Walmart store.

Since its founding by Sam Walton (1918–1992) in 1962, Walmart's success story has consistently been based on three fundamental principles: it offers (almost) everything anyone could want, at the cheapest possible price, in the same shop. Although Walmart is increasingly involved in distributing goods directly to its customers via online sales, consumers still flock to its so-called 'supercenters,' behemoths of around 16,000 square meters plonked down in vast carparks scaled up to handle peak shopping periods. Strictly speaking, there is nothing utopian about Walmart whatsoever—it does not put forward a social or political blueprint for a better world, nor do its buildings attempt to contribute to the civic virtues of the city—instead, Walmart is a cathedral of consumption. In a word, Walmart represents cornucopia, not utopia. Cornucopia is symbolized through history by goat's horns (*cornu*) overflowing with food (*copia*). In short, Walmart buildings are now the *cornu*, and the *copia* is all the stuff of contemporary life.

Among urban designers, particularly card-carrying members of the Congress for the New Urbanism, the contemporary landscape of 'big-box' retail outlets that serves suburbia is socially, environmentally, and aesthetically reprehensible. In terms of the suburban landscape it dominates, Walmart can thus be seen as a bastardization of architect Victor Gruen's (1903–1980) mid-century vision of suburban shopping malls as cultural centers. Instead of railing against suburbia as most architects do, Gruen accepted and tried to anchor suburban sprawl with retail centers that included the arts, public gathering spaces, and congenial buildings. It was Sam Walton, however, who best understood that American consumers would happily forsake the civic virtues of good design for a parking spot and a bargain.

Be that as it may, Walmart is not oblivious to criticism. Even if seriously addressing the quality of the public realm that their buildings deleteriously impact remains a bridge too far, Walmart is now the biggest producer of solar energy in the United States and it has recently promised to phase out the sale of battery cage eggs by 2025. One wonders, then, what else Walmart could do if it were to conduct an ethical and environmental audit of all of its products.

See Also: Suburban Backyard (76), Amazon Fulfillment Center (160), Freshkills Park (240)

33°56’11.5”N 84°01’33.8”W

200 m

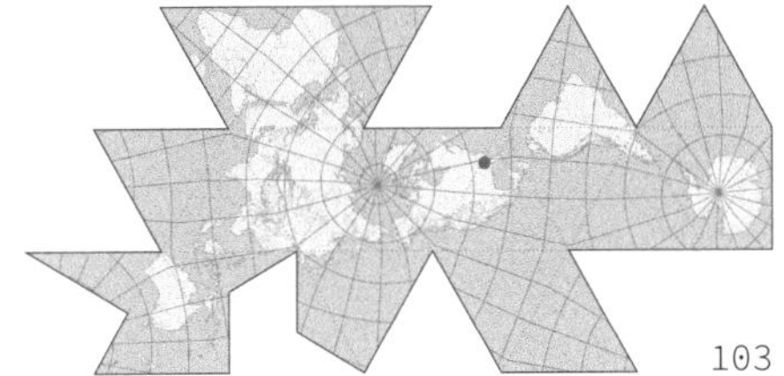

Bos-Wash Megaregion

United States

The United Nations defines a city as a settlement containing 300,000 or more people. Today's so-called megacities are defined as having a population of ten million or more. When megacities sprawl and merge with other cities over a large geographic region, the phenomenon of such large-scale urbanization is known as a megaregion. The accepted definition of a megaregion is not based on a certain population threshold, but rather by the fact that it can be seen as a continuous ribbon of electric lights at night by a satellite.

In his 1961 book *Megalopolis*, French geographer Jean Gottmann identified the first megaregion stretching from Boston to Washington, or 'Bos-Wash' as it would later become known. Gottmann waxed lyrical that this vast urban conglomeration including Washington, Baltimore, Philadelphia, New York, and Boston represented a new kind of spatial order in the history of civilization. There are now 29 recognized megaregions in the world—in Japan, China, India, Europe, and the United States. These megaregions have all formed organically; that is, they were not planned to become megaregions—they just happened. Because of this lack of planned intent, megaregions are not strictly speaking utopian, but they are lauded as incubators of innovation in a global economy. They also tend to have good transportation and communications systems and offer a wide range of employment opportunities and lifestyle options. Because megaregions have been identified as cultural and economic powerhouses, some nations, not least of all China, are trying to incentivize their growth.

What has been largely missing from discussions about the utopian characteristics of megaregions is that their economic and cultural success is ultimately dependent on the health of the environment in which they take root. While scholarship and policy related to megaregions typically focuses on a megaregion's bright lights, it is the dark matter of the landscape—its soil, water, vegetation, and wildlife—that ultimately underpins and sustains a megaregion. It is axiomatic that without a healthy ecosystem there can be no healthy city and no healthy society. Accordingly, planners working in megaregions are at pains to incorporate 'ecosystem services' (air, water, soil, and other natural freebies) into the megaregion's economic calculus.

The utopian prospect of megaregional urbanization—or rather, its 'ecotopian' prospect—is not only that the megaregion is attractive for large numbers of people to come together and create wealth and culture, but that it might also coexist symbiotically, not parasitically, with its regional landscape. Such a city really would be a new kind of spatial order in the history of civilization.

See Also: Suburban Backyard (76), Welwyn Garden City (98), Masdar City (118)

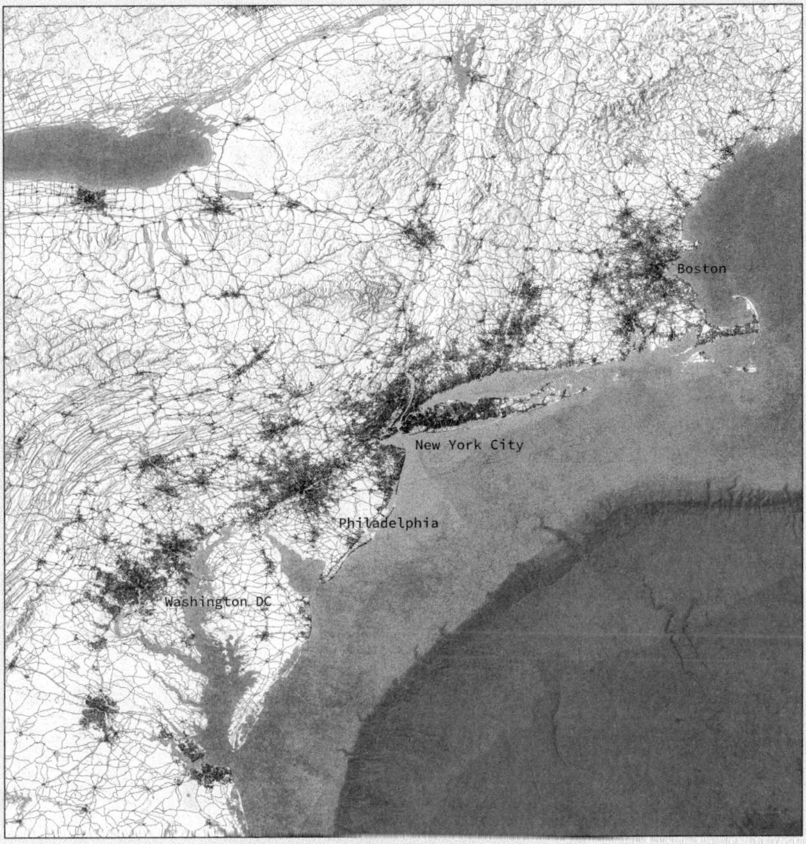

Boston

New York City

Philadelphia

Washington DC

40°42'46.0"N 74°00'22.0"W

400 km

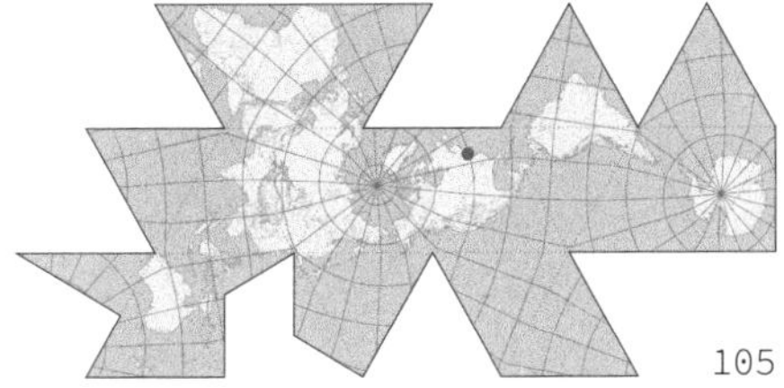

Pruitt-Igoe
Missouri, United States

In the first half of the 20th century, the dominant global architectural organization was the Congrès Internationaux d'Architecture Moderne (CIAM). Its members, many of the most prominent architects of the time, believed that mass produced, high-rise buildings of concrete and glass surrounded by generous parkland was *the* future. Not only would this system efficiently house burgeoning populations and manifest equality, it would also celebrate the rationality, efficiency, and aesthetics of the machine age. Modern people would, they assumed, be happy to live in small, sunny, airy apartments with views over greenery and amenities at their doorstep. It all made perfect sense. In practice, however, the CIAM utopia became a dystopia of jerry-built boxes surrounded by car parks. While some apartments received an excess of sunlight, others were permanently in the shadows and residents found themselves staring across forlorn open space to a building that was a mirror image of the one they themselves were entrapped in.

Such was the situation at the housing estate of Pruitt-Igoe, in St Louis, a development consisting of 33 eleven-story buildings designed by architect Minoru Yamasaki according to the textbook CIAM design principles outlined above. Originally, Pruitt was planned for the black community and Igoe for the white, but as the whites moved out to the suburbs, most of the housing estate became occupied by people of color. Occupancy peaked at 91% in 1957, but because money from rent was not enough to cover maintenance costs, by the 1970s Pruitt-Igoe had become derelict. So degraded had the estate become that authorities decided to evacuate the residents, and, at 3:32 pm on the afternoon of July 15th, 1972, the Pruitt-Igoe housing estate was detonated. Today the estate is but a trace on the ground (indicated in red opposite) and the land is being reclaimed by a weedy urban forest.

Critics used Pruitt-Igoe as evidence of the negative consequences of big government and the welfare state; others blamed the design and the principles on which it was conceived for dehumanizing a community. Although the CIAM had folded over a decade earlier (1959), architecture critic Charles Jencks declared the demolition of Pruitt-Igoe as the definitive end of modernism, and the beginning of post-modernism, in architecture. From this point on, planners turned away from the legacy of the CIAM and instead looked to the urban design critic Jane Jacobs, whose 1961 book *The Death and Life of American Cities* argued that traditional architectural character, small-scale public spaces, and vibrant streetscapes were the essential ingredients of good cities.

See Also: Suburban Backyard (76), Welwyn Garden City (98), Levittown (100), Seaside (110), Medellín (112), Kilamba (122)

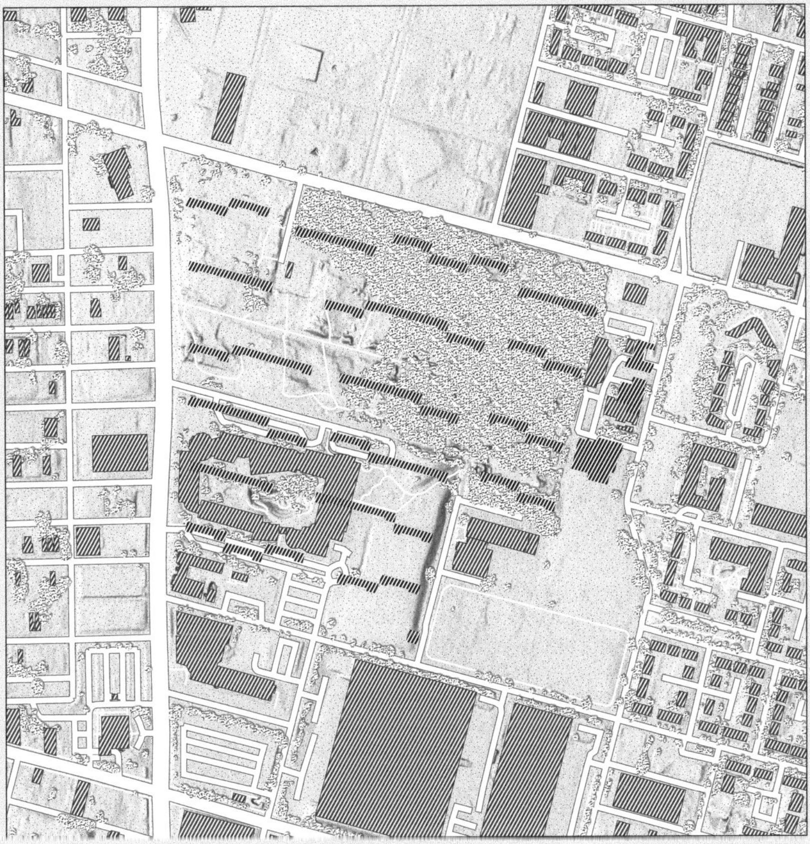

38°38’30.5”N 90°12’33.7”W

400 m

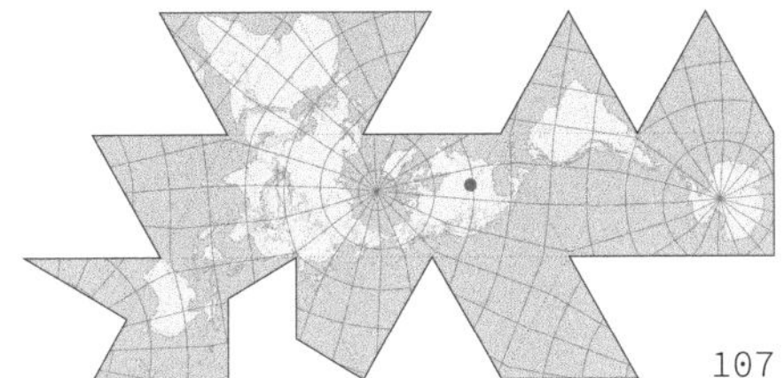

Chandigarh

India

After Lahore, the original capital of the Punjab, became part of Pakistan in its partition from India in 1947, the Indian government decided to build a new capital named Chandigarh. In a bid to create a symbol of India's future as a modern nation, Prime Minister Nehru hired the most famous architect of the day, Charles-Édouard Jeanneret (1887–1965), otherwise known as Le Corbusier, aka 'the crow.'

Le Corbusier had by this time built a global reputation railing against traditional forms of organic urban growth, proposing instead a modern new world of glass and concrete towers set in generous green spaces. This, he argued, should be applied to development the world over in a way that is "totally uncompromising." Indeed, to make way for his vision of the modern world, even Paris—which he referred to as a scab on the surface of the earth—would have to be bulldozed. As he had done previously in his hypothetical city designs, Corbusier's plan for Chandigarh was based on the metaphor of the human body. The capital buildings (courts and parliament) in the north constitute the head, the central business district is the heart, and the industrial and educational zones constitute the appendages.

Because skyscrapers were unaffordable, Corbusier lowered the building heights of the new city; but because he simultaneously maintained his belief in vast green spaces, his plan for accommodating 500,000 people spread far and wide. While it looked good in plan—a grid with ribbons of green space woven throughout—in reality, it was a city for cars in a country of pedestrians. Because of its scale, even now, as a city of 1.2 million people, Chandigarh, while greener than most Indian cities, feels empty and over scaled.

Nehru's Indian utopia was one of wealth and equality for all, something he thought could be achieved through rational planning by government. In northern India this dream was symbolized, and partially realized by Chandigarh's modernism. In a similar vein, today, Prime Minister Modi boasts of building 100 new 'smart cities' as quickly as possible. Learning from history—Chandigarh, Canberra, Brasilia, and Abuja—to name but a few, the smartest thing to do might first be not to automatically associate progress with brand new urban development. For his part, it is noteworthy that Le Corbusier, for all his proselytizing about the modern, chose to retire to a log cabin on the French Riviera.

See Also: The United Nations (96), Pruitt-Igoe (106), Seaside (110), Auroville (114)

30°45’00.0”N 76°46’48.0”E

5 km

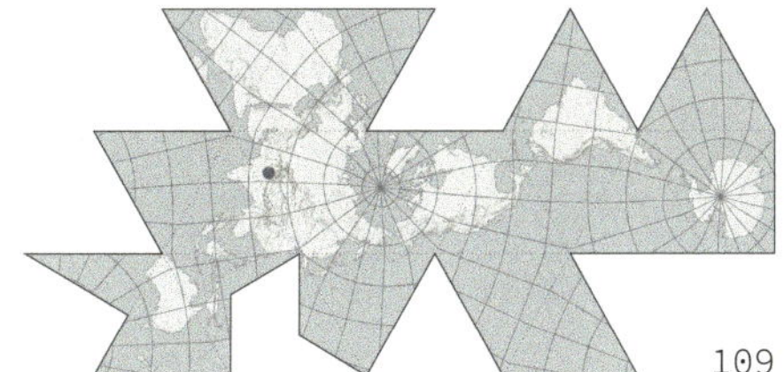

Seaside

Florida, United States

Despite all appearances to the contrary, the little resort town of Seaside on the Florida panhandle is a controversial place. Established in the early 1980s, it was the first and most high-profile example of an urban design movement known as New Urbanism organized under the aegis of the Congress for the New Urbanism (CNU). Spearheaded by architects Andrés Duany and Elizabeth Plater-Zyberk in the United States, and Rob and Léon Krier (along with now King Charles III) in Europe and England, the New Urbanists believe that the early 20th-century vision of the modern city (towers in the park) as promulgated by the Congrès Internationaux d'Architecture Moderne was profoundly mistaken. Their other whipping boy is suburban sprawl—for them it is ugly, unwalkable, car-dependent, anti-social, and unsustainable.

According to the new urbanists, designers should instead look to medieval and Baroque European towns and small-town America for inspiration and guidance on how to create places that are compact, pedestrian friendly, and rich in vernacular character. In prosecuting this reformist agenda, Seaside is Exhibit A. The brainchild of developer Robert Davis and architects Duany Plater-Zyberk and Co., Seaside has more than 400 cottages and condos, 20 restaurants, and 40 shops and galleries all built in a similar style drawn from old towns in the American south.

Seaside has ignited and polarized debate about what makes for good urban design today. For its acolytes, Seaside shows how design can create a strong sense of place. For its critics, because Seaside is socially homogenous, expensive, kitsch, and disconnected from the real economy, it cancels itself out as a model of any relevance to urbanism more broadly.

Perhaps the best way to evaluate Seaside is through the eyes of film director Peter Weir, who chose the town as the set for his 1998 film *The Truman Show*. In the film the main character, Truman, lives an obsequiously happy life and never leaves the town; that is, until he learns that both the town and his life are elaborate fakes created by a reality TV show. The film ends with Truman's heroic escape, where he rows across a fake ocean, climbs a set of stairs and exits through a door in the backdrop of a fake sky. We can assume, then, that Truman finds himself in a car park outside a film studio with generic American sprawl beyond. In other words, everything the new urbanists are against is paradoxically the landscape of his liberation.

See Also: Levittown (100), Bos-Wash Megaregion (104), Pruitt-Igoe (106), EPCOT (124), Cumbernauld Town Centre (180)

30°19’19.1”N 86°08’31.8”W

400 m

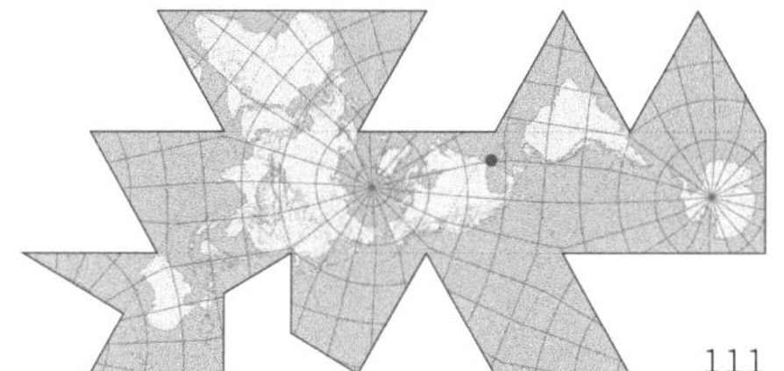

Medellín

Aburrá Valley, Colombia

The city of Medellín in Colombia was founded by the Spanish in 1616. The city's economy has historically revolved around gold, coffee, and, in the late 20th century, cocaine. In the grip of Pablo Escobar's eponymous drug cartel in the 1980s and early 1990s, Medellín earned a reputation as the murder capital of the world. Remarkably, in 2013, just 20 years after Escobar was gunned down by American-funded paramilitaries, Medellín was hailed as the most innovative city in the world by the Urban Land Institute (ULI).

How this transformation happened is due to a combination of good political leadership and good urban designers working together to improve the quality of life for people living in Medellín's poorest communities in the city's sprawling informal settlements. The catalyst for this was Mayor Sergio Fajardo's (2004–2008) concept of Social Urbanism. Instead of razing the self-constructed *favelas* (slums) and replacing them with government-issue housing, Fajardo, along with academics, community workers, and design professionals, not only accepted the intractable reality of informal settlements, he praised them. The informal settlements were recognized for their strong sense of community, their social and aesthetic vibrancy and their high levels of material resourcefulness and sustainability—qualities that planners everywhere strive to achieve in formally designed and developed cities. This is not to romanticize the favelas, it is to recognize that what they needed was not wholesale replacement, but improved accessibility and the provision of basic services.

Consequently, innovative forms of public transportation such as cable cars and escalators to negotiate Medellin's steep topography were retrofitted into the favelas. Anchoring institutions such as schools, medical centers, and libraries, as well as small parks, were also carefully inserted into the rambling favelas and quickly became hubs for a renewed sense of civic pride. With these tangible changes the favelas became safer and more productive.

Nearly half of Colombia's 50 million people live in informal settlements, as do around two billion people worldwide. Medellín is a beacon of hope that these typically overlooked and under-served settlements can begin to provide security and opportunity for their occupants. Indeed, for the bulk of urban history humans have constructed their own settlements without top-down planning. If anything, it is the modern planned city, not the unplanned city, that is the aberration.

See Also: Levittown (100), Pruitt-Igoe (106)

6°17’39.9”N 75°32’53.9”W

500 m

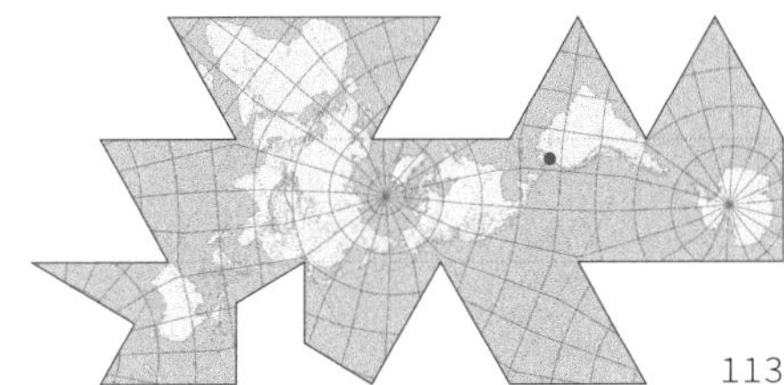

Auroville

Viluppuram, India

Utopian cities often have a distinct geometric order. This emphasis on form begins with Plato (428–348 BCE), who wrote "the city will never know happiness unless its draughtsman are artists who have the divine as their pattern." Each of the 54 cities comprising Thomas More's utopia, conceived in 1516, had four equal sectors with 30 houses in each neighborhood in straight rows. In 1547, Italian architect Filarete planned 'Sforzinda,' a starshaped city radiating from a "House of Vice and Virtue" at its center. The ground floor was a brothel and the top floor was an observatory (which, per Plato, equaled virtue). Thommaso Campanella's 'City of the Sun' followed suit in 1602 by being prescribed as a series of concentric circles, and in 1619 Johannes Valentinus Andreae proposed 'Christianopolis' in the form of an expanding series of squares.

Planned according to the template of a spiral galaxy, Auroville, founded in 1968, extends this tradition to the 20th century. Auroville is anchored at its center by the Matrimandir (Temple of the Mother), a golden geodesic sphere serving as a non-denominational temple devoted to meditation. The various arms of the spiral are demarcated by streets and buildings. Auroville's spiral was intended to contain four sectors: the international, the cultural, the industrial, and the residential, each radiating from the Matrimandir out into a surrounding greenbelt. As indicated by dashed red lines on the adjacent plan, the spiral's sectors have not materialized. The few buildings that have been built according to the spiral plan are marked in black lines.

Originally planned for 50,000 people, Auroville today has around 3,000 permanent residents. Aurovillians believe in communal ownership, lifelong education, youthfulness, beauty, peace, unity, and a non-religious form of divine consciousness. The city was founded by 'The Mother' Mirra Alfassa (1878–1973) and stems from her own theory of the evolution of consciousness as derived from her mentor, Sri Aurobindo (1872–1950). Today Auroville is a vibrant community aiming for self-sufficiency through organic food production, forestry, soil conservation, water and waste management, and alternative energy production. The problem that bedevils Auroville's harmony, however, is ironically the plan itself. The community is divided between those who want to stick to and complete the original template of the spiral, and those who prefer to let the community evolve in a more haphazard manner.

See Also: Chandigarh (108), Burning Man (116), BedZED (128), Freiburg im Breisgau (130)

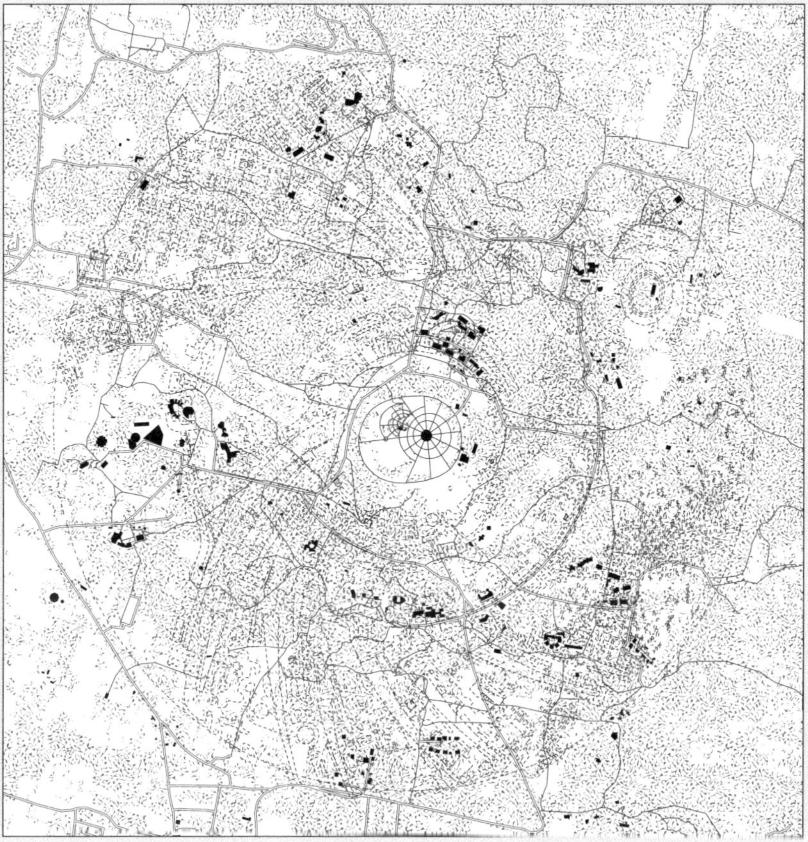

12°00’25.3”N 79°48’38.2”E

1 km

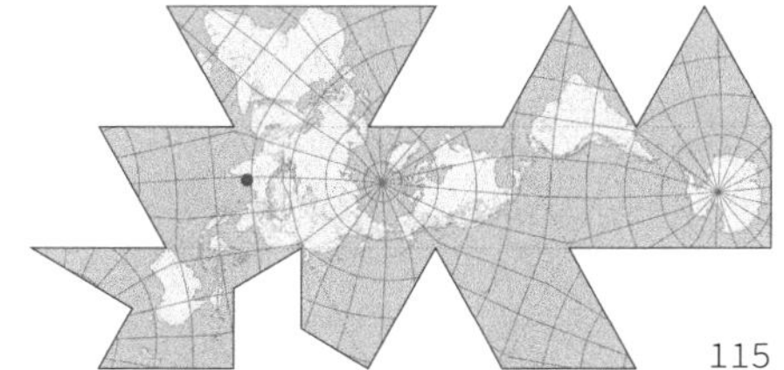

Burning Man
Nevada, United States

The Burning Man Festival has its roots in a summer solstice celebration that artist Mary Grauberger used to host in the mid-1970s at Baker Beach in San Francisco. A feature of these events was that Grauberger would ritualistically burn her sculptures. Burning Man founder Larry Harvey was a regular at these pagan gatherings and, in 1987, he partnered with Jerry James to continue and wildly expand the tradition Grauberger had begun. A total of a dozen people attended the first event hosted by Harvey and James. Today, Burning Man takes place on the flats of Black Rock Desert in Pershing County, Nevada, more than 300 kilometers from its original location and attracts over 70,000 revelers each year.

The physical footprint of Burning Man is known as Black Rock City and it exists for exactly three months of each year. Within this footprint, the actual Burning Man festival comes to life for just one intense week prior to and including Labor Day. The festival is renowned for its extraordinary array of large-scale ephemera and costumery related to each year's theme. The themes are typically enigmatic concepts such as "Mysteria," "Psyche," or "The Wheel of Time"; the theme for 2022 was "Waking Dreams." Each year the layout of the pop-up village begins from the so-called 'Golden Stake' that marks the location for a sculpture of 'The Man'—the flammable icon of the event. Continuing a deep historical tradition of using pure geometric forms to mark out utopian ideals, the template for Black Rock City is a circle inside a pentagon. Everything in the ephemeral village—roads, neighborhoods, and infrastructure—is laid out according to the template.

Because its denizens engage in labor-free bacchanalia and its mission statement is to produce positive spiritual (not political) change, Burning Man could be categorized as paradisiacal or cornucopian, but because it takes the form of a prototypical city it is decidedly utopian. Its utopian vision is spelled out through its ten-point charter: radical inclusion, gifting, decommodification, radical self-reliance, radical self-expression, communal effort, civic responsibility, participation, immediacy, and finally, leaving no trace.

Despite the appearance of mayhem during the celebrations, Burning Man operates under strict rules. Behavior is policed, territory is defined, and everything is under surveillance. Then, once the party is over, everything that makes Burning Man possible—all the shelters, infrastructure, and works of art—are removed, to make a clean slate for next year's event. This is particularly apt because if there is one thing utopia requires above all, it is a tabula rasa.

See Also: Auroville (114)

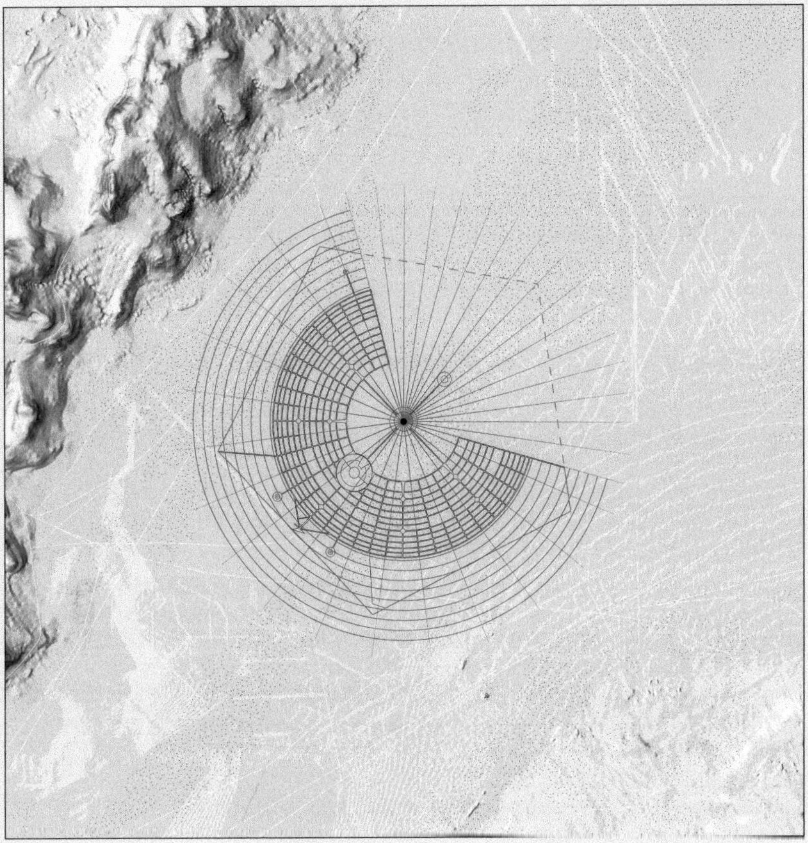

40°47’10.7”N 119°12’23.1”W

4 km

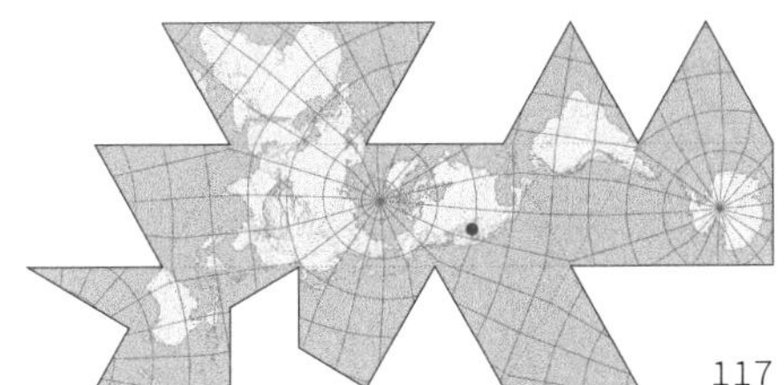

Masdar City

Abu Dhabi, United Arab Emirates

Throughout history cities have grown organically in landscapes where resources were plentiful, where trading routes intersected, and wherever their rulers said they should. The recent phenomenon of rapid urbanization in the United Arab Emirates is an unlikely case of all three—the ruler is Khalifa bin Zayed Al Nahyan, the resources are petroleum and natural gas, and the trade routes are now global flows of capital. Having exhausted the cliché of the skyscraper as a sign of progress, in 2006 the UAE announced a new, highly symbolic project—the world's first carbon neutral, car-free, zero-waste city. At the time this was unprecedented.

Designed by the one of the world's most reputable architecture firms, Foster and Partners, along with MIT's Technology and Development Program, 'Masdar,' meaning 'source,' was evidently serious about being a breakthrough project. Conceived for 50,000 people, the plan for the new city covered 6 square kilometers and was estimated to cost somewhere around $20 billion. The project was couched in experimental terms, with the aim of developing a replicable model of sustainable urbanism and related technologies, which the UAE could then export to the rest of the world.

Construction on Masdar City began in February 2008 and the first buildings devoted to its educational core—the Masdar Institute—were completed and occupied by October 2010. However, due to the impact of the global financial crisis, Masdar's completion has now been pushed out to 2030. Originally slated for 1,500 businesses with 60,000 day workers specializing in the production of environmentally friendly products, by last count fewer than 2,000 people were employed in Masdar, and only a few hundred students live on site.

These numbers don't read like a success story and the hype surrounding the project has made it hard to separate fact from fiction, but the project's use of architecture and urban form to support solar energy, create thermal comfort, recycle water, and promote walkability is, at least in this part of the world, something of a breakthrough. Despite its struggles, the high-tech, innovative ethos of Masdar lives on in similarly ambitious projects such as 'The Line' in Saudi Arabia, Toyota's 'Woven City' in Japan, and most recently 'Telosa' conceived by an ex-Walmart executive for 'somewhere' in the desert of the United States. For their critics these projects are little more than a rebranding of real-estate speculation as ecotopian; for those actually working on designing their new urban systems, they are important opportunities to test innovations.

See Also: BedZED (128), Freiburg im Breisgau (130)

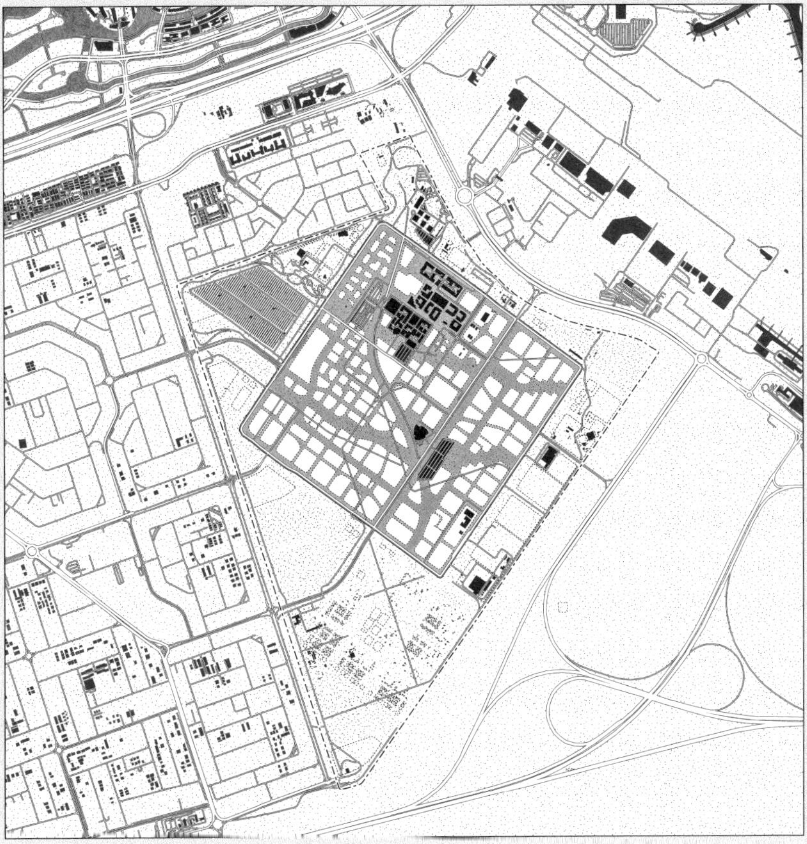

24°25'32.4"N 54°36'54.0"E

2 km

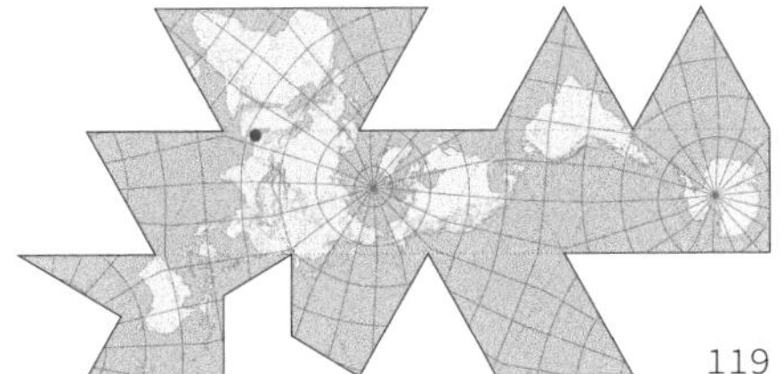

Burj Khalifa
Dubai, United Arab Emirates

The crown for the world's tallest building is typically related to hotspots in the global economy. It was in the United States for much of the 20th century and then in East Asia before returning to the Arab world for the first time since the 14th century when the Pyramids of Giza were usurped by the Lincoln Cathedral in England. Today, standing at 828 meters, the Burj Khalifa tower in Dubai holds the crown. It has been the tallest building in the world since 2009 when it beat out the Taipei 101 in Taiwan.

Designed by Chicago-based architecture firm, Skidmore, Owings, and Merrell, the construction of the Burj Khalifa's tapered metal and glass tower cost an estimated $1.5 billion. Its design is supposedly inspired by regional cultural references like mosque minarets and desert flowers, as well as by Frank Lloyd Wright's 1957 concept drawings for the Illinois Sky-City in Chicago. The construction of the Burj Khalifa capped off two decades of relentless development in the region where, under a model of 'borrow and build,' Dubai grew from a relatively unknown enclave to a soaring corporate conglomeration.

Though the Burj Khalifa has been celebrated for its design and engineering achievements, the problem for it—as for all skyscrapers—is how it meets the ground and impacts public space. The Burj Khalifa's solution to this problem was to simply transform the surroundings into the world's biggest shopping mall. Covering an area of over 200 football fields, Dubai Mall includes a massive aquarium, over 1,000 retailers and an Olympic-sized ice skating rink. One of the more intriguing and perhaps fitting items in the mall is the so-called 'Dubai Dino,' a 24-meter-long skeleton of a dinosaur (*Diplodocus longus*) originally unearthed in Wyoming and thought to have died from drought. The Burj Khalifa, like all big development in Dubai, is also inevitably associated with the city's reputation for harsh labor conditions. Most of Dubai's construction workers are low-paid migrant workers from South Asia who work in extreme conditions and live in shanty towns at the edges of the desert.

Plans to take the Burj Khalifa's crown for the tallest building in the world abound. Currently it is expected to be eclipsed by The Bride of the Gulf, a 1,152-meter tower that is set to rise from the ashes of war-torn Basra in southern Iraq.

See Also: Masdar City (118), Water Desalination Plant (148), The World (216)

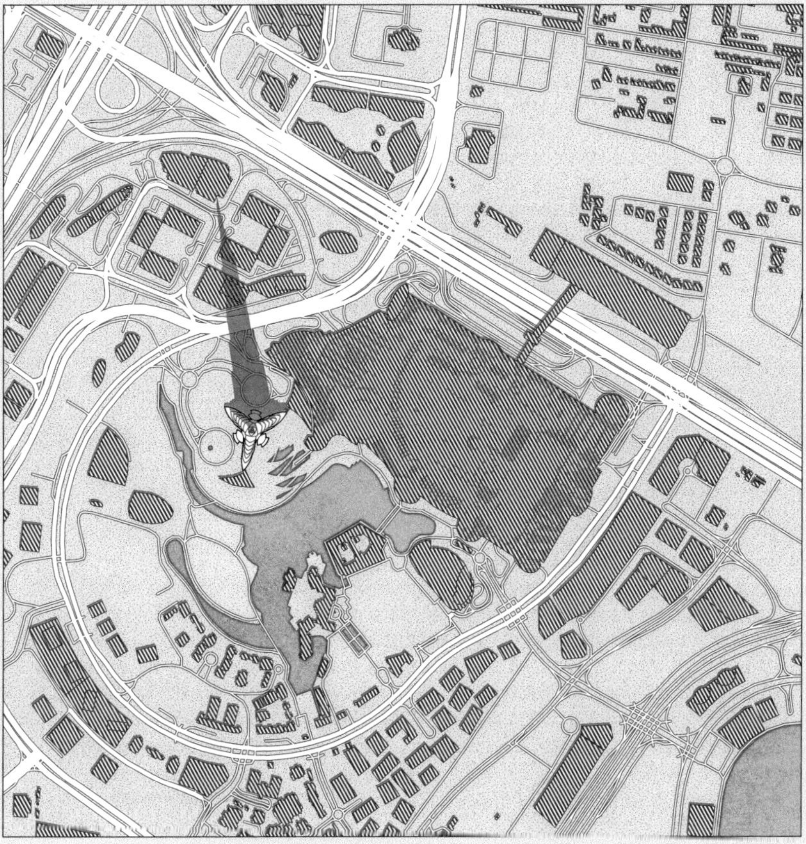

25°11’44.5”N 55°16’33.6”E

500 m

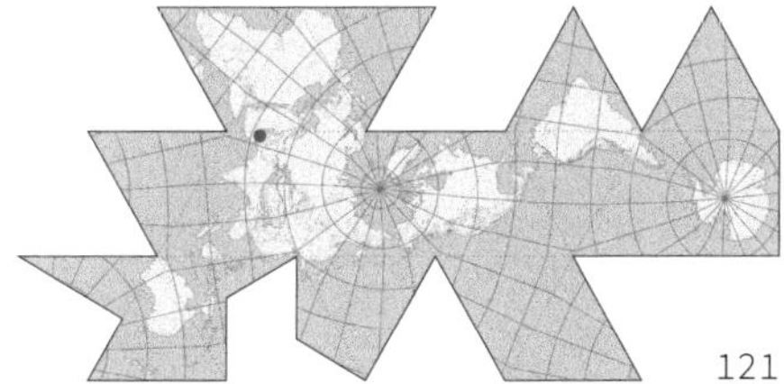

Kilamba
Luanda, Angola

The capital of Angola, Luanda, is the fastest growing city in Africa. Founded in 1576 by Portuguese explorers as São Paulo da Assunção de Loanda, it is one of the oldest colonial cities on the continent. Luanda served as the capital of the global slave trade right up until abolition in 1836. Over five million Angolans were sold to markets, primarily in Brazil, also a Portuguese colony. The city's most recent growth relates to lucrative oil and diamond trades, as executives take up residence in new apartments and the poor stream in from across the nation, crowding into informal settlements (*musseques*). At the same time as half its population lives on $2 a day, Luanda now has the dubious honor of being one of the most expensive cities in the world. It is also one of the most corrupt.

In 2002, China issued a communiqué that it would help rebuild Angola after 27 years of civil war. In exchange for the rapid development of housing and infrastructure, the Chinese would be paid in oil from the nation's overflowing wells. In 2008, Angolan president José Eduardo dos Santos pledged to build one million homes in four years across five new cities. One of these new cities is Kilamba on the outskirts of Luanda.

Kilamba was planned in China according to a stock-standard Chinese urban design template: a large grid, wide streets, and repeated building typologies. With its own electricity supply, the new city could boast street lighting, telecommunications, pressurized tap water, and a functioning sewer system. Kilamba's current population is around 150,000 and the aim is to reach 750,000, but because it is all brand new and lacks any small-scale commercial space, the city feels lifeless. For some, this is a welcome reprieve from the interminable chaos of African cities, for others, it represents a dehumanized, elitist enclave with no sense of place.

According to recent United Nations data, there are just under 1.2 billion people living on the African continent. By 2050 this number is projected to double, and by 2100 to reach something in the order of 4.4 billion. It is little wonder, then, that Africa is experiencing a wave of large-scale speculative urban developments. Like Kilamba, the majority of these projects are located almost exclusively in peri-urban, greenfield sites and come with hyperbolic rhetoric and spectacular imagery of gleaming urban futures. Utopia's new shore is Africa.

See Also: Levittown (100), Pruitt-Igoe (106), Masdar City (118)

8°48’55.7”S 13°13’44.5”E

20 km

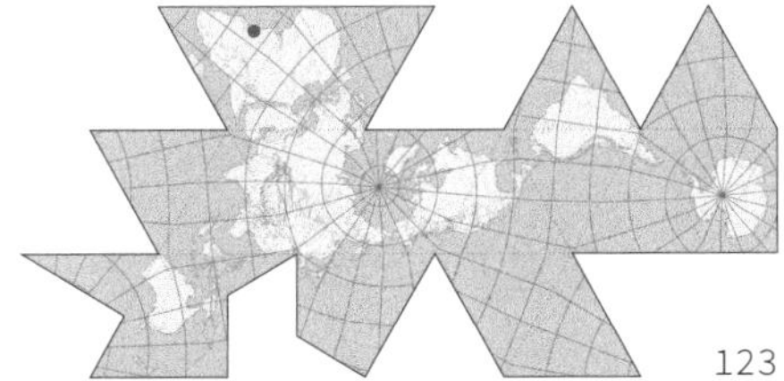

EPCOT

Florida, United States

Opened in 1982, the Experimental Prototypical Community of Tomorrow (known as EPCOT) is one of four theme parks in Walt Disney World, Florida. In his later years, EPCOT was Walt Disney's obsession, his magnum opus. Motivated by the specter of urban blight, riots, pollution, and congestion in American cities, Disney, with his inimitable optimism, believed he could create a perfect city from scratch. And what better place to do it than on his own 10,000 hectares of swampland in Florida where his 'imagineers' could make up their own rules. Probably inspired by Buckminster Fuller's 1960 concept of placing midtown Manhattan under a geodesic dome, Disney's vision of the ideal city was for 20,000 people to live and work inside a massive plastic bubble. In this way the micro-climate could be controlled and the city sanitized and protected from external threats. For Disney, this experiment in utopianism was not only a matter of getting things right on earth, but a prelude for colonizing space in a race against the Russians.

The idea of EPCOT as a genuinely utopian spatial and social experiment died with the man himself in 1966. Although still branded as experimental and prototypical, EPCOT opened in 1982 as a theme park where utopian ideas about the future are presented as edutainment. As well as displays about how technology will solve all our problems, EPCOT's big attraction is that eleven different cultures are showcased in microcosm so Americans can avoid the hassle and expense of having to travel overseas to experience the real thing. The original concept of the overarching dome congealed into a geodesic sphere at the park's entrance named "Spaceship Earth"—an homage to Fuller's book *Manual for Spaceship Earth* about how he thought humans must learn to manage the earth as if it, too, were a closed system like a spaceship. The building houses an audio-animatronic ride (originally designed by the science fiction writer Ray Bradbury) which takes visitors on a 15-minute journey through the history of the universe, culminating in the triumph of human reason and a bright future.

Paradoxically, while EPCOT is not the utopia Disney intended, the corporation's imagineers have more recently taken Disneyland's clean, main-street version of small-town America and used it as the basis for designing real-world towns. The first of these, named Celebration, also in Florida, opened in 1996. Celebration was not marketed as an experimental utopia, but simply as "the happiest place in America." Be that as it may, the media couldn't help but report Celebration's first murder and its first suicide with a touch of *schadenfreude*.

See Also: Seaside (110)

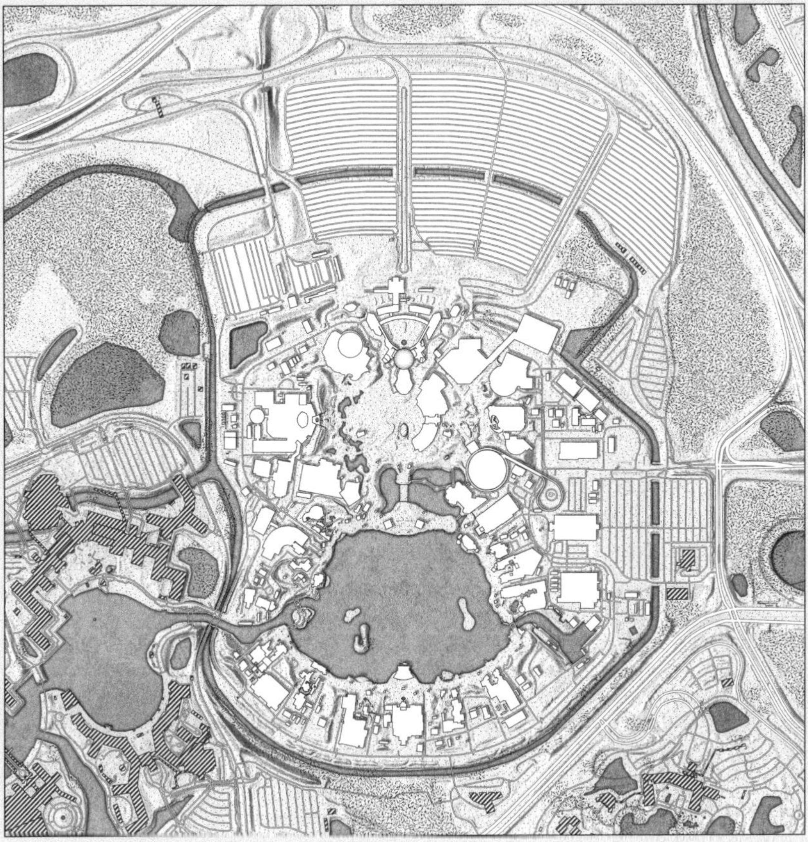

28°22'31.1"N 81°32'57.9"W

1 km

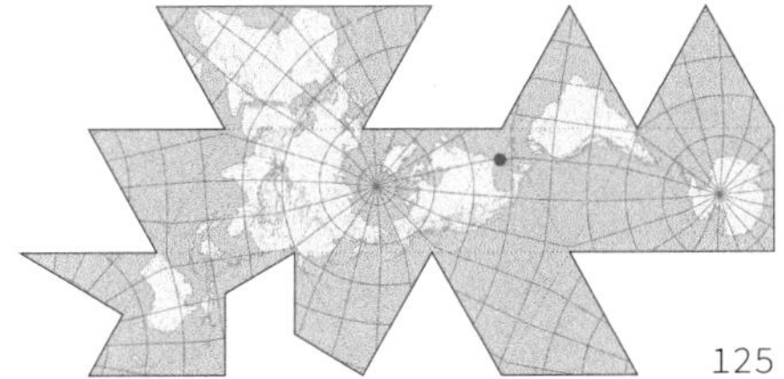

Biosphere II
Arizona, United States

Biosphere II was an experiment to see if, and for how long, a small group of humans could live within an entirely artificial, self-contained ecosystem. The pet project of a group of entrepreneurial hippies along with a team of scientists, Biosphere II's mission was reported in the media as everything and anything from saving the world to seeding new ones.

As it happened, eight 'biospherians' or 'terranauts,' as they were variously referred to, entered the enclosure in designer space suits on September 26th, 1991 and didn't come back out until two years later. Reports vary, but by the time they reemerged, the artificial ecosystem for which they were responsible—featuring microcosms of the earth's major biomes—had almost completely collapsed. All pollinating insects had died, cockroaches had overtaken, and oxygen levels were dangerously low. In addition to this ecological decline, the 'crew' (four men and four women) had splintered into factions and were plagued by 'he said, she said' scandals. On a more positive note, as a scientific experiment the biospherians did achieve 83% food self-sufficiency and some individuals recorded some significant health improvements.

Though originally touted as the greatest scientific experiment since the moon landing, in 1999 *Time Magazine* called Biosphere II one of the 50 worst ideas of the 20th century. Either way, much was learned about our capacity—or rather, our incapacity—to design and then manage the complexity of an ecosystem in a closed environment. Above all, Biosphere II reminds us that the only reason Biosphere I (the earth) works so well is that it is an open system with billions of years of practice fine-tuning its interrelated systems in a way that ensures the survival of the whole.

The moral of the story is of course that we can't reproduce the sophistication of the earth's ecosystem and therefore we should be more grateful for and caring of the earth system, which provides everything we need to survive for free, every day. Not to be humbled, the fantasy of living in high-tech terrariums is alive and well in Dubai where Sheikh Mohammed bin Rashid is funding a third Biosphere experiment in a cluster of space domes known as 'Mars Science City.'

See Also: The Eden Project (50), EPCOT (124), Space Garden (302)

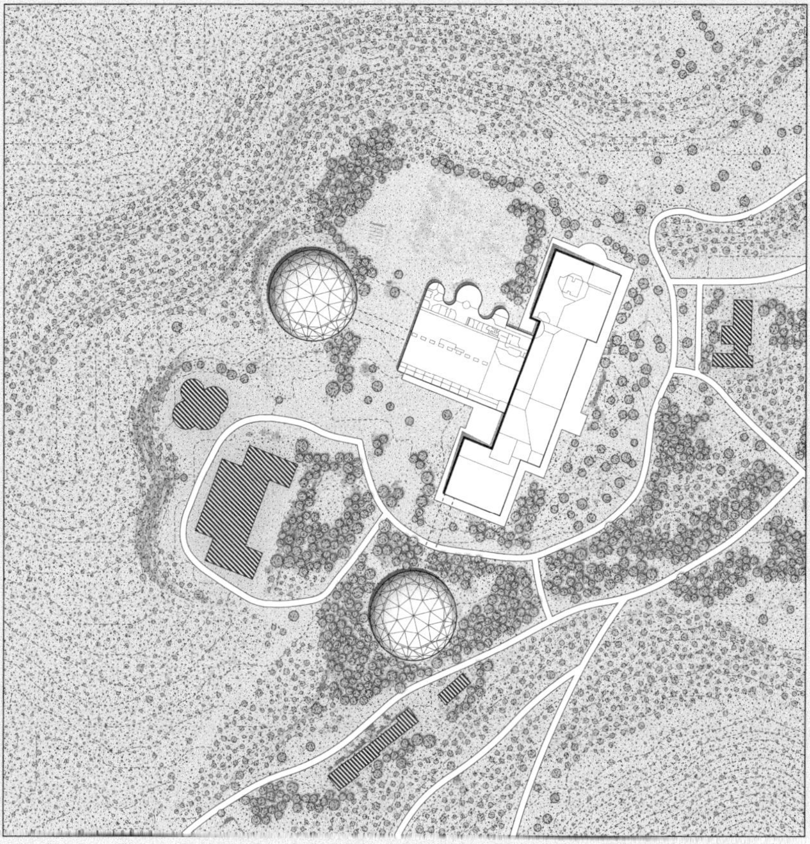

32°34’41.4”N 110°51’06.9”W

200 m

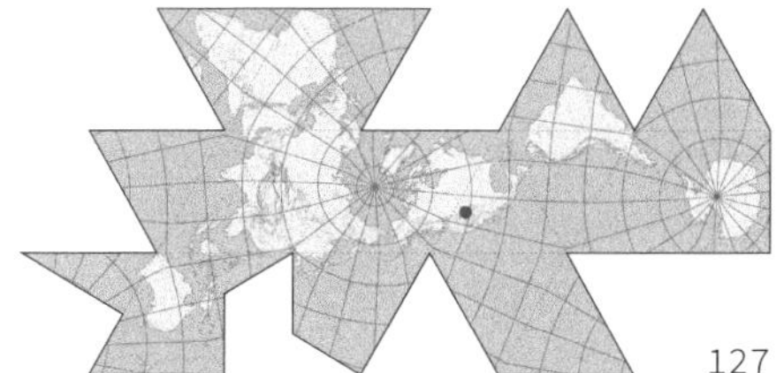

BedZED

South London, England

Conceived in 1997 and completed in 2002, Beddington Zero Energy Development (BedZED) is an 'eco-village' in the Borough of Sutton, just south of London. The 1.6-hectare site is a former sewage works, cleaned up and retrofitted as a residential project with 119 dwellings for 250 people. What distinguishes BedZED from other housing developments is that the design and construction of the project, and the lifestyles of the people who live there, aim to exist within a 'one planet' ecological footprint. This means that an individual's level of consumption is limited to the amount derived from dividing the earth's resources by its total population. The magic number is around 2 hectares per person; that is, everything you need to survive including all your waste should be derived from and contained within 2 hectares of land—about four football fields. The average English ecological footprint is 4 hectares per person, which is to say that by the 'one planet' standard the average English citizen is consuming twice as much as the earth can equitably sustain. Put simply, BedZED is about doing everything it can to cut that figure in half.

Taken seriously, this is a complex design parameter for any development to meet and a difficult ethical commitment for its residents to live up to, but BedZED's has certainly tried. For example, all its building materials were vetted for their own ecological footprints and, insofar as possible, sourced locally. Homes are designed with space to produce food and work from home. Roofs are both solar and green to harvest energy and water and provide insulation, and additional energy is produced on site through a biomass incinerator. Rainwater is stored, and gray water is cleaned and reused.

So, has BedZED met its one planet goal? Not quite. While it does very well with regard to minimizing water and energy use, there is not enough space on the BedZED site to significantly reduce its food-related footprint. Similarly, sewage is not treated on site, and some residents do need to travel for work. Overall, however, it is estimated that a BedZED resident's energy use and waste *is* close to half that of the average UK resident, and their carbon footprint is about one-fifth less, which is not only environmentally virtuous but also translates into cost savings for residents. The knowledge gained through the creation of BedZED is now being exported worldwide with 'one planet communities' springing up in Europe, Australia, Africa, and America.

See Also: Masdar City (118), Freiburg im Breisgau (130)

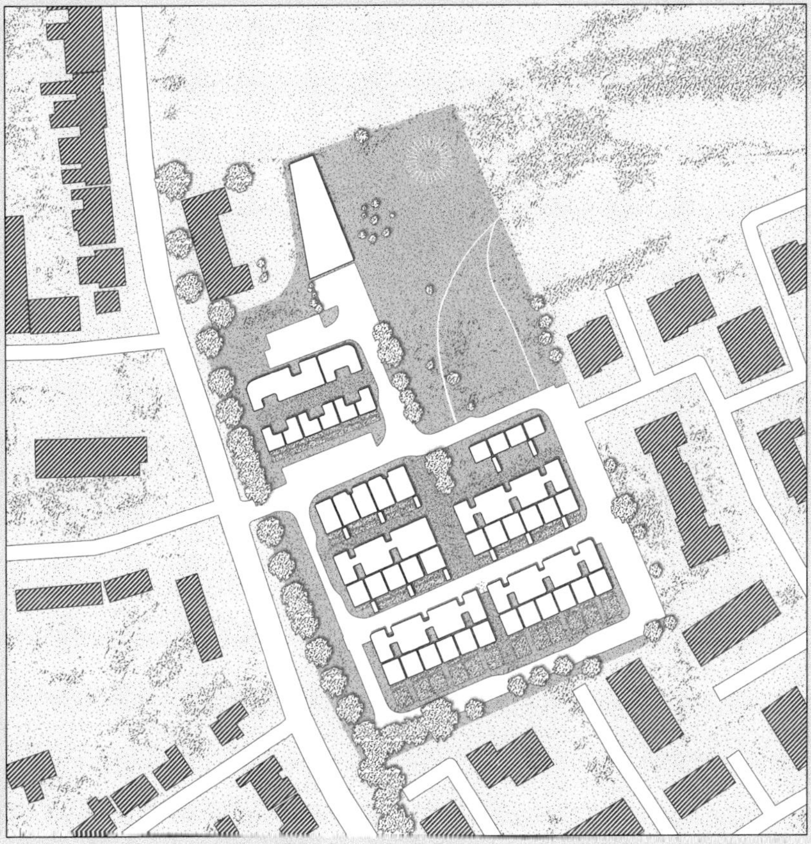

51°22’55.5”N 0°09’21.7”W

100 m

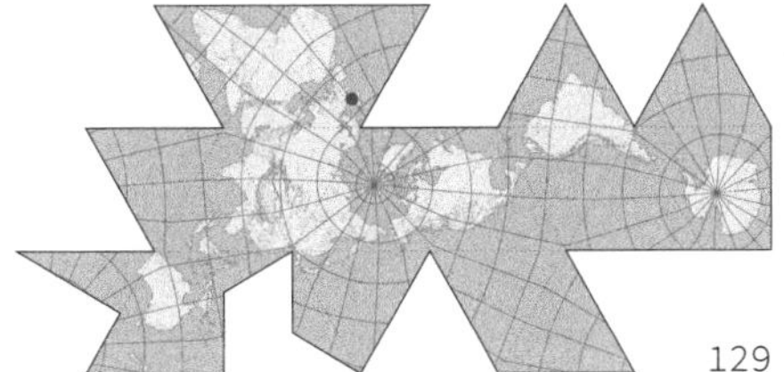

Freiburg im Breisgau
Germany

Small medieval towns such as Freiburg im Breisgau in southwest Germany survived for centuries off predominantly renewable, organic resources. Though at times tenuous, and by no means easy or completely benign, these towns did strike a balance with their surrounding landscape and formed a resilient network of urbanism across much of Europe. In a word, by our standards, these old towns were *sustainable*.

The expansion of markets through imperialism and colonialism, fueled by the Industrial Revolution, changed all that. Based on a conceptual framework that nature is primarily a resource for human exploitation, the forces of mechanization, population growth, and wealth creation turbo-charged urban development globally. Scholars refer to this now as planetary urbanization and the broad consensus is that our cities and their supply chains need to be redesigned so that they become more sustainable. This means they need to function within certain environmental limitations. The question is how to do this without naively invoking a return to the Middle Ages.

We are seeing the beginnings of an answer to this in a series of urban design experiments in contemporary European cities. Hafen City in Hamburg, the districts of Ørestad and Sluseholmen in Copenhagen, Bo01 in Malmö, Hammarby Sjöstad in Stockholm, Low2No in Helsinki and, as illustrated opposite, the enclave of Vauban in Freiburg, are all managing to combine modern lifestyles with significantly improved environmental performance.

As a demonstration project of more ecological ways of building and living, Vauban began in 1993 when a group of like-minded residents envisioned the conversion of an old French military base into a car-free, energy efficient, solar powered 'eco-city.' The community opened its first group of houses in 1998 and as of 2020 the district has just over 5,200 residents. Vauban boasts the production of more energy than it consumes and has plans for expansion into neighboring Dietenbach, which aims to become Germany's, if not the world's, first fully carbon-neutral community. Following this lead, the entire city of Freiburg now aims to be carbon neutral by 2050. No doubt it helps that Freiburg is a Green Party stronghold, but the bigger picture here is that projects like these are necessary design experiments pointing to the evolution of the city from a wasteful machine to a closed-loop, sustainable ecosystem.

See Also: Masdar City (118), BedZED (128)

47°59’42.0”N 7°51’00.0”E

5 km

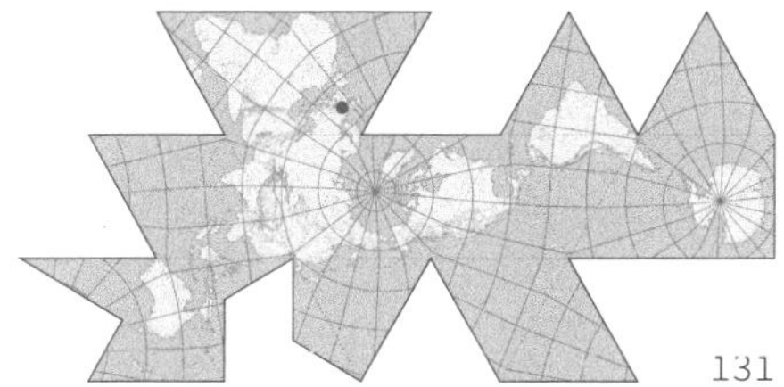

Machines

To satisfy their desires, humans have a Promethean propensity for extending their physical ability with tools. As the ancient Greek story goes, Prometheus, the god of foresight, is asked by Zeus to create humans (the *anthropos*) so that he would have some entertaining pets. He commands Prometheus to give the *anthropos* just enough intelligence to make them interesting, but not so much that they would use their wits to usurp the gods. For that reason, Zeus also specifically instructs Prometheus not to give humans the tool of fire. Prometheus disobeys this instruction and humans proceed to build a world on their own terms, doing effectively what Zeus feared they would. For his disobedience Prometheus is chained to a cliff for eternity and through Pandora's box all the ills of the world are unleashed upon humanity. The moral of the story is not only that humans have become gods, but also that technology's attraction is also its curse.

What interests us in this chapter is not the array of tools humans have invented, but the *landscape* of technology itself. This landscape takes its most pronounced shape with the agricultural revolution and the emergence of large-scale urbanization. Cities themselves are forms of technology—meta-machines generating constant innovation related to minimizing labor, winning wars, alleviating environmental pressures, and enshrining power. Until the Industrial Revolution, cities and their surrounding farmlands were predominantly made of wood, stone, and ceramics: they were powered by water, wind, animals, and the human body. Underpinning it all was fire, but in the late 18th century this fire became an inferno.

The engines of the Industrial Revolution were the catalysts for railways, factories, cars, airplanes, cargo ships, bulldozers, crop harvesters, and power plants. Today these machines form a global network fired by fossil fuels. And it is here, in its modern incarnation, that the parable of technology shifts from the Promethean to the Faustian. In exchange for superhuman powers, Johann Wolfgang von Goethe's quintessentially modern character, Faust, signs his soul over to the devil and becomes a megalomaniac. In a premonition of the 20th century, Faust uses his powers to build a tower so high that he can see out from it to infinity, only to realize—and regret—that its construction has destroyed everything around it. This is what Karl Marx would theorize as creative destruction—the contradiction at the heart of the modern age.

In this chapter we visit lands that bear witness to this creative destruction. We visit places where the latter outweighs the former, but we also visit sites where there is hope that technology can yet be used with modesty to restore a depleted earth. But make no mistake, the landscape of technology is not sentimental. Technology's favorite place—like utopia—is always the future, and today that future has a digital horizon and its leading protagonist is neither Prometheus nor Faust—it is the cyborg. As the name suggests, the cyborg is a combination of the cybernetic and the organic—a new hybrid of nature and technology. The cyborg is a human body augmented with prosthetics that opens onto a world of science fiction where intelligent machines not only merge with human bodies, but threaten to replace them altogether. The landscape of technology in this new world is one where the whole planet is now a kind of cyborg.

Bulldozer

International

It has been calculated that humans now move more earth than the earth's natural processes combined. And not just a bit more, it is something in the order of ten times more. Ipso facto, the key tenet of the Anthropocene is that humans have themselves become a geological force of nature. More than anything, this is due to one machine—the mighty bulldozer.

The first bulldozers appeared in 1908 in the United States and they've been refined, enlarged, and mass-produced ever since. Technically, the bulldozer is a combination of a large blade (or bucket in the case of front-end loaders) and hydraulic circuitry powered by a diesel engine and directed by a skilled driver. Inspired by the German military invention of the tank, one of the key breakthroughs in the story of the bulldozer is the replacement of wheels with a rotational tracking system so as to drive through difficult terrain without getting bogged.

The bulldozer has been used with military logic to clear the way and prepare the ground for freeways, farms, factories, and suburbs. With thick chains stretched between them, bulldozers can work in tandem to clear a forest in minutes. Bulldozers also invaded our cities, ploughing historical urban fabric into the ground to make way for modern development. They are now tearing down rainforests for palm oil plantations and being prepared to move into the oceans and strip mine the sea bed. We even have baby bulldozers scuttling about on Mars.

As a verb, to bulldoze means to achieve an impact through brute force. Underpinning its brutality is the fact that the word stems from the American south where a 'bull dose' originally meant to give an extreme flogging to a slave. In 1968 the 'earth artist' Walter de Maria hung a vast canvas painting in bulldozer yellow in the Dwan Gallery in New York City. On the yellow painting was a small plaque that read "the color men use when they attack the earth." But as we reckon with the destructive social and environmental consequences of this machine, we must also acknowledge that it has freed animals and humans from grueling labor. Whether the bulldozer can be turned around and used to help restore some of what it has hitherto bulldozed is now the question.

See Also: Polymetallic Nodule Extractor (168), Palm Oil Plantation (246), Perseverance Mars Rover (304)

2 m

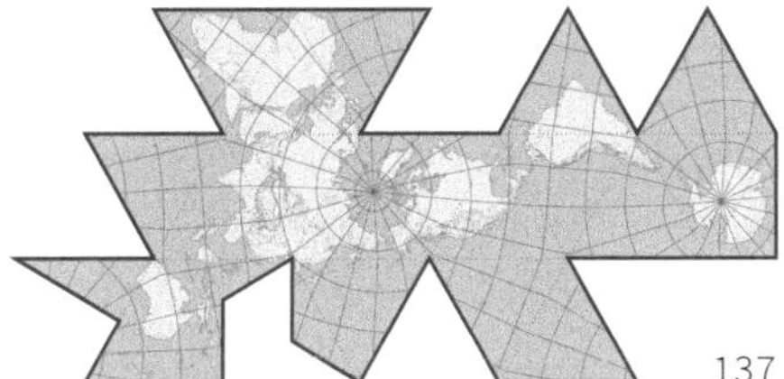

Bahrain Formula 1 Circuit

Southern Governorate, Bahrain

Whether it be swimming, walking, running, horse-riding, driving cars, or blasting off in rocket ships, mobility in all its forms has been ritualized and celebrated throughout history. It is only since the Industrial Revolution, however, that speed—moving faster and making things faster—has become a primary goal in many aspects of life. As a measure of efficiency and the optimization of the relationship between form and function, increased speed is—rightly or wrongly—synonymous with evolutionary improvement, and those who excel at it are hailed as heroes.

The speed limit at the start of the 19th century in England was 4 miles per hour on the open road and 2 miles per hour near towns. In 1829 a major breakthrough occurred with George Stephenson's invention of 'Rocket'—a steam locomotive that reached what for many at the time was a frightening speed of 30 miles per hour. Steam-powered mobility dominated the 19th century until 1985, when Carl Benz created a motorcar with a combustion engine that ran on coal gas. The first major car race came nine years later in France (Paris to Rouen), with racing cars averaging around 12 miles per hour. In 1897, the first driver of these new machines was killed in an accident in London. Well over a million people now die in car-related accidents every year.

The world speed record stands at 763 miles per hour and every year at the Bonneville Salt Lake in Utah, speedsters fire up massive, custom-made machines and drive them in straight lines across the salt flat to try to beat it. The ballet of machined speed, however, is the Grand Prix Formula 1, overseen by the Fédération Internationale de l'Automobile. In Formula 1 racing, the most exceptionally skilled humans are squeezed into high-tech exoskeletons to push the outer limits of the laws of physics.

For some of course, the sight of men in toy cars going very fast around in circles is juvenile. For others, the Formula 1 is the apotheosis of human ingenuity, skill, and raw power. Certainly, in the age of climate change, the veneration of fossil-fueled machines burning rubber on bitumen in desert landscapes to advertise polluting industries is becoming somewhat harder to sustain. In response to this, the entire global operation of the annual Formula 1 extravaganza now aims to become carbon neutral by 2030—whatever that really means. As Mahatma Ghandi once quipped, "speed is irrelevant if you are going in the wrong direction."

See Also: Tesla Gigafactory (162), Athabasca Oil Sands (192)

26°01’55.5”N 50°30’53.5”E

800 m

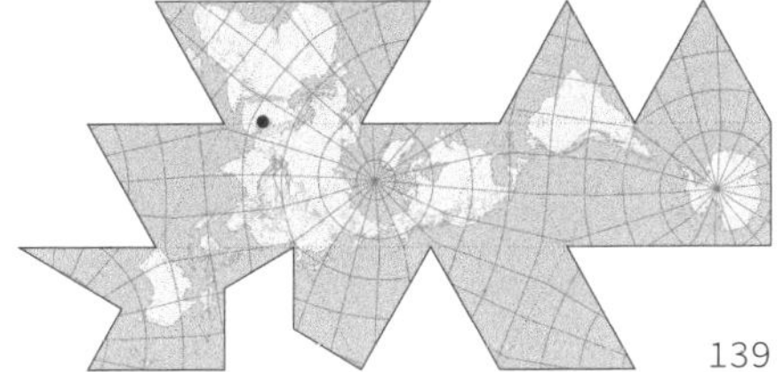

Fertilizer Production Plant

Damietta Free Trade Zone, Egypt

The elements nitrogen (N), phosphorous (P), and potassium (K) are essential for plant life. Until the 20th century, farms were fertilized by organic materials rich in these elements, such as nitrogen-fixing legumes, manure, urea, blood and bone, guano, and phosphate rock. Toward the end of the 19th century, however, it was obvious that supplies of these natural fertilizers were inadequate to the task of feeding a burgeoning global population.

In the early 20th century, German chemist Fritz Haber was researching chemical weaponry for the German government when he discovered a way of combining methane gas, water, and other reactants and catalysts to yield ammonia (NH_3) and its derivative, ammonia nitrate (NH_4NO_3). Carl Bosch took Haber's discovery to an industrial scale, making prodigious amounts of nitrogen cheaply available for fertilizer, explosives, and many other modern products. By taking nitrogen freely from the air and 'fixing' it for plants to easily absorb, Haber and Bosch set the stage for the Green Revolution of the mid-20th century when machinery, new crops and fertilizer were combined under the aegis of large-scale agribusiness to feed the world. With secure food supplies, the human population has since tripled and continues to grow.

The expansion of cropland has been devastating for the world's forests. That said, the damage has been contained to a far smaller land area than that which would be required to the feed the same number of people in the absence of industrial fertilizers. This raises the question of the degree to which food security and population growth are causally related. It seems self-evident that more food sustains more people, who in turn make more people requiring more food. And yet, as farms are industrialized the land requires fewer workers and people move to cities where rates of childbirth typically decline.

In terms of feeding people, the Haber-Bosch process is something of an industrial miracle. However, requiring around 500 degrees Celsius to work its magic, the process is energy intensive and consequently has a large carbon footprint. Problems also arise as the application of synthetic fertilizers to farmland kills off the bacterial life in soils, rendering them dependent on the constant input of more fertilizer. As well as killing the soil's microbiology, nitrogen (and phosphate) leaches into waterways and causes algal blooms. These blooms strip oxygen from lakes, rivers, and oceans, leading to hypoxia, otherwise known as 'dead zones,' where no marine life can exist.

See Also: The Four Rivers of Paradise (52), GIS Crop Harvester (142), Greenhouse Agriculture (144), Ocean Dead Zones (252)

31°28’03.4”N 31°46’31.8”E

300 m

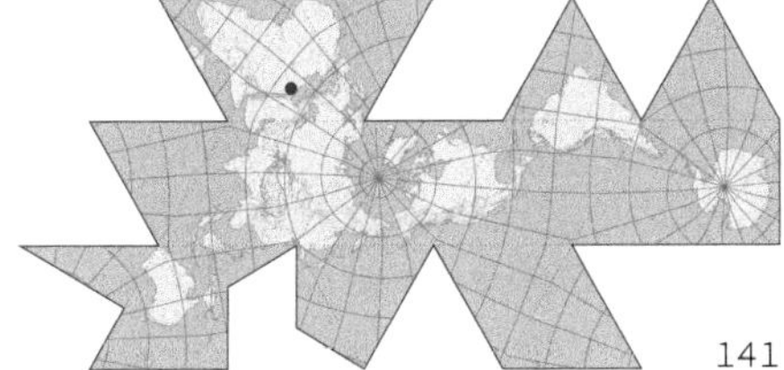

GIS Crop Harvester

International

Since its advent in Canada in the 1960s, GIS (Geographic Information System) and remote sensing make it possible to use a global network of satellites to locate anything on the surface of the earth accurately. In large-scale industrial agriculture this technology allows machinery such as planters, combine harvesters, and sprayers to steer by themselves. By establishing the boundaries of a field in GIS, the machines conform to the topography and the boundaries of the field they are working. Because farms are now typically rigged with sensors and networked into systems that constantly monitor environmental conditions and crop development, the machines can also adjust their every action to precisely suit local conditions. If a farm is rigged with sensors, its water and fertilizer needs can be more precisely determined and the farm's environmental impacts such as nutrient runoff and carbon emissions can be monitored. Where information isn't available at a suitable degree of resolution, farmers can now fly drones over their properties and program in-situ sensors to gather their own data as input to then guide the machines.

Where humans are involved they function as intermediaries between data and the land, responding in real time to input the optimal settings for the machines. The cab of a tractor in this kind of farming now has many different monitors depending on the operation, or it has no cab at all. This robotic farming applies best to the relatively homogenous, geometric forms of large-scale agricultural production, but hand-held datapads are becoming more useful for smaller, family farms that also produce much of the world's food.

Such technologies are generally used to optimize efficiency. While this can improve productivity and profit, and lower costs for consumers, if the social and ecological problems that bedevil industrial agriculture are not also being addressed then high-tech farming is a losing game. Farmers today need to address depleted soils, the over-reliance on pesticides and herbicides, high nutrient runoff, the poor treatment of animals, the reliance on fossil fuels and government subsidies, poor food quality, and not least of all, the demise of rural communities. It seems romantic, however, to think a global population of eleven billion or more people in the late 21st century will be fed through a return to small-scale farming—even if that is possible and desirable, it too will need to be a highly technological landscape. The challenge is how to use technology to help restructure the contemporary industrial agricultural landscape so its productivity is maintained, but its long-term viability is improved.

See Also: The Four Rivers of Paradise (52), Ogallala Aquifer (54), Greenhouse Agriculture (144), Ocean Dead Zones (252)

20 m

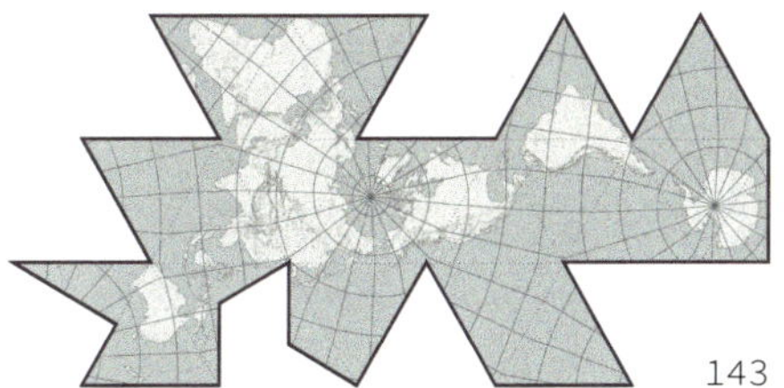

Greenhouse Agriculture

El Ejido, Almería, Spain

At least since antiquity it has been known that plant growth can be accelerated in controlled micro-environments. For example, to satisfy emperor Tiberius's appetite for cucumbers, gardeners worked out they could be produced all year if the plants were grown under sheets of mica. Seventeenth-century aristocratic gardens such as Versailles included glass buildings (orangeries) so that citrus could be cultivated in winter. The Gardens of Sansouci in Potsdam, outside Berlin, had terraces of glass cabinets for growing grapes. By the late 19th century, small glass houses, also known as greenhouses, had become a common part of suburban gardens.

The mass production of greenhouses is indebted to the surgeon and amateur horticulturalist Nathaniel Bagshaw Ward (1791–1868), who developed the Wardian Case, a portable glass cabinet designed to protect delicate plants from the cold and the heavily polluted air of Victorian London. Ward speculated that his cases could improve the diet of the urban poor and offer a therapeutic benefit to their owners. Ward's cases also helped the British Empire move plants around the world, not least of all tea plants from China to begin the plantations in India. Known now as 'plant factories,' today's glass (or plastic) greenhouses are machines finely tuned to maximize agricultural yield. For example, due to its greenhouses the tiny nation of the Netherlands is now one of the world's largest exporters of agricultural produce. Spain, from which the example opposite is drawn, has over 20,000 hectares of greenhouses. As well as producing vegetables, the out-of-season flowers in the world's florist shops are largely sourced from climate-controlled greenhouses in the Netherlands, Colombia, Ecuador, Ethiopia, and Kenya.

Although on occasion there is reference in the media to 'frankenfarms,' this new form of high-tech agriculture—with much of the work being done by robots—is generally a good news story. Indeed, if by virtue of hyper-production in greenhouses the sprawling footprint of global food production can be reduced, then land can be freed up for things like forestry for carbon sequestration and habitat restoration for biodiversity. Greenhouse production is, however, limited to flowers and vegetables, not the broadacre crops that constitute the bulk of our calorie intake and also feed animals for meat production. The land area of these crops will only be reduced by producing artificial meat products in factories, and the task of convincing the public to forego meat in favor of these products is undoubtedly a very challenging one.

See Also: Fertilizer Production Plant (140), GIS Crop Harvester (142), Aquaculture (146), Harris Ranch (186)

El Ejido
Aguadulce
Roquetas
de Mar
Almerimar

36°44'27.4"N 2°44'54.2"W

20 km

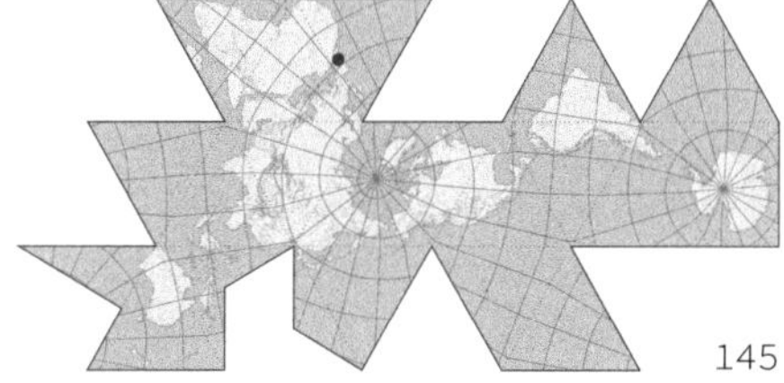

Aquaculture
Pulandian Harbor, Tudao, China

Today we hear regularly that the oceans are overfished. Under the veil of water, the once bountiful ocean is now a trawled desert. With depleted oceans, it is now up to fish and shrimp farms to satisfy the growing global demand, and for the first time in history, in 2014, humans consumed more seafood produced in farms than caught in the wild. Fish and shrimp farming is now a massive global monoculture where industrialized food pellets and hormonal regulation ensures a constant supply. For example, 99% of salmon are now produced in open water pens and genetically engineered so they eat all year and put on the bulk consumers have come to expect.

Farmed fish and shrimp are not, however, without their problems. Just as forests are cleared for farms on land, mangroves—which incubate much aquatic life—are cleared for industrialized aquaculture along the coast. The farmed fish and shrimp are also highly susceptible to certain viral, bacterial, and fungal diseases and outbreaks can be passed on to native populations. To manage disease, producers use large amounts of antibiotics and chemicals, which not only go into the seafood we eat, but discharge into coastal estuaries, impacting other marine organisms. Additionally, as some farmed fish invariably escape their pens and interbreed with wild fish, the genetic diversity of native populations is being rendered less diverse and therefore less resilient.

There is nothing new in humans engineering environments to mass produce seafood. Traces of the oldest traps to harvest freshwater eels from around 6,600 years ago have been uncovered in Australia. The integration of fish production into rice paddies in China is also an ancient practice. Roman villas often had *piscinae*, productive fishponds, built into their designs. Carp were domesticated in the Middle Ages and kept in ponds, and large fishponds were built into aristocratic European and English estates to supply their owners with fresh food. When the sustainable production and consumption of aquatic life began to falter in the mid-19th century, the first industrial-scale fish farms, known in France as *piscifactoire* (fish factories), distributed fish eggs to help repopulate depleted waterways worldwide. Today, while new technologies are helping to increase aquaculture yields and nutritional values, species escaping from fish farms threaten marine biodiversity through competition with native species for scarce food and habitat resources, sometimes becoming dominant in ecosystems and, together with overfishing of species in some habitats, creating the same risk of monoculture as we have on the land.

See Also: Greenhouse Agriculture (144), Harris Ranch (186), Ocean Dead Zones (252)

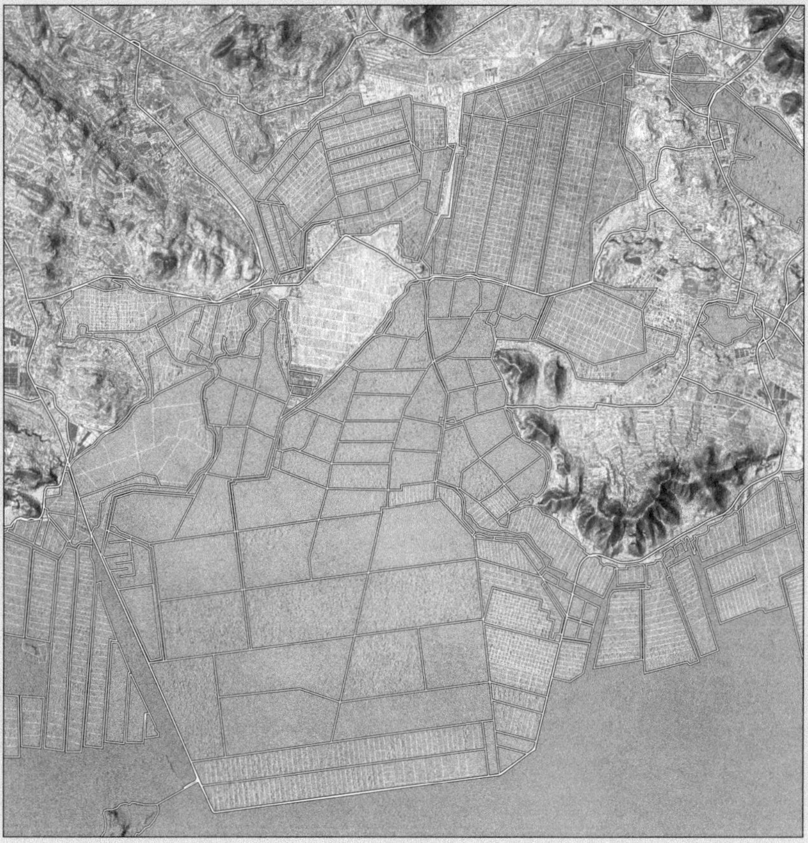

39°21’56.9”N 121°35’11.6”E

5 km

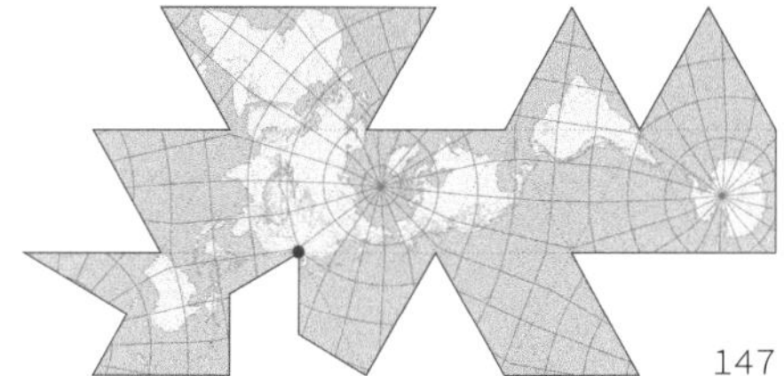

Water Desalination Plant

Al Jubail, Saudi Arabia

Though the world has lots of water, 97% of it is salty. Despite having bodies that are also salty (due to our evolution from the sea), humans can only drink fresh water. Because of this, human settlements have only ever taken root and endured in places with an adequate freshwater supply, or in places such as today's Los Angeles or Beijing, to which fresh water can be redirected cost effectively. The historical relationship between settlement and water has, however, now been significantly loosened by the advent of desalination plants—typically massive machines that convert salty water into potable water. Desalination plants can augment water supplies to existing cities as they outgrow their naturally occurring water sources and become vulnerable to drought. They can also serve entirely new settlements, more or less anywhere, so long as these settlements are not too far inland or upland.

The desalination of ocean water—something ocean-going birds and mangroves mastered long ago—has a long history. Sailors have long been adept at boiling seawater and condensing the steam into drinkable fresh water for lengthy voyages. However, it is only in the late 20th century that the technology of desalination has become viable at a range of scales. A desalination plant works by sucking in seawater (at a rate fish can escape from), preheating it, and then passing it through thin-film composite polymer membranes via a process known as reverse osmosis. The waste product, brine, is then pumped back into the ocean and the fresh water is pumped overland to consumers. At the scale required to supply major cities, desalination plants and their related distribution systems are energy intensive and expensive to build and run: the example opposite in Saudi Arabia cost $3.8 billion in 2014. In such regions the dream of using desalination to green the desert is periodically touted, but generally the return on investment is prohibitive, not to mention that messing with ecosystems on such a scale could further destabilize the planet's weather.

Because they provide the essential source of all life, desalination plants are generally popular with the public. Criticism relates to the way in which they are a techno-fix for water shortages that really demand behavioral and systemic changes whereby water is valued more highly and used more carefully. For fear of its provenance, people generally react negatively to recycled water, forgetting that all the water on earth has already cycled through many living (and dead) things, many times over. We are, as it were, drinking Caesar's piss whether we like it or not.

See Also: The Four Rivers of Paradise (52), Ogallala Aquifer (54)

26°54’01.8”N 49°46’36.3”E

2 km

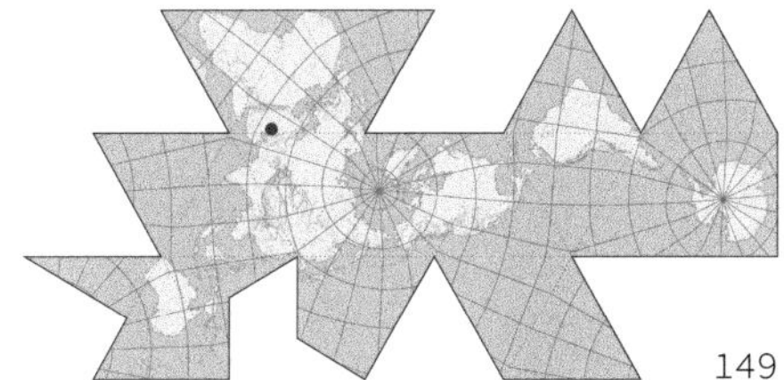

Three Gorges Dam

Hubei Province, China

China is an ancient hydraulic civilization. Water flows across the Chinese landscape from the Tibetan Plateau in the west and spreads rich silts throughout the lowlands of the east. By carefully and ingeniously managing this flow, Chinese culture has thrived for over 5,000 years. Reflecting this, Chinese metaphysics—known as *feng shui*—is based on studying the movement of wind (*feng*) and the flow of water (*shui*) and locating things accordingly. Together *feng* and *shui* constitute *chi*, the vitality that courses through the land and through human bodies, weaving them together in Chinese mysticism as one. The ancient lore of the land is that water can be redirected and slowed, but not stopped. Like many things in contemporary China, however, this traditional wisdom bends to the prerogatives of the modern nation-state and every Chinese leader since Sun Yat-sen first raised the idea back in 1919 has promised to dam the Yangtze River and convert it into electricity.

Construction of the Three Gorges Dam began in 1994 and was completed in 2006. In order to make way for its 1,080-square-kilometer reservoir, two cities, 114 towns, and 1,680 villages were drowned. Over 1.4 million people were forcibly displaced. Whether the great dam prevents flooding is a subject of debate, but there is no question as to the merits of the 22,500 megawatts of electricity it pulses out across the nation. Chinese cities and factories are ablaze with electrons.

The environmental impacts of the Three Gorges Dam include draining downstream ecosystems, increased landslides, and the blocking of sediment flow and fish migration. Because of its gargantuan size, the Three Gorges Dam presents the additional problem of exacerbating earthquakes by literally squashing its underlying geology. Its 39 trillion kilograms of water has even caused a slight wobble in the rotation of the earth.

The dam has also had a profound cultural impact by drowning settlements that had existed since the Zhou and Han dynasties (1046–220 CE). Residents of Zigui, once home to the famous poet Qu Yuan (340–278 BCE), were moved 37 kilometers southwest to 'New Zigui.' Reports suggest that some like the new apartments and abundant electricity the Communist Party has provided as compensation. Others are evidently traumatized by the submersion of their ancestral homes in the name of progress.

See Also: The Four Rivers of Paradise (52)

30°49’14.0”N 111°00’33.0”E

2 km

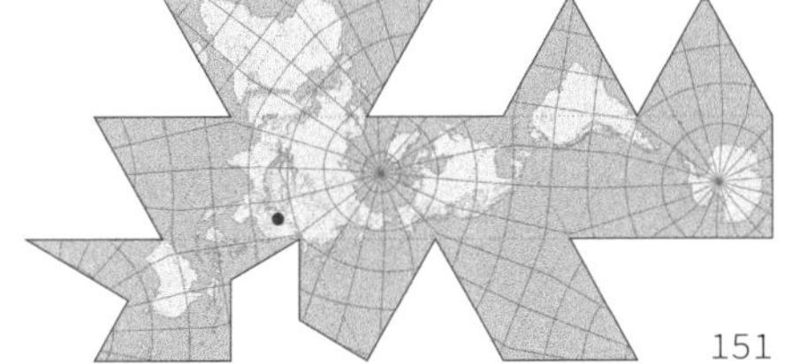

United Downs Geothermal Well
Cornwall, England

The earth system is powered by external heat from the sun and internal heat from its molten core. Upon its magma float the world's seven tectonic plates, each around 100 kilometers thick. Across their surfaces we turn the soil, plant crops, and build our cities. Digging into their strata we also tap their fossil fuels, their minerals, and their aquifers wherever we can find them. What we haven't successfully done—at least not yet—is tap the almost inexhaustible supply of heat that is within the tectonic plates themselves.

And for obvious reason. Except for odd spots where it bubbles up to the surface as hot springs, geysers, or fumaroles, the earth's 4.5-billion-year-old internal combustion engine has simply been too hard to get to and too hot to handle even if we did. Since we derive heat from other sources it has also been unnecessary, but as the cultural and economic transition from fossil fuels to renewables accelerates, geothermal energy is beginning to receive the attention it requires in order to make it a viable source of energy. And the prize is great—unlike sun, wind, and rain, geothermal is the only truly consistent renewable energy source on earth.

The example of the United Downs Deep Geothermal Power Project opposite takes advantage of the geology of southwest England, which has the highest subsurface heat flow in the United Kingdom. This system comprises two wells: an injection well, which pumps brine into natural fault lines heating it to 170–190 degrees Celsius, and a production well, which pumps it back to the surface to power a turbine. This one plant is capable of powering 10,000 homes per year.

But here's the rub. Geothermal energy is limited to regions where heat, water, and geological porosity coincide by providence. The amount of energy extracted is also limited to the depth of the bore and the degree of heat the system can handle. Measured dollar for dollar and joule for joule, a coal burning, carbon belching powerplant is still very hard to beat. But this is now changing. As geothermal systems have developed whereby liquid flows through a closed loop and can reach greater depths, their yields improve significantly, and the wells can be located more or less anywhere. This presents the prospect of providing baseload power and heat anywhere on the face of the earth around the clock, without pollution or greenhouse gases. Drill, baby, drill.

See Also: Fântânele-Cogealac Wind Farm (154), Bhadla Solar Park (156)

50°13’47.2”N 5°09’56.8”W

200 m

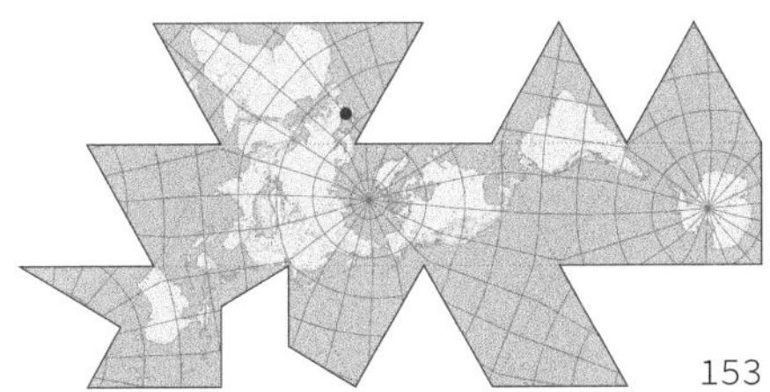

Fântânele-Cogealac Wind Farm

Fântânele, Romania

Sandwiched between the surface of the earth and the vacuum of outer space, the atmosphere is alive with constant movement generated by heat and air pressure differentials. Always somewhere between chaos and equilibrium, the winds chase each other around the world, driving ocean currents, sculpting the land and distributing heat, moisture, dust, nutrients, pollen, and pollution.

The ancient Greeks called these winds the *Anemoi*: Boreas is the north wind, Zephyrus the west wind, Notus the south wind and Eurus the east wind. We know them today as the polar easterlies, westerlies (roaring forties), horse latitudes, and the trade winds. Each of these winds has shaped the destiny of humans. We have harnessed them for sailing, milling, cooling, and pumping and built our cities where they are propitious. But what concerns us now, above all, is how to catch the wind and generate clean energy so as to minimize our reliance on fossil fuels. Although hampered by the vested interests of the fossil fuel industries, wind power, like solar and geothermal, is becoming more efficient and cost effective. A large wind turbine can produce enough electricity to power up to 1,000 homes and predictions are that by 2050 one-third of the world's electricity needs could be met by wind.

Spanning an area of over 1,000 hectares, the Fântânele-Cogealac Wind Farm in the province of Dobruja, Romania is the world's largest wind farm. These are seriously big machines—the blades of the turbines have a diameter of 80–100 meters (the size of a football field). The farm accounts for 10% of the total green energy production in Romania and local farmers who lease their land to the industry have been able to continue farming while deriving extra income. Even so, wind farms like this face problems: they not only require consistent wind, they also meet with resistance because they are so visually intrusive and create hazards for birds and bats. For these reasons wind farming is increasingly turning to offshore locations where winds blow largely unimpeded, and where they are beyond the range of NIMBYs.

See Also: Three Gorges Dam (150), United Downs Geothermal Well (152), Bhadla Solar Park (156)

44°36’50.5”N 28°32’54.0”E

3 km

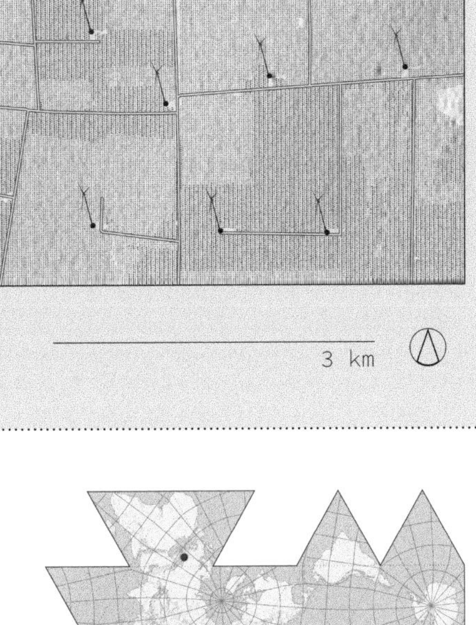

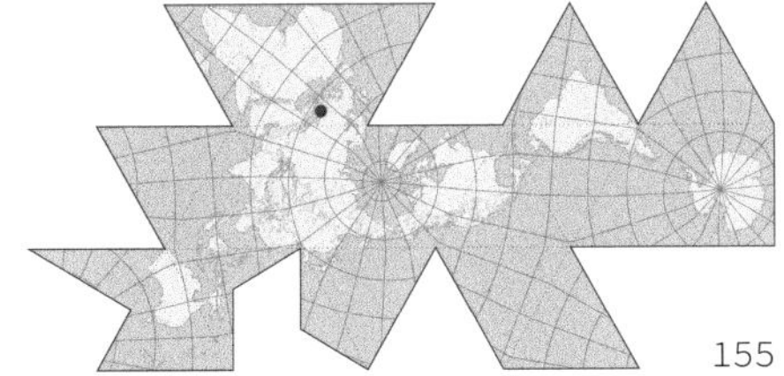

Bhadla Solar Park

Rajasthan, India

Three billion years ago plant cells learned how to capture sunlight and use it to release electrons from water and add them to carbon dioxide to build their bodies. In the process of performing this extraordinary molecular trick, oxygen is released as a waste product. Photosynthesis thus creates both the food and the oxygen that sustains life on earth. Even the fossil fuels that give humans their current superpowers are compressed plants built from sunlight that was converted into forests some 300 million years ago.

As fossil fuels become increasingly untenable due to their carbon emissions, or simply run out, we need to find alternative forms of energy if we are to maintain high-powered, industrialized cultures. As it happens, the sun provides the earth with more energy in a day than humanity uses in a year, so it is little wonder that technology should now try to emulate plants and capture this energy directly from the source.

The technological versions of green leaves are dark purple and known as photo-voltaic (solar) panels. Far simpler than a leaf, but considerably more efficient and durable in terms of the energy it can harvest, a solar panel is a thin pane of silicon, or similar material, that can conduct a flow of electrons in one direction. The biggest version of this created to date is in the Thar desert in Rajasthan, where sunshine is both abundant and consistent. Covering an area of 5,700 hectares, the Bhadla solar park has a capacity of producing 2,245 megawatts, enough to run a small city. With today's level of solar technology we'd need a total solar surface area of around 30 million hectares or 5,263 Bhadlas to power the world.

Getting cheaper and more efficient all the time, the solar panel is an icon of a cleaner, greener world. Even so, they don't grow on trees. Photovoltaic panels have a 20–30 year lifespan and the minerals and metals such as lead, copper, aluminum, tellurium, and cobalt required to produce them are sourced through mining, as well as the recycling of scrap materials, both of which have a bad reputation for exploitation of labor and pollution of the environment. Solar energy's capacity to replace fossil fuels is also limited to the capacity to store the energy in batteries or in other forms.

See Also: Three Gorges Dam (150), United Downs Geothermal Well (152), Fântânele-Cogealac Wind Farm (154), Chernobyl Reactor #4 (200)

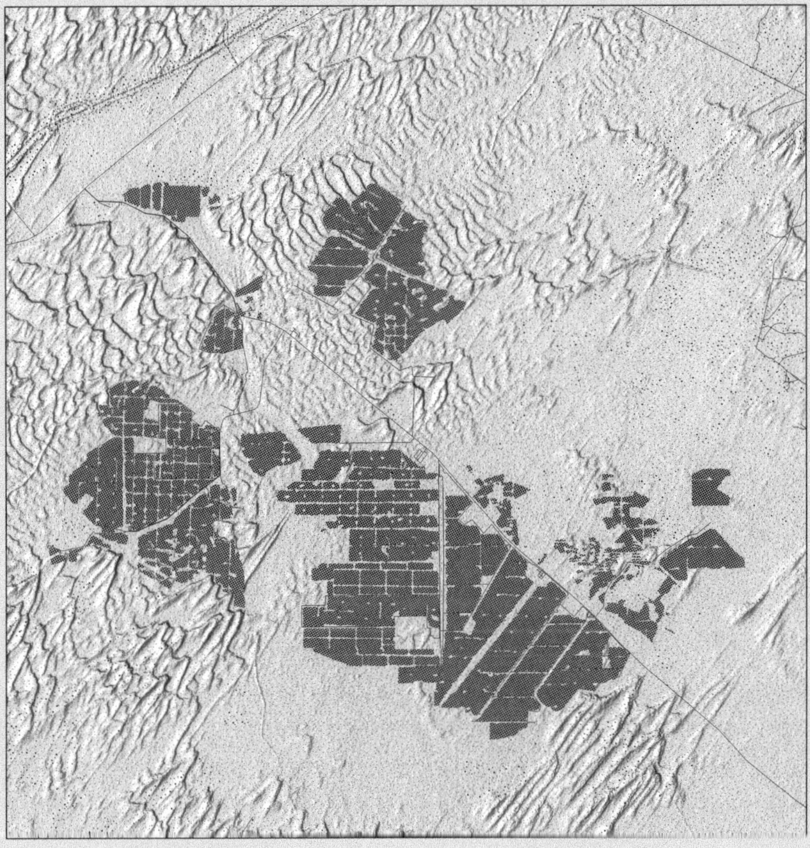

27°31’05.0”N 71°55’46.1”E

5 km

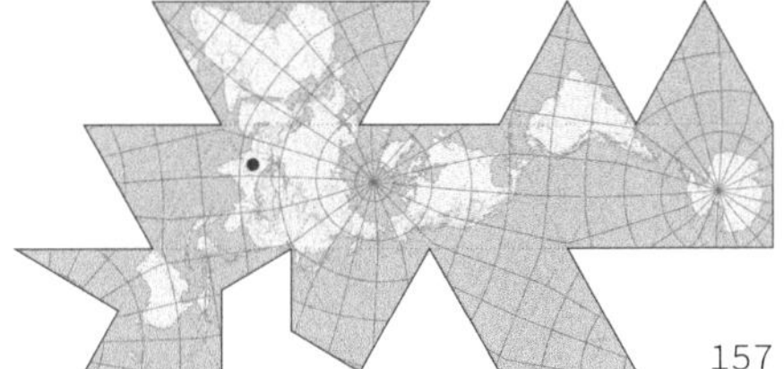

Direct Air Carbon Capture Plant
Reykjavík, Iceland

Because we are pumping carbon dioxide (CO_2) into the atmosphere at a rate beyond which the earth system can absorb it, there is an urgent need to now find ways of augmenting the earth system's natural carbon sequestration processes. Emerging technologies of direct air capture (DAC) coupled with geologic sequestration have the potential to remove significant amounts of carbon from the atmosphere and put it back into the subterranean places from whence it originally came.

Basically, the DAC system is a very large air filter in which air is pushed through chemicals using fans. These chemicals bind with CO_2, stripping the carbon from the air while leaving nitrogen and oxygen untouched. The resultant compound, carbamate or carbonate, depending on the type of chemical filter used, is then treated with heat, pressure, or more chemicals to extract pure CO_2 gas and lime (CaO) through a process called calcination.

The CO_2 filtered from the air can then be converted into a liquid and pumped back into sedimentary rock basins around 800 meters below the surface, ideally through some of the very bores through which the fossil fuels were extracted in the first place. As is happening in the new geothermally powered Climeworks DAC plant shown opposite, CO_2 can also be injected into basalt rock formations only 400 meters or so beneath the earth's surface. In this scenario carbonated brine is injected into cavities in the basalt and becomes limestone over time. Alternatively, CO_2 can also be locked up by adding it to certain industrial wastes, opening opportunities for carbon capture infrastructure to be established on decommissioned mining and industrial lands.

Because this new infrastructure is being actively promoted by some of the same companies that caused global warming in the first place, climate activists worry that it will cause complacency and even exacerbate fossil fuel extraction. Another concern is that to make an impact a lot of DAC machines will be needed and this will blight the landscape. In this vein, a common retort to the use of DAC machines is why not just use trees? While it is true that trees are natural carbon sequestration machines, there simply isn't enough terrestrial space for the number that would be required. Trees also die and burn, and when they do their stored carbon is released, defeating the purpose. It will not be one thing alone that gets the carbon genie back in the bottle, but one thing is for sure, direct air capture promises to be a big part of it.

See Also: Stratospheric Veil (218)

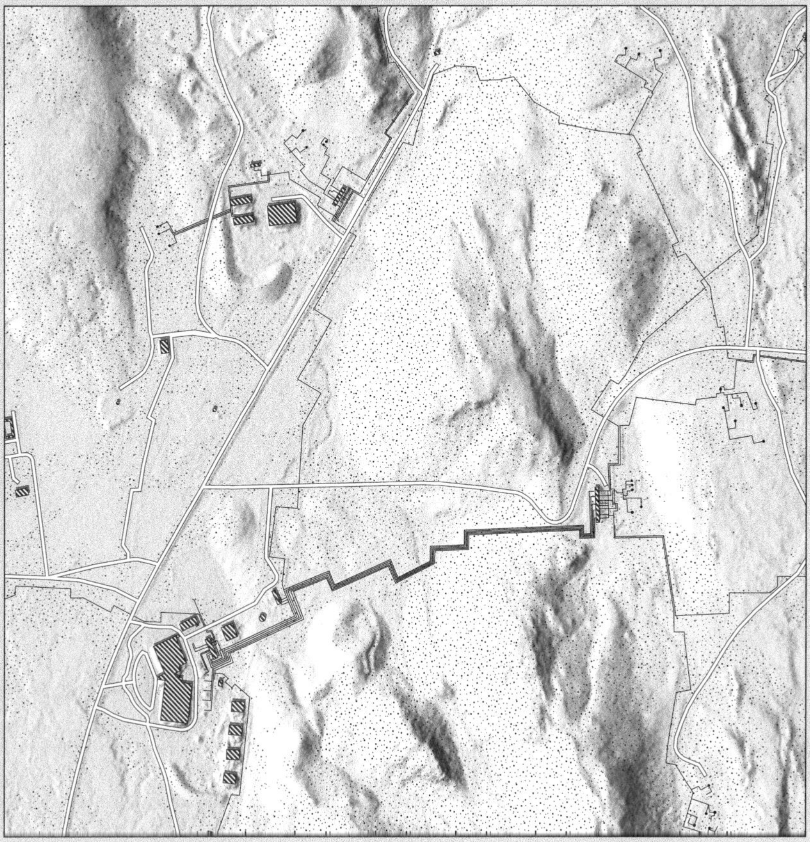

64°02’36.4”N 21°22’51.3”W

1 km

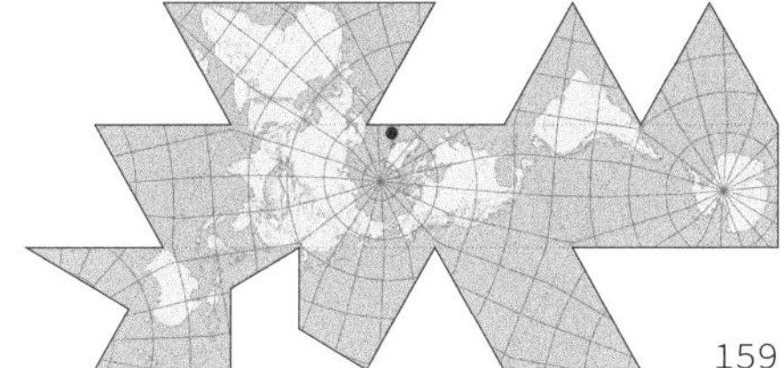

Amazon Fulfillment Center

California, United States

At the time of writing there are over 280 Amazon fulfillment centers worldwide. Each center is usually at least 70,000 square meters (think 16 footballs fields) but some are even double that size. A fulfillment center is a labyrinth of shelves, conveyors, robots, and humans all working in sync to scan, sort, and send packages. The whole system is designed by algorithms to maximize the speed with which items can come in from suppliers, be packaged into cardboard boxes, padded with pressurized plastic cushions, and sent out to online consumers. Amazon's *raison d'etre* is to be able to deliver anything to anyone, anywhere, as quickly as possible. Put another way, Amazon aims to be in total control of delivering everything to everyone, everywhere.

Given the extremely mechanistic and logistical nature of this enterprise, Amazon has been investing heavily in robotics. As of 2019, Amazon had more than 200,000 mobile robots working in warehouses. For some the specter of robots taking over entirely is logical, for others it's frightening. Newer fulfillment centers that have robots do reduce some of the physical toll on workers, who sometimes walk over 20 kilometers per day on concrete floors, but human workers also report an increase in repetitive strain from other tasks as they struggle to keep up with the robots.

Despite resisting the unionization of its labor, Amazon does try to make a good workplace for humans. It's hard, however, to imagine how the company's slogan "work hard, have fun, make history" that greets workers every day really applies to the situation the employees find themselves in. Working hard is clear, but what is meant by fun and history in this context is questionable. While it's a stretch to claim that stacking boxes is fun, Amazon does have some grounds to say it's making history. Amazon fulfillment centers do represent a new phase, if not the apotheosis, of the Industrial Revolution and, for consumers to be able to shop for almost everything without moving from their homes, is also certainly a historical first. So too is the creation of a proletariat that now goes to work every day to move everything but make nothing. What Amazon doesn't declare in its daily mantra, however, is that in addition to working hard, having fun and making history, employees should also strive to behave less like humans and more like the robots they share the factory floor with.

See Also: Walmart Supercenter (102), Tesla Gigafactory (162)

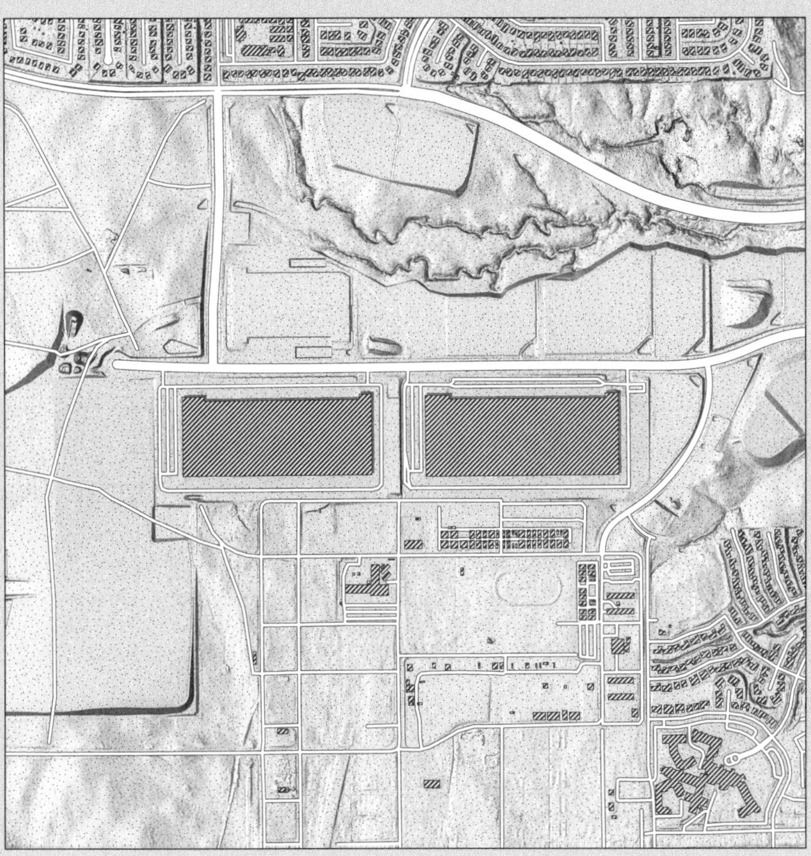

33°52’47.8”N 117°18’08.2”W

800 m

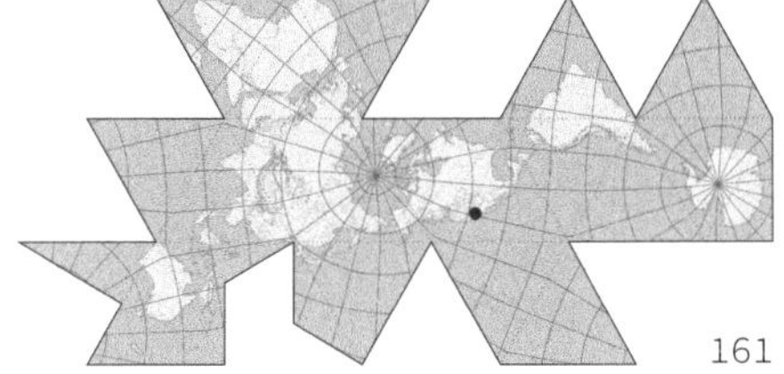

Tesla Gigafactory
Nevada, United States

Celebrity entrepreneur Elon Musk has a knack for taking mundane things like tunnels, cars, and in this case, factories, and making them seem exciting. In a culture where bigger is still better, the gigafactory ('giga' meaning billion) is a prime example of his Midas touch. The concept is simple: raw materials in one end, finished cars out the other, no middlemen. This perfect business model—a kind of hyper-Fordism—is, however, yet to fully materialize.

Due to the climate crisis and desire to reduce fossil fuel emissions, there is a growing demand for electric cars. As the world's largest producer of electric vehicles, Musk's company Tesla is aiming to produce more than 500,000 cars per annum. Meeting this target gave rise to the concept of the gigafactory and in June 2014, Tesla broke ground for the first of these behemoths near Sparks in the state of Nevada. The site was chosen because Nevada offered Tesla $1.25 billion in tax breaks over a decade, along with a big flat chunk of land with water rights and lots of sunshine. At close to 177,000 square meters, the Tesla Gigafactory is, at the time of writing, about 30% complete. Modular by design, it will continue to expand until it can truly claim to be the biggest building ever built.

Today the gigafactory mainly produces batteries and electric motors and already has more battery production capacity than the rest of the world's automakers combined. Placing the battery manufacturing process inside the same building as the rest of the car production simplifies the production process, increases productivity, and reduces costs. The building's solar roof is expected to power the entire operation, but the promised geothermal and wind power components have not yet materialized. A 10-million-gallon water tank supplies chilled water for air conditioning and cooling some of the robotics. The vast floor plate of the factory is magnetized to help guide the robots.

Although bereft of conventional forms of architectural merit, the gigafactory is to our age what the pyramids were to the Egyptians. Both are monuments to cult-like figures and both express the values of their respective cultures. Where they differ, however, is that the pyramids will still be there long after the gigafactory is swept away by the desert, leaving nothing but a vast magnetized concrete slab for future archeologists to ponder.

See Also: Walmart Supercenter (102), Bahrain Formula 1 Circuit (138), Amazon Fulfillment Center (160), Data Center (164)

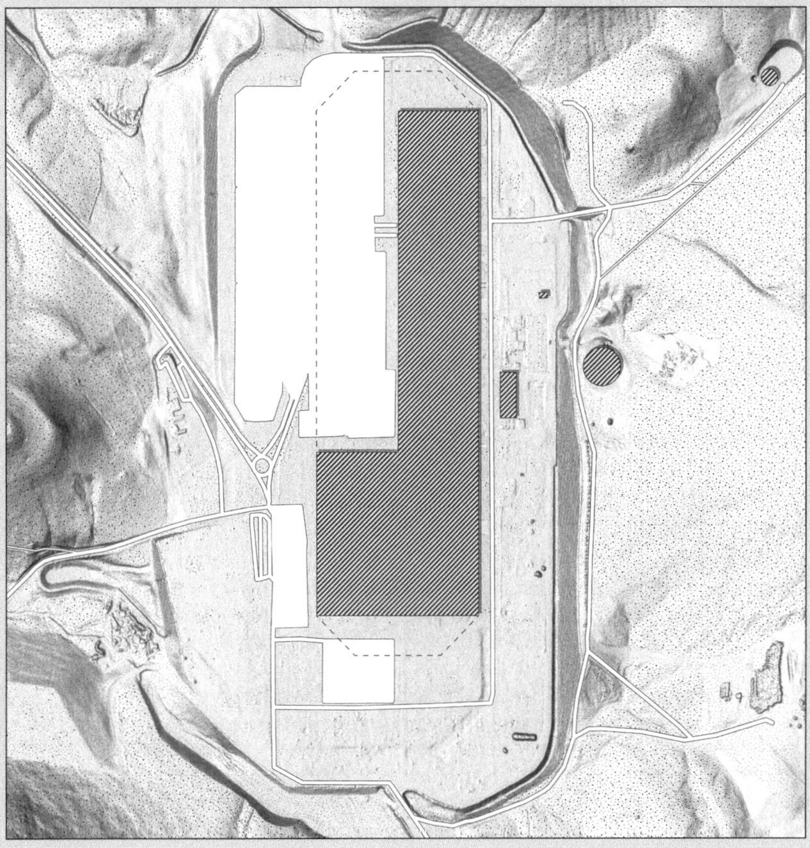

39°32’18.5”N 119°26’24.2”W

500 m

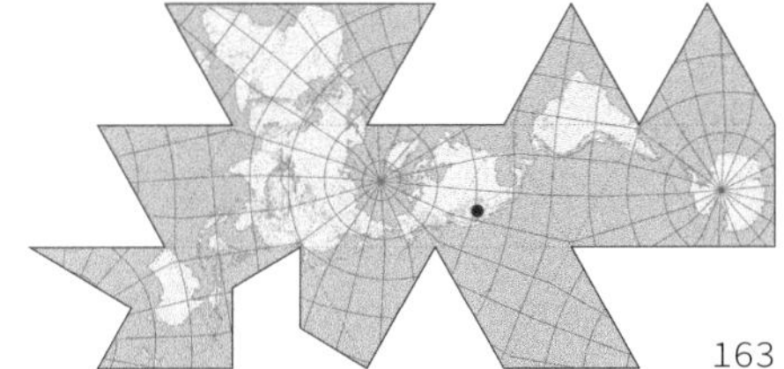

Data Center

Nevada, United States

What the Amazon fulfillment center is for stuff, the data center is for information. It too makes nothing, but stores and transfers everything—everything digital that is. Data centers are the synapses and memory of the internet. Data centers play the stock market, mine Bitcoin, stream movies, host video games, back up businesses, run computationally intensive models of things like climate change or machine learning, store Google's webmap, and keep every Facebook and Twitter post ever sent.

Big companies either have their own data centers—Walmart's 'Area 71' in Jane, Missouri, is an impressive example—or they rent space from service providers such as global tech company Switch. Switch recently opened Tahoe Reno 1 as the first of seven in its 800-hectare Citadel Campus in Nevada. With more than 120,000 square meters of space, Tahoe Reno 1 as shown opposite is one of the world's largest datacenters. Tahoe Reno 1 is a part of Switch's so-called SUPERLOOP, an 800-kilometer multi-terabyte fiberoptic network that connects Switch's clients to more than 40 million people in less than 10 milliseconds.

In addition to anonymity and security, data centers require vast amounts of energy to keep the servers constantly running. Tahoe Reno 1 for example, requires up to 130 megawatts of power, and at full buildout, the Citadel Campus will require up to 815 megawatts of power. Globally, data centers use an estimated 200–250 terawatt hours (TWh) of electricity per year, the equivalent of New Zealand. This figure excludes the exponentially growing power demands for blockchain technologies such as NFTs (non-fungible tokens) and cryptocurrency, which would add another half (~100 TWh) on top. Some projections expect that demand for electricity to sustain digital culture will reach nearly 3,000 TWh by 2030. By comparison, today the entire world generates about 3,500 TWh through wind energy and 1,800 TWh via solar.

Data centers can be thought of as architectural icons of the digital age. While we will always visit cathedrals, museums and libraries, it is extremely unlikely that any of us will ever visit a data center. This is not only because they are typically remote, camouflaged and fortified, its also because there is nothing for humans to see or do in them: they barely even have any employees. Data centers are just big, air-conditioned sheds chock full of servers. They are utterly mechanistic and inhuman, and yet, in their memory banks they contain every single emoji ever sent.

See Also: Apple Park (48), Microchip (268), Smartphone (270)

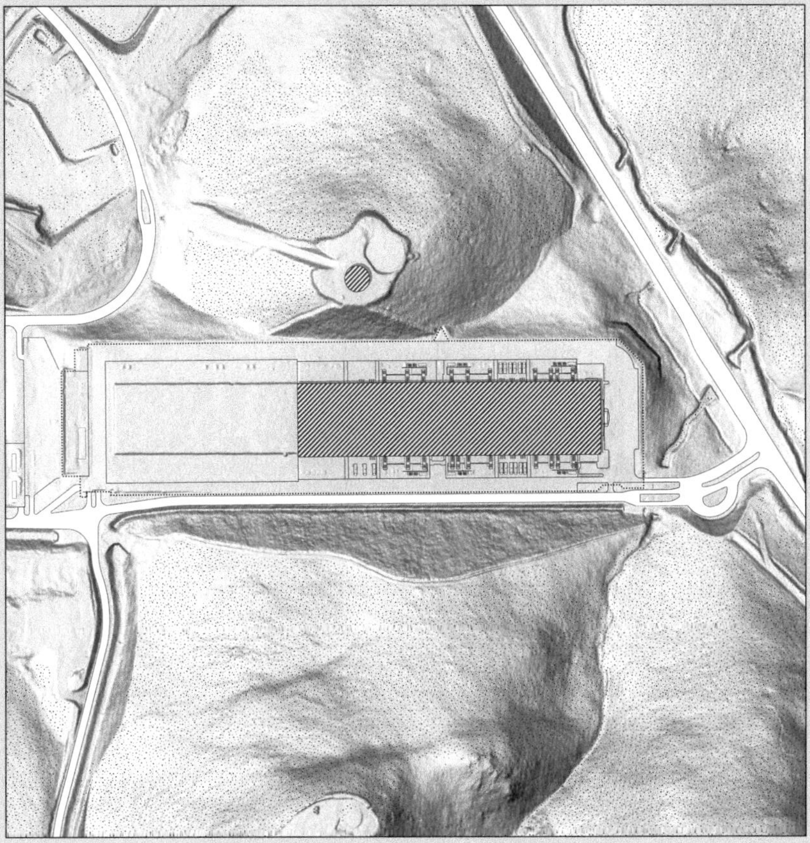

39°30’50.6”N 119°28’26.2”W

300 m

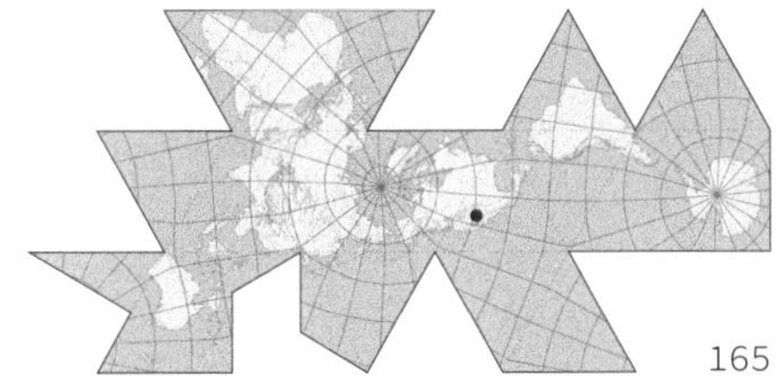

Salar de Uyuni Lithium Mine

Uyuni Salt Flat, Bolivia

Bolivia's Salar de Uyuni (salt flats of Uyuni) cover 10,000 square kilometers of the Andean high plains in South America's Lithium Triangle, a region rich in lithium deposits that also includes parts of Argentina and Chile. Historically the area has been used for table salt, harvested by the native Aymara people, but since the 1980s, state-owned and multinational corporations have built (and abandoned) mining operations across the Salar. The Salar de Uyuni flats hold nearly half the world's supply of lithium (5.4 million tons of a global total of 11 million). Known as white gold, lithium is essential to making batteries and its value is rising with the increased demand for electric cars and high-tech devices.

The lithium is found in a mineral-rich brine just below the saline crust of the salt pans. The extraction process is relatively simple and low cost: miners drill holes in the flats to access the brine and deposit it in evaporation pools for 12 to 18 months after which time lithium remains in bright yellow-green pools. This is then converted into powdery white lithium carbonate for battery makers.

Though electric cars are a promising example of relatively clean energy—a technological advancement with the potential to greatly reduce our reliance on fossil fuels and to decrease carbon emissions—the lithium battery powering a Tesla is not without its own damage to the environment. As with most mining operations, the extraction process requires large amounts of water, a scarce resource in the arid climate of the high plains where local farmers and inhabitants already face difficulty accessing adequate water supplies. Lithium mining also uses toxic chemicals that can cause contamination of local waterways. These localized social and environmental problems need then to be weighed against global progress toward lowering carbon emissions, as well as the income the mining industry brings to the nations involved.

Lithium mining and the production of clean, green goods for the First World also brings the persistent problem of global inequity into stark relief: the cheapest Tesla, for example, is around five times the average annual income of a Bolivian.

See Also: Tesla Gigafactory (162), Polymetallic Nodule Extractor (168), Smartphone (270)

20°34’04.1”S 67°22’44.5”W

5 km

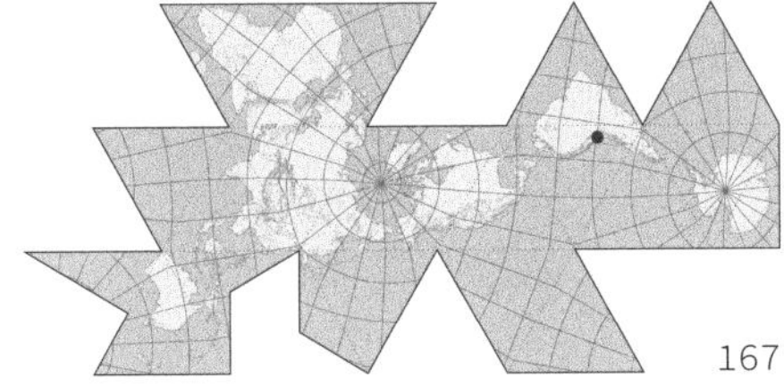

Polymetallic Nodule Extractor
International

To reduce our dependence on fossil fuels, the green energy and technology industries require an increasing quantity of raw materials such as manganese, lithium, and cobalt. The problem, however, is that these materials are quite rare. Consequently, polymetallic nodules, polymetallic sulfides, and polymetallic cobalt-rich ferromanganese crusts on the seabed have come into focus.

As of 2021, the International Seabed Authority has authorized 30 contracts to explore the viability of long-term seabed mining operations. The Patania II, shown opposite, is a 25-ton prototype nodule collector designed to operate on the abyssal plains of the deep ocean floor. The machine is an underwater bulldozer-cum-vacuum cleaner connected to a mothership at the surface via a 5-kilometer-long umbilical cord. The mothership directs the machine's work, filters the slurry it sucks up, extracts the valuable nodules, and then returns the bulk of the material back to the ocean.

For the miners, the ocean floor is not only attractive because of the mineral rich nodules, but also because the mining operation can happen beyond the watchful eye of the public. Indeed, at these depths the whole process takes place in total darkness, so whatever happens down there we will have to take the miners' word for it. But we know how this goes. History teaches that the process of extraction almost inevitably requires the decimation of the source environment. It also teaches that nature is not just inert matter that can be manipulated without consequence. What we now know to be true, and can model economically, is that everything in an ecosystem works to provide us with 'ecosystem services,' that is free services such as fresh air, water, and food that would otherwise be extremely expensive, not to say impossible for us to manufacture ourselves. The ocean provides these services, and the ecology of the ocean floor is intrinsic to its overall health and vitality.

There may well be sections of the ocean floor where some level of disturbance has minimum impact, where the benefits will outweigh the costs. But if we have learned anything from mining the land, it is that we should transparently analyze all the risks before we go in and destroy this last frontier under the cloak of darkness.

See Also: Salar de Uyuni Lithium Mine (166), Nauru Island (188)

4 m

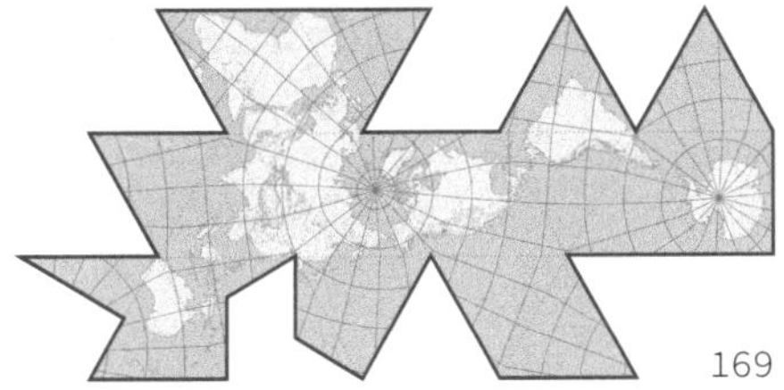

Sand Motor

The Hague, the Netherlands

Owing to erosion from wind and ocean currents, much of the Dutch coastline has shifted inland over the past millennium. To secure the nation against further incursion, in recent times sands have been dredged from the North Sea and used to bolster the Netherlamds' beaches and dunes. To make this massive dredging process more efficient, Marcel Stive, professor of coastal engineering at Delft University of Technology, developed the idea of a beach nourishment program that uses the natural power of waves, currents, and wind to do the work of distributing sand along the Dutch coastline. This harnessing of natural forces to do mechanistic work is a new form of engineering known as nature-based solutions and the Dutch Sand Motor (Zandmotor) is one of its best examples.

The way the Sand Motor works is that instead of constantly shipping dredge material up and down the coast, it is stockpiled in one strategic location from which, over time, the natural processes (littoral drift) of the coast does the work of distributing it. A decade after the project was initiated, nearly 3 million cubic meters of material initially deposited at the site of the Sand Motor (the bulge in the coastline visible opposite) has been attenuated into a slender band of material stretching far along the coast. The distributed material forms a natural barrier to the effects of storm surges as well as sheltering a network of shallow coastal bays that serve as a further buffer to the ocean.

In contrast to the short lifespans of more conventional methods, the Sand Motor continues to slowly but surely replenish the coast for 20 years or more without the need for further intervention. In addition to its primary purpose of stockpiling and distributing sand, the Sand Motor is also designed as a destination for recreation, and an area of habitat restoration for coastal biodiversity. While the idea of getting nature to do much of the work of beach and dune replenishment seems simple enough, its realization is only made possible by the capacity to model complex coastal processes and extrapolate these into the future with accuracy. The Sand Motor is above all a practical project extending a long Dutch tradition of shaping the land and managing water. But so too, the Sand Motor is a monument to the epoch of the Anthropocene, an age defined by the fact that humans now move more raw materials than the earth itself does. The beauty of the Sand Motor is that in this case, humans and the earth are moving materials in concert.

See Also: Spiral Jetty (258), Global Sea Level Rise Monitoring (282)

52°03’18.9”N 4°11’23.5”E

800 m

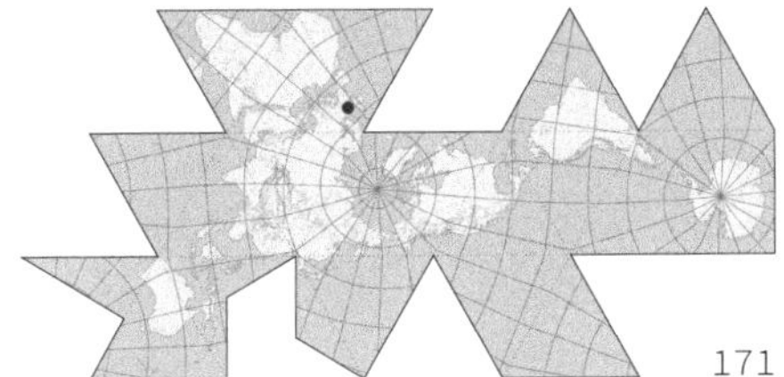

Tree Planting Drones

International

With the world losing around 10 million hectares of forest each year and the rate of desertification due to overgrazing and climate change increasing, the task of restoring landscapes on a scale and at a pace commensurate with the crisis is daunting. It's not just the sheer scale of the work that needs to be done, it is also the physical complexity of that which is being restored. Ecosystems might look simple—a swamp here, a forest there—but they are not. Ecosystems are complex, highly evolved systems. They are easy to burn and bulldoze but they are extremely hard to put back together again.

Perhaps technology can help. For example, in the last decade, unmanned aerial drones have become an important part of reforestation and afforestation efforts. With drones, some companies are claiming an ability to reseed up to 60 hectares of land per day and rehabilitate land eleven times faster and one-third cheaper than traditional methods of restoration. The drones are also especially good at gathering data about site conditions prior to, and after restorative efforts have taken place. This can also include the surveillance of illegal practices of extraction in protected and restored areas.

Because they work with seeds rather than propagated nursey stock, the problem with restoration-by-drone is that the rate of successful seed propagation is limited. And even when the seeds do propagate en masse it is important to note that landscapes are not restored just because they have been replanted and then appear green. For example, plantations of a single or only a few different species do not automatically inculcate and sustain biodiversity. Irrespective of whether it is done by drone or by human hand, planting vegetation in denuded landscapes is just the first step in reestablishing healthy, self-sustaining, ecological processes.

This (2020–2030) is the UN Decade of Ecosystem Restoration. This means governments, NGOs, and communities are redoubling their efforts to galvanize funding, marshal labor, and work out how best to restore depleted ecosystems to some semblance of health. But where conservation once conjured images of picturesque scenery and park rangers, the future conservation landscape will likely be one in which a labor force of robots fans out across degraded lands to prepare the soil and signal to the drones overhead to release their seeds. Thereafter, technology will certainly play a role but it will be humans who have the skills and the passion to nurse these lands back to life.

See Also: Yellowstone to Yukon Initiative (58), Guanacaste National Park (66), GIS Crop Harvester (142), COTSbot (214)

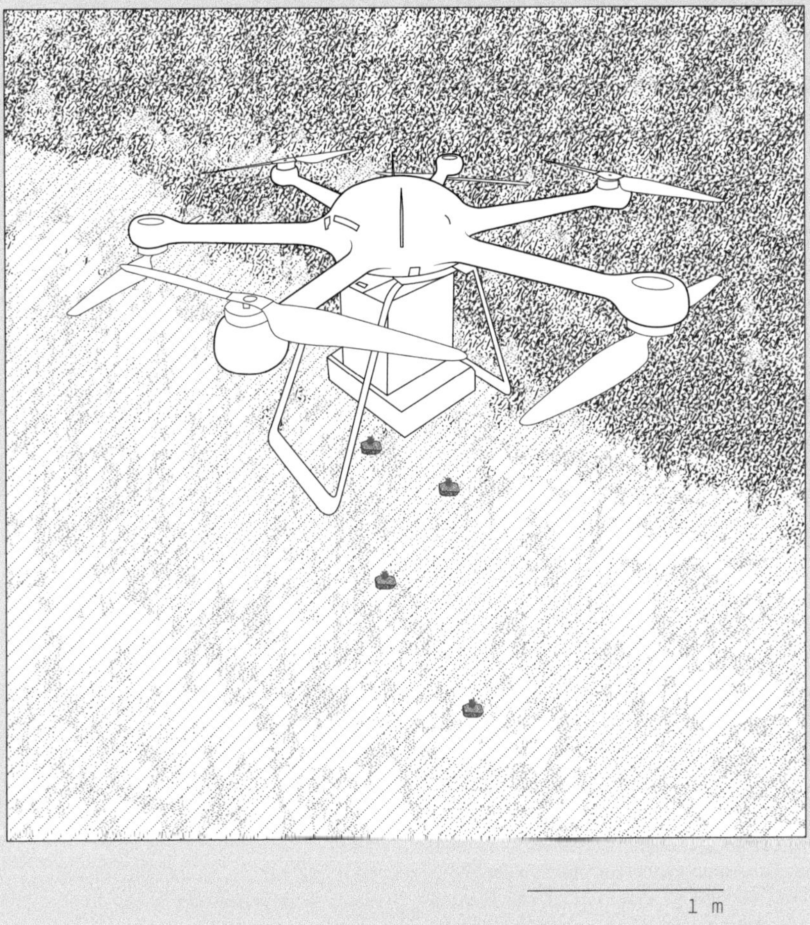

1 m

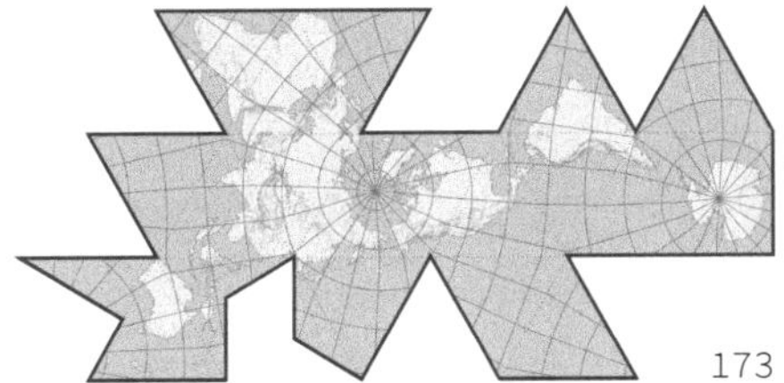

Launch Complex 39

Florida, United States

Space flight has been mathematically feasible since Newton's laws of motion accurately described moving bodies in the late 17th century. It wasn't until the mid-20th century, however, that humans could muster the 37 million horsepower of thrust required to break the earth's gravitational field, and also engineer a container to protect human cargo while doing so. The first person in space was Russian cosmonaut Yuri Gagarin, in 1961. In the same year, President Kennedy charged NASA with landing an American on the moon within a decade. To do so the Americans needed to not only build a very big rocket, they also needed a propitious place from which to launch it.

Merritt Island, a national park off the coast of Florida, was chosen as the site to construct the so-called 'moonport,' officially known as 'Launch Complex 39' (LC39) at the Kennedy Space Center. Despite unpredictable local weather, in terms of the physics of space flight Florida is a good spot on the earth's surface to launch from. Merritt Island is also far enough away from major population centers to minimize any collateral damage in the case of an accident.

In its short history LC39 has seen momentous events. The launch of Apollo 11, which catapulted Neil Armstrong, Buzz Aldrin, and Michael Collins to the moon, took place here on July 16th, 1969. This represented a highpoint of human ingenuity and cemented America's position as the 20th century's preeminent global superpower. It could be argued, however, that the Apollo 8 flight a year earlier was equally, if not more, important, for it was on that flight that Will Anders took the photograph 'Earthrise.' This image of the earth from afar altered humanity's cosmological sense of place by showing the earth as a small blue orb in the void of space.

LC39 has also borne witness to great tragedy. It was here that the Space Shuttle Challenger exploded in 1986, taking the lives of seven astronauts as a stunned global audience watched in real time. As part of a recently renewed era of space travel, the Kennedy Space Center is now preparing the Artemis program, which aims to land the first women on the moon by 2025. Of late, interest in extra-terrestrial adventure has burgeoned as celebrity entrepreneurs compete to offer various forms of space tourism. NASA, along with some of these entrepreneurs, also now looks to Mars as humanity's next stop. If that happens we will probably depart from the thick concrete slab that is LC39.

See Also: Landsat (300), Space Garden (302), Perseverance Mars Rover (304), Voyager Spacecraft (306)

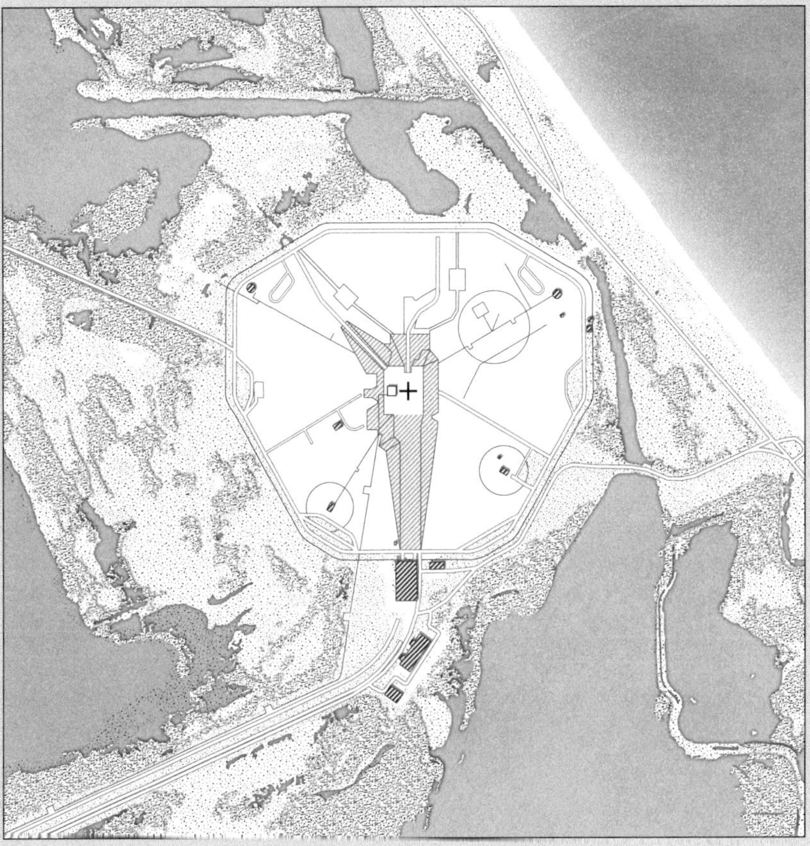

28°36’27.3”N 80°36’15.3”W

800 m

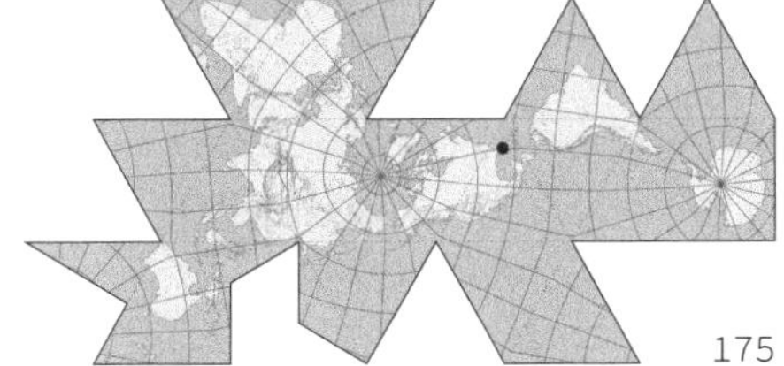

Monsters

The character of the monster takes many forms across many cultures. There are the *yokai* in Japan, the *wangliang* in China, the *rakshasas* in India, vampires in Transylvania, and, of course, Satan waiting for you with open wings to welcome you into hell. Rising up in our dreams, lurking in dark forests, written into lore, and now manufactured in mass media, monsters embody our deepest fears and fascinations.

In mythic literature—starting with Gilgamesh who confronts a scale-covered beast with bull horns and a snake-head penis—the hero must overcome the monster. Only then can the Manichaean struggle between good and evil that animates the universe be turned from violence and destruction to kindness and construction. But what of the modern world, that which 17th-century philosopher Thomas Hobbes described as a kind of new Leviathan?

In the modern world two additional classes of monster come to the fore. The first, introduced to us in Mary Shelley's Frankenstein in 1818, are the monsters we create, and the second, introduced by Sigmund Freud a century later, are the ones we see in the mirror. The monsters we will focus on in this chapter are environmental versions of the first variety, and yet it is also possible to understand these as extensions of the second.

What Frankenstein's monster teaches is not (only) that we shouldn't have transgressed natural limits or theological taboos in the first place, but that we have to take responsibility for the consequences when we do. Translated into practical terms this means returning to the wastelands of the modern world and doing the hard work of now repairing the landscape. This is what is meant by the United Nations' declaration that this is now the Decade of Ecosystem Restoration (2020–2030).

Getting busy with the work of environmental restoration is all well and good, but things get more complicated when we turn to our own reflections. As Judith Schalansky writes in her 2020 book, *Atlas of Remote Islands*, "[t]here is no untouched garden of Eden lying at the edges of this never-ending globe. Instead, human beings travelling far and wide have turned into the very monsters they chased off the maps" (p. 19). The origin of the word, *monstrum* means to warn, not just to frighten. In other words, monstrosities serve as omens of what the world could yet become if we don't make peace with our monsters.

Cumbernauld Town Centre

Cumbernauld, Scotland

The purpose of architecture is to create functional *and* beautiful structures. At best, architecture not only keeps the rain out, it surrounds us with exalted forms of aesthetic experience and edifies the human spirit. In the 20th century, however, with new theories of modern living and clients fixated on profit, the profession of architecture has bequeathed to us a spectacular array of monstrosities.

To give the best of these the publicity they deserve, the Carbuncle Awards—the equivalent of the Ig-Nobels in the sciences—were inaugurated in 2000 by the Scottish magazine *Urban Realm*. Of all the winners over the last two decades, the Cumbernauld Town Centre in Lanarkshire, Scotland holds the dubious honor of being awarded the Carbuncle of the Year award not once, but twice.

The theory behind Cumbernauld Town Centre's award-winning design was that of a megastructure, a term coined in architectural discourse in the early 1960s. The idea of the megastructure is that instead of one building being dedicated to one function—say a school or a church—the megastructure serves as a modular, structural system that can be extended to include any and all functions. Taken to its logical extreme, a megastructure could contain an entire city and it was in this form that architects found it most exciting.

As a pure architectural concept, the dream of the megastructure is that it could merge two seemingly incompatible worlds: on the one hand the rational and systematic, and on the other the pluralistic and diverse—each compensating for and supporting the other. But if there is one thing that characterizes modern architecture above all else, it is that what is good in theory was often not so good in practice.

Ahead of its time, Cumbernauld was conceived in the late 1950s as a new town of around 50,000 people. Instead of a conventional town with individual buildings on streets and public spaces defined by buildings, the megastructural approach of which it is emblematic was to lift everything up off the ground and pack it into one (mega)structure. Hailed as a design breakthrough at the time, it is a brutalist concrete shopping center perched over a road and connected to carparks by elevated walkways. While its all-in-one configuration enables certain efficiencies, and offers citizens protection from the region's harsh weather, it appears as a hulking foreign object in the landscape—a classic carbuncle.

See Also: Walmart Supercenter (102), Burj Khalifa (120), Tesla Gigafactory (162)

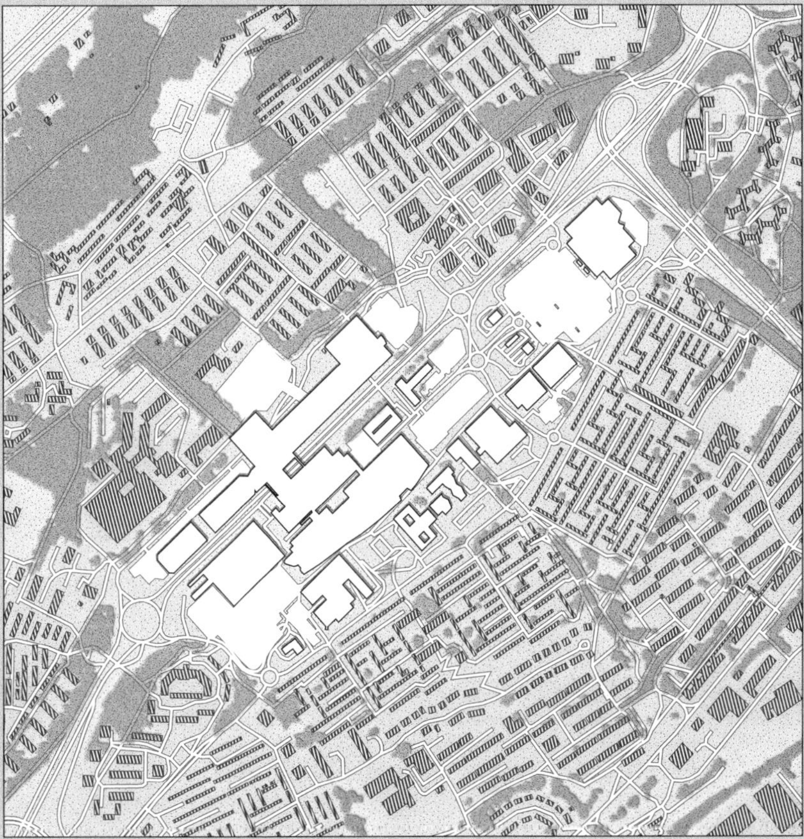

55°56’48.6”N 3°59’25.5”W

500 m

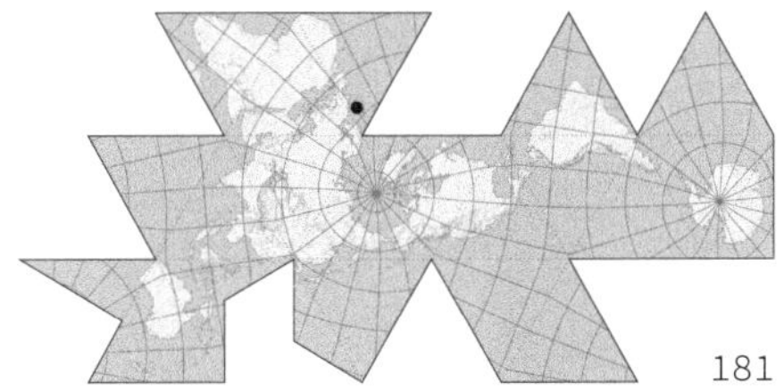

Griffith Park
California, United States

Indelibly branded by its Hollywood sign, Griffith Park is a rugged 1,700-hectare urban wilderness in the midst of Los Angeles. The land was originally gifted to the city by Colonel J. Griffith and his wife Tina Mesmer in 1896. A century earlier the land had been stolen from the indigenous Tongva people and made into Rancho los Feliz, the property of José Vicente Feliz who, with three soldiers and 44 settlers, founded the city of Los Angeles in 1781. In 1863, on the occasion of receiving nothing in the will of Feliz's descendent Don Antonio Feliz, his blind teenage niece and house keeper Doña Petranilla reportedly exclaimed: "The wrath of heaven and the vengeance of hell shall fall upon this place." Legend has it the park has been haunted ever since by what is known as Feliz's curse.

Certainly, going by the historical record, an extraordinary number of bad things have happened in Griffith Park. Animal sacrifices, suicides, murders, and prostitution are all apparently commonplace. The park has also been host to some inauspicious developments, such as a prison farm, a POW camp, and a lot of LA's trash. Today, however, the park boasts many visitors due to the presence of the LA Zoo, the Griffith Observatory, the Greek Theater, and, of course, that sign.

Which brings us to the park's current superstar—an adult mountain lion known as 'P22.' Unless someone put him there, ecologists believe that around 12 years ago P22 travelled 80 kilometers or so from the Santa Monica mountains and crossed freeways 101 and 405 to take up residence in the park. P22 was first captured on film in early 2012 by wildlife biologist Miguel Ordeñana, but he really shot to fame when photographer Steve Winter photographed him for *National Geographic* with the Hollywood sign perfectly framed in the background. Despite having never been seen by the 10 million or so people who visit the park every year, P22 enjoys an iconic status.

P22 is a local hero, but without any hope of a female mate, he is also a tragic character. LA is now building an 87-million-dollar wildlife crossing over the 101 freeway to help reconnect the habitat for mountain lions, but this won't help P22, who is isolated further west in Griffith Park. Luckily, P22 has plenty of rats to eat in Griffith Park—if he were to take down an Angelino, his status as hero would very quickly shift to that of monster.

See Also: Yellowstone to Yukon Initiative (58), Oostvaardersplassen (62), Wildlife Tags (294)

34°08’14.0”N 118°17’39.8”W

5 km

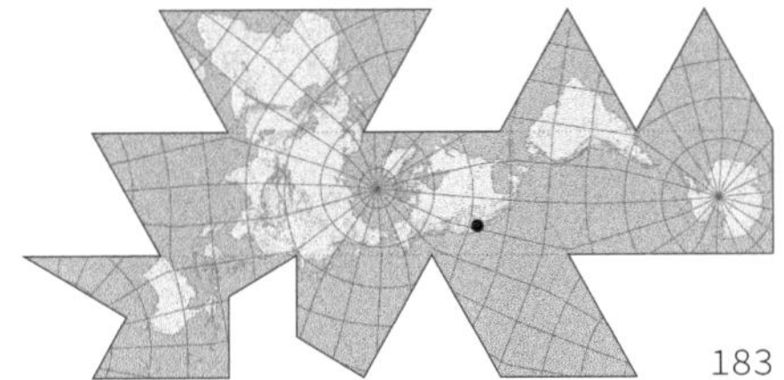

Pleistocene Park

Sakha Republic, Russia

Established in 1989, Pleistocene Park is a rewilding experiment in Siberia. The term rewilding means the reintroduction of certain species back into ecosystems from which they have been extirpated. It can also mean restoring ecosystems by kick-starting ecological processes and thereafter minimizing human involvement. Both forms of rewilding can attract controversy because they manifest ideas of nature with which some might not agree and also because rewilding needs space, which competes with the interest of humankind. Paradoxically, it can be argued that rewilding is now in human interests because it leads to a biodiverse ecosystem, something without which we cannot survive.

Pleistocene Park is a particularly interesting case of rewilding. The brainchild of Russian ecologist Sergey A. Zimov, the project drew global media attention due to his proposal to resurrect the woolly mammoth from DNA samples and restore it as a keystone species in the Siberian steppe. Zimov argues that 'charismatic megafauna' such as the mammoth are essential to recreating and then maintaining the grasslands because they break up and manure the soil. Once the mammoth (and other animals such as musk oxen, elk, horses, bison, sheep, and reindeer) disappeared, due to a combination of climate change and hunting, so too did the grasses, allowing a shrubby tundra to gradually replace the steppe.

As well as a desire to reconstruct ecological balance—something often criticized as nostalgic—there is a more urgent and compelling reason to rewild the Siberian steppe. Under its surface is permafrost—a sleeping giant full of undecomposed material kept in suspended animation by the frozen ground. As this ground thaws because of a warming climate, the natural processes of decomposition resume and release methane, a greenhouse gas much worse than carbon in terms of its heat-storing ability in the atmosphere. In short, if the Siberian permafrost thaws, climate change could radically accelerate.

Zimov argues that by bringing back the big animals and returning the landscape to grassland it would increase the albedo (reflective capacity) of the land preventing the buildup of a blanket of snow, which in turn will drop the land's temperature, thus maintaining the top layers of permafrost where, incidentally, most of the methane is. Pleistocene Park is where Zimov is testing his hypothesis, and while he hasn't yet brought back the mammoth, he has reintroduced other animals and shown that by returning the land to grasses, its temperature does in fact drop, so that the methane stays trapped in the permafrost.

See Also: Oostvaardersplassen (62), Svalbard Global Seed Vault (260), Frozen Zoo (262)

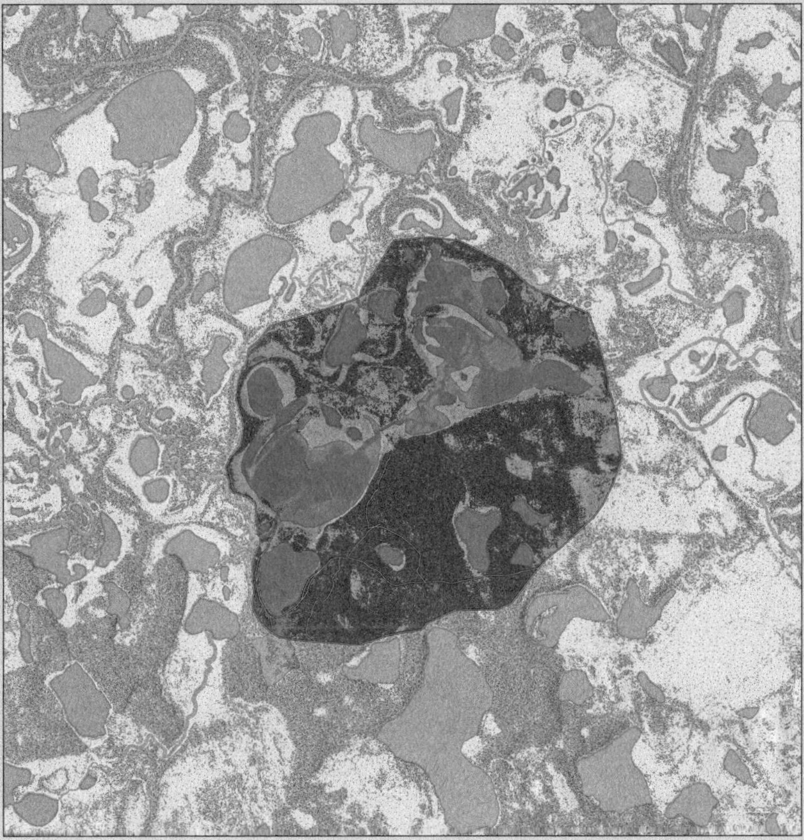

68°30’46.5”N 161°30’21.6”E

300 m

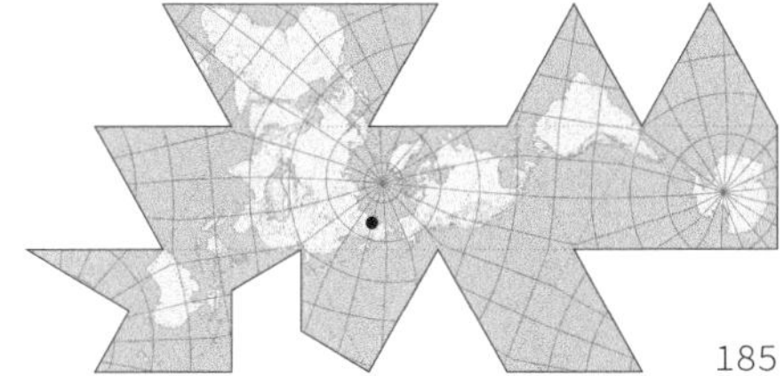

Harris Ranch
California, United States

Concentrated Animal Feeding Operations (CAFOs) are large treeless landscapes of holding pens, feedlots, abattoirs, and effluent basins designed to optimize the mass-production of meat and other animal products. In terms of providing low-cost food for billions of people worldwide, CAFOs are extremely efficient, but when all their industrialized inputs and outputs are tallied and the welfare of the animals is also taken into account, CAFOs are the stuff of nightmares.

Able to process over 250,000 cows and provide up to 150 million pounds of red meat to grocery stores and restaurants per annum, Harris Ranch in Fresno County, California represents the state of the art in concentrated animal feeding operations. The ranch has over 2,000 hectares of outdoor corrals to hold and feed its bovine inventory. After 120 days, by which time the average beast will fatten up to around 600 kilograms, the cattle are slaughtered. To reduce their anxiety, the animals are funneled to their death through a maze designed by renowned animal behavioralist Dr. Temple Grandin. Although documentation from animal activists suggests the animals *are* stressed, this concession to their state of mind alone makes Harris Ranch better than most. Relatively speaking, cows have it good compared with other concentrated feed lot animals. Many chickens and pigs, for example, never see the light of day or feel the earth beneath their feet.

In addition to issues of animal cruelty, CAFOs are also synonymous with a host of environmental problems related to the vast quantities of feed they require at one end of the operation and the toxic waste they produce at the other. Growing grain to feed the world's livestock is now the largest single land use on the planet. The proliferation of animals to keep pace with growing populations and their desire to eat meat also requires deforestation, which causes biodiversity loss and high carbon emissions. The animals then erode and compact soil, pollute water with nitrous oxide and ammonia, and expel over one third of all anthropogenic-related methane into the atmosphere.

Immediate measures to counteract the negative and largely unregulated landscape impacts of the global livestock trade relate to more strict protection of wildlands and pricing mechanisms to improve land and water management. Culturally, trends toward vegan diets and the possibility of a transition to biotech food production decoupled from animals promise a future that is less wasteful and less cruel.

See Also: Ogallala Aquifer (54), Fertilizer Production Plant (140), GIS Crop Harvester (142)

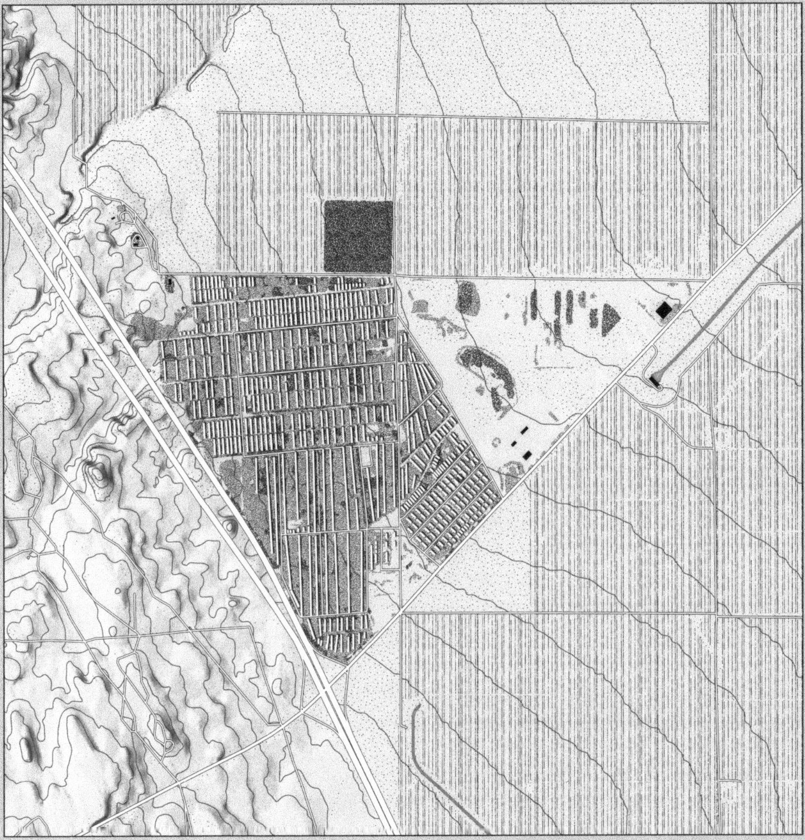

36°18’22.7”N 120°15’58.0”W

1 km

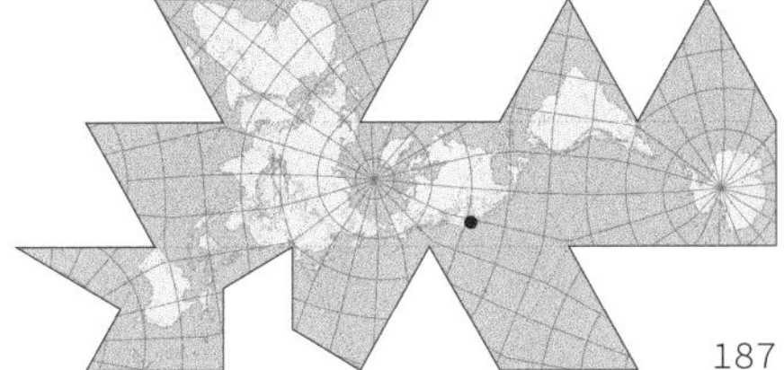

Nauru Island

Republic of Nauru, Oceania

Until 1900, no one knew that the island of Nauru in the Pacific was a big lump of phosphate, the essential ingredient in modern fertilizer. A mix of Polynesian and Micronesian peoples have lived on tiny Nauru island for around 3,000 years, engaging in aquaculture and the subsistence farming of coconuts and pandanus. Before Christianity arrived, Nauruans idolized a goddess, and the culture and economy were based on *bubutsi*, meaning 'to share.' The early Europeans who dropped anchor referred to it as 'Pleasant Island.'

Problems began, however, when whalers and pirates traded guns and alcohol for food and water. From 1878 the guns were used in a ten-year civil war that historians say lacked any political reason other than that one act of violence begat another. Germany annexed the island in 1888 until it was captured by Australian troops in 1914 who, along with the United Kingdom and New Zealand, promptly sized up the phosphate reserves for excavation. A year later, an influenza epidemic killed one-fifth of the Nauruan population. In World War II, to spite the allies, the Germans torpedoed the island's phosphate mining infrastructure before the Japanese occupied the island and removed 1,200 Nauruans as POW laborers for their other projects in the Pacific—working many of them to death. As a Japanese outpost, in World War II the island was bombed by the Americans.

After the war, Nauru became a UN Trust Territory and eventually gained its independence in 1968. With independence, the Nauruans took over the phosphate trade from the Australians after declining their offer to relocate the entire population to a new island in Australian waters. The Nauruans instead focused on prizing out the last of the phosphate for themselves. The plan was that with the sale of the remaining phosphate, Nauru would build a financial nest egg for its 10,000 or so citizens. For a while this seemed to be working—in the 1970s Nauru had the highest per-capita GDP in the world. As is so often the case with mining booms, however, the money was squandered. Now the nation is beholden to aid and worse, takes rent money from the Australian Government for holding Australian asylum seekers in a notoriously brutal detention center. With the island's ecosystem devastated, no work, and the highest rates of obesity and diabetes in the world, Nauruans have little left to share. Given there is now nothing of value on the island, Nauru is now advocating for deep sea mining in its waters.

See Also: Banwa Resort (80), Fertilizer Production Plant (140), Polymetallic Nodule Extractor (168)

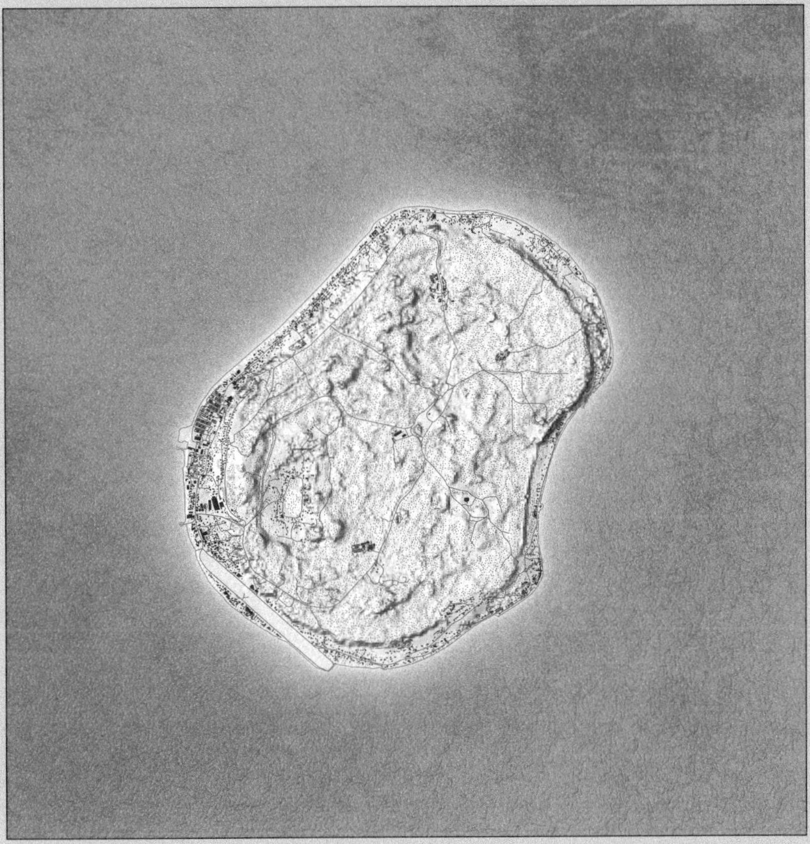

0°31’35.3”S 166°56’06.3”E

500 m

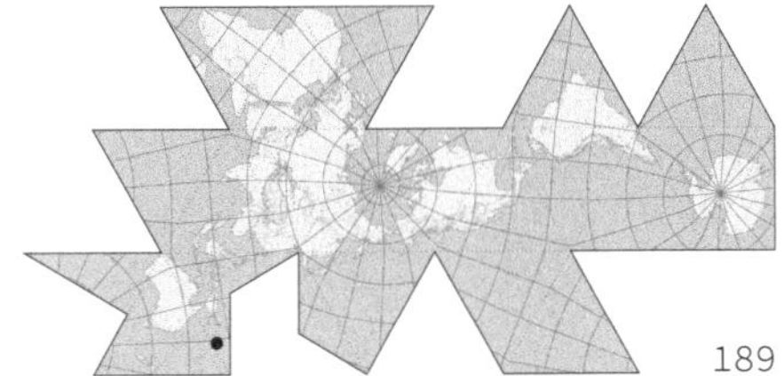

Mountaintop Removal Mining

West Virginia, United States

The classic image of coal mining is strong men with blackened faces hammering rock deep inside the earth. The image of coal mining in regions like Appalachia, where coal is distributed as a thin layer just under the surface of the land, is blowing the tops off mountains. Mountaintop removal mining (MTR) emerged when the oil crises of the 1970s triggered an increase in demand for coal, prompting open-cut mining with bigger machines and fewer workers. In the 1990s, MTR rapidly expanded because it gave access to a form of relatively low-sulfur coal, a 'cleaner' coal, which paradoxically became desirable because of amendments to the US Clean Air Act that had tightened carbon emission limits.

MTR is exactly what it says it is: to a depth of around 250 meters, entire mountain tops are detonated and the coal then extracted from the rubble. First, the forest is burnt and clear felled. Then the topography is detonated and the coal-bearing rock trucked out for processing. The remaining rubble is pushed down into valleys or dumped back into the area of what used to be a mountain top. In theory, the land is then revegetated. Alas, even when regulations are enforced and there is some money left to conduct genuine restoration, the landscape left in the wake of this form of mining is akin to band-aiding an amputation. The extraction obliterates the forest ecology of the mountaintop, and the dregs clog the valleys. The process of exploding the geology of the mountains also covers the region in toxic dust and the process of washing the coal pollutes waterways with a slurry of heavy metals such as arsenic, mercury, lead, and chromium. In short, this is mining at its crudest and most destructive.

Research indicates that communities living in MTR regions are more prone to a range of serious health issues that cannot be ascribed only to lifestyle. As natural gas (through the fracking boom) takes over as a cheap energy source and emissions targets bite, King Coal is finally now being usurped. Despite a brief burst of activity under the banner of "Trump Digs Coal," the industry in America, as elsewhere, seems destined for extinction, leaving decapitated mountains, clogged, toxic waterways, and broken communities in its wake.

See Also: Athabasca Oil Sands (192), Fracking Wells (194)

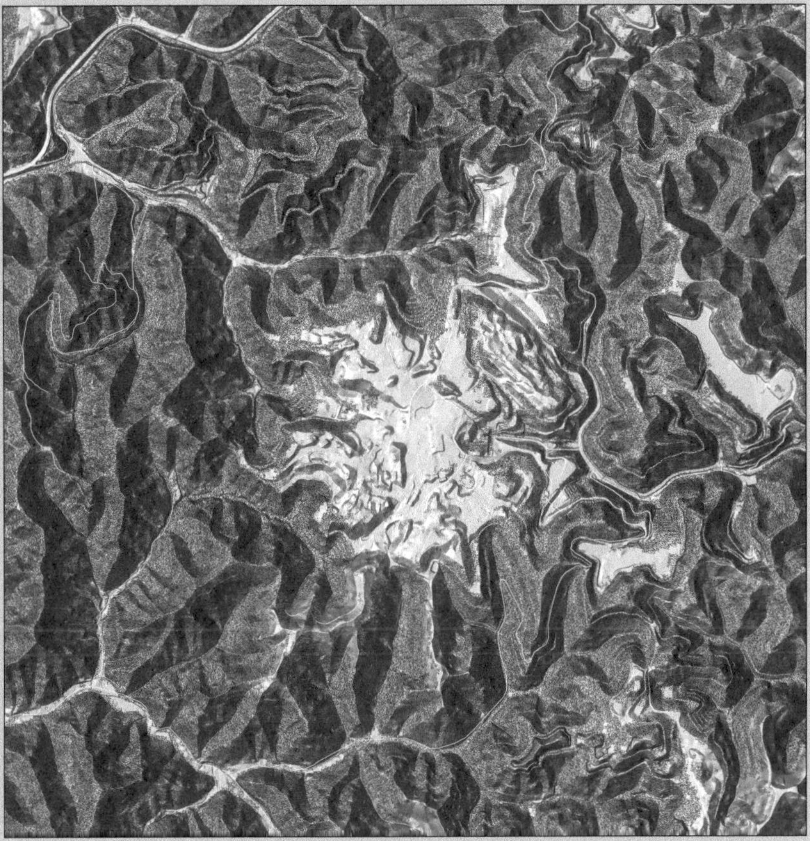

37°45'27.5"N 82°06'59.9"W

2 km

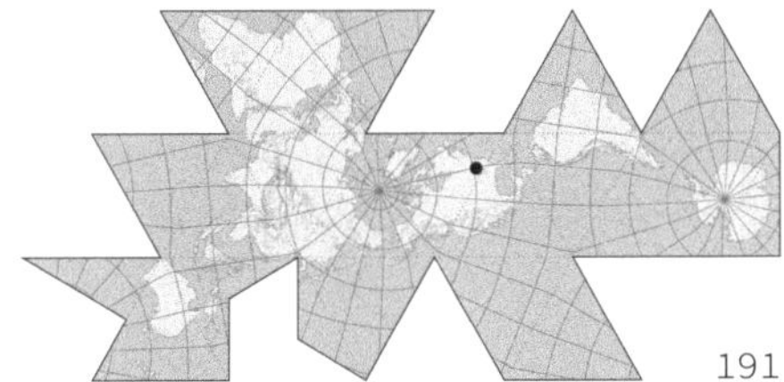

Athabasca Oil Sands

Alberta, Canada

Around 50 meters deep and spread over a vast land area, Alberta's Athabasca oil sands are a naturally occurring admixture of rocks, sand, clay, water, and bitumen. Bitumen is a form of crude oil that is too dense to flow on its own. Used by indigenous people to waterproof canoes, the potential of the oil sands as an energy resource was first noticed by colonists in the early 20th century.

The challenge of extracting this resource is threefold: first, the oil in the bitumen is mixed in with sand and clay. Second, it lies directly under Canada's largely intact boreal forests and muskegs (peat bogs) and so wherever mining takes place, the forests and bogs are necessarily obliterated. Third, mining in Athabasca has met with fierce resistance and there is really no way the industry can put a good spin on the apocalyptic imagery of seething tar pits and menacing machines destroying pristine forests. These challenges notwithstanding, the incentive of a vast oil supply is proving irresistible.

Believe it or not, in the 1950s the crack-pot plan was to denotate nuclear bombs under the oil sands in the hope that the heat would separate the oil from the sand. This, it was pointed out, ran the risk of igniting the whole thing and turning it into glass, not to mention the nuclear fallout. Today, the sands are separated from the oil by a process of flushing the bituminous sludge with hot water and caustic soda. The oil is then siphoned off and piped to refineries, the sands are returned to fill in the mine's excavation, and the wastewater is held in tailing ponds where it is treated.

Mining oil sands is profitable but risky—the pipelines can leak, the mine sites are hard to restore to any semblance of a viable ecology, and, above all, the tailing ponds are brimful with extremely toxic liquid. Inevitably, some of this wastewater leaches into the groundwater and wends its way into the Athabasca River, mutating if not killing all forms of life it comes into contact with. The mining process not only requires large amounts of water to flush the bitumen, it also requires massive quantities of natural gas to power the whole operation, adding significantly to Canada's carbon footprint. Of course, mining the oil sands also contributes significantly to the Canadian economy, but as it does so it also undermines Canada's righteous promotion of climate change action on the world stage. Canada is not alone in being hypocritical in this regard.

See Also: Mountaintop Removal Mining (190), Fracking Wells (194), Cancer Alley (204)

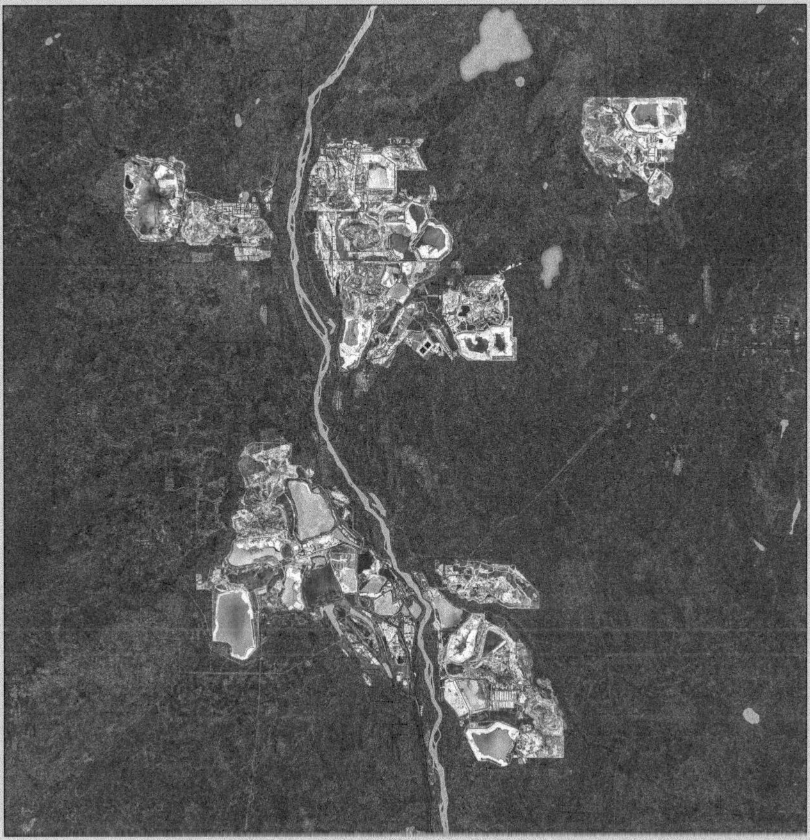

57°09’07.0”N 111°36’08.3”W

30 km

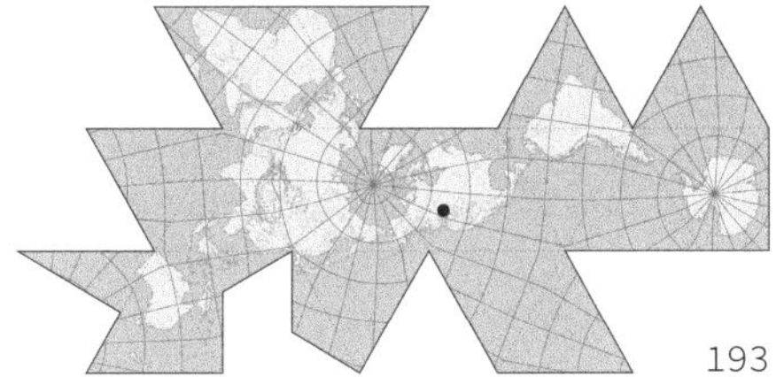

Fracking Wells
Oklahoma, United States

'Fracking' is a new word, meaning to hydraulically fracture the earth to release a flow of fossil fuels. The process is as crude as it sounds: by pumping a slew of chemicals, water, and sand at extreme pressure into the bowels of the earth, its geology can be cracked open to release pockets of oil and gas. The idea is not new—the first US patent for putting an explosive device in an oil well to improve flow was granted in 1865—but knowing precisely where to frack and then to do so profitably, is.

From the 1990s onward, the technique of modern-day fracking was developed by Texan oil magnate and environmental philanthropist George P. Mitchell. Instead of just drilling down to pierce a bubble suspended in the geological strata, Mitchell combined hydraulic pressure with both vertical and horizontal drilling so gas trapped in shale seams could be released in greater abundance. This has since proven to be a technique applicable to vast areas of the United States and beyond. As such, fracking has created booming regional economies and is credited with helping secure America's 21st-century energy independence.

Fracking is now deployed worldwide, but it is controversial for several reasons. First, it involves pumping enormous quantities of toxic chemicals into the ground, which risks contaminating water resources. Second, because fracking uses prodigious amounts of water in its processes, local water resources wherever it takes place are depleted. Third, the wastewater requires, but doesn't always receive, careful treatment. Fourth, the fracking rig and the related water retention basins and long-distance piping significantly disturb the landscape's visual character. And finally, critics argue that the success of fracking for fossil fuels (predominantly natural gas) further defers the necessary energy transition to truly renewable energy supplies. For these reasons some regions have banned fracking. For most—particularly farmers on whose land fracking takes place—the temptation of easy energy and fast money are just too great.

Mining has always been a dark art. Prior to the rationalization of landscape as a mere resource to serve the purposes of the Industrial Revolution, minerals were thought of as living veins in the earth's body. As such, the violent nature of mining was ritualized in order to appease mother earth and assuage the miner's guilt associated with defiling her body. Today, however, we think nothing of forcing chemicals into the earth's bones, to snap them open so we can suck out the last drops of carboniferous marrow.

See Also: Mountaintop Removal Mining (190), Athabasca Oil Sands (192)

35°44’26.0”N 99°32’53.2”W

3 km

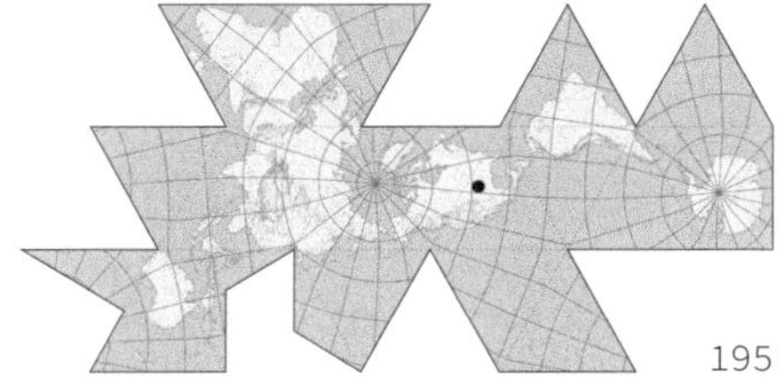

Vozrozhdeniya Island
Kantubek, Uzbekistan

Vozrozhdeniya Island is located in Uzbekistan, on the border with Kazakhstan. Originally, the island was located within the Aral Sea, but following a Soviet Union project that dammed the sea's feeder rivers in order to use the water for agriculture, the Aral rapidly receded. Considered one of the major environmental disasters of recent times, by 2010 what had once been the world's fourth largest lake had effectively disappeared, and with it Vozrozhdeniya Island.

Until the early 20th century, Vozrozhdeniya Island was a small fishing village. In 1948, the Soviet Union's Red Army decided to use the island as a military research complex for testing and developing bioweapons such as anthrax, smallpox, plague, brucellosis, and tularemia. In 1954, it was enlarged and renamed Aralsk-7, the epicenter of Soviet biological warfare research. Aralsk-7 was renowned in the intelligence community for its scale and scope, as well as for breaching international conventions on biological warfare. The complex was kept top secret and erased from any Soviet maps. To this day, the full inventory of the kinds of germ warfare invented and trialed at Vozrozhdeniya are unknown.

What is known is that there have been numerous instances of accidental release of biological agents from Vozrozhdeniya, including weaponized smallpox in 1971, the plague in 1972, and anthrax spores mixed with bleach and dumped into pits in 1988. That same year, over 50,000 antelope died in the vicinity in the span of one hour. Anthrax spores, known for their longevity, can survive for hundreds of years when buried underground.

In 1991, following the dissolution of the Soviet Union, the island was abandoned and the facility's equipment hastily and inappropriately disposed. The small town of Kantubek associated with the facility was evacuated and is now a ghost town. In recent years there have been pledges to clean up the land, and although there has been a steady return of plants and animals to the area it is still considered unsafe for humans.

Given its ascendancy as the preeminent global economic system, capitalism is generally associated with and blamed for environmental despoliation. This is not unwarranted, but sites like Vozrozhdeniya show that capitalism's antithesis, socialism, at least in its 20th-century form, also has an appalling track record of environmental mismanagement.

See Also: Runit Dome (198), Chernobyl Reactor #4 (200), Onkalo Spent Nuclear Repository (202)

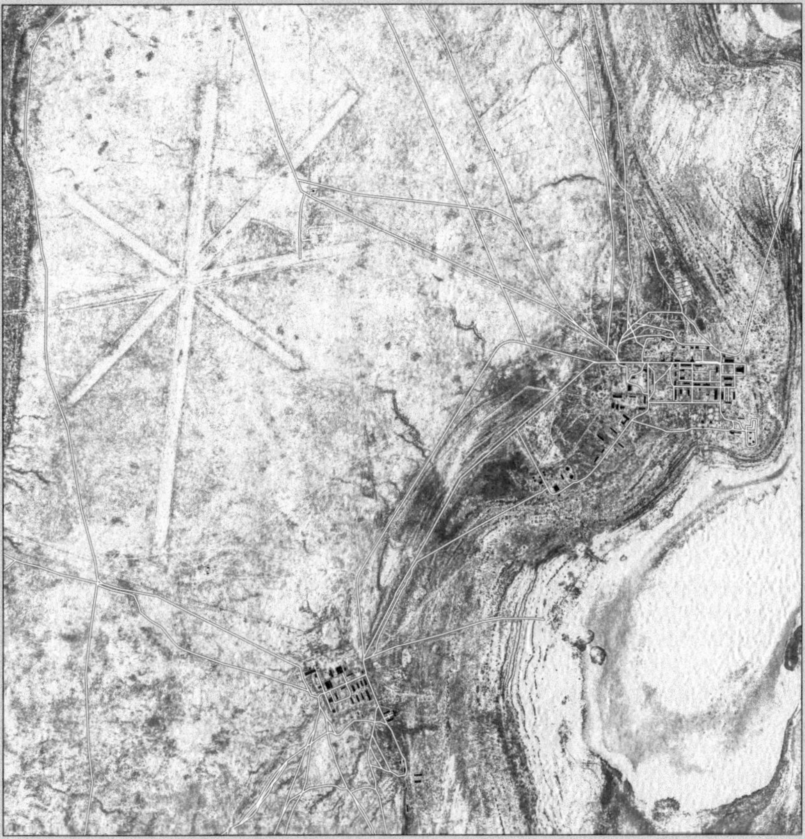

45°09'29.8"N 59°17'46.7"E

2 km

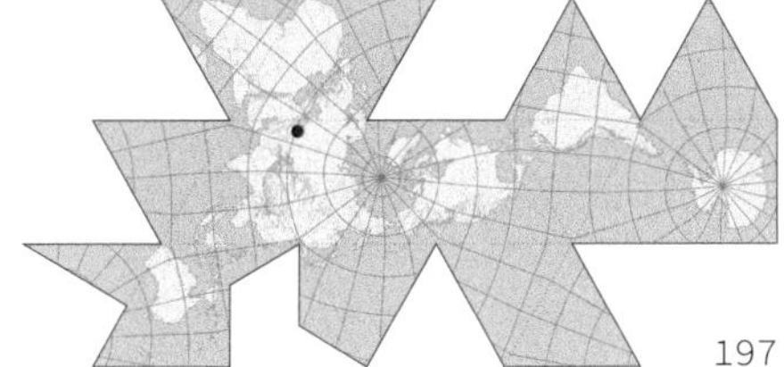

Runit Dome
Enewetak Atoll, Marshall Islands

Located between Hawaii and the Philippines, Enewetak Atoll in the Marshall Islands is a 120-kilometer-long atoll demarcating the rim of an ancient volcano. It was held by the Japanese from 1914 until taken by the United States in 1944, who used it as a nuclear testing ground until the completion of the clean-up operation in 1980. Between 1945 and 1958, 67 nuclear tests were conducted on the Enewetak and Bikini Atolls. The biggest test was 1,000 times that of the bomb dropped on Hiroshima. Videos record American officials telling the local Marshallese prior to the tests that their forced exile to make way for the tests was for the greater good; the tests were, they said, all part of "God's plan."

The Marshall Islands were originally chosen because of their remoteness, low population, calm weather, and the expectation that the predominant winds would reliably blow nuclear fallout away from where people lived. This, however, was not always the case and there are reports of local children being excited by what they thought was snow falling on them. In fact, it was incinerated coral and nuclear fallout.

The cleanup of the atolls by a team of 400 American soldiers started in 1977 and took three years to complete. Around 73,000 cubic meters of polluted material, including the island's entire layer of topsoil and chunks of extremely toxic plutonium from a bomb that failed to detonate, were dumped in the so-called Cactus crater on Runit Island. Once full, the crater was then capped with an 18-inch-thick concrete dome, now referred to by locals as 'the tomb.' Given assurances it was safe, the original inhabitants of Enewetak returned to the island in 1980. Some have reported significant health problems, as have the American soldiers who conducted the cleanup. Some moneys have been paid to the Marshall Islands as compensation, but American soldiers with health-related issues have not yet been compensated.

Haunted by their recent past, the Marshall Islanders are now bracing for and planning evacuation from the effects of sea level rise. The rising waters will not only wash away the history of thousands of years of human inhabitation, it will also flush the contents of the tomb into the ocean. It is little wonder, then, that the dystopian novelist J.G. Ballard chose Enewetak as the setting for his short story *Terminal Beach*, in which the main character becomes a monster.

See Also: Chernobyl Reactor #4 (200), Onkalo Spent Nuclear Repository (202), Doom Town (232)

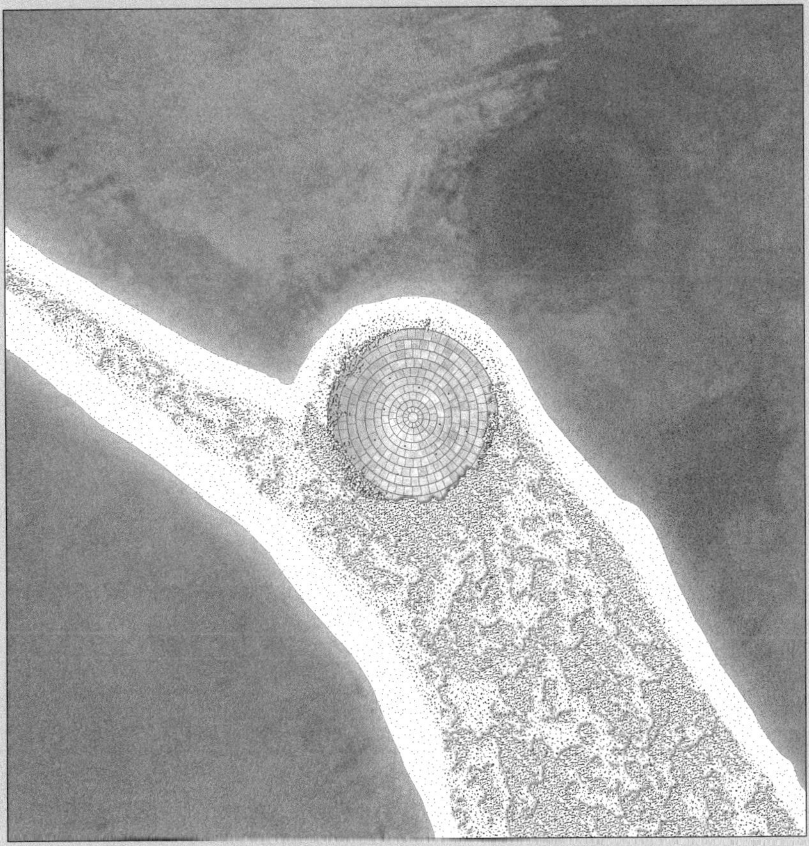

11°33’08.7”N 162°20’51.3”E

200 m

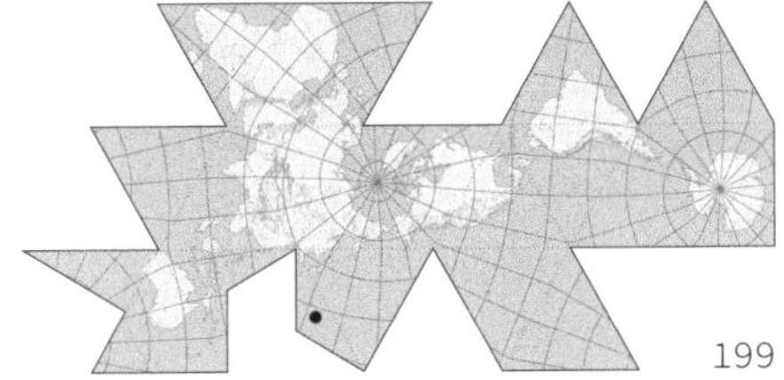

Chernobyl Reactor #4

Pripyat, Ukraine

At 1:23 am on April 26th, 1986, an explosion filled the sky over the small Ukrainian town of Pripyat. The town was constructed by the Soviet Union in 1970 to house workers from the Vladimir Lenin (aka Chernobyl) nuclear power plant. Thirty-four hours later the first buses arrived to evacuate everyone. People were told to leave their belongings as they'd only be away for three days. In all, over 200,000 people were evacuated, never to return.

With the explosion, over 100 different types of radioactive particles spread through the atmosphere, reaching as far as Ireland in the west and the Himalayas in the east. Simultaneously, corium, a lava-like slurry of uranium and plutonium, burrowed down deep into the labyrinthine complex of reactor #4. Soviet officials eventually declared a 30-kilometer no-go zone, known as the Chernobyl Exclusion Zone (CEZ), around the reactor. It remains one of the most radioactively contaminated areas in the world.

To prevent the dispersal of radioactive matter, the reactor was initially covered in concrete. This is a process the industry refers to as entombment and reactor #4 is now known as the sarcophagus. With international support, the sarcophagus has since been enclosed in a 'New Safe Confinement Unit,' a massive steel barrel, constructed adjacent to the site and then rolled into place on tracks. Inside the barrel are cranes and related mechanisms that can be remotely maneuvered to pick through the ruins of radioactive material as the clean-up continues.

Despite varying reports as to the level of risk, the CEZ has become a somewhat macabre tourist attraction with Pripyat playing the role of a modern Pompeii. Tourists also come to get a glimpse of what the world would look like without us, as an unruly wilderness has taken over the zone. Scientists too are fascinated by the resurgent life in the zone, documenting and analyzing its emergent ecology. While the vegetation looks healthy enough, scientists are reporting increased genetic mutations in birds, butterflies, and other insects, along with declining populations of certain species. Mutation and mortality are also well documented in the human population, especially among 'liquidators'—the people who have worked on containing and cleaning up Chernobyl.

Currently there are concerns of a potential build up to another explosion as neutrons strike and split the nuclei of the remaining uranium atoms, creating volatile energy. In this sense the sarcophagus is not a container for the dead, but something very much alive. In fact, it will be alive for at least the next 20,000 years.

See Also: Runit Dome (198), Onkalo Spent Nuclear Repository (202), Doom Town (232), Thermonuclear Experimental Reactor (278)

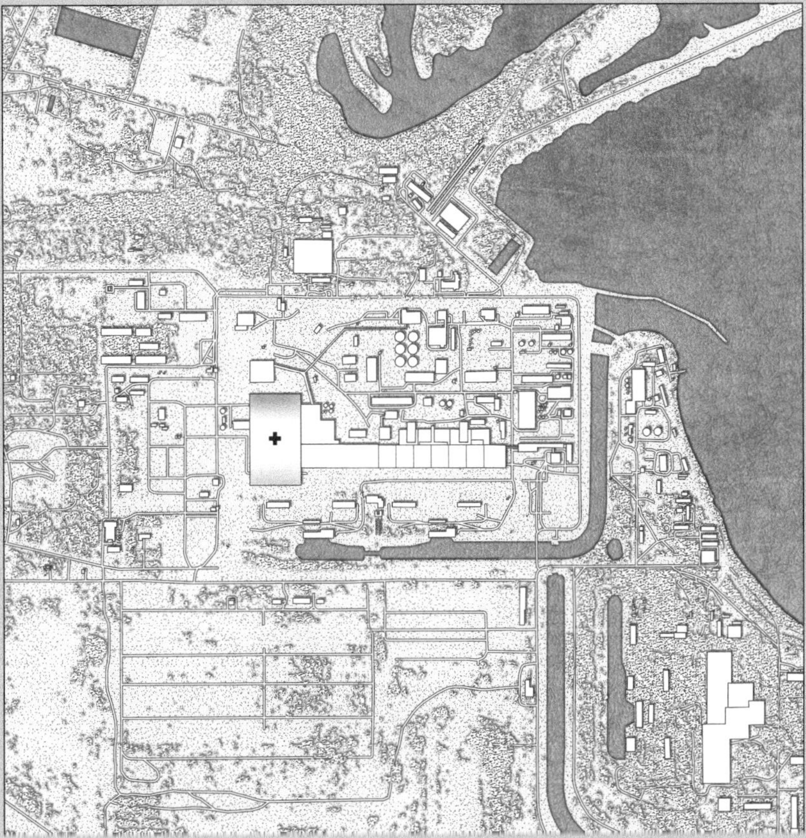

51°23’23.0”N 30°05’55.3”E

800 m

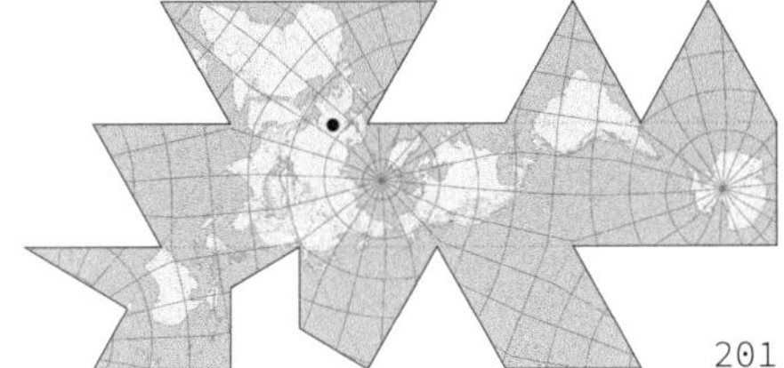

Onkalo Spent Nuclear Repository
Olkiluoto, Finland

Onkalo in Finnish means an animal burrow. But not just any burrow—it specifically means one you wouldn't want to put your hand into. The onkalo referred to here is Finland's soon-to-be-completed Spent Nuclear Fuel Repository, a 7-kilometer-long tunnel that spirals 500 meters down into some of the most stable rock on earth. The reason for this massive subterranean burrow is that, according to Finnish law, any spent nuclear material must be disposed of within the nation's borders.

As of 2025, copper canisters containing pellets of spent nuclear fuel will be entombed in Onkalo. The 4.5-meter-long canisters will be individually set in clay, which serves as a natural cushion against any geological disturbances. Onkalo has the capacity for 5,400 canisters, the expected sum total of Finland's nuclear waste for the next 150 years. The canisters are buried deep so that a future ice age will not rip open the burrow, but not so deep that changes in the bedrock from the earth's internal forces might disturb them.

There are currently 450 nuclear power stations worldwide, and the long-term treatment of their radioactive waste has always presented the industry with a big problem. Not only is nuclear waste a kind of monster in the public imagination, it's also very hard to find politically acceptable, affordable, safe, long-term places to put the stuff. Temporarily, the waste can be kept in pools of water, but for long-term disposal deep burial is considered the best option. Alternatives such as sinking it into the earth's ice caps or blasting it out into space are currently prohibited by international law.

Ice ages may come and go, scraping back everything on the earth's surface, but the canisters buried deep in the earth at Onkalo will be there, unmoved, for 100,000 years. At least that's the idea. But even if that does play out as planned, what then? Who or what will one day put their hand in this 21st-century burrow?

See Also: Runit Dome (198), Chernobyl Reactor #4 (200)

61°14’06.5”N 21°28’55.6”E

300 m

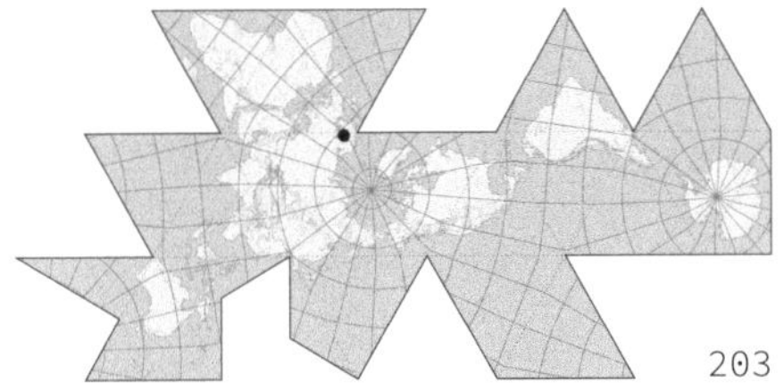

Cancer Alley

Louisiana, United States

Previously known as 'the chemical corridor,' Cancer Alley refers to a 136-kilometer stretch of the Mississippi River between Baton Rouge and New Orleans where hundreds of petrochemical plants, oil refineries, and related industries are clustered. If it's plastic it probably came from here or a place just like it. Cancer Alley in Louisiana is a region where residents are predominantly black and poor and where the risk of absorbing carcinogenic toxins emitted by the industries is notoriously high. In Cancer Alley there can be anything up to 50 different toxic chemicals floating around in the atmosphere and water at any given time. Back in 1976, when Coast Guard divers tried to collect sediment samples from the river, their hands developed second-degree burns from handling the material.

The exact degree to which the region is cancerous is debatable, but no one would deny that according to the data a lot of people do get really sick here. You only need to look at the monstrous refineries spewing their waste into the Mississippi's fetid swamps to sense the risk of living here. Whichever way you look at this landscape, there is something wrong with the picture—the combination of heavy industry, old plantation lands, poor residential areas, weedy vegetation, and putrid waters reflect a culture with a dark history of exploitation where the commitment to free enterprise is oftentimes antithetical to public health.

In environmental justice activism, Cancer Alley is referred to as a 'sacrifice zone.' The term comes from National Sacrifice Zones, areas that, during the Cold War, were polluted by nuclear testing and thus sacrificed for the greater good. So, what is that greater good today? As well as pointing the finger at the petrochemical industry, we, the consumers of cheap plastic products and cheap energy are all co-creators of Cancer Alley and places like it the world over. In a post-fossil fuel world, all the petroproducts we use—along with their industrial supply chains—will need to be redesigned with higher regard for human and environmental health. To undo and redesign a world now so thoroughly entangled in fossil fuels and plastics is surely one of the greatest technical and cultural challenges of the 21st century, and how well we do it will determine whether we are entering a new ecological era or a second dark age.

See Also: Freshkills Park (240)

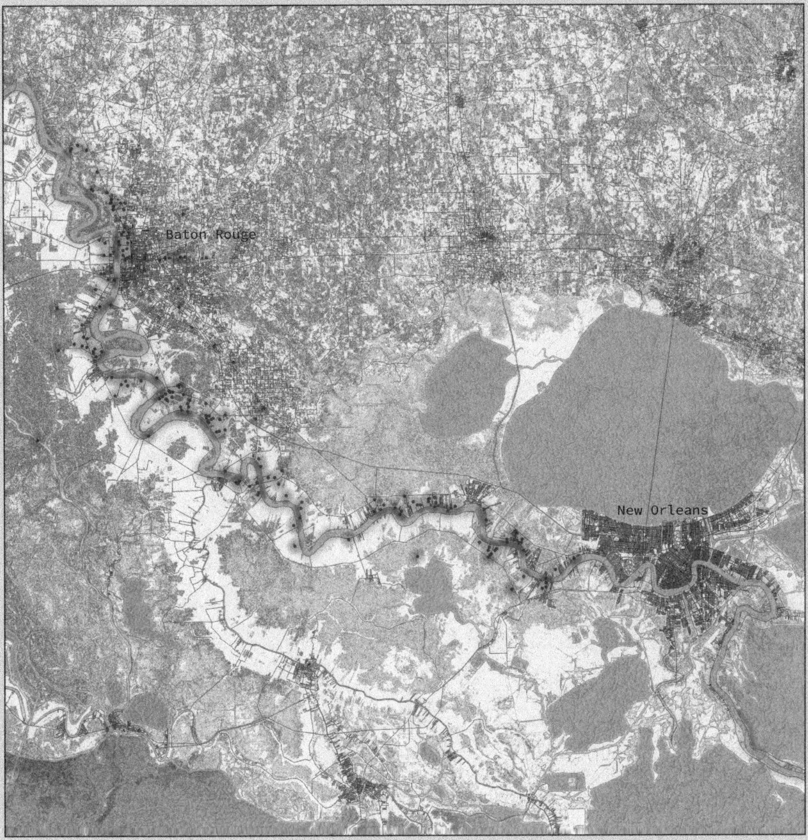

Baton Rouge

New Orleans

30°29'1"N 91°10'50"W

100 km

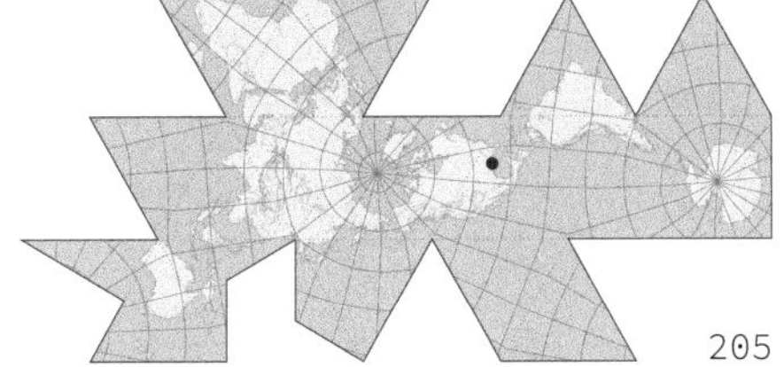

Louisiana State Penitentiary

Louisiana, United States

America has over 2.3 million people incarcerated in more than 7,000 so-called correctional facilities. In addition to those behind bars, at any given time there are another 840,000 on parole and 3.6 million on probation, many of whom are spiraling through the system for low-level offenses and misdemeanors. Many of these people are poor, black, or brown. Their experience in the criminal justice system can have the adverse effect of worsening their poverty and, in turn, increasing their liability to commit crime.

Of America's vast carceral landscape, Louisiana State Penitentiary, aka 'Angola,' is one of if not the most infamous. Set on an old plantation in the floodplain of the Mississippi, Angola is a 7,300-hectare (around the size of Manhattan) maximum security prison farm holding over 6,300 adult male inmates. Because the state of Louisiana has the nation's harshest sentencing laws, many of the inmates are 'lifers.' Angola is also home to the state's (male) death row inmates.

As if it were a township, Angola has its own fire station, airfield, wastewater treatment plant, museum, stadium, multiple churches, and its own cemetery. It also has residential enclaves for the staff, who are referred to as 'free men.' Inmates not in solitary confinement or on death row live in dormitories (named after trees) instead of individual cell blocks. Angola even has its own newspaper (The Angolite) and a radio station and holds a popular rodeo several times a year where the public pay to see inmates attempt to ride wild horses and angry bulls.

Although the prison has a long history of brutality, overcrowding, and bloodshed, from 1995 to 2016, with Burl Cain as Warden, statistically Angola became a less violent place. This was controversially achieved through a combination of religious indoctrination and hard labor. Working the land, for which the inmates are paid anything between 4 and 40 cents an hour, is mandatory in Angola. Critics argue the prison is conducting a modern form of slavery, others defend the role of manual labor in the physical and psychological lives of the inmates.

The real question, of course, is how and why did all these men get into Angola in the first place? To answer that, America's structural inequality and racism comes into focus as an ongoing injustice that has its roots in the colonial ground on which prisons like Angola now stand.

See Also: Black Lives Matter Plaza (94), Öncüpinar Accommodation Facility (206)

30°57'11.0"N 91°35'14.4"W

3 km

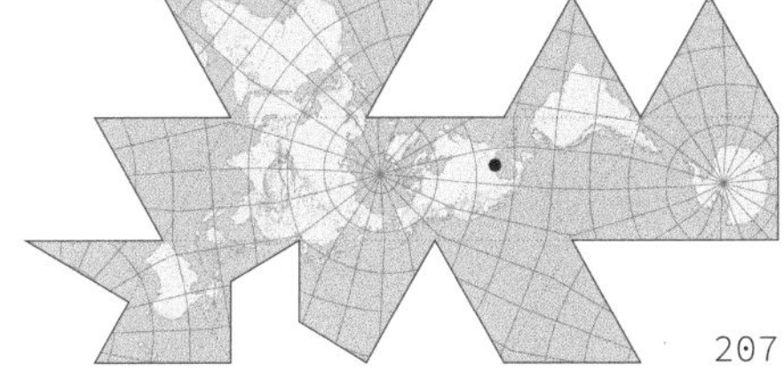

Öncüpinar Accommodation Facility
Kilis, Turkey

As of 2022 there are 82.4 million forcibly displaced people in the world. Over one-third of these are children and 26.4 million are refugees, meaning they have been forced to leave their country in order to escape war, persecution, or natural disaster. More than two-thirds currently come from Syria, Venezuela, Afghanistan, South Sudan, and Myanmar. By far the largest cohort, 6.8 million, are Syrian. Forty-eight million are internally displaced people, meaning that because they have not left their homelands, they are not technically refugees with rights under the Geneva Convention.

Most refugees will eventually integrate into their host nations, but initially—and often for many years thereafter—they languish in camps, designed as temporary installations in accordance with UNHCR design guidelines. Building camps in host nations is often politically and practically problematic: too close to existing settlements can cause tension with locals, and too far away makes camps hard to service and exacerbates the sense of isolation and alienation refugees inevitably experience. Similarly, the design of the camps themselves is complicated by the fact that on the one hand their level of acceptance by the host nation is linked to the political promise of their ephemerality, and yet on the other, camps can exist for many years and even grow into permanent towns. In short, the problem for refugee camps is that they are caught in both a spatial and temporal limbo. This in turn profoundly impacts the psychology of those seeking refuge, many of whom are already traumatized by the events that led to their refugee status in the first place.

The Öncüpinar Accommodation Facility for 16,000 Syrian refugees at Kilis in southern Turkey has dealt with these issues in two ways. First, it is sited just meters inside the Turkish side of the border with Syria and surrounded by a prison-grade perimeter wall. Second, while it is meant to be a temporary installation, it nonetheless comprises solid buildings, which could be considered an upgrade from tents. But because these buildings are mass produced and set out in grids on a vast concrete tarmac, the camp feels like so much cargo awaiting shipment. Through its design, therefore, Öncüpinar has a weird sense of permanent impermanence—it appears frozen in time yet also ready to be moved.

See Also: Louisiana State Penitentiary (206), Auschwitz (228)

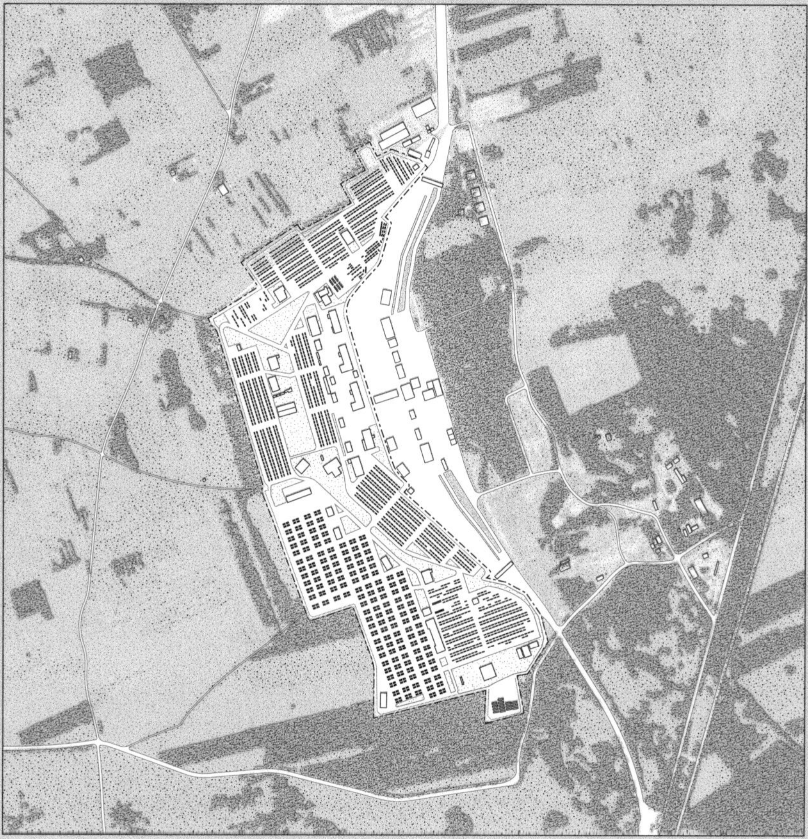

36°38’49.0”N 37°04’59.0”E

500 m

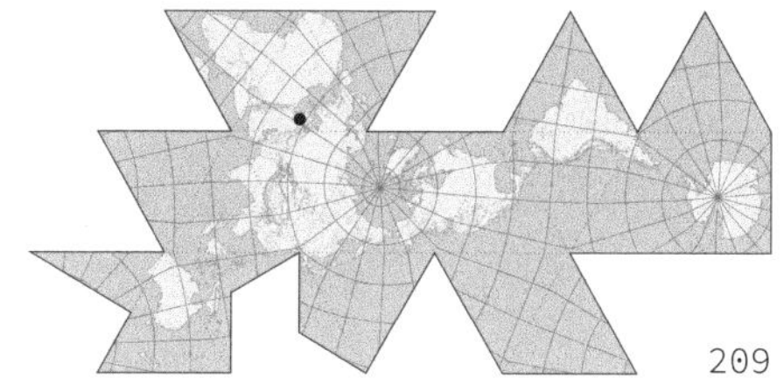

USA-Mexico Border Wall

United States & Mexico

All animals, including humans, define their territory in some way. To reinforce property rights, the boundaries of settled peoples have typically taken the form of built structures such as fences and walls. Remarkably, in today's globalized economy where tourists, goods and information flow across boundaries with relative ease, there are now more walls between nations than ever before. Serving the purposes of military defense and controlling immigration, today 48 out of a total of 195 nations have physical border walls of one sort or another.

One of the most prominent of these is the USA-Mexico border wall. The border between the United States and Mexico is 3,110 kilometers long—1,052 kilometers of it is fenced, some of it is defined by natural barriers, and the rest is unfenced. The border and what exactly flows across it, is a constant source of political debate in American politics, but this reached new heights of hyperbole in 2016 when the controversial candidate for President, Donald J. Trump promised to build a "big, beautiful, black wall" for the entire length. He claimed this would stop the flow of illicit drugs and protect America against what he portrayed as an inexorable dissolution into crime, chaos, and the Latino gene-pool. In the end, for all his braggadocio and a price tag of $15 billion, Trump only added 64 kilometers of new wall—a fitting monument to a presidency unscrupulously based on inciting fear of the other.

Even in the absence of a real wall, and no matter whether it is overseen by Democrats or Republicans, the USA-Mexico border is a very real, and heavily policed division. It is an enduring symbol of a world divided between the rich North and the poorer South, between the colonizer and the colonized, the haves and the have nots. It is a line across which America can make its geopolitical plays at will, and across which it can regulate flows of cheap resources and cheap labor in its own self-interests.

For the individual aspiring to a better life, the USA-Mexico border is a perilous threshold. Contrary to the enduring myth, for those who successfully cross the border, the promise of liberty and wealth in 'El Norte' can just as likely mean persecution, exploitation, and personal tragedy. This century, due to the sociopolitical ramifications of climate change, waves of human migration are expected to increase. No doubt so too will the number of cynical politicians ready to incite fear and tout walls to protect us from the barbarians.

See Also: Israel-Palestine Border Wall (212)

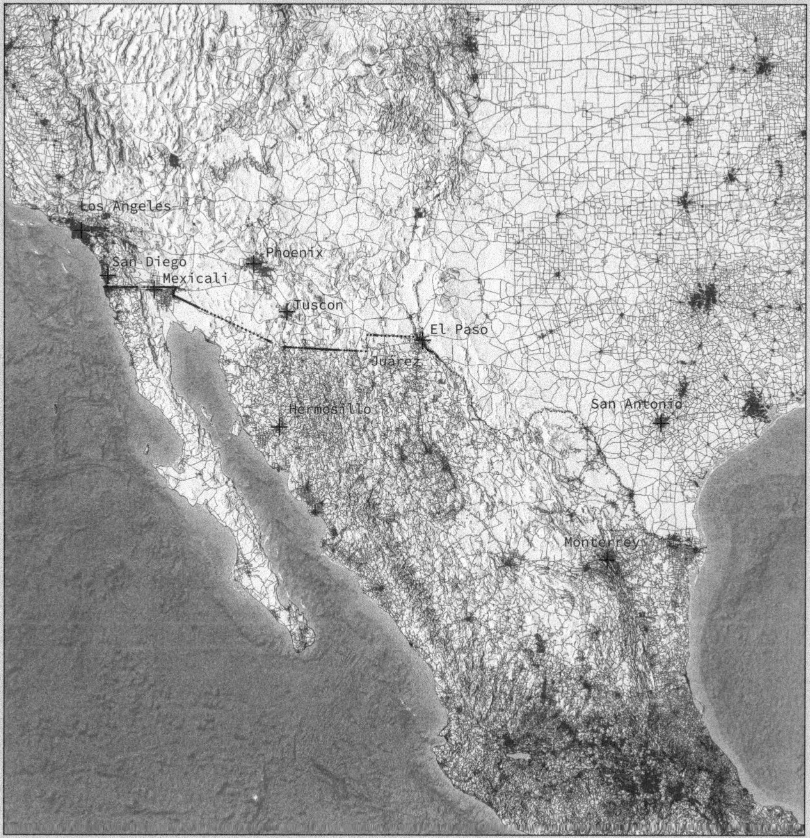

Los Angeles
San Diego
Mexicali
Phoenix
Tuscon
El Paso
Juárez
Hermosillo
San Antonio
Monterrey

29°29’45.9”N 106°52’16.2”W

1,000 km

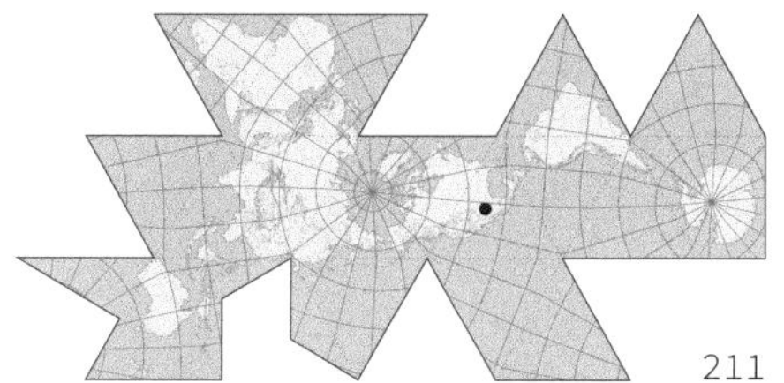

Israel-Palestine Border Wall

Israel & Palestine

The region of Canaan (the Levant) is probably the most complicated, contested, and storied landscape in the world. Overlaid on an even deeper history of semi-nomadic Neolithic settlements, in recorded history the region has been variously occupied by the Egyptians, Israelites, Hittites, Assyrians, Babylonians, Hellenes, Romans, Byzantines, Persians, Arabs, Crusaders, Ayyubids, Mamluks, Ottomans, Germans, and English. Today, the region is constituted by the nations of Lebanon, Syria, Israel, Palestine, Egypt, and Jordan.

According to their own story in the Old Testament, God (Yahweh) promised the land of Canaan to the Israelites, motivating their exodus from Egypt and subsequent conquest of the region in the 13th century BCE. Centered on the city of Jerusalem, throughout history the Kingdom of Israel has in turn been periodically attacked, plundered, occupied, and its peoples repeatedly terrorized, incarcerated, and evicted. For different yet connected reasons, all three Abrahamic religions—Judaism, Christianity, and Islam—hold Jerusalem to be sacred. The Jewish temple was first built, and according to Judaism, will again be built there. For Christians, Jerusalem is holy because Jesus was crucified and resurrected there, and for Islam, it was from Jerusalem that the prophet Muhammed ascended to heaven.

In the early 20th century under British rule, the territory known then as Palestine (now Israel) saw an increase in its Jewish population. After the Holocaust, in 1947, the UN agreed to split Palestine into Jewish and Arab states, with Jerusalem placed under international jurisdiction. Arising from constant tensions, war between Jews and Arabs broke out in 1948, and again in 1967, whereafter Israelis strengthened their grip on Jerusalem by annexing East Jerusalem and constricting Palestinians into an archipelago of settlements in the West Bank (of the River Jordan) and the Gaza Strip on the Mediterranean coast. The international community generally considers the West Bank to be Arab territory under military occupation by Israel. For Palestinians a West Bank free of Israeli forces is the prerequisite for, and basis of, any future Palestinian State.

Today, Israel largely controls what happens in the West Bank. As such it stands accused of illegally building Jewish settlements on Arab land, exploiting the West Bank's ecological resources, and oppressing its Arab population. For their part, Palestinians in both Gaza and the West Bank stand accused of launching consistently murderous terrorist attacks on Israeli citizens. Consequently, the Israeli government fenced off Gaza with a 65-kilometer wall in the 1990s and has now completed much of a 708-kilometer wall in, and around, the West Bank.

See Also: USA-Mexico Border Wall (210)

Tel Aviv

Jerusalem

Gaza Strip

31°27’19.1”N 35°00’44.9”E

200 km

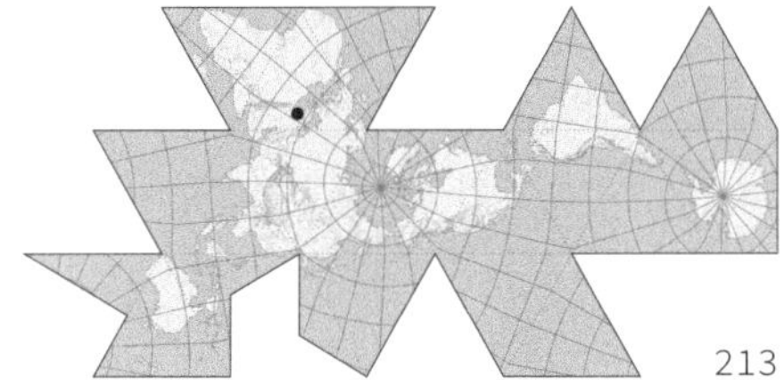

COTSbot
Great Barrier Reef, Australia

What rainforests are to the land, coral reefs are to the ocean. The Amazon of reefs is the Great Barrier Reef off the northeast coast of Australia. At 2,300 kilometers long, the Great Barrier Reef is the largest living structure on earth. Not only is the Great Barrier Reef a rich marine ecosystem, it is also a vitally important source of tourist revenue for its host nation. Without human intervention, however, the crown-of-thorns starfish could literally suck the life out of the entire thing.

Crown-of-thorns starfish (*Acanthaster planci*) feed on coral polyps (*Scleractinia*), secreting digestive enzymes that allow it to absorb nutrients from the coral tissue. This process leaves the coral vulnerable to algae infestation, causing death. In this way a single starfish can kill up to 6 square meters of living coral reef per year. Because starfish bodies can regenerate after injury, they are hard to kill by conventional means. They also reproduce rapidly, with females producing 1,000 million eggs in their five-year lifetime. The starfish are not an invasive species as one might expect—their proliferation is linked to increased nutrients in the water from agricultural runoff and the overfishing of their natural predators in the food chain.

In an effort to stop the proliferation of the starfish, scientists at the Queensland University of Technology have designed the COTSbot (Crown-Of-Thorns Starfish Robot). Just over 1 meter long, the robot uses sonar to navigate through the intricate reefs and recognizes starfish through its image-analyzing neural net. Once spotted, a needle-capped pneumatic arm injects 10 milliliters of poisonous bile salts into the starfish. With 99.4% accuracy, a single COTSbot can kill more than 200 starfish in a six-hour mission.

There is something monstrous about the starfish mindlessly proliferating and killing the reef. There is also something monstrous about the COTSbot in turn killing them, but perhaps the biggest monstrosity of all in this situation is that such a beautiful thing as the coral reef is now threatened, not just by starfish, but by irreversible changes to the chemistry and temperature of the ocean caused by human-induced climate change. This is not to say we should send in robots to kill the humans who perpetuate this crime, it is to recognize that ultimately, we, not starfish, are the problem.

See Also: Fertilizer Production Plant (140), Aquaculture (146), Ocean Dead Zones (252)

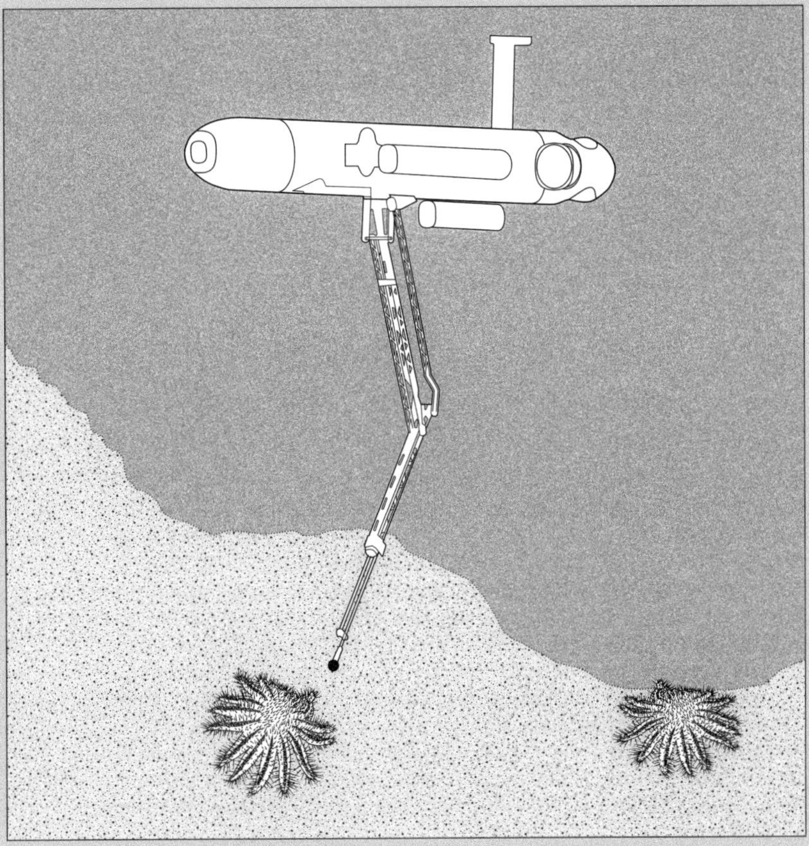

18°17'0"S 147°42'0"E

1 m

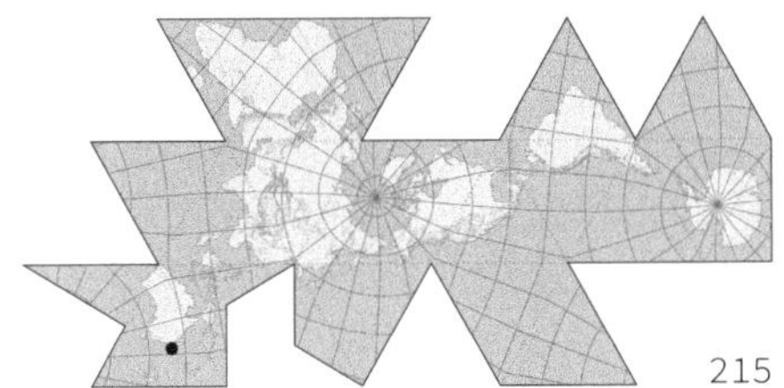

The World

Dubai, United Arab Emirates

It is one of the defining characteristics of the Anthropocene that humans now move more earth than the planet's natural processes do. A part of this is our propensity for dredging material from the ocean to create new land for development. Filling in wetlands is an ancient part of city-making, but it is only in the 20th and 21st centuries that the scale of such earthworks has reached epic proportions.

A prime example of this is Dubai where, since 2001, the coast has been refashioned as a form of graphic design for satellites. It all began with the Palm Jumeirah in 2001, then came The World in 2003. After this came two more palms; Diera in 2004 and Jebel Ali in 2006, with the *coup de grace* of The Universe launched in 2008. But scribbling on napkins and scribbling on oceans are two very different things: Diera, Jebel Ali, and Palm Jumeirah are incomplete, much of The World is a windblown wasteland, and The Universe was cancelled a year after it began.

Of all these strange shapes The World is arguably the most monstrous. Barely recognizable, nations and continents are sandy blobs and while there have been plenty of ideas for what to do on these islands, little has materialized. The World began with Dubai's Crown Prince, Sheikh Mohammed bin Rashid al Maktoum, building a big house on Greenland, then gifting it to Formula 1 racing legend Michael Schumacher. Despite having no water nor electricity, an Austrian developer is pushing forward with the 'Heart of Europe'—a theme park featuring European villages and snow-lined streets. The Australian blob is slated to become a resort. Sweden plans a hotel. America might yet become something called 'Coral Island' and Ireland was all set to become a big Irish pub before its developer went broke. Oddly enough, the Lebanese piece of The World, which includes a private club, is the only commercial success story so far.

Had the scribblers of these supergraphics known their urban design history, they would have taken heed that the last time this kind of thing happened was in 1593 when the Venetian Republic built a city, *ex nihilo* outside Venice. The city was designed by architect Vincent Scamozzi as a perfectly geometric nine-pointed star. So unpopular with residents was the brand-new city that in order to bring it to life, criminals were pardoned if they agreed to live there. And its name: Palmanova!

See Also: The United Nations (96), Burj Khalifa (120), EPCOT (124), Bulldozer (136), Landsat (300)

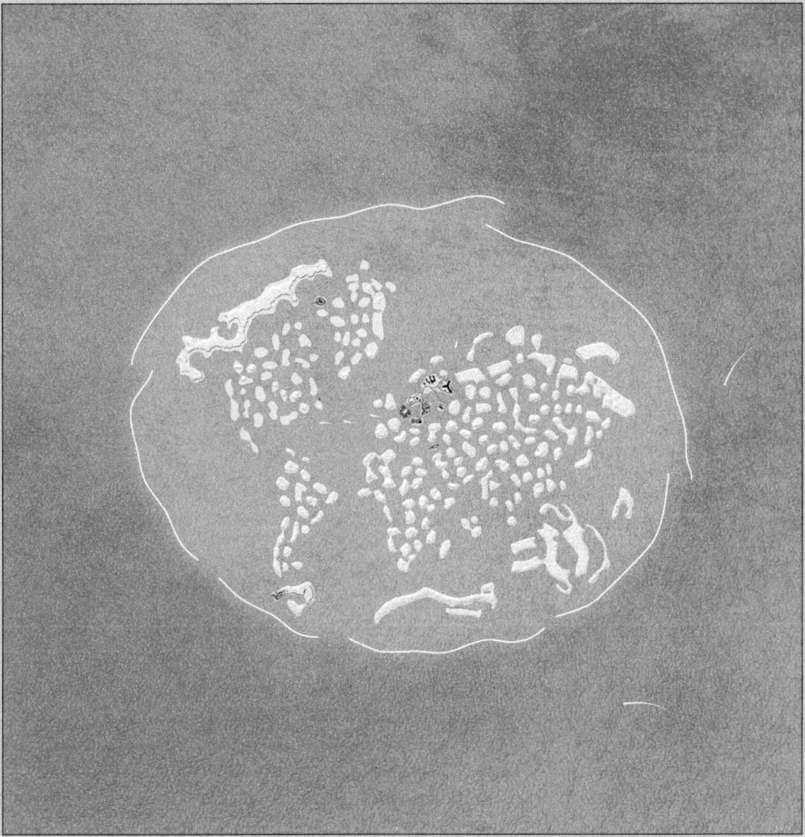

25°13’37.0”N 55°10’07.7”E

5 km

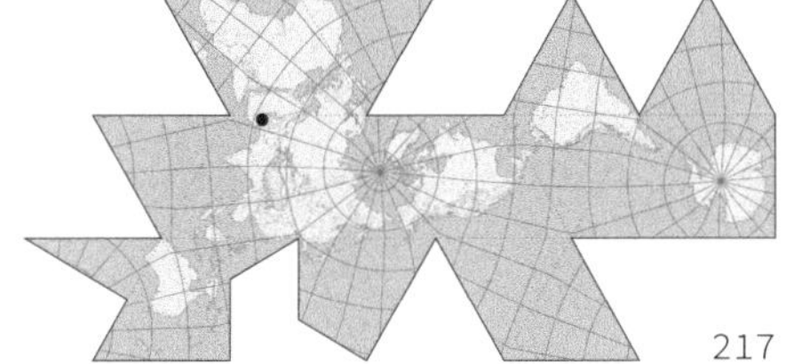

Stratospheric Veil

International

This is the only thing we encounter on the tour that doesn't actually exist—at least not yet. There are two reasons for allowing its inclusion. The first is that monsters often don't really exist, but more importantly, this particular monster—the creation of a stratospheric veil to block out some of the sun's heat to help stabilize the earth's temperature—might well come to exist sometime soon and it needs to be vigorously debated before it does.

The ideas of orbiting sun-shades around the earth, or chemically enhancing cloud cover, or the injection of sulfates (aerosols) into the stratosphere to deflect sunlight back into space, should strike the fear of God into mere mortals. But before we panic, consider that the idea of a stratospheric veil does have some things going for it. Comprised of sulfuric acid suspended in tiny water droplets some 20 kilometers above the earth, the veil is relatively easy to manufacture. Just one ton of sulfur suspended in the stratosphere can deflect enough sunlight to offset the global warming effects of one million tons of carbon emissions. If multiplied, such a veil could quickly reduce global temperature, which would forestall arctic sea-ice melt, saving cities and estuarine ecosystems from imminent flooding. Reduced temperatures could also help prevent desertification and crop losses associated with global warming. Finally, even if it doesn't work out exactly as intended, the veil can always be removed by simply letting the sulfur particles fall to earth and not renewing them with more.

That said, here are the reasons you should panic: a stratospheric veil could destabilize global weather and stop the monsoon, which would automatically put more than a billion people at risk of starvation. Sulfur particles may also damage the ozone layer and as they fall to earth, they will compound pollution-related health problems and further acidify the oceans. The veil may also work too well and, by cooling the planet, fast forward us into a new ice age. But, perhaps its biggest problem is the question of how it would be regulated. Who sets the temperature and who is then going to take the blame for all the weather-related catastrophes we used to blame on God? Either way, the really interesting thing about the geoengineering monster—and what makes it the *sine qua non* of the Anthropocene—is that the sky God we fear now is us.

See Also: Direct Air Carbon Capture Plant (158), Mauna Loa Baseline Observatory (280), Global Sea Level Rise Monitoring (282)

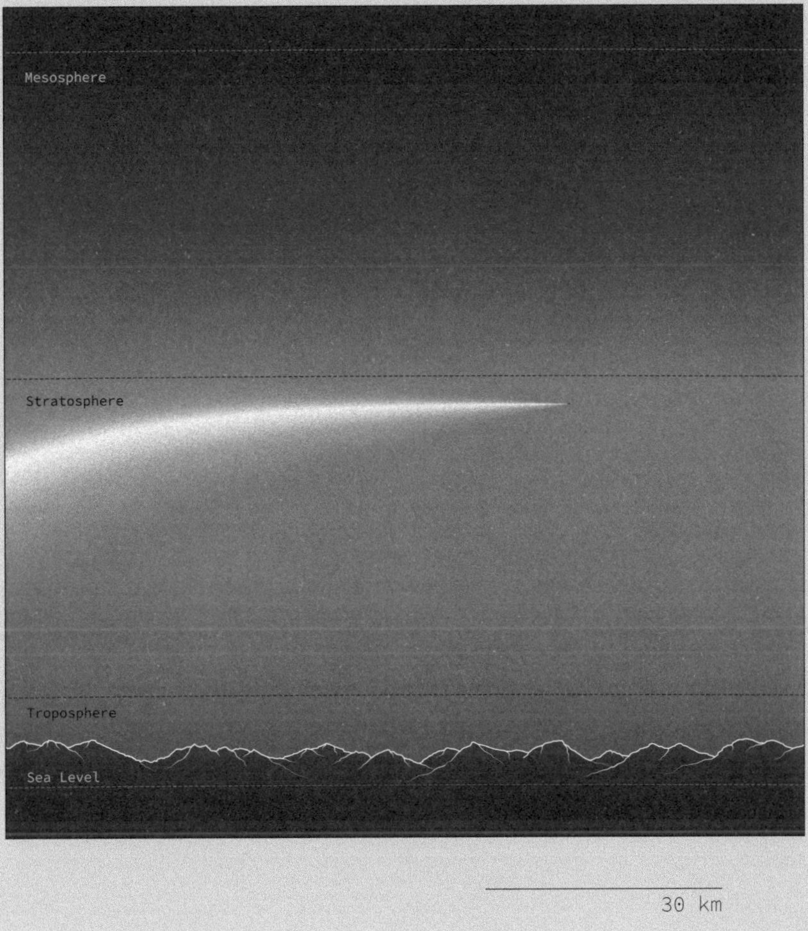

Mesosphere

Stratosphere

Troposphere

Sea Level

30 km

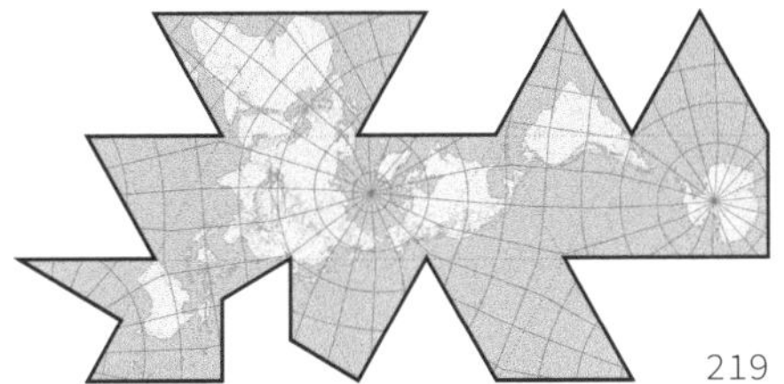

Ruins

Ruins take many forms—fossils, artifacts, earthworks, graves, buildings, even entire cities. Ruins are marked on maps as places of pilgrimage and preserved in museums for posterity. Just as it was for the Grand Tourists, the Roman Forum—a field of little more than stones and weeds—is still a major attraction. In addition to ancient Rome, today's travelers will also try to tick the Valley of the Kings, Stonehenge, and Angkor Wat off their 'must see' lists. What is it with us and ruins?

Of course, ruins fascinate us because they are portals to other cultures and other times. But visiting ruins isn't just about time-traveling to exotica, it is about encountering the inexorable power of time itself. To linger at the edge of the ruin is to step up to the brink of time without being swallowed by its vortex—to broach death. This is what 17th-century painter Nicolas Poussin points to when he has a shepherd notice his own shadow cast over the words *Et in Arcadia Ego*—meaning that even in Arcadia death cannot be defied—inscribed into the side of a tomb. It was this romantic melancholy that the Grand Tourists sought out, even going so far as to construct fake ruins on their picturesque estates when they returned home from their travels.

The Grand Tourists also sought out etchings by 18th-century master Giovanni Battista Piranesi, whose obsession with ruins is unrivaled in the history of art. To enhance the poetics of his subject and assert Christianity's ascendance over paganism, Piranesi's etchings forensically reconstruct iconic fragments of classical architecture in various states of ruination. We can also find this theme of Christian progress writ large in the new world.

Thomas Cole's 19th-century epic painting *The Oxbow*, for example, shows the stormy wilderness of the American West being actively replaced with farms, buildings, and clear skies. This none too subtly expressed America's manifest destiny, the construction of a new world free from the ruins of the old. In hindsight we now see that this colonial conceit led to the ruination of ecosystems and the indigenous cultures they sustained.

Just prior to painting *The Oxbow*, Cole illustrated what he understood to be the entirety of history in five monumental canvases. Titled *The Course of Empire*, the series begins with wilderness, moves to pasture, then to the great city and its destruction. It ends with ruins being reclaimed by nature. The question Cole was asking of his young nation was whether it could avoid this classical, cyclical notion of history and force it instead into the straight line of progress. This question is as relevant today as it was then. Perhaps even more so.

Sticking to the rule of only including 20th- and 21st-century destinations in this tour, there are no blockbuster archeological sites in the pages that follow; rather, the ruins in this chapter have been chosen because they represent the social and environmental violence of the times. Above all, they relate to the Anthropocene's most melodramatic of themes—the dread that human-induced climate change could set in motion the ruination of the entire world. And we need only look up at the moon to see what that ruin looks like.

But who do we think we are? Is it not an insult to the mighty earth—churning through ice ages of ruination and rebirth many times over—to think we could really ruin it? On the other hand, if—as is often glibly stated—it is true that humans have now become gods, then it would be irresponsible to think we couldn't.

Heavy Loadbearing Body

Berlin, Germany

Recalling the Roman historian, Publius Cornelius Tacitus (98 CE) who wrote of an ideal Germanic society, Adolf Hitler planned to rename Berlin, Germania. The centerpiece of Germania, planned by Hitler and his loyal architect Albert Speer, was a grand axis titled 'The Avenue of Splendors.' It was punctuated by an 'Arch of Triumph' at one end and terminated by the so-called 'People's Hall' at the other. The Arch of Triumph was to be around three times bigger than the Arc de Triomphe in Paris and the People's Hall was to be 16 times bigger than St Peter's in Rome, the largest domed structure ever built.

No one questioned how any of this was to be paid for. For Hitler, Germania was the prize of the nation's inevitable conquest of Europe. This, of course, is not how things played out, and while Hitler fawned over his model of the new city, Berlin fell to the Russians. Neither the arch, nor the dome, nor the avenue linking the two were built.

Before that, however, what Speer and his team of engineers did tell Hitler was that if any of these trophies were to be built then they needed to first be confident that Berlin's swampy soils could support them. Which brings us to the *Schwerbelastungskörper*, literally translated as the 'heavy loadbearing body,' or more simply put—a foundation.

At 14 meters high, 11 meters wide and weighing around 12,000 tons, this particular foundation is something to behold. The solid concrete behemoth served as a simulation of the weight that needed to be supported if Hitler's monuments were to be built. The way it works is that the cylindrical *Schwerbelastungskörper* sits on top of a further subterranean concrete structure with passages and rooms designed for measuring the exact degree to which the whole thing would sink into Berlin's damp soils. Indeed, after several years of conducting this experiment, what Speer learned was that the gravitas of Hitler's vision was literally more than the earth could take.

Too heavy to move and too thick to break up, the *Schwerbelastungskörper* sits today in the midst of a Berlin residential district; the perfect anti-monument to the megalomania and ruination of the Third Reich.

See Also: Potsdamer Platz (92), Teufelsberg (226), Auschwitz (228)

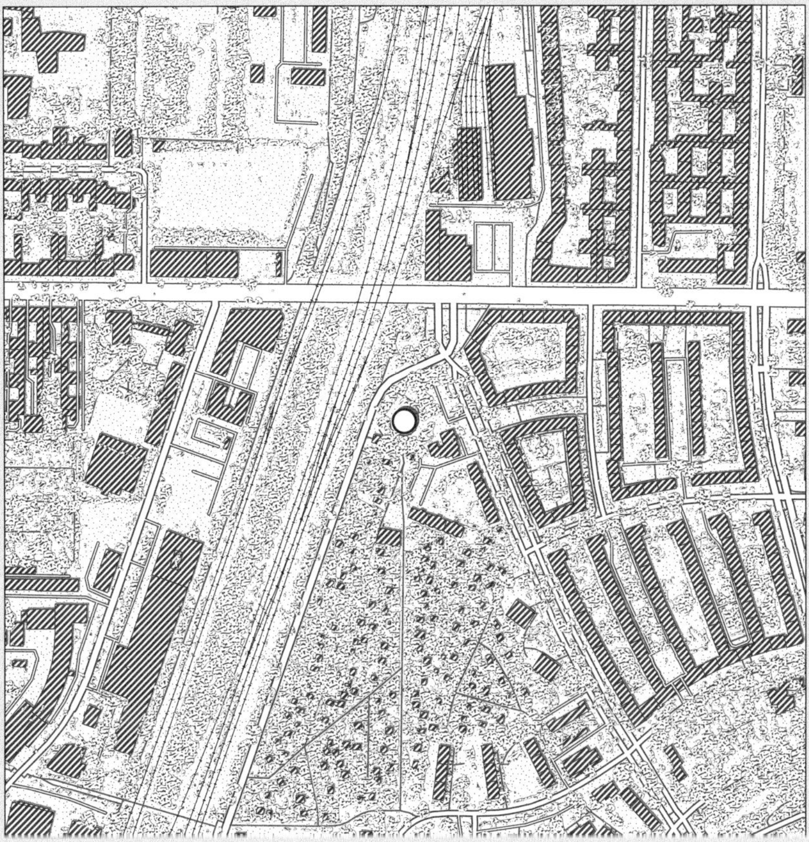

52°29’02.4”N 13°22’17.8”E

400 m

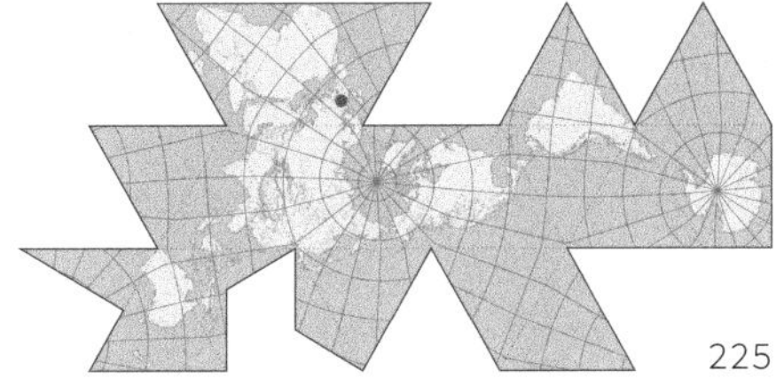

Teufelsberg

Berlin, Germany

After World War II, in Berlin *Trümmerfrauen* (rubble women) removed 26 million cubic meters of war-torn rubble and piled it up in the Grunewald forest to the west of the city. The result is known as Teufelsberg: the Devil's Mountain. Because it offers some elevation in an otherwise flat city, Teufelsberg is a public attraction, a place to taboggan, fly kites and just look out over the great, gray mass that is Berlin. As the weather and use wear down Teufelsberg's topsoil, porcelain fragments and broken bricks from old Berlin apartments protrude through to the surface.

Teufelsberg's sinister qualities are compounded by the fact that it covers an incomplete Nazi technical academy and is just a stone's throw away from the fascist 1936 Olympic Stadium ensemble, which Hitler designed as a spearhead pointing at Moscow. During the Cold War (1945–1989), again due to its elevation, Teufelsberg supported a radio surveillance center run by the United States and British governments. Its geodesic domes spied on and interupted communications throughout Eastern Europe.

Buildings such as the Teufelsberg surveillance center, and later the large rotating Daimler (Mercedes) Benz symbol crowing the glitzy commercial center of West Berlin, projected the West's military and financial prowess to the East. For their part, the East Germans responded with their own symbology—a 365-meter-high *Fernsehturm* (television tower) perched on the Alexanderplatz in East Berlin. The tower was close enough to West Berlin to send a message that communism could also produce spectacular architecture, but far enough away that when East Germans peered out from its observation deck, the West looked unimpressive.

In the symbolic volleying that was played back and forth across the Berlin Wall, the West pointed out that every day when the sun set it caused the façade of the tower to shimmer with what appeared to be a large Christian cross. Since communism has no truck with religion, this unintended affect of the tower's façade was an embarrassment for the East Germans. Another way to see it is that the East was indeed holding up a cross to Teufelsberg and this—even if only short-lived—put the East on the right side of history.

See Also: Potsdamer Platz (92), Heavy Loadbearing Body (224), Auschwitz (228)

52°29'51.0"N 13°14'28.0"E

2 km

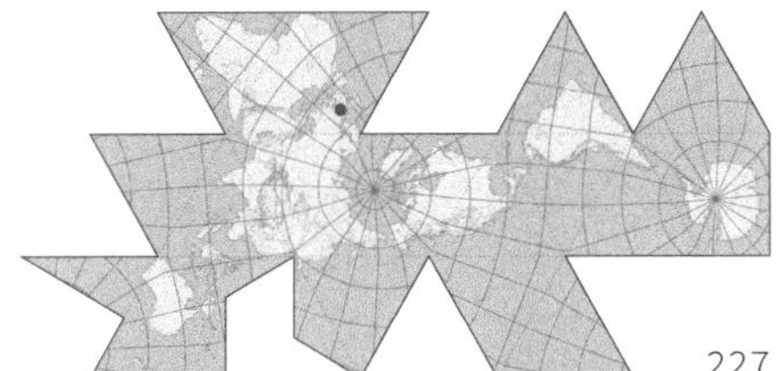

Auschwitz
Brzezinka, Poland

The Auschwitz Concentration Camp or 'death camp' was one prominent part of a vast network of over 1,000 prisons created by the Nazis under the rule of Adolf Hitler between 1933 and 1945. Specifically, in the period 1941–1945, known as the Holocaust, over six million Jewish people, gypsies, homosexuals, and other prisoners of war were murdered by the Nazis in these prisons with ruthless, industrial efficiency. At Auschwitz alone, at least 1.1 million people were murdered.

Upon arrival at the camp, prisoners were greeted by a sign that read *Arbeit macht frei* (work sets you free). They were then tattooed with a number, shaved, disinfected, and separated into those who would be worked to death, and those—mainly women, children, and the elderly—who would be killed forthwith in gas chambers. The bodies, ransacked for anything of value, were then burned in one of the five crematoriums on the site. A small number of prisoners were set aside as subjects for a range of unethical medical experiments.

The Holocaust is widely regarded as the darkest period in Western history: its cultural and political ramifications have reshaped the world and our understanding of human nature. It has underpinned the creation of the modern state of Israel and the identity of postwar Germany and Europe beyond. The events of the Holocaust, how it came to be, who was complicit, the methods used, and above all, the specious racism and nationalism on which it was based, remain critically important subjects to this day. What happened at Auschwitz also reminds us of other genocides that have occurred since: a list including, but not contained to, Bangladesh (1971), Uganda (1971–1979), East Timor (1974–1999), Cambodia (1975–1979), Guatemala (1981–1983), Kurdish Iraq (1986–1989), Yazidi Iraq (2014–2019), Rwanda (1994), Bosnia (1995), Darfur (2003–), and Myanmar (2017–).

In addition to the enduring ruins of Auschwitz in Poland, two of the strongest tributes to the victims of the Holocaust are to be found in Berlin, the city from which Hitler and his henchmen administered the genocide. The first is the Jewish Museum by architect Daniel Libeskind and landscape architects Lützow 7, and the second is the Memorial to the Murdered Jews of Europe by architect Peter Eisenman, artist Richard Serra, and landscape architect Laurie Olin. Both these memorials are testament to the ongoing German project of not just apologizing for the past, but actively building a society in which it cannot be repeated.

See Also: Potsdamer Platz (92), Öncüpinar Accommodation Facility (206), Heavy Loadbearing Body (224), Teufelsberg (226)

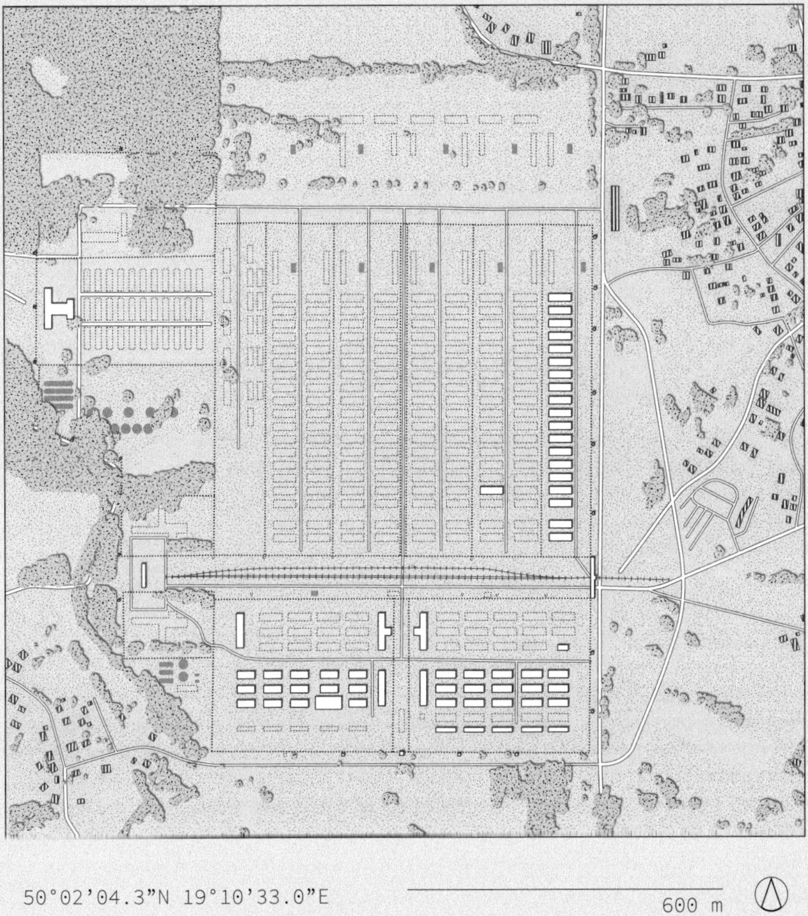

50°02’04.3”N 19°10’33.0”E

600 m

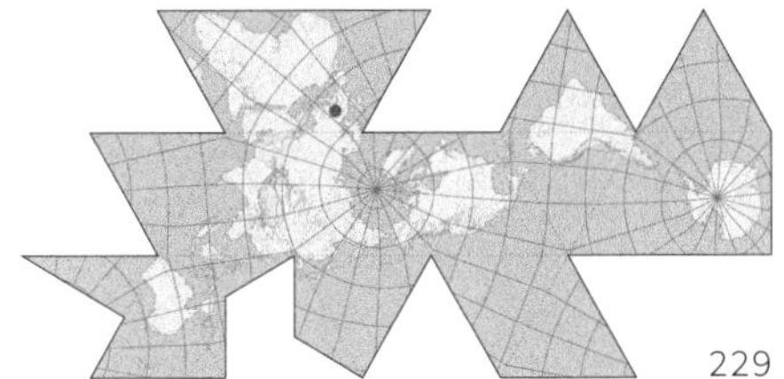

Emscher Landscape Park

Ruhrgebiet, Germany

In the heart of Germany's former industrial powerhouse, the Ruhrgebiet, a 450-square-kilometer parkland, has arisen from the ashes. The catalyst for the Emscher Landscape Park was The International Building Exhibition (Internationale Bauausstellung, or IBA), a recurring event that brings together funding, planners, and communities to focus on topical social and environmental issues in different regions throughout the country. The IBA is a form of development authority, but its focus is culture, before real estate. In the case of the Ruhrgebiet, under the rubric of IBA, a range of events took place from 1989 to 1999, generating ideas for urban renewal. The big idea for the Ruhrgebiet, and the key to its remarkable success, was to prioritize public open space and environmental restoration as the basis of the region's postindustrial future.

Because the Ruhrgebiet had long been dominated by coal mining and steel manufacturing, by the end of the 1980s its landscape was heavily polluted and unsuitable for recreation. Seventeen municipalities—many of which began as worker towns based on Ebenezer Howard's 'Garden City'concept—adopted the IBA's plan to create a new east-west green corridor along the Emscher River connecting seven existing north-south green corridors created back in the 1920s.

The aim of this combined area, now called the Emscher Landscape Park, was to improve the environmental quality of the landscape, shift public perception of the former industrial region, and incentivize new investment. Within the overarching regional plan, municipalities developed their own local projects for specific places. Over the last three decades transportation routes have been turned into a network of pedestrian and cycling pathways, waterways have been restored to health, and industrial ruins have been retrofitted as attractive and exciting public spaces.

One of the most iconic projects of the many that now make up the Emscher Landscape Park is Duisburg Nord, a park designed by landscape architect Peter Latz in 1991. Here the ruins of a coal and steel production plant have become the structure for plant growth, communal events, recreation, and a design that poetically acknowledges Germany's industrial heritage. Emscher Landscape Park has now become a model for turning industrial ruins into user-friendly green spaces the world over.

See Also: Freshkills Park (240), Tudela Culip Restoration Project (256)

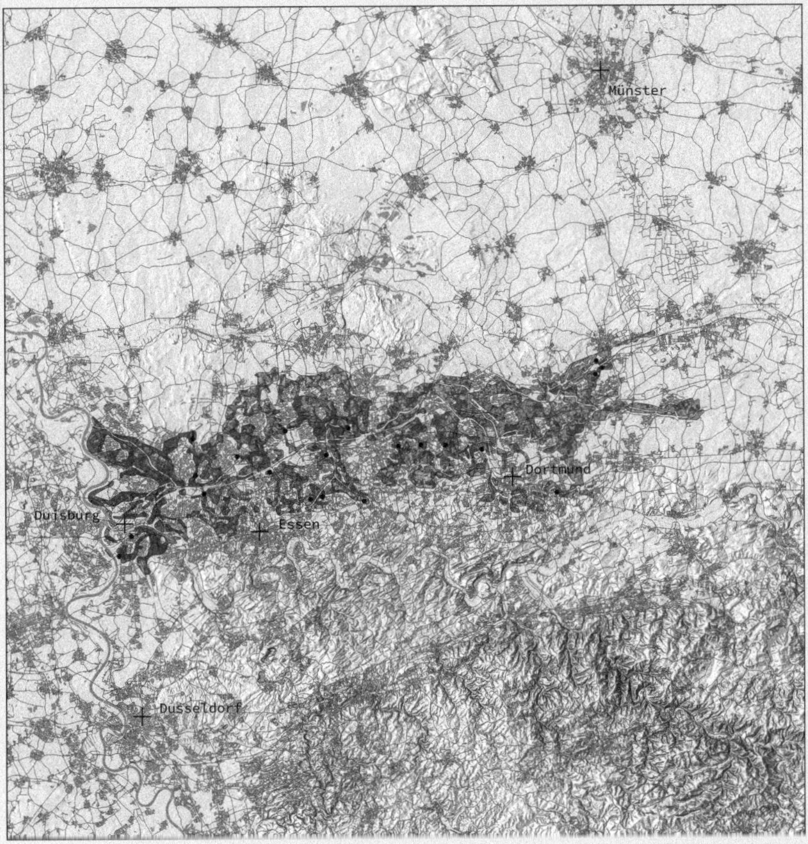

Münster

Dortmund

Duisburg

Essen

Dusseldorf

51°29’34.2”N 6°54’03.6”E

40 km

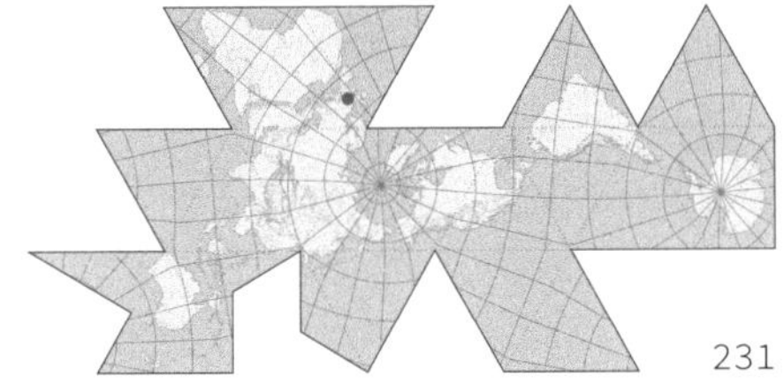

Doom Town

Nevada, United States

The United States Atomic Energy Commission first began testing atomic bombs at its Nevada Test Site, now known as Doom Town, in 1950. Originally referred to as 'Survival Town,' the faux town functioned as a place to test how basic infrastructure and other paraphernalia sampled from domestic American life could withstand nuclear blasts.

The Nevada Test Site covers approximately 3,522 square kilometers of desert and mountainous terrain in which 928 nuclear tests occurred, 828 of them underground. The atmospheric tests were so intense that the mushroom clouds could be seen from almost 160 kilometers away in Las Vegas. The fall-out from the tests was routinely carried by winds across St. George and southern Utah and has since been linked to upsurges of cancer rates in those regions.

The before and after images from the Doom Town tests are seared into the consciousness of 20th century popular culture. Before the blast, pristine mannequins of white middle-class American families sit happily in their neat 1950s kitchens; after the blast they are strewn across the room, twisted and broken, their contented facial expressions eerily unchanged. These images of suburban Armageddon capture a *zeitgeist* where American postwar bravado barely concealed growing Cold War anxiety. The message these scenes sent was that the American dream can be yours, so long as you follow military instructions.

In the late 20th century, a sense of security in the suburbs was paradoxically linked to the buildup of nuclear arsenals on both sides of the Cold War under a shared policy of Mutually Assured Destruction, otherwise known as MAD. In essence, MAD means that if you fire your nukes, we will fire ours, and then we're both history, so let's not even start. So far, this appeal to the lowest common denominator has worked and much of the world has enjoyed a sustained period of relative peace.

The buildup of nuclear weaponry is today governed internationally under two treaties: the Nuclear Nonproliferation Treaty of 1968 and the Comprehensive Nuclear Test Ban Treaty of 1996. Despite these treaties, the world's nuclear-armed states (United States, Russia, China, England, France, Israel, Pakistan, and India) now possess a combined total of about 13,080 nuclear warheads, of which 90% are split between the United States and Russia.

See Also: Runit Dome (198), Chernobyl Reactor #4 (200), Onkalo Spent Nuclear Repository (202), Vivos xPoint (234)

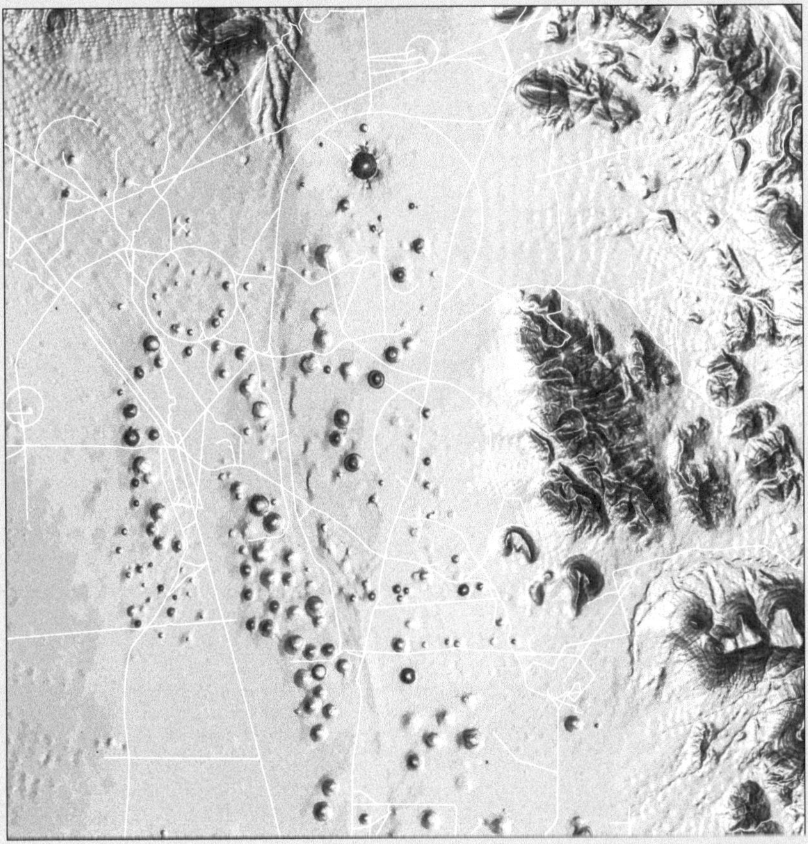

37°04’25.0”N 116°02’12.0”W

4 km

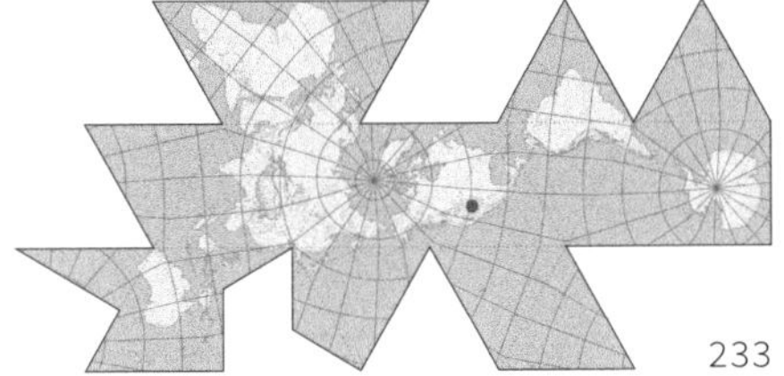

Vivos xPoint

South Dakota, United States

Stressing that it is far away from sea level rise, volcanic eruption, nuclear targets, as well as the crime and anarchy of big cities, the Vivos xPoint bunker complex advertises itself as a refuge from the apocalypse. The project's advertising targets so-called 'preppers,' people specifically preparing to survive some imminent disaster.

The complex is retrofitted into a former US Army Black Hills Ordnance Depot that previously served as a storage facility for munitions and chemical weapons, including nerve, sarin, mustard, and VX gas. The featureless landscape of the depot is pock-marked with 575 earth-covered, concrete bunkers, each able to withstand an internal blast threshold of 500,000 pounds.

Although not originally constructed for human settlement, according to the advertising each of the bunkers can accommodate up to 24 people. Buyers can purchase a bunker and retrofit it themselves, or Vivos, the Californian company specializing in real estate for preppers around the world, can do it for them. Some bunkers are set aside for community amenities such as a cinema, restaurant, a hydro and aquaponics facility, and headquarters for the private on-site security service.

With around 200 bunkers already sold, some families and individuals have moved in and made the former depot their permanent home. Interviews with these residents indicate that while they are fully aware of the unorthodox nature of their circumstance, they express optimism about their future; not only will they survive the apocalypse, they feel part of a new community. In this sense, the preppers consider themselves not just as pioneers of this bleak landscape, but pilgrims of a future in which either they will be the only survivors, or one in which they will have to fend off others who will want to take what they have.

In troubled times prepping is big business. There is now a global market in high-security underground living with much of it aimed toward the luxury end of the scale. As Vivos's advertising says, "only the prepared will survive." Indeed, but one has to wonder how suffering in the present so as to be ready for an even grimmer future really makes any sense. From the prepper's perspective, of course, this is far more rational than being unprepared. One can also assume that it makes preppers feel special.

See Also: Doom Town (232)

43°09’48.3”N 103°56’41.2”W

4 km

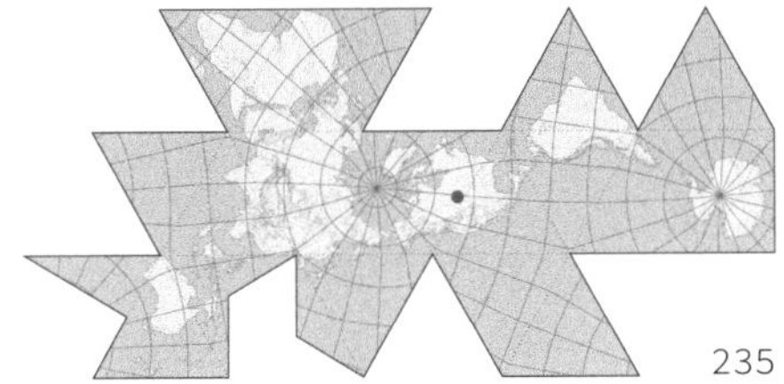

Vietnam Veterans Memorial

Washington, DC, United States

The Vietnam Veterans Memorial in Washington, DC, commemorates the period from November 1st, 1955 to May 15th, 1975, in which America was at war with North Vietnam. The memorial design was determined by an open competition launched in 1980. The brief stipulated that the memorial would be 1) reflective and contemplative in character, 2) harmonious with its site and environment, 3) make no political statement about the war itself, and 4) contain the 58,320 names of all those Americans who died or remain missing. From 1,421 entries, Maya Ying Lin, a 21-year-old architecture student at Yale University, was selected as the winner.

Lin's design, which would prove to be extremely controversial, was unlike anything else in Washington's otherwise white, neoclassical ensemble of figurative sculptures, obelisks, and temples. The design is a black V shape defined by two black granite walls incised in the earth. One arm of the V points toward the Washington Memorial, the other toward the Lincoln Memorial. Each arm is 75 meters long and reaches 3 meters below grade at the apex of the memorial where they meet. Each wall comprises 72 highly polished black granite panels listing the names of the dead according to the year of their death.

The memorial was controversial because of its perceived symbolism. A massive black gash in the ground was seen as something shameful and negative, particularly by veterans and those on the political right. For others, the fact that there was nothing overtly nationalistic or heroic about Lin's design was precisely its virtue. For admirers of the work, it is an original and daring work of art that honestly reflects the tragedy of the Vietnam War. Played out in the national spotlight, the debate concerning the memorial's symbolism became so vexed that a compromise was only reached through the addition of a figurative sculpture, *The Three Servicemen*, by Frederick Hart, and, sometime later, an American flag.

Perhaps what should now be added to the memorial is an acknowledgment of all the Vietnamese who also lost their lives and whose country was left in ruins when the last helicopter left Saigon on April 29th, 1975.

See Also: World Trade Center (238)

38°53’27.9”N 77°02’51.6”W

60 m

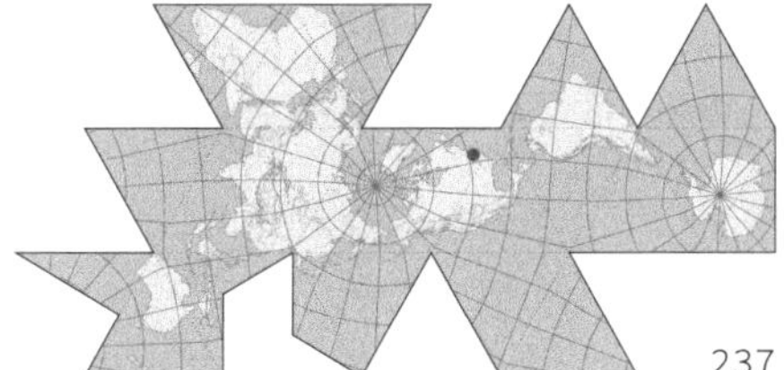

World Trade Center

New York, United States

The World Trade Center—two massive buildings in the financial district of lower Manhattan—was opened in 1973 and destroyed by terrorist attack on September 11th, 2001. That morning, two Boeing 767 jets were hijacked and flown directly into the twin towers of the center, killing 2,606 people in the buildings and 157 on board the planes. A third plane struck the Pentagon in Washington, killing another 189, and a fourth crash-landed in a field in Shanksville, Pennsylvania, killing 40 people. The attacks—carried out in retaliation for American foreign policy in relation to the oppression of Muslims—were orchestrated by Al Qaeda, a militant Sunni Islamist network founded by Osama Bin Laden.

After the harrowing cleanup operation of the World Trade Center and the removal of the rubble to Freshkills on Staten Island, the question was what to do with the site and how to commemorate what had happened. This was both an existential question and an urban design question—a question of balancing the need for meaningful commemoration with the real estate value and practicalities of a busy, working city.

Daniel Libeskind, an architect renowned for the poetic and spiritual qualities of his hitherto largely conceptual architecture, was appointed to develop the master plan—a framework for the redevelopment of the 6.5-hectare precinct. In his plan, Libeskind was adamant that the footprints of the two former towers should remain as memorials within a large public open space. The design of this public space, the centerpiece of the redevelopment precinct, was put to open international competition in 2003.

The winner was an unknown architect, Michael Arad, who then partnered with renowned landscape architect Peter Walker to refine and construct the winning design. The design is a simple public plaza of oak trees set in paving at street level with the two footprints of the twin towers left as deep voids clad in black granite. Water pours down into the voids from all sides. The cavernous voids can be looked into, but not entered. At the plaza level the voids are framed by a granite balustrade in which the names of the dead are inscribed. In the grid of new oaks that shade the plaza, there is a Callery pear, the one tree that, remarkably, survived the attack. Within the memorial plaza, this one tree has become a shrine and a symbol of New York City's resilience. For some, this tree, alone in a new park without the two massive voids of the original towers, would have been enough to carry the symbolic burden and the depth of pain that is 9/11.

See Also: Vietnam Veterans Memorial (236), Freshkills Park (240)

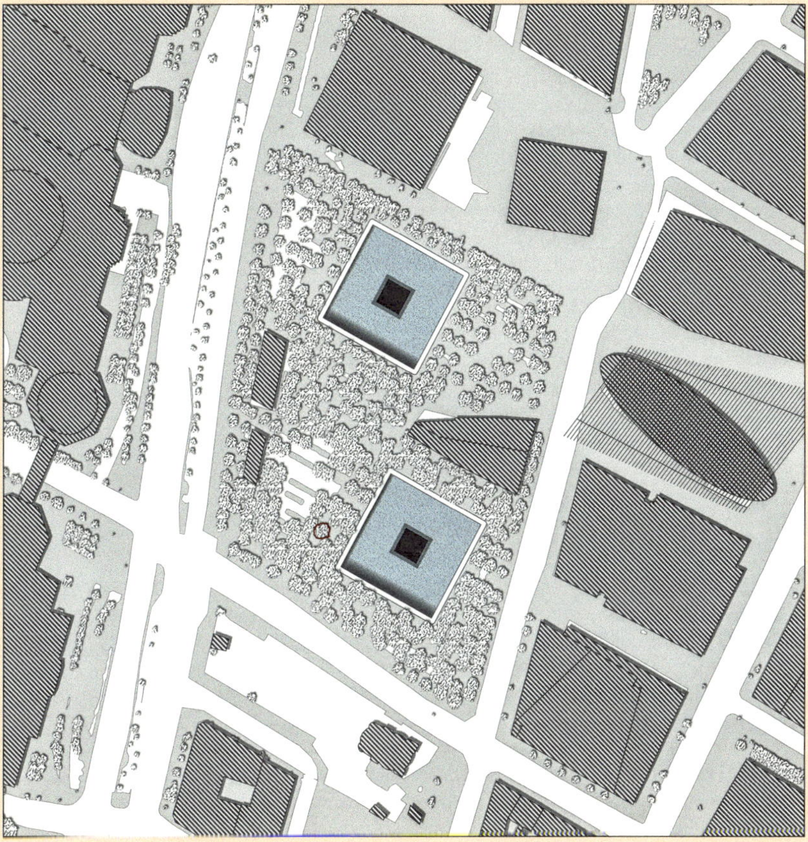

40°42’41.6”N 74°00’47.6”W

200 m

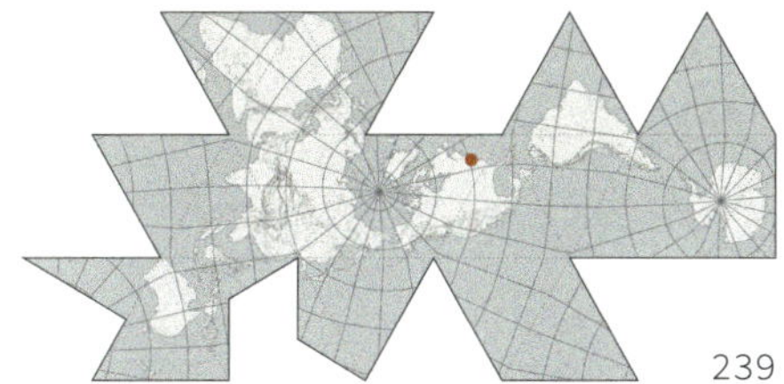

Freshkills Park

New York, United States

The ruins of the World Trade Center's twin towers were trucked 40 kilometers south of Manhattan to the Freshkills landfill site on Staten Island. These materials capped the final phase of the landfill operation that had grown from a height of 1 meter above sea level in 1948 to a peak of 69 meters, covering an area three times the size of Central Park. Absorbing the daily refuse of New York City, Freshkills held the unenviable title of the world's largest pile of trash, until 2003 when it was declared a parkland.

The alchemy of converting toxic waste to parkland is, however, no simple thing. To do so, landscape architect James Corner and his team devised a 30-year plan. Typically, landfill sites are contained within a membrane, fitted with piping to exhume the methane they produce, then covered in topsoil and revegetated. Freshkills, however, was too big for this approach and so the plan for its transformation had to be such that the park would effectively heal itself through consecutive phases of plant growth, each building on the previous. Today, after almost two decades of trial and error, Freshkills Park has a thin veneer of grassland and some patchy clumps of young trees. Although still seeping toxins and exhaling methane, the land now has a pulse and the landscape is slowly, but surely, building up its ecological vitality.

What is perhaps most interesting about the Freshkills landscape experiment is that it fits into none of landscape architecture's traditional aesthetic classifications. It is neither beautiful, picturesque or sublime. The landscape design is in this regard almost anti-design: it doesn't try to look pretty or scary. It doesn't greenwash its past, but nor does it wallow in its history. It doesn't preach to its visitors or make big claims about its future. In a word, Freshkills is banal. At a glance, it looks today like any generic, low-maintenance open space, but if you stay a while the topography, the scrappy vegetation, the small methane outlets, and the views from the park back across to New York combine to give the place an uncanny quality. In a subtle way, the banality of Freshkills is a dark mirror to our world of conspicuous consumption, an anti-monument to the depleted landscapes of the Anthropocene, and a stark reminder of just how difficult it is to breathe life back into them.

See Also: Walmart Supercenter (102), Amazon Fulfillment Center (160), World Trade Center (238)

40°34’36.3”N 74°11’05.4”W

2 km

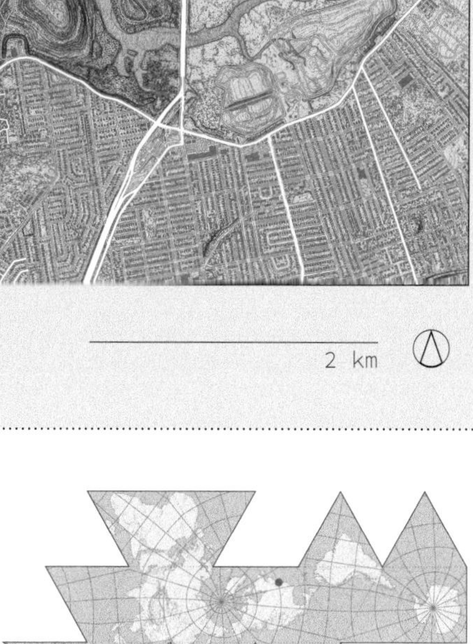

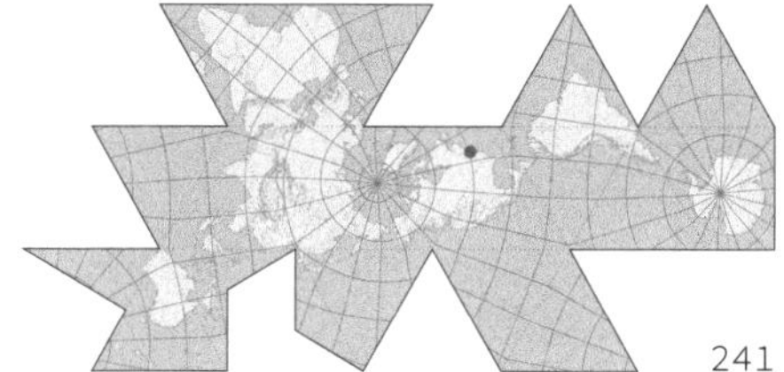

Agbogbloshie E-Waste Site
Accra, Ghana

Mass-produced modern products perform two particular tricks. The first is that they appear as if by magic with no trace of their material histories, and the second is that they become obsolete by design, requiring replacement. This throwaway culture is inculcated by the advertising industry forever stoking capricious desires and greenwashing the entire process wherever it can. These attributes of modern production reach their apotheosis in the digital age. As a consequence, e-waste (old phones, computers, tablets, TVs, lamps, refrigerators, washers, shavers, microwaves, etc.) is the fastest growing waste stream on the planet. The UN reported a record 53.6 million metric tons of this junk in 2019, a figure expected to rise to 75 million metric tons by 2030.

Much of this material ends up in landfills and while some of it is recycled close to its point of sale, most enters a global market where it is shipped to impoverished communities in Africa, Asia, India, and South America for sorting. Located 2 kilometers west of Accra's main financial center, the district of Agbogbloshie contains what is probably the largest informal e-waste recycling site in the world.

Adjacent to one of Ghana's largest slums, Old Fadama, a majority of the workers in Agbogbloshie are rural migrants and kids. Equipped with nothing more than hammers, chisels, and their bare hands, a workforce of around 10,000 people scavenges through the e-waste, breaking it down, burning off plastic casings, and prizing out every last bit of aluminum, steel, brass, and copper. In the process, mercury, lead, cadmium, arsenic, beryllium, thallium, bromine flame retardants, (hydro)chlorofluorocarbons, and dioxins are released into the environment. These elements and chemicals seep into the workers bodies, into the soil, into adjacent waterways, into the animals that also roam the trash, and into the air as plumes of toxic black smoke. The spoils are then fed back into a global system of middlemen to eventually be recycled into new e-products. On one level this system is highly efficient; on another, the economic disparity that it underscores between the original consumer and the recycler is obscene.

Despite Ghana's attempts to ban the import of e-waste and the European Union's attempts at mitigating its export, the lack of policing and the lucrative nature of the business ensures that sites like Agbogbloshie exist. The big tech companies are aware of this dark side to their shiny white products and the more their consumers come to understand the Dickensian nature of these global supply chains, the more likely things are to change.

See Also: Apple Park (48), Microchip (268), Smartphone (270)

5°33'14.6"N 0°13'40.7"W

500 m

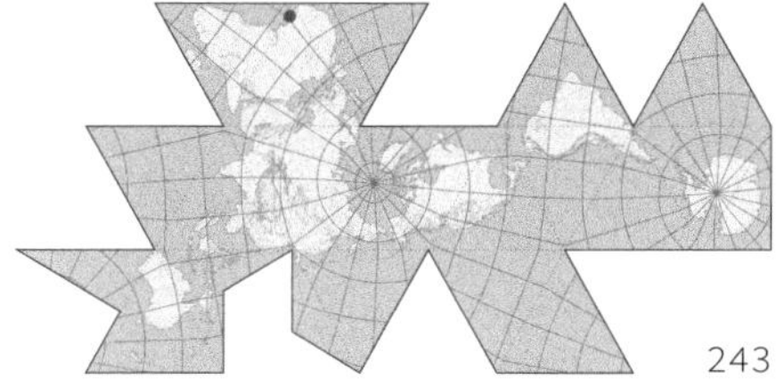

The Rainbow Warrior

Matauri Bay, New Zealand

On July 10th, 1985, an operation named 'Satanique' by the French secret service entered its final phase. Their mission was to disable a thorn in their government's side—the environmental NGO Greenpeace. The next day, Greenpeace's ship *Rainbow Warrior*—a global symbol of environmental activism—was to lead a small armada of vessels to Mururoa Atoll in the South Pacific where the French were testing nuclear weapons. In what was later described by New Zealand Prime Minister David Lange as an act of terrorism, shortly before midnight the *Rainbow Warrior*, docked in Auckland, was detonated with high-powered explosives attached to its hull by the French secret service.

The second of two explosions not only destroyed the *Warrior* beyond repair, but it also killed Greenpeace photographer Fernando Pereira, who was on board at the time. Two of the agents involved were eventually arrested and sentenced to ten years for manslaughter, and after months of embarrassing denial, the French government finally confessed to, and apologized for, planning and executing the attack, which was personally authorized by French President François Mitterrand. Among other diplomatic efforts to repair relations, France paid $8.2 million to Greenpeace, with which it promptly purchased a new protest vessel, the *Rainbow Warrior II.*

Later in 1985, 13 Pacific island nations, including Australia and New Zealand, signed the Treaty of Rarotonga, declaring much of the South Pacific a nuclear-free zone. Although France also signed the treaty it did not abide by its terms. The French conducted eight more tests at Mururoa before ratifying the Comprehensive Nuclear-Test-Ban Treaty in 1995. *Rainbow Warrior II* protested these tests, though this time the vessel was seized rather than destroyed.

The original *Rainbow Warrior* was scuttled in New Zealand's Matauri Bay, near the Cavalli Islands, on December 12th, 1987. Functioning now as an incubator for marine life and a dive site, the ruins of the *Rainbow Warrior* are an icon of environmental protest. In a pyrrhic victory for Greenpeace, the nuclear test site at Mururoa was fully dismantled in 1996. Today, *Rainbow Warrior III* continues Greenpeace's mission of peaceful protest with a focus on lobbying against deep sea mining.

See Also: Polymetallic Nodule Extractor (168), Runit Dome (198), Ocean Dead Zones (252)

36°50’32.7”S 174°46’17.7”E

20 m

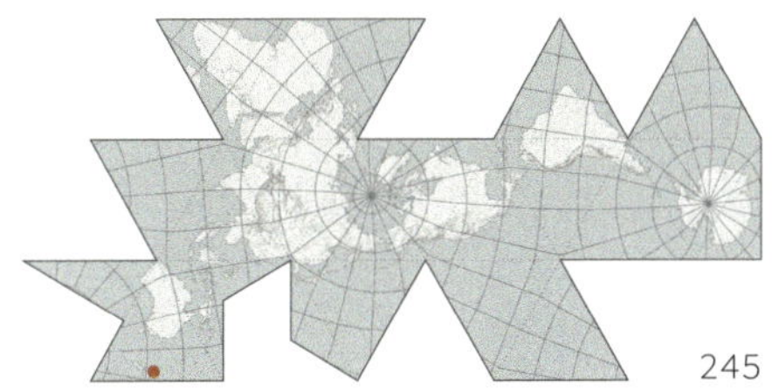

Palm Oil Plantation

Agusan del Sur, Philippines

The Dutch first transplanted the African oil palm tree (*Elaeis guineensis*) from Africa to Java in 1848 and the British shipped it to Malaysia in the 1870s. With the capacity to produce 7,250 liters of highly versatile (trans-fat free) oil per hectare, per year, the oil palm has become by far the best producer of vegetable oil on the planet, and Indonesia and Malaysia are now its two top producers. Palm oil is now Indonesia's largest export product.

Palm oil production accelerated when, at the turn of the century, the United States and the European Union championed it as a biofuel replacement for fossil-based fuels to help reduce carbon emissions. Alas, in their enthusiasm for biofuels, the fact that the production of palm oil meant the clearance of lowland tropical rainforest was overlooked. Soon after the US congress and global markets endorsed palm-based biofuels, much of Kalimantan (Borneo)—one of the world's last truly great remaining rainforests—was promptly slashed and burned. The shame of it is not only that biodiversity is lost, but also that by cutting down the forest more carbon is released than the derived biofuels would themselves ever compensate for. Furthermore, like all plantation-based products, the corporate monoculture of palm oil requires the submission of indigenous people and local communities. This is a process governments valorize as providing jobs and lifting rural people out of poverty. Maybe, but with the loss of biodiversity also comes the loss of culture.

Palm oil is now out of favor as a biofuel, but its use in myriad products is ubiquitous. It will almost certainly be found in cosmetics, pizza dough, ice cream, detergent, cookies, margarine, soap, shampoo, instant noodles, bread, chocolate, and of course pre-fried foods such as chips and nachos, and so on. Today the world uses around 70 million metric tons of palm oil per annum, a figure expected to double by 2050. So, unless someone can soon bioengineer an oil that doesn't come from palms, it follows that the decimation of the world's remaining rainforest will also double. Despite their nice appearance—orderly lines of healthy palms—palm oil plantations are ecologically and culturally ruinous.

See Also: Camp Leakey (68)

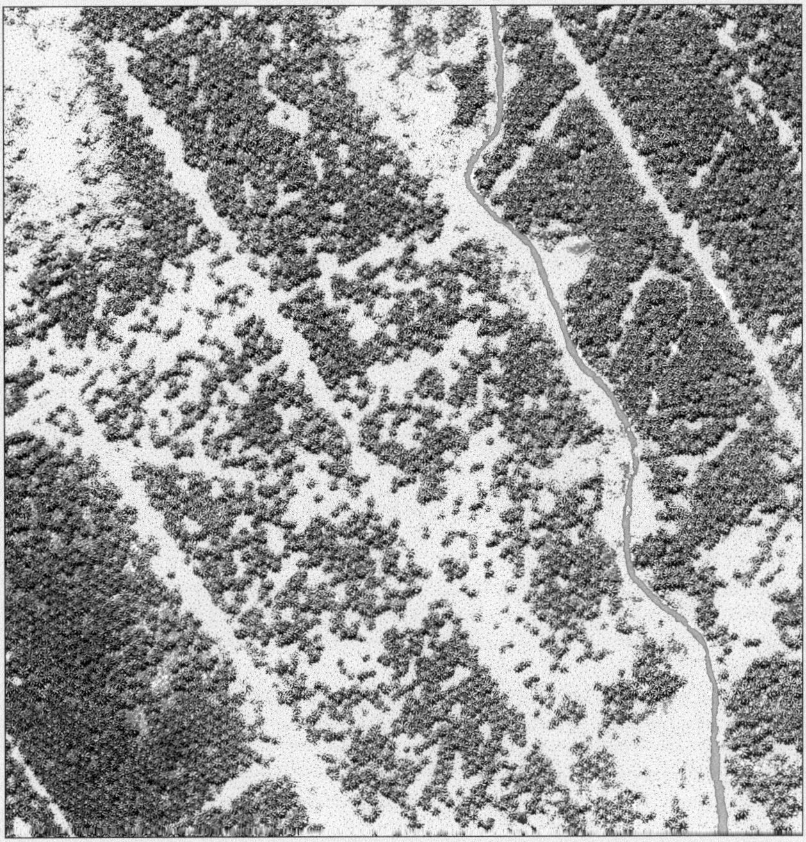

8°23’19.7”N 125°59’12.4”E

300 m

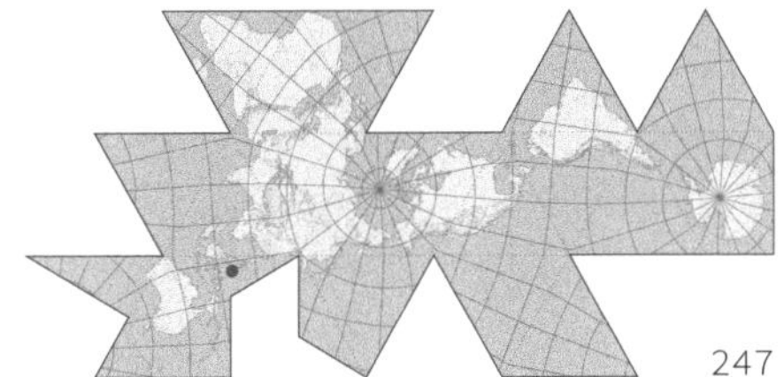

Great Pacific Trash Vortex

Pacific Ocean

Plastic is derived from oil. The raw material of oil is broken down into basic chemical compounds such as ethylene, propylene, and butylene. These are then recombined to form long polymer chains, which are mass-produced as pellets to be melted together and molded to make virtually anything. Plastic is cheap, functional, and, above all, durable. Look around your home or workplace—much of it is plastic. In just over a century of production, humans have created more than 6 billion tons of plastic.

The problem with plastic waste is that it doesn't go away. Much of the 6 billion tons that has been produced is now littered throughout the world's ecosystem. The ruins of our culture are not the stones of great buildings, they are little bits of plastic. The most insidious of these are microplastics in the world's oceans. Although at this point numbers become meaningless, it is estimated that there are over 5 trillion bits of microplastic in the world's oceans.

Fine fibers and fragments of polyamide, polyethylene, and polyethylene terephthalate collect in the vortexes of the world's five main ocean gyres. The largest of these is the Pacific Trash Vortex, the eye of the North Pacific Gyre that coagulates debris from North American and Japanese waste. The two main items in this gyre are the plastic shopping bag—invented in 1965—and the water bottle, 500 billion of which are sold every year. As these ocean plastics disintegrate down to the molecular scale of their polymers and remain suspended in the upper reaches of the water column, they appear as tasty morsels to marine organisms. Having entered the food chain, the microplastics then build up in organisms leading eventually to organ failure. Passing through the hierarchy of the food chain, some of the plastics eventually make their way into human bodies, but most of the material settles on the ocean floor and is eventually folded back into the earth's crust from whence it originally came.

Although innovation toward truly harmless, biodegradable plastics is stymied by commercial interests in maintaining the status quo, in a positive turn of events, consumers are increasingly reluctant to use plastic bags and water bottles. There are also a range of products made of ocean plastics now being successfully marketed for the very reason that they are helping to clean up the ocean's trash vortexes. The challenge is then keeping these improved products from also making their way back to their source.

See Also: Freshkills Park (240), Deepwater Horizon Oil Spill (250), Ocean Dead Zones (252)

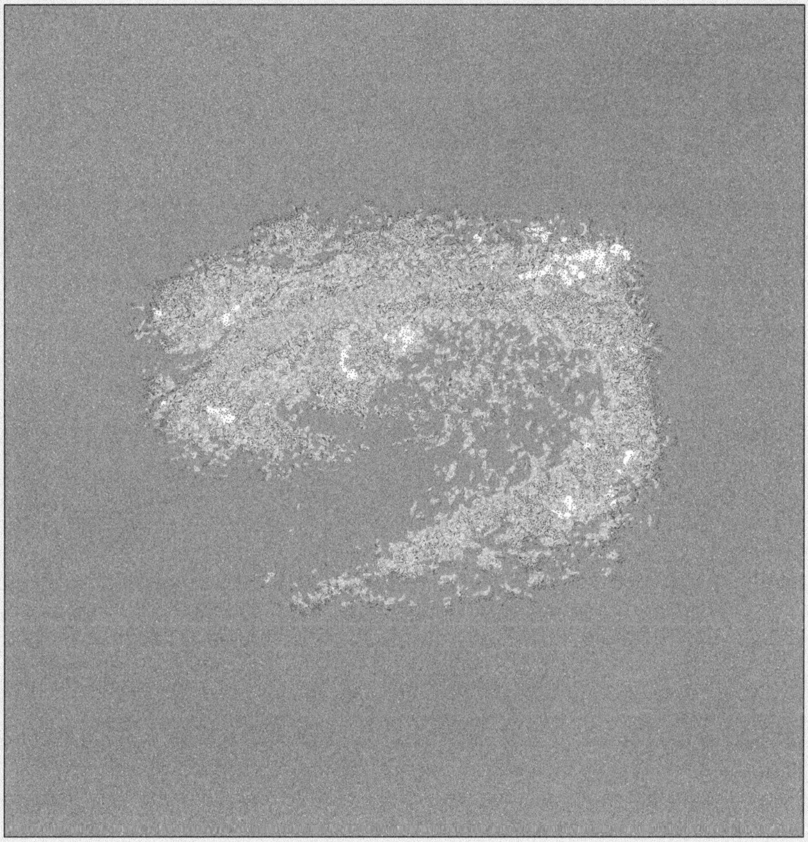

0°0'0"N 160°0'0"W

300 km

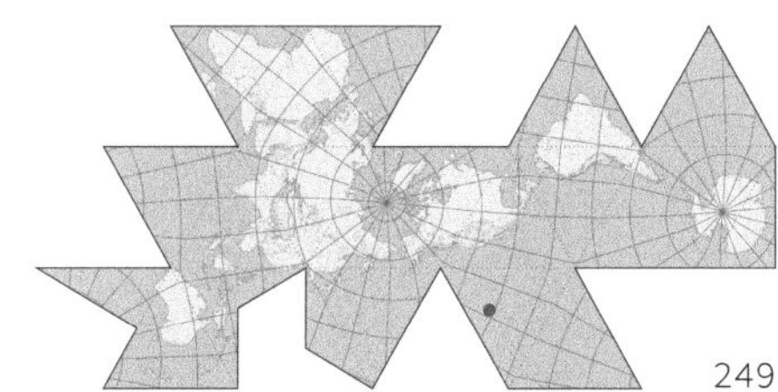

Deepwater Horizon Oil Spill

Gulf of Mexico, North America

The Gulf of Mexico is one of the richest and most productive oil and gas regions in the world. There are about 4,000 oil platforms off the coast of Louisiana, Texas, and Mississippi at any given time. From these rigs there is an average of 80 uncontrolled oil blowouts spilling around 330,000 gallons (1,250,000 liters) of oil into the Gulf every year. A major fire occurs on a rig every three days.

Drilling for oil is a dirty and dangerous business at the best of times, but nothing compares to what happened April 22nd, 2010. That day a bubble of methane gas shot up through the drill column of the Deepwater Horizon rig owned and operated by Transocean, drilling for BP. The bubble broke through several seals and barriers before exploding, killing 11. The rig burnt and sank, causing the largest marine oil spill in history. By July of that year, it was estimated that close to 5 million barrels of oil had leaked into the gulf, with only about the equivalent of 800,000 barrels safely recouped. After a series of attempts, on September 19th, 2010—some five months after it began—the well was finally sealed, and the flow abated. The spill resulted in a 149,000-square-kilometer oil slick. Oil and tar were smeared across 1,770 kilometers of shoreline in Mississippi, Alabama, and Florida. Wildlife suffered immensely from the spill. Studies of the impacts on whales, dolphins, birds, and turtles are shocking. Fish in the Gulf show evidence of contamination by polycyclic aromatic hydrocarbons (PAHs) to this day.

The cleanup required 1.8 million gallons (almost 7 million liters) of dispersants, used to emulsify the oil so bacteria could more easily metabolize it. BP created a $20 billion fund for those affected by the spill, which was depleted by 2013. The trial involving BP, Transocean, and Halliburton set the parties liable for 3.19 million barrels of leaked oil and ended in a settlement with BP of an additional $20.8 billion. At last count, in 2020, the total expense of the ongoing cleanup has reached $71 billion.

Addicted to the superpowers oil has given us, humans are now a danger to themselves and everything else on the planet. As ecotheologian Thomas Berry once said, there is a very good reason why the earth kept oil sealed deep in the ground. He also said the earth is a very good bookkeeper; it doesn't count dollars, but it keeps track of every molecule.

See Also: Athabasca Oil Sands (192), Fracking Wells (194), Great Pacific Trash Vortex (248)

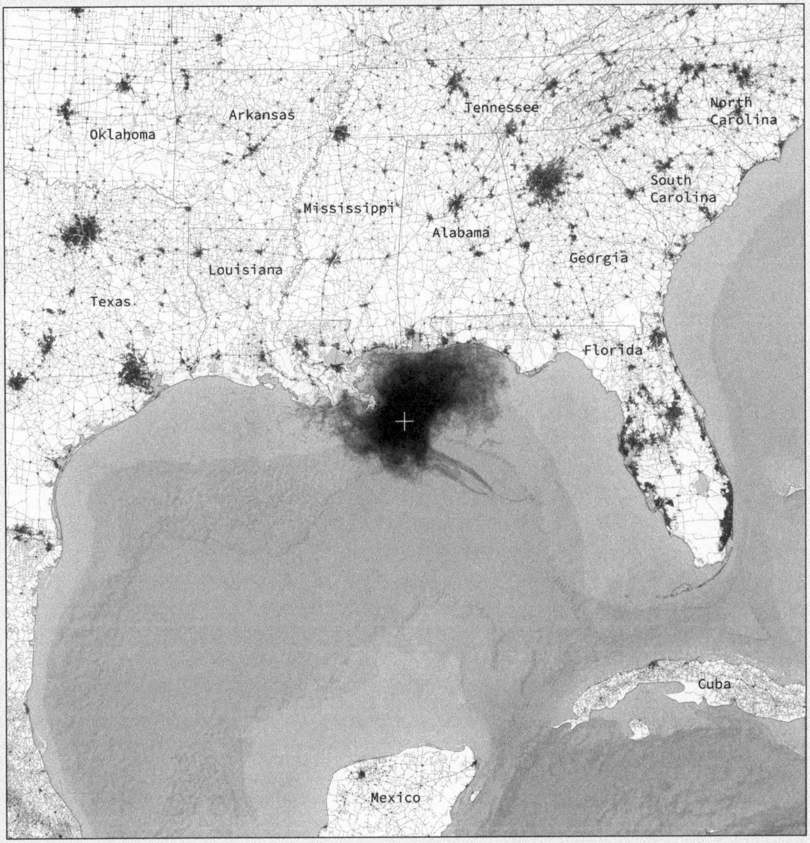

Oklahoma
Arkansas
Tennessee
North Carolina
South Carolina
Mississippi
Alabama
Georgia
Louisiana
Texas
Florida
Cuba
Mexico

28°44'17.3"N 88°21'57.4"W

800 km

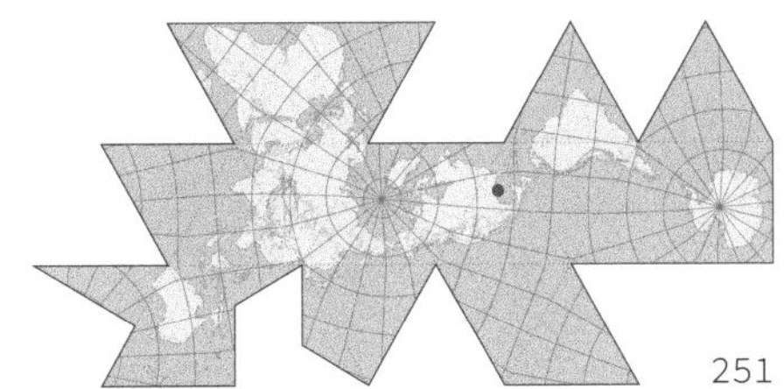

Ocean Dead Zones

International

There are now hundreds of so-called dead zones in the world's oceans. Dead zones are caused by an increased amount of nitrogen and phosphorus from agricultural and urban areas entering the water. This enriched water causes phytoplankton, microscopic cyanobacteria, and algae to proliferate exponentially. These microscopic organisms become so numerous that they block out the light, killing aquatic plants. When the plants and, in turn, the phytoplankton, cyanobacteria, and algae die, their decomposition consumes whatever oxygen is left in the water. This process is known as eutrophication—a hypoxic or anoxic condition in which aerobic life cannot survive. Prime examples of dead zones include large portions of the Baltic Sea, the Gulf of Mexico and the Gulf of Oman.

Because dead zones in the ocean are not obvious—the nicest looking water can have no life in it—public awareness of the issue is hard to raise. What does, however, attract public attention regarding the health of the marine ecosystem is the loss of mangroves and coral reefs, both of which are also killed by eutrophication. This is compounded by coastal development, oil spills, changes to tidal conditions, and the harvesting of mangrove wood for the production of charcoal for cooking and heating. Coral reefs and mangroves are invaluable to the marine ecosystem because they incubate and harbor extraordinary levels of biodiversity. By filtering silt and runoff, mangroves also serve to protect offshore coral reefs, and, inversely, they function as storm-surge barriers that enhance the resilience of coastal settlements threatened by sea level rise.

Improvements to the world's water quality require the protection and restoration of habitat at the scale of water catchments, the management of agricultural runoff, stormwater retention and filtration, and the treatment of industrial waste and domestic sewerage prior to its discharge into waterways. Above all, there needs to be further designation of coastal protected areas, focusing on mangroves and reefs under the UN Convention on Biological Diversity. Currently only 6.5% of the world's oceans have a protected status; the agreed global target is to reach 10%.

See Also: The Four Rivers of Paradise (52), COTSbot (214), The Rainbow Warrior (244), Great Pacific Trash Vortex (248), Deepwater Horizon Oil Spill (250)

0°N 0°W

10,000 km

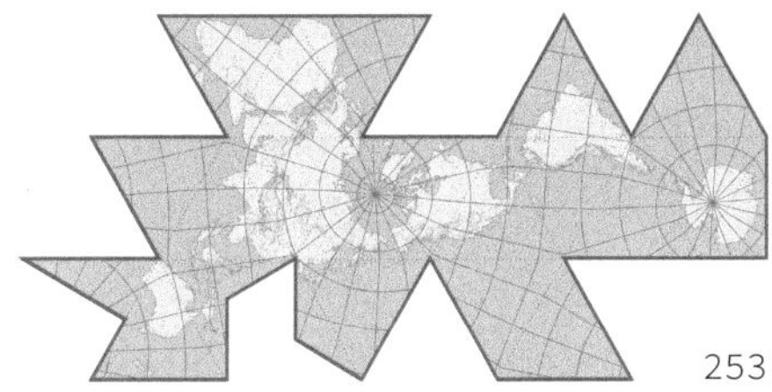

MOSE Floodgates

Venice, Italy

It is in Venice that this tour and the original Grand Tour cross paths. From the 10th to the 17th century, Venice accrued the wealth to commission some of Europe's finest art and architecture. Indeed, in the unlikely context of a muddy lagoon, the city itself is a work of art of exceptional beauty and ingenuity. Built on wooden piles sunk into the clays of a tidal basin, Venice has always had to deal with the natural phenomenon of *acqua alta,* or high water. Today's challenges are twofold: first, due to tectonics (and aquifer depletion, which has now been prohibited) Venice is slowly but surely sinking into the mud. Second, global sea level rise due to climate change is causing more frequent and higher levels of flooding than the city can handle, and this is only predicted to get worse.

At its inception in 1992, the MOSE (Modulo Sperimentale Elettromeccanico) project—a series of retractable flood gates in the areas where the Adriatic meets the Venetian Lagoon—was broadcast as Venice's savior from *acqua alta.* Billions of dollars over budget, 15 years late, and bedeviled by corruption, the 78 segments of the various gates are now completed. When not in use, the gates lie flat under the water, and, when needed in a storm event, they fill with air and pivot into an upright position to form a vertical barrier between the open ocean on one side and the lagoon on the other. Then, as the storm event and its related surge of water subsides, the gates fill with water and sink back down to their horizontal, underwater position.

Early tests indicate that the Venetian gates do work as intended, but the big fear is that the whole project has been designed and built to what many believe is an underestimation of future sea level rise. If this is so, then in the not-too-distant future the gates will need to be almost always in an upright position, separating the lagoon from the ocean. This will not only interrupt shipping, but since most of Venice's waste goes into the lagoon via the city's canals, the city will effectively be trapped in its own toilet. Not only is this unseemly and unhealthy, but because human effluent and storm water is high in nitrogen and phosphorous it will also lead to algae blooms, which will choke out the aquatic life of the broader lagoon ecosystem. Given all this, could it be time to think the unthinkable—to leave the gates open and allow Venice to gracefully become a ruin?

See Also: Ocean Dead Zones (252), Global Sea Level Rise Monitoring (282)

45°20’04.3”N 12°19’42.2”E

4 km

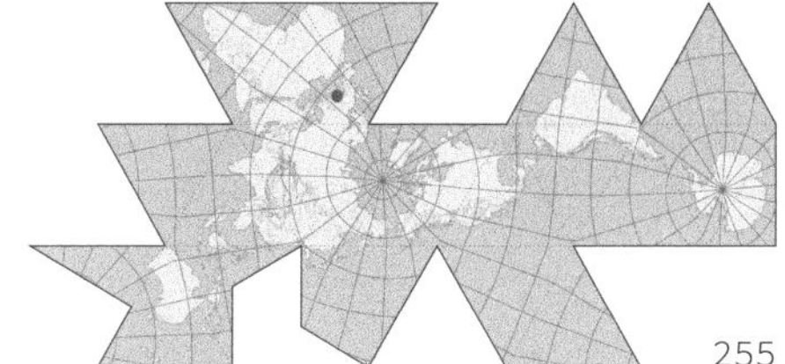

Tudela Culip Restoration Project

Cadaqués, Spain

Absorbing a burgeoning global tourist industry, the Spanish coast has been relentlessly developed since the 1960s. Anecdotal evidence suggests that a majority of the tourists don't come for Spanish culture per se, rather, they are in pursuit of what is known in the industry as the 4 S's - sun, sea, sand, and sex. Since the general orientation of the tourist's gaze is toward the horizon, developers in Spain have gotten away with creating a lot of cheap, ugly buildings in which to accommodate the northern hoards at competitive price points. However, as Spain began its long, hard recovery from the Great Spanish Depression (2008–2014)—caused, not incidentally, by real estate speculation—a backlash against selling Spain short with bad design has emerged.

A powerful example of this is the Tudela-Culip restoration project on the site of a former Club Med resort at Cap de Creus on the Costa Brava, an hour north of Barcelona. The project is fascinating because the brief for the designers was not so much about what to do, but what to 'undo.' The brief given to landscape architect Martí Franch was to remove the 430 buildings and related infrastructure (shown in red opposite) from the sprawling resort and to restore the 90 hectares of coastal landscape to its original character.

For Franch, however, to just remove the resort and pretend the land is pristine would be dishonest. For him, as for most landscape architects, the land is a palimpsest and good design can, and should, acknowledge its historical layers. This, they argue, gives people a sense of place, and a sense of time, in an otherwise disorienting modern world. Consequently, although the resort has been removed, Franch has left certain traces of its existence, along with other references to how this landscape is locally understood and its use throughout history.

In the absence of the resort, Franch's design carefully choreographs a visitor's movement through the landscape. For example, the design reveals how local fisherman use the land to navigate and leads visitors to discrete vistas, which influenced the region's most famous artist, Salvador Dalí. The design also invites users to take occasional detours—to lose themselves in the landscape. The Tudela Culip Restoration project is a masterclass in good design undoing bad design, and it sends a powerful message not only to the rest of Spain's disfigured coastline, but to a world in which low-quality development continues to run rampant.

See Also: Time Landscape (82), Potsdamer Platz (92), Global Sea Level Rise Monitoring (282)

42°19’29.3”N 3°18’01.8”E

300 m

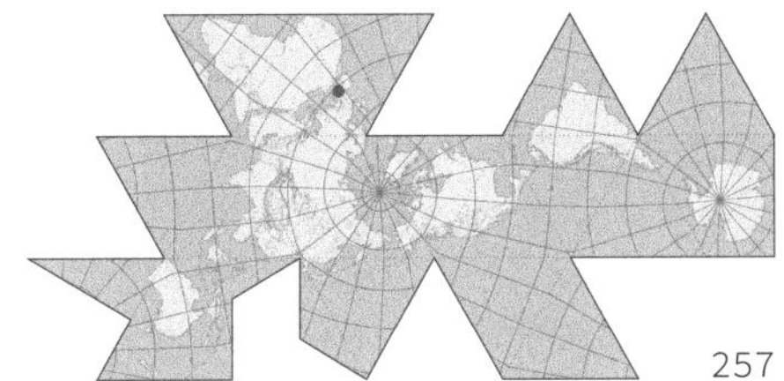

Spiral Jetty
Utah, United States

The need humans have to inscribe forms of orientation into the surface of the earth runs deep. Take, for example, the standing stones of Stonehenge, the Nazca lines in the deserts of southern Peru, and the Serpent Mound earthwork in Ohio, all of which functioned to locate their respective cultures within specific narratives of cosmological space and time. In the mid-20th century, in a move away from the commodification of art, a small group of American and British artists returned to these primal landscapes as inspiration and began to similarly use the raw material of the earth as the medium for their works of art. This movement became known as land art.

The land art movement was formalized in October 1968 when one of its leading proponents, Robert Smithson, curated a group exhibition titled *Earthworks* at the Dwan Gallery in New York City. Included in the exhibition were works by Michael Heizer, Walter de Maria, Dennis Oppenheim, Robert Morris, Sol Lewitt, and Claes Oldenburg, all of whom would go on to have significant careers. Soon after the show, with the gravitas of their ideas now understood by the art world, two of the most notable examples of the genre were constructed: in 1969 Heizer carved *Double Negative*—two massive voids into a remote mesa outside Las Vegas; and a year later, Smithson created his magnum opus, *Spiral Jetty*—a 457-meter-long, 4.5-meter-wide spiral in the Great Salt Lake in Utah.

The figure of the spiral is archetypal. We find spirals throughout nature and art history. Smithson's interest, however, was less with the symbolism of spirals or landscape's pictorial qualities and more with the material processes by which the biophysical world changes over geological time periods. Smithson's art engaged forces and processes such as erosion, sedimentation, and dissolution; in a word, Smithson was fascinated with entropy—the process by which things lose energy and form over time.

After a few years of intense production, making maps, texts and proposals for more earthworks, in 1973 Smithson died in a plane crash while conducting reconnaissance for *Amarillo Ramp*, an earthwork in Texas. With his turn to the earth as the subject and medium of his art, Smithson was a prescient artist who developed an aesthetic of the Anthropocene decades before the term even existed.

See Also: Time Landscape (82), Garden of Cosmic Speculation (86), Roden Crater (296)

41°26’15.6”N 112°40’07.9”W

200 m

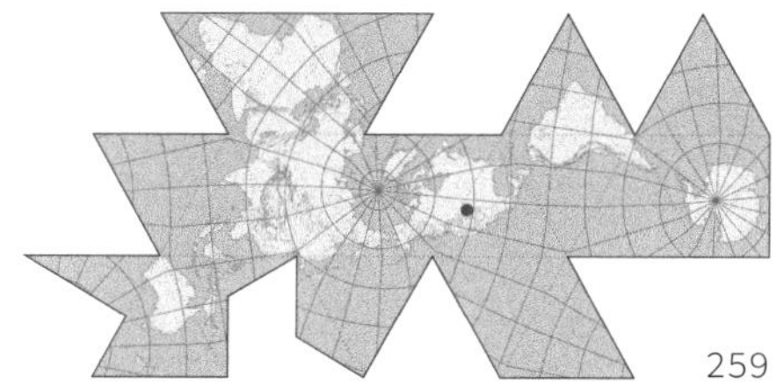

Svalbard Global Seed Vault

Svalbard, Norway

Author and naturalist Henry Thoreau referred to seeds as 'the perfect alchemists.' Indeed, seeds beget the plants without which the earth's ecosystem would revert to microbial sludge. More immediately, without the seeds of agricultural crops to plant each year, most of humanity would not survive. To ensure that that never happens, the Svalbard Global Seed Bank—opened by the Norwegian government in 2008—collects and protects a comprehensive global collection of crop seeds. The seed bank has been nicknamed the 'doomsday vault' because it serves as an insurance policy against the ruination of the world's other 1,700 seed banks.

Located 1,300 kilometers north of the Arctic Circle, the seed bank is built 120 meters into solid rock on an island in the Svalbard archipelago. The seed bank's remote location was chosen as one of the safest places in the world for the cold storage of seeds. The permafrost keeps temperatures in the vault around minus 18 degrees Celsius, even if power for refrigeration is cut. Based on ongoing donations from around the world, the bank now contains seeds from more than 4,000 plant species. Exempting genetically modified seeds, which are prohibited from the collection, the vault has the capacity for 2.25 billion seeds.

Most of the world's seed banks were established in the 1970s and 1980s as it became clear that the Green Revolution, while increasing global food supply, was also reducing genetic diversity. The United Nations Food and Agriculture Organization (FAO) estimates that 75% of crop biodiversity has already been lost. Though it is difficult to quantify what this means, it is widely understood that conserving agricultural biodiversity is the best protection against future blights like pests, diseases, and climate change. As well as its practical function, the Svalbard seed bank's concrete form, designed by architect Peter Søderman, and its cathedral-like window by artist Dyveke Sanne, function as powerful symbols of our anxious times.

See Also: Fertilizer Production Plant (140), GIS Crop Harvester (142), Frozen Zoo (262)

78°14’07.9”N 15°29’28.6”E

100 m

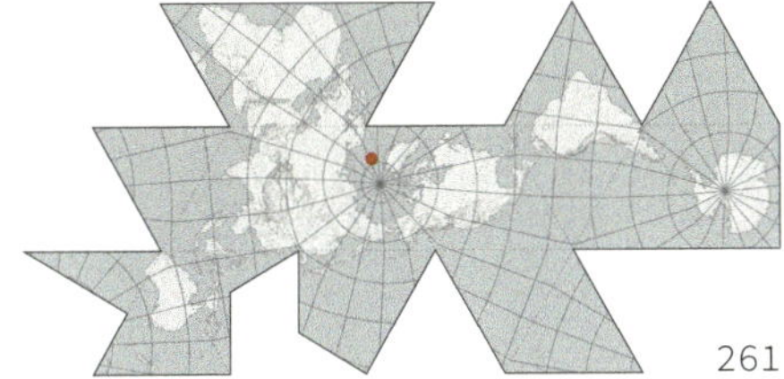

Frozen Zoo

California, United States

It was the Persians who first gathered animals into *pari-daiza* (walled gardens), not, however, so they could be admired and protected, but so they could more conveniently be hunted. So too, the Romans were fond of collecting exotic animals only to then slaughter them for entertainment in the colosseum. The first recorded menagerie—where animals were sustained for viewing—was in the Tower of London in the 13th century. This was followed by the spectacular menagerie at the court of Versailles in the 17th century, but it wasn't until the 19th century that zoos started to proliferate as urban attractions for the general public. In the 20th and 21st centuries zoos have rebranded themselves as scientific institutions serving the higher purpose of conservation. As such, all contemporary zoos wrestle with the conundrum of having to incarcerate animals in order to protect them, and struggle to find the right balance between entertainment, education, and zoological research.

The Frozen Zoo gets around the traditional zoo's contradictory nature by avoiding living animals altogether. Instead, at the Frozen Zoo the only thing in captivity is an animal's genes and the only thing to see are cryogenic canisters. Starting in the 1970s, the Frozen Zoo was the brainchild of geneticist and pathologist Kurt Brenirschke at San Diego Zoo's Beckman Center for Conservation Research. With mixed results, various test cases from the Frozen Zoo have been born. The challenge for these test-tube animals is not only to be born without birth defects, but to learn how to survive and then pass that knowledge on to their offspring.

From Frankenstein's monster to Jurassic Park, the warning is that only God, (or, if you prefer, evolution) has the power to make life, and we interfere with this power at our own risk. Now, however, if we are to preserve life from an extinction event paradoxically being caused by us, it seems we have no choice but to intervene. Of course, both Frankenstein's monster and Jurassic Park come with artistic license, but in contemporary biology truth can be at least as strange as fiction. For example, the idea of bringing back the woolly mammoth from frozen DNA in Siberia—a project known as Pleistocene Park—is very real. The frightening thing about this frozen ark is not what monstrosities it might give birth too, but the fact that for its contents to be thawed out, the world will have become an ecological ruin.

See Also: The Eden Project (50), Pleistocene Park (184), Svalbard Global Seed Vault (260)

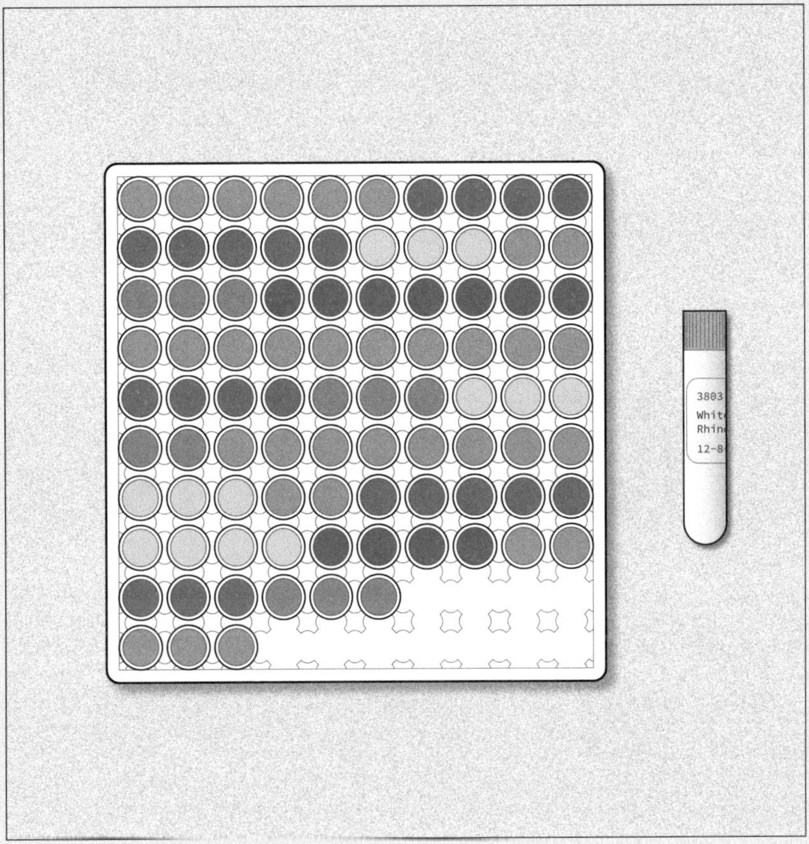

32°44’10.7”N 117°08’57.8”W

5 cm

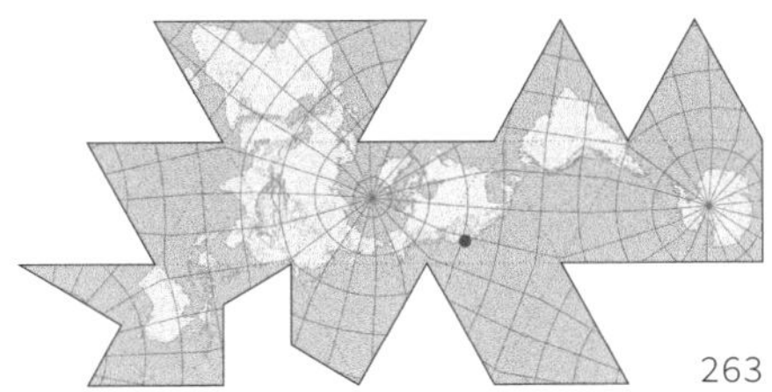

Instruments

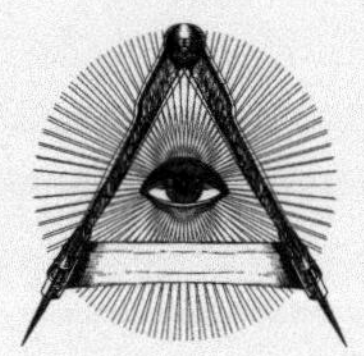

Deploying techniques developed over billions of years of evolution, our bodies function as hypersensitive instruments constantly registering and translating a flood of stimuli. It is only by processing this sensory information through taste, touch, vision, hearing, and smell that we can survive in, and make some sense of, the world around us. The sensory apparatus of the human body has now been extended and enhanced through technology to reach all corners of the world.

For example, in 240 BCE, with the simplest of instruments and most elegant of experiments—two sticks casting shadows in two distant places measured at the same time—Eratosthenes proved the earth was round. Through telescopic observation, Galileo proved what Copernicus had already surmised in 1543—that the cosmos was heliocentric, not geocentric. Today, Voyager 1 sends back little beeps from 14 billion miles away and we can see light arriving from the very birth of the universe itself. We can also 'see' inside the atom, measure the movements of tectonic plates, track cancer cells, and, perhaps most importantly, gauge the number of carbon molecules in the atmosphere. The faith vested in instruments is the belief that to measure the world is to know it, and to know it is to potentially control it.

The instruments that matter most right now for us as tourists of the Anthropocene are the ones planted in the living tissue of the earth. For it is these instruments (sensors) that provide us with feedback about the rapid environmental change that is occurring around us, and in part because of us.

What these instruments are telling us is that the earth system, on which we depend for our survival, might now be careening out of control. And while history teaches that we can't control nature or predict the future, we can at least react to the stimuli and attempt to control ourselves. This is how nature becomes culture and how culture learns that it is nothing without nature.

Microchip
International

In 1822, English inventor and mathematician Charles Babbage tried to build a 'Difference Engine'—a machine he claimed would make calculations without error. Before the government gave up on the project and cut his funding, the (hand-cranked) engine had grown to 2.4 meters tall, weighed 15 tons, and had 25,000 metal parts. Undeterred, Babbage then conceptually designed a second machine, a programmable 'Analytic Engine' replete with memory and branching logic. Although it wasn't built in his lifetime, it is generally regarded as the first computer and in a pyrrhic victory for Babbage, in 1989 the British Museum built the Difference Engine exactly to his specifications and it worked perfectly!

The early computers of the 20th century were, like Babbage's machines, behemoths that filled large rooms. The turn toward making computers small began in 1947 when a group of scientists at Bell Telephone Laboratories developed point-contact transistors, leading to Jack Kilby's portable calculator in 1967. This was followed a year later by Robert Noyce's invention of the microprocessor, where transistors and resistors were etched onto a tiny 'chip' of wafer-thin semiconducting material, such as silicon or germanium.

Although digital consumer products have tended to get smaller over time, in order to perform massively complex calculations and simulations of things like climate change or global pandemics, we need very big machines—the so-called supercomputers. Supercomputers are ensembles of many computers working together in parallel configuration. The biggest and best in the world today is Japan's Fugaku petascale supercomputer in Kobe. A vast room of black boxes, it can reach around 500 petaflops of processing power at any one time, meaning it can conduct about 500 quadrillion operations a second.

Of course, Fugaku, or any computer for that matter, can far exceed what any individual human brain could ever calculate, but for all its processing might Fugaku's mental capacity is only about 40% of what a human brain can process. For a computer with today's technology to rival a human brain it would need to be as big as a city block, and would require a power plant for its energy and a river to cool its circuits. Given this, it is extremely unlikely that a human mind will be fully downloaded into a computer any time soon, as Hollywood and some futurists would have it. On the other hand, microchips have entered human bodies for medical and other reasons, and the line between innate and digitally enhanced intelligence is becoming increasingly blurred.

See Also: Apple Park (48), Data Center (164), Agbogbloshie E-Waste Site (242), Smartphone (270)

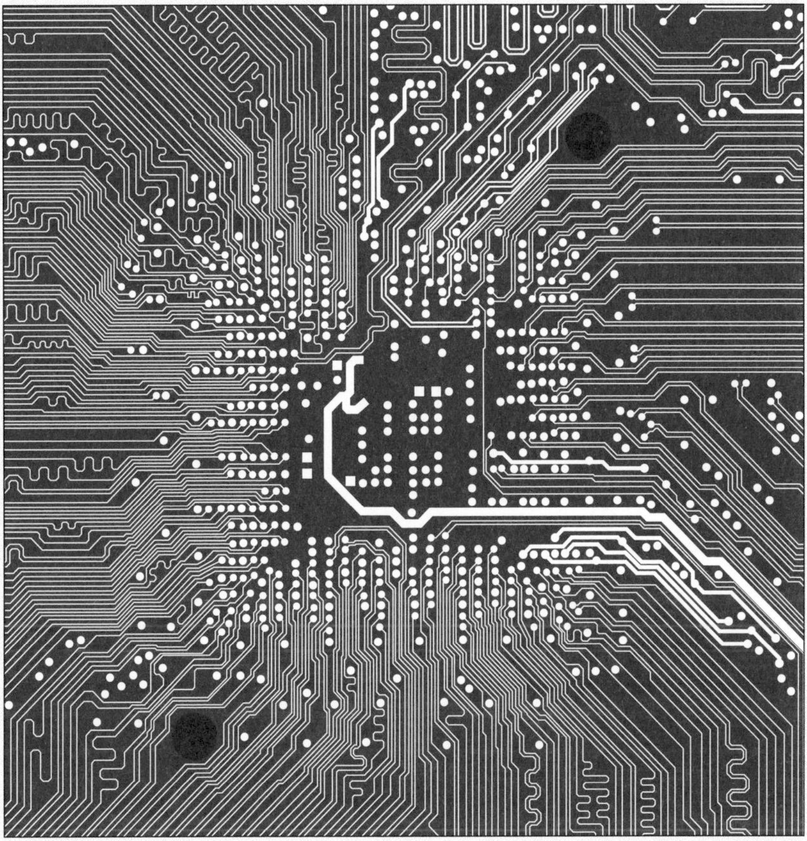

32°44’10.7”N 117°08’57.8”W

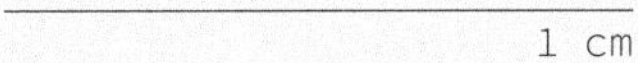

1 cm

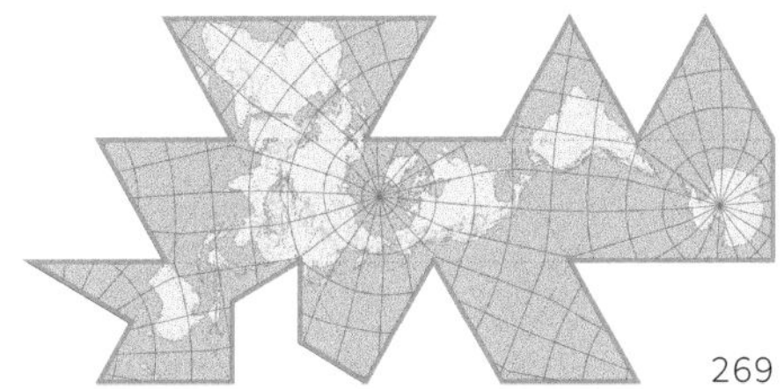

Smartphone
International

A smartphone is a hand-held, mobile communications device that enables humans to communicate with one another and access the internet. Since the debut of the iPhone in 2007, over 14 billion smartphones have been sold worldwide, primarily in countries where consumers can afford the average $750 price tag, plus the phone and data plans they then require.

The development of the smartphone was enabled by the recent miniaturization of transistors down to submicron levels, a transition from analog to faster digital wireless (mobile) networks, and the invention of the lithium-ion battery. Their commercial success is due to consumer desire to be both connected and mobile in a world where local person-to-person relationships have expanded into, if not been entirely replaced by, a global, digital sense of community. Digital technology has also been successful because it has been able to create an aura around itself that is clean and green. It is worth noting, however, that a 129-gram phone requires 34 kilograms of ore to be mined by industries with reputations for exploitation and pollution. Similarly, the global black market in recycling electronic goods through impoverished sectors of society in the Global South is disturbing. In response to some of this, Apple's iPhone 13 reportedly uses 100% recycled rare earth elements. Apple is also using upcycled plastic water bottles for its antenna lines and the company aims to completely remove all plastic packaging by 2025. Apple also promises to be entirely carbon neutral by 2030, though we have yet to discover what this will truly mean in practice.

Many studies have explored how mobile devices have influenced human behavior and social norms. For those born in the 21st century who know nothing different, the smartphone is an essential—not to say natural—extension of their minds and bodies, and even a temporary separation from the device can cause anxiety. For a minority of critics, the device and the social media platforms it provides access to are a narcissistic threat to the authenticity of face-to-face communication and causal to a range of emerging social pathologies.

See Also: Apple Park (48), Data Center (164), Agbogbloshie E-Waste Site (242), Microchip (268)

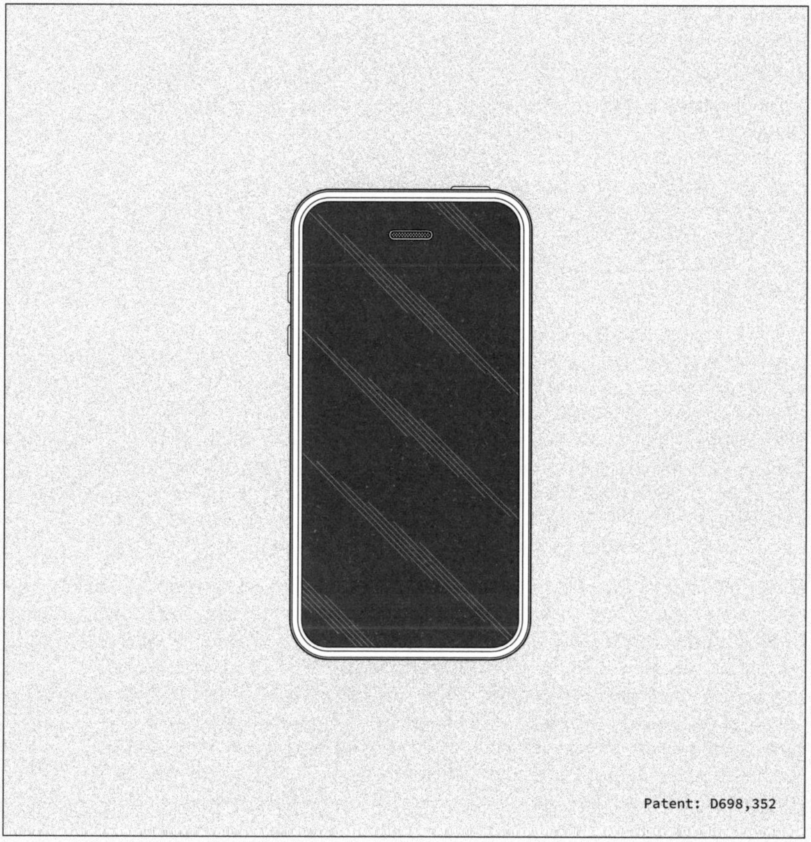

Patent: D698,352

32°44’10.7”N 117°08’57.8”W

5 cm

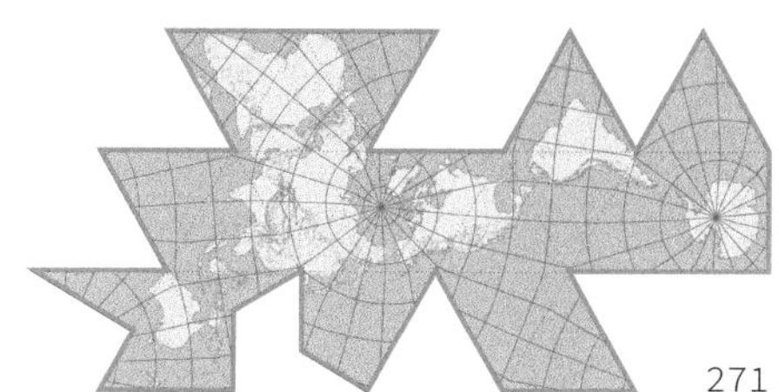

Magnetic Resonance Imaging

International

Although there are ancient Indian and Chinese records of anatomy, and unpublished Greek studies purportedly from as far back as the 4th century BCE, it was Galen of Pergamon in the 2nd century CE who first systematically created a compendium of human anatomy. Based on extrapolations from his work with animals and wounded gladiators, Galen's work was detailed but ultimately inaccurate. His descriptions were somewhat advanced by Islamic physicians such as Avicenna in the 11th century and the Jewish polymath Maimonides in the 12th century.

It was Leonardo da Vinci in the 15th century who, with better access to cadavers, made the first really accurate human anatomical images. Da Vinci laid the aesthetic groundwork for Andreas Vesalius, a Belgian who, in the following century, was able to dissect and analyze corpses consistently and objectively. The publication of his complete account of the human body *De Humani Corporis Fabrica Libri Septem* (*On the Fabric of the Human Body*) in 1543 laid the solid foundation for the discipline of modern anatomy. In the centuries to follow, in the name of science, custom-built theatres for dissections (of dead humans) and vivisections (of live animals) became commonplace.

In the 21st century, instead of using scalpels to open windows to the workings of the human body, we have MRIs—magnetic resonance imaging machines. MRI machines have enabled the study of the human body, living or dead, in unprecedented detail. The way MRIs work is that the machine's heavy-duty magnets, coupled with radio waves, affect the behavior of hydrogen atoms in a body. These can be detected and translated into cross-sectional and three-dimensional images. These images don't just show bones and tissue as with x-rays, they can record body functions in real time. They can also peer into the folds of the human brain.

If you can lie still, suppress the claustrophobia, and tolerate the heavy metal noise, an MRI machine can provide you with highly detailed imagery of your entire body. Although they probably will be one day, MRIs are not yet like photo booths for cheap, fast, personal use. If you do happen to find yourself in an MRI machine it probably means something is wrong with you; but better to be slid into its magnetic tube than to be hoisted onto the vivisection table to get a look at what it is. Whereas other advanced body imaging such as PET scans (positron emission tomography) and CT scans (computerized tomography) can reveal an increasing array of cancers, MRI imaging is the crucial instrument for reengineering our broken bodies.

See Also: Landsat (300)

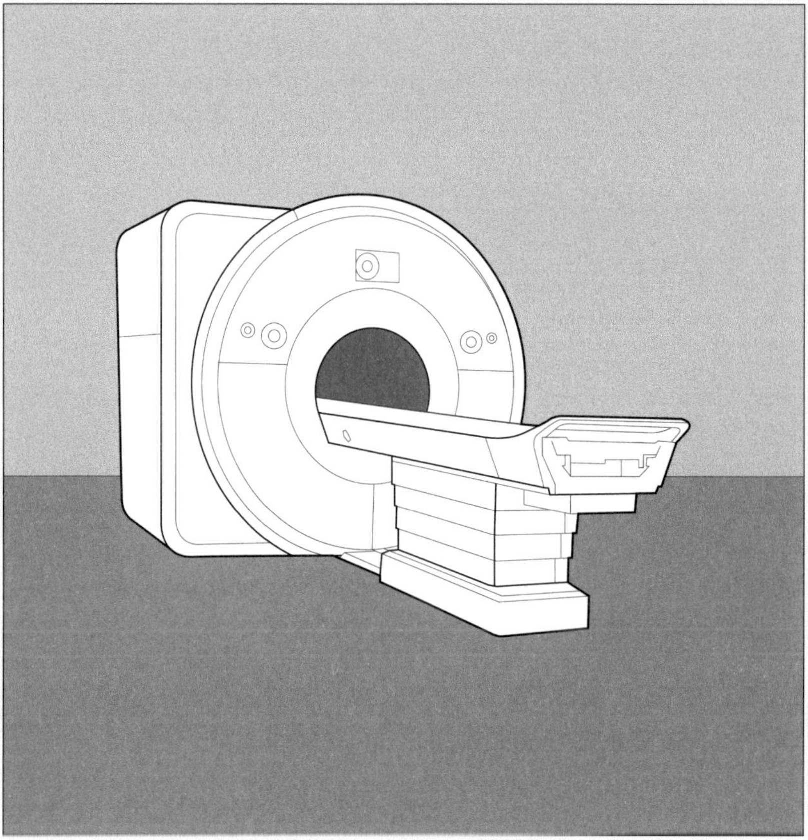

32°44’10.7”N 117°08’57.8”W

1 m

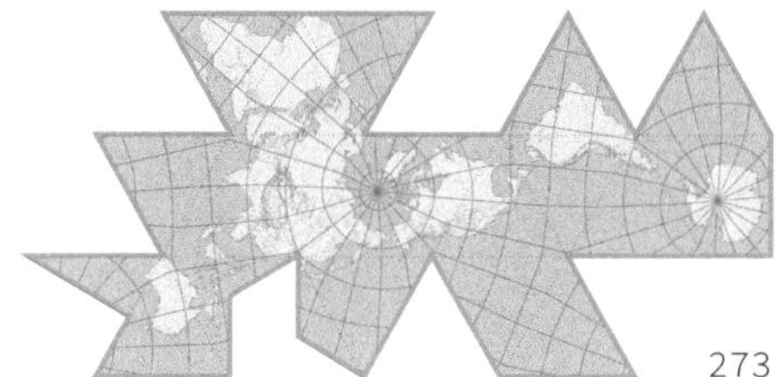

Large Hadron Collider

France & Switzerland

Starting in 1954 with the maxim that it would never do research for the military, the European Center for Nuclear Research (CERN) concerns itself with the study of interactions between subatomic particles using an instrument called a Large Hadron Collider. The collider is a cluster of magnetic, subterranean, vacuum tunnels inside of which particles are accelerated close to the speed of light and smashed into one another. The collisions occur in four detectors spaced out along the collider, which is 27 kilometers long and 100 meters underground across the border of France and Switzerland. Each of the four detectors has specialized capabilities to help physicists sort through the shrapnel of the collisions in the hope of finding new clues as to the mysterious inner workings of matter. The purpose of this is to try to discover how the universe built itself and how it holds itself together.

In the collider, beams containing 300,000 billion hadrons (particles containing quarks, such as protons and neutrons) stream in opposite directions at a speed of 11,245 laps per second. At this speed a particle travels 303,315 kilometers or 7.5 times around the earth in one second. The particles are so minuscule that the chance of any two colliding has been described as shooting two needles from 10 kilometers apart and expecting them to hit head on. The collider's *raison d'etre*, however, is that it massively increases the odds of this occurring; indeed, it can guarantee it. At full tilt, the collisions in the collider equate to the force of two trains hitting head-on at a speed of 150 kilometers per hour concentrated into a tiny space. The energy produced in these collisions is apparently similar to those that existed a trillionth of a second after the Big Bang, in something called the quark-gluon plasma.

Famously, the researchers at CERN recently discovered the Higgs boson, the 17th particle as predicted by the Standard Model—the collection of theories that embodies our current understanding of particle physics. The Standard Model is, however, far from providing a complete picture of the nature of matter. We still don't know how the four main forces—gravity, electromagnetism, and the strong and weak forces—interlock, nor do we know what makes up the 95% of the mass of the universe that we can't see, the so-called dark matter and its related dark energy. To help crack open these riddles, an even larger collider is now being planned.

See Also: Super-Kamiokande Neutrino Detector (276)

Gex

Meyrin

46°14’01.7”N 6°02’46.7”E

5 km

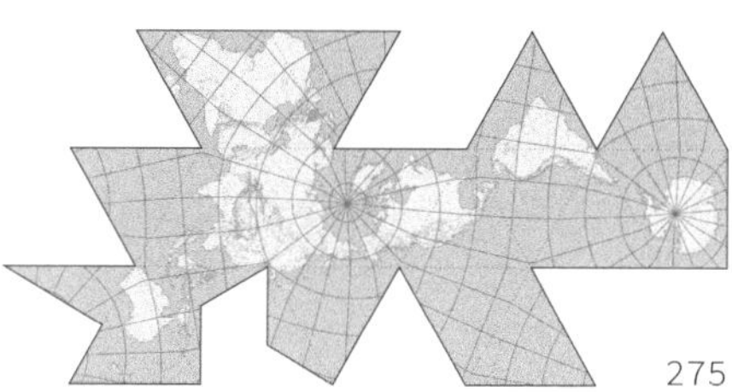

Super-Kamiokande Neutrino Detector

Mount Ikeno, Gifu, Japan

Embedded one kilometer below the surface of Japan's Mount Ikena is an instrument designed to detect neutrinos, some of the smallest particles in existence. Produced by nuclear fusion occurring in the sun, neutrinos are almost massless and can pass through matter at near the speed of light. As you read this, neutrinos are streaming through your body, indeed, they are constantly streaming through the entire planet. Most other particles, including light and cosmic radiation, cannot do this.

Scientists cannot see a neutrino as a thing unto itself, but they can see the result of its occasional interaction with other particles as it whizzes by. Seeing these results is the sole purpose of the Super-Kamiokande, a ten-story-tall cistern filled with pure water and lined with over 11,000 glass bulb reflectors. The Super-Kamiokande is an environment especially created so that nothing ever happens; or rather, when something does happen, it can't be anything other than a neutrino interacting with the water as it passes through. This interaction is recognized by flashes of so-called Cherenkov radiation, something that specifically occurs when a neutrino interacts with a molecule of water. Through the reflectors, which detect the radiation, scientists can know the trajectory and so-called 'flavor,' of the neutrino.

By understanding how neutrinos change their flavor and interact with other matter, scientists hope to understand the phenomenon of leptogenesis, the fundamental asymmetry between matter and antimatter in the universe. The fact that neutrinos have an infinitesimally small bit of mass is most likely the reason for this asymmetry, and probably the reason why the universe has any matter at all. Because neutrinos, unlike other subatomic particles, cannot be broken down into any further parts, they are considered the absolute building blocks of matter. In other words, neutrinos probably hold the key to understanding how this universe created matter in the first place.

See Also: Large Hadron Collider (274)

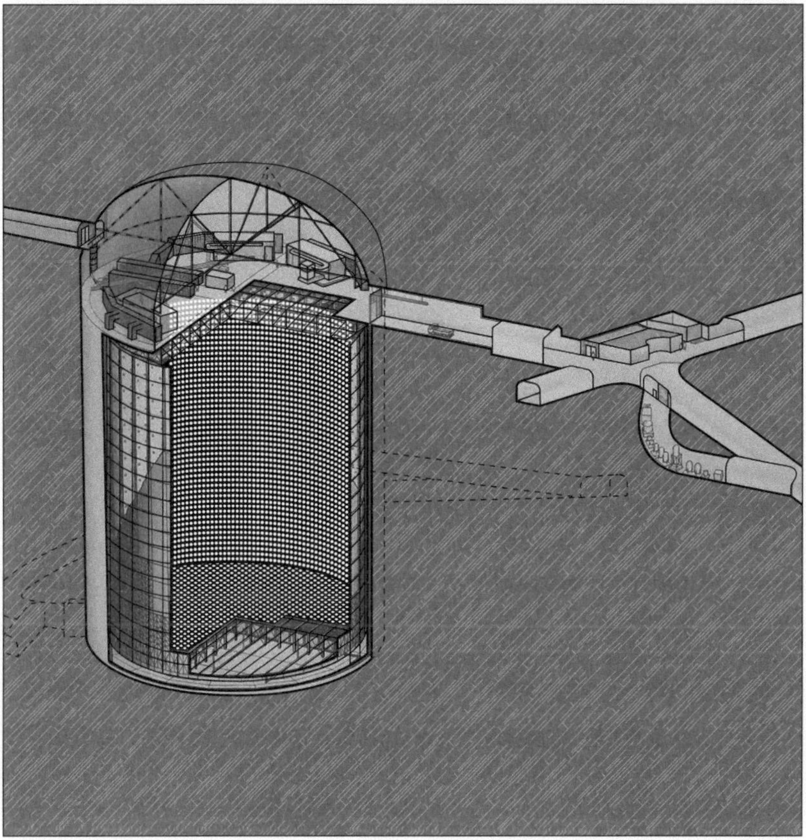

36°25’32.6”N 137°18’37.1”E

40 m

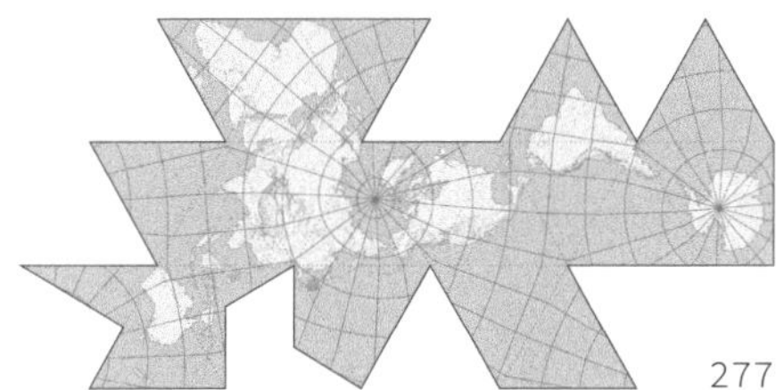

Thermonuclear Experimental Reactor

Saint-Paul-lès-Durance, France

In the south of France, an international team of scientists from 35 countries is building an experimental machine that weighs as much as the Titanic to perform something called the 'deuterium-tritium operation.' With the prize of clean and sustainable energy as the inspiration, the International Thermonuclear Experimental Reactor (ITER) will attempt, through this operation, to do synthetically here on earth what stars do naturally in the heavens. The ITER fusion reactor is not designed to make power and feed it into the electrical grid, it is only a research project, a step in a much longer process toward ultimately creating a viable fusion reactor that would produce cheap, clean, plentiful electricity.

In this experimental method to create fusion power, a doughnut-shaped device heats two isotopes of hydrogen deuterium and tritium to 150 million degrees Celsius, merging them into a plasma ten times hotter than the Sun. The plasma is contained by magnetic fields generated by coils kept at 4° Kelvin above absolute zero, the point at which particles that normally make heat through their movement grind to a halt. Around this is the added insulation of the largest vacuum chamber in the world. With the deuterium-tritium operation not scheduled until 2035, it might be the middle of the century before there is enough evidence to support fusion reactors as a viable option for the generation of electricity,

In most attempts at fusion, the energy input has been greater than the energy output, but in a major breakthrough at the Lawrence Livermore National Laboratory in California in 2022, a small power gain was achieved. The ITER, however, hopes to achieve a 10-fold power gain. This means, for example, that by inputting 50 MW, fusion would produce 500 MW for a 400 to 600-second-long pulse. At this rate, within ten minutes such fusion would produce nearly as much energy as some land-based wind farms produce in a year. If these kinds of numbers are ever achieved, then fusion could well save a carbon-saturated, energy-hungry world just in the nick of time. At least that's the hope.

See Also: United Downs Geothermal Well (152), Fântânele-Cogealac Wind Farm (154), Bhadla Solar Park (156), Chernobyl Reactor #4 (200)

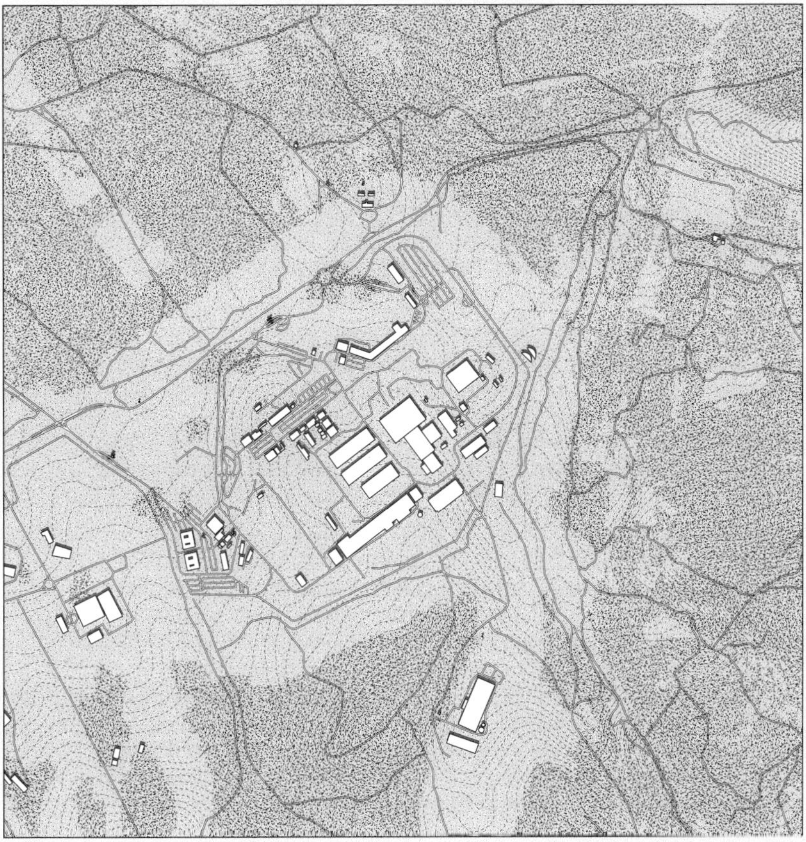

43°42’29.9”N 5°46’38.7”E

1 km

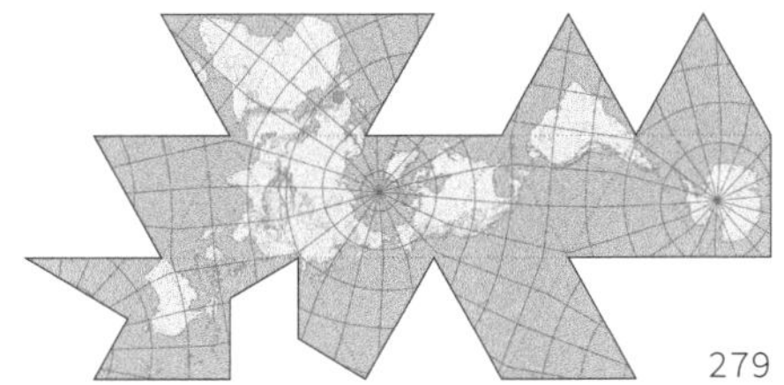

Mauna Loa Baseline Observatory

Hawaii, United States

Rising 4,170 meters above the Pacific Ocean, Mauna Loa (long mountain) is the largest active volcano on earth. And perched right on top is the world's oldest instrument for measuring carbon dioxide (CO_2) levels in the atmosphere. The Mauna Lao Baseline Observatory was established by the United States Weather Bureau in 1956 and directed by Charles David Keeling until his death in 2005, whereafter his son, Ralph Keeling, assumed the directorship. The observatory has measured atmospheric CO_2 levels consistently and accurately since 1958.

Publishing his first data in 1960, Keeling suggested that the world's CO_2 levels were steadily rising and that this was probably due to burning fossil fuels. By the 1970s the data he gathered formed what is now known as the Keeling Curve, quite probably the most frightening representation of the biophysical world ever produced. The curve shows CO_2 levels rising from 313 parts per million in March 1958 to 420.78 in June 2022. In other words, it shows humans slowly, but surely, cooking a planet.

Keeling was not the first person to say that levels of atmospheric CO_2 were rising—that honor can be shared among the late 19th-century chemist Svante Arrhenius, the early 20th-century amateur British meteorologist Guy Stewart Callender, and, in the mid-20th century, Keeling's boss at the Scripps Institute of Oceanography, Roger Revelle. But it was Keeling who—through his own custom-made infrared gas analyzer—really proved CO_2 buildup beyond doubt. He also discovered that CO_2 levels change seasonally; they rise in winter and drop in summer. Rightly, he surmised that this was due to the cycle of vegetation growth in spring and decay in autumn taking place on a planetary scale. In effect, Keeling discovered and measured the rhythm of the earth breathing.

Because of Keeling's persistence, often without government support for his work, we now know the 'inconvenient truth' of climate change. Because of Keeling's rigor, Mauna Loa is a towering monument to the scientific method. With its volatile weather above and churning lava below, it is also a monument to the precarity of the Anthropocene.

See Also: Direct Air Carbon Capture Plant (158), Global Sea Level Rise Monitoring (282)

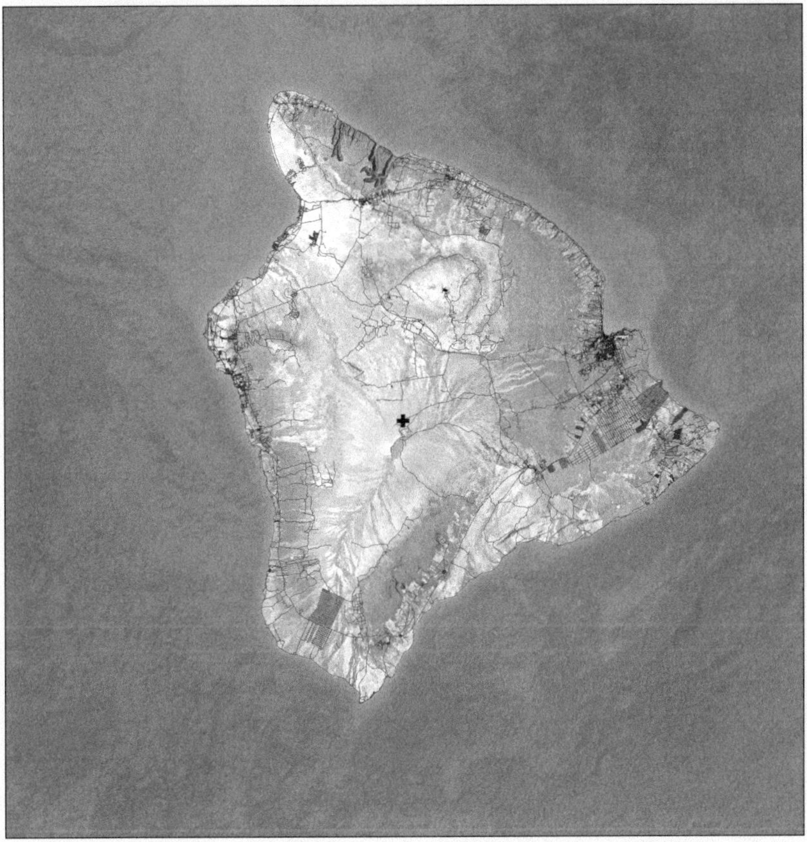

19°32’10.3”N 155°34’34.7”W

100 m

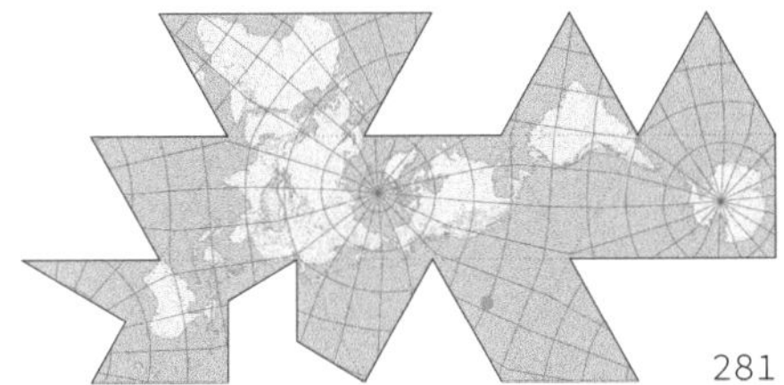

Global Sea Level Rise Monitoring

International

If the earth had been a perfect sphere, the ocean would evenly cover the entire planet to a depth of about 4 meters. Because of topographic variation, however, the oceans cover just over 70% of the earth's surface.

The level of the ocean changes in relation to the periodicity of ice ages and how much water is locked up as ice. For example, sea level is now 120 meters higher than it was 20,000 years ago when a far icier world than ours had vast land bridges, allowing species to migrate around the world. Inversely, in warmer periods the oceans have been anywhere between 6 and 30 meters higher than where they currently are. If all the earth's ice were to now melt, sea level would rise by something in the order of 70 meters. This of course would reshape the world and completely drown most major cities and their infrastructure.

Because of global warming, sea levels are currently rising by about 3.3 mm (+/- 0.3 mm) per year. The rate of change is also apparently accelerating. If it continues as such, the Intergovernmental Panel on Climate Change predicts between 0.6 and 1.1 meters of global sea level rise by 2100 (about 1.5 centimeters per year). To monitor this change, the Global Sea Level Observing System was established in 1985 by the Intergovernmental Oceanographic Commission of UNESCO. As indicated on the map opposite, the Global Sea Level Observing System contributes to the Global Ocean Observing System through the collection of data gathered from 290 tide gauges sited on coasts and islands around the world.

Adapting to rising sea levels involves four general strategies: first, the construction of defensive structures such as sea walls and levies; second, creating so-called nature-based solutions that involve a combination of preserving and reconstructing coastal landscapes so they absorb rising waters and buffer settlements from storm surges; third, designing buildings and infrastructure that rise above incoming waters; and fourth, mass retreat from the coastline. Ultimately, it's the latter that will have to happen, and governments will have to plan this retreat in a rational and timely manner. How exactly to do this is becoming one of the most complicated urban planning conundrums of the times.

See Also: Ocean Dead Zones (252), MOSE Floodgates (254), Mauna Loa Baseline Observatory (280)

10,000 km

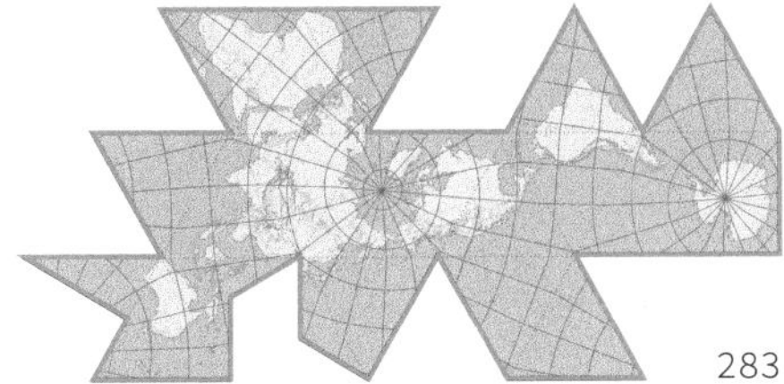

Fendouzhe Deepwater Submersible

International

In November 2020, China reported that it had broken its national record for the deepest manned dive into the Mariana Trench in a new titanium submersible called Fendouzhe, or 'striver.' Using sound waves to navigate in the dark, Fendouzhe touched down at 10,908 meters below sea level and three divers spent about six hours using its robotic arms to collect samples.

China has been conducting manned deep-sea exploration since 2012. The purpose of these expeditions is ultimately to discover new resources. Ye Cong, the chief designer of the submersible, said that it will help China draw a better 'treasure map' of the deep sea. Commentary posted to the People's Daily WeChat account, a news outlet that is understood to be the Communist Party's official mouthpiece, discussed global competition to find and mine rare earth resources from the seafloor as an important motivator for their deep-sea research program. Rare earth resources are used to make high-tech products like smartphones, and missile and radar systems. China already produces many of these commodities and is looking to the ocean to maintain its dominance.

The ocean floor is governed by the International Seabed Authority (ISA), an autonomous international organization established under the 1982 United Nations Convention on the Law of the Sea. The ISA's purpose is to mitigate the damage of seabed mining, not prevent it altogether. Delegates from 168 member states convene every year to identify where mining will be permitted, issue licenses, and draft a Mining Code containing technical and environmental standards. The Code was expected to be issued in mid-2020, but nothing has been released to date.

Once the Mining Code is released it will likely open up large sections of the seafloor to mining. It is expected that vast areas of seafloor will be dredged every year and that China will likely be the first country to start this work. Mining the seafloor may reduce some of the negative environmental and social impacts associated with rare earth mining on land, but the potential ramifications of destroying underwater ecosystems are not well studied or understood. Fendouzhe is the forward scout of a new frontier of extraction.

See Also: Polymetallic Nodule Extractor (168)

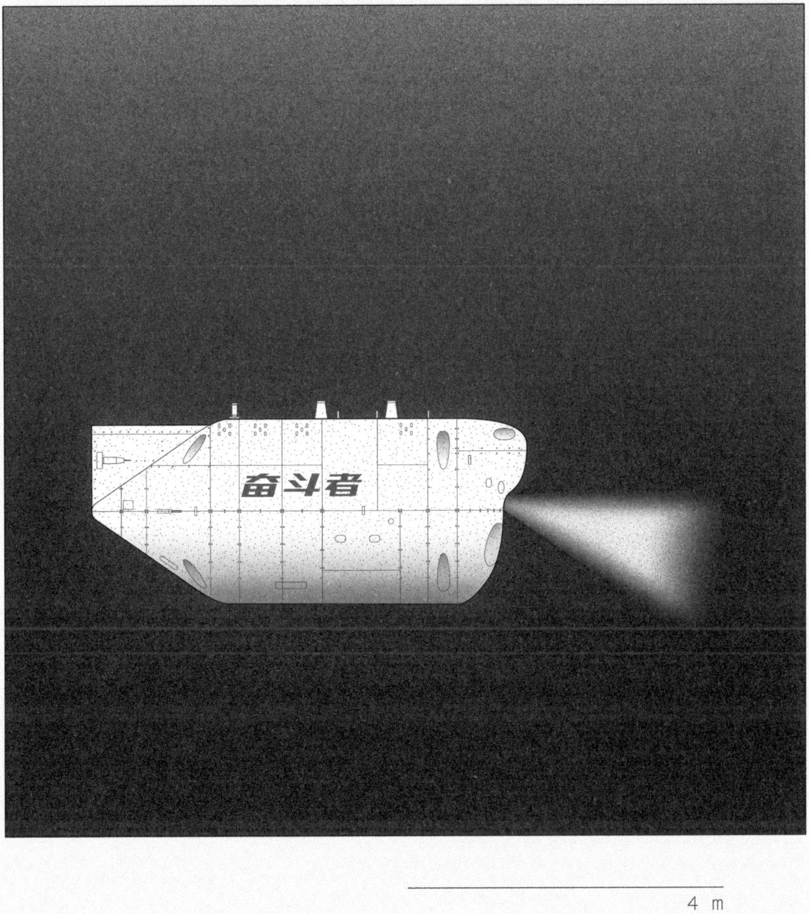

4 m

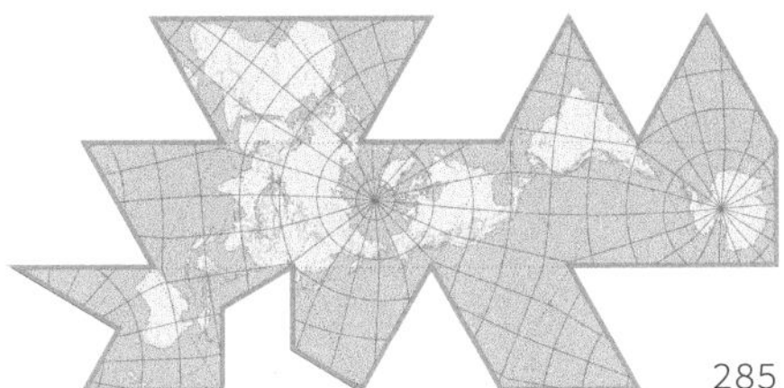

Greenland Ice Core Project
Greenland

A key to understanding how the earth system works as a whole and then working out how we might better fit into it, is to understand the carbon cycle—specifically, how carbon is exchanged between, and held within the atmosphere, the soil, plants, and, above all, the oceans. When atmospheric carbon dioxide (CO_2) levels are high, plants are big, oceans levels are high and temperatures warm. Inversely, when CO_2 levels are low, the earth hibernates in ice ages. The rhythm of ice ages coming and going is the fundamental rhythm of life on earth.

However, now that we have upset that rhythm nothing could be more important than trying to understand the consequences. To do this, predictive models of future climate behavior are extrapolated from our knowledge of past conditions. Logically, the more accurately the historical climate record is known, the greater the veracity of our forecasting is likely to be.

One way to gain accurate readings of climate history is to drill core samples from ice. Ice sheets form in layers as each snowfall is compressed. In this layered ice are trapped small bubbles of air, each preserved as a snap-frozen record of the atmospheric conditions of the very day the bubble was formed. Along with the ice itself, these bubbles are time capsules that we can tap into to learn about climatic conditions at the time.

At several kilometers deep, the Greenland ice sheet is in this way an archive of the last three million years of environmental history and from 2007 to 2012, scientists from 14 nations converged on this icy archive. Over five years, the North Greenland Eemian Ice Drilling Project (NEEM) recovered over 2.5 kilometers of core samples reaching back 120,000 years to the Eemian interglacial period. By studying the bubbles from the Eemian, scientists have been able to confirm that an increase in CO_2 levels similar to our own led to significant temperature increase. The NEEM is just one of a number of ice core projects, shown opposite, undertaken since the 1990s to uncover important historical climate data frozen in time.

Whereas under normal circumstances the earth system would just continue to freeze and thaw, the concern now is that it could get locked into a thaw and, through positive feedback, cross a point of no return and continue to overheat. This would add another dead planet to the solar system—only this time, one created by us.

See Also: Mauna Loa Baseline Observatory (280), Halley VI Research Station (288)

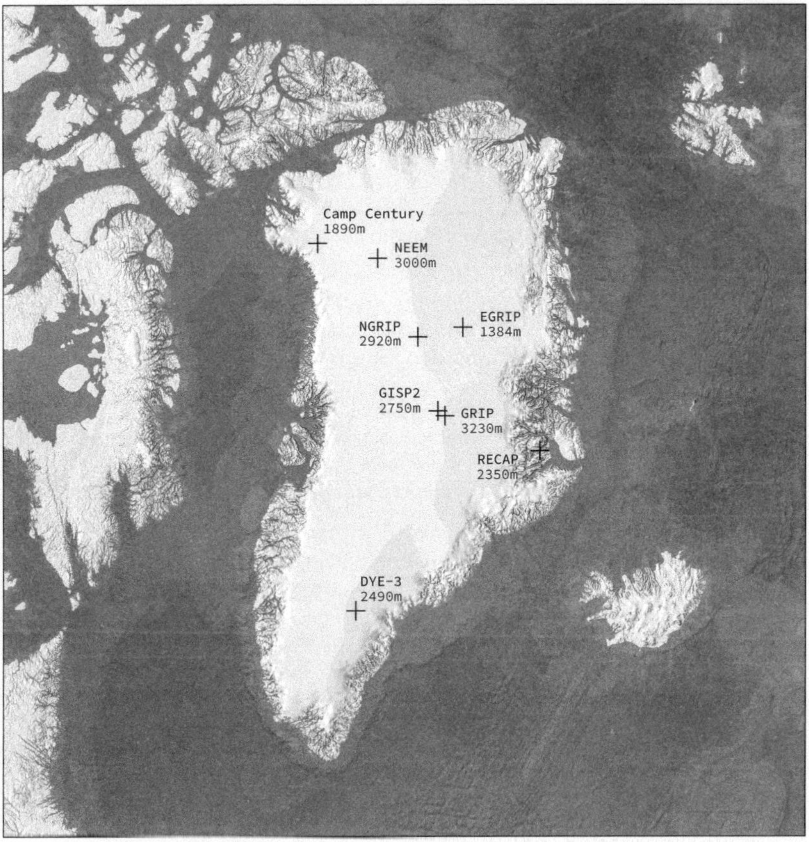

Camp Century
1890m

NEEM
3000m

NGRIP
2920m

EGRIP
1384m

GISP2
2750m

GRIP
3230m

RECAP
2350m

DYE-3
2490m

79°00’00.0”N 50°00’00.0”W

1,000 km

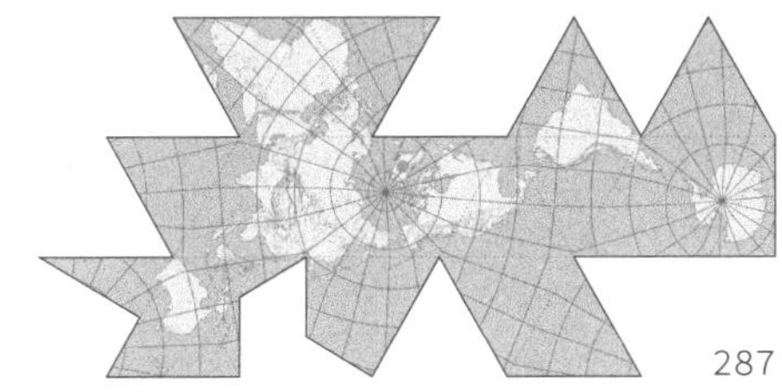

Halley VI Research Station

Brunt Ice Shelf, Antarctica

In 2004, the British Antarctic Survey launched a design competition for a new structure to replace the Halley V research station on the 130-meter-thick Brunt Ice Shelf, which floats on the Weddell Sea in Antarctica. Faber Maunsell and Hugh Broughton Architects won the competition with a modular design, featuring buildings with hydraulic legs and retractable skis to keep the modules above the snowline and make them easy to move should the station need to relocate.

Built in Cape Town by Petrel Engineering, the Halley VI research station officially opened on February 5th, 2013, and consists of eight modules that include laboratories, accommodation for up to 70 people, energy generation, a command module, and a garage to service an array of machines used to conduct field work and move the modules if necessary. The design features spaces that encourage social interaction, using a color and materials palette to enliven the more than 100 days of total darkness that residents of Halley VI experience every year, and the many days where venturing outside is ill advised.

With an array of instruments inside and beyond the station itself, scientists at the facility study climate change, sea level rise, space weather, ice shelf dynamics, and atmospheric conditions contributing to the Space Environment Impacts Expert Group, SPACESTORM, and the World Meteorological Organization's Global Atmospheric Watch. Halley VI also measures the gradual drift of the Brunt Ice Shelf itself so as to learn more about so-called calving events, when ice sheets break up. Scientifically, Antarctica is of interest as an index of global climate change and also because its extreme environment makes it akin to conditions on other planets. Most notably, in 1985 the hole in the ozone layer was discovered from Halley.

Currently, there are more than 70 permanent research stations in Antarctica, representing more than 29 countries. Each country has signed the Antarctic Treaty, committing to the preservation of the ecosystem and peaceful cooperation with other signatories. The 'international continent' of Antarctica is ostensibly politically neutral, but with so many countries vying for research time and territory, it is also increasingly scrutinized as a resource that could be subject to sovereign or commercial claims. Perched on tenterhooks, as if it has indeed landed on another planet, Halley VI creates a striking image of human presence in an unforgiving and austere icescape, one that is slowly, but surely, melting.

See Also: Mauna Loa Baseline Observatory (280), Greenland Ice Core Project (286), Critical Zone Tree (290)

75°34’04.8”S 25°30’60.0”W

100 m

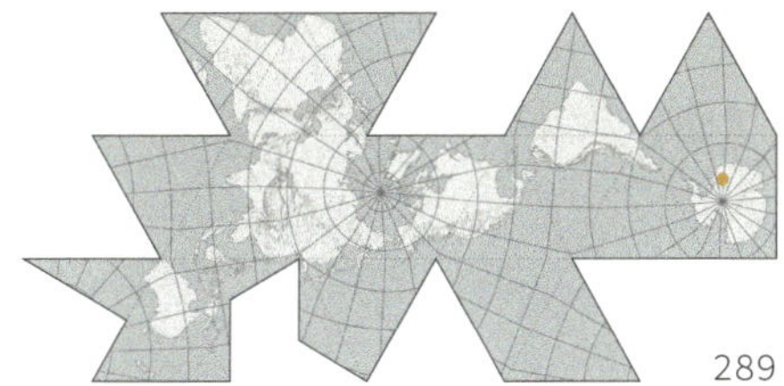

Critical Zone Tree

Sierra National Forest, California, United States

Measured from the top of the tallest tree to the bottom of the water table deep in the ground, the so-called 'critical zone' is the thin bandwidth of living tissue that enwraps the earth. Combining research on the complex interactions between the atmosphere, water, soil, and living things, critical zone science seeks to not only to explain how the earth functions as a self-regulating whole, but also to understand how human actions affect it.

Critical zone science is conducted through a global network of cooperative Critical Zone Observatories (CZOs)—field stations in both urban and remote landscapes where coordinated experiments on various aspects of the earth's biophysical functions are undertaken. For example, in the Southern Sierra Critical Zone Observatory within the Sierra National Forest in California, scientists outfitted a white fir (*Abies concolor*) with hundreds of instruments to better understand how the tree gathers, uses, and releases water in a variety of different conditions. Fitted with an array of sensors, the whole tree becomes a kind of advanced technological instrument.

Instead of studying things as objects in isolation, the subject of the science being conducted through the instrument of the Critical Zone Tree is the relationship between the tree and its environment—how they reciprocally contribute to, and are dependent on, one another. Sadly, due to infestation by bark beetles, which have flourished in unusually dry conditions related to climate change, the fir died before the six-year study of its physiology could conclude. It was 65. Back in the calmer days of the Holocene, the fir would have lived to the ripe old age of at least 300.

CZOs also fit into a global network of International Long Term Ecological Research (ILTER) sites and an affiliated community of researchers. Whereas the science of ecology once focused on the wild places without humans, many ILTER sites are now including the human component in their analysis. This is an important conceptual shift because it situates humans as a part of nature. It is also possible to see the emergence of CZOs and ILTERs as the beginning of a new science of the earth system, which treats the earth and humanity as symbiotic—even as one body. In his rhetorical analysis of climate change, atmospheric chemist and author of the Gaia hypothesis James Lovelock has said the earth now has a fever. But instead of seeing humanity as a virus, Lovelock urged that we take responsibility and become what he referred to as "doctors of planetary medicine." The CZOs will help provide the right diagnosis.

See Also: Mauna Loa Baseline Observatory (280)

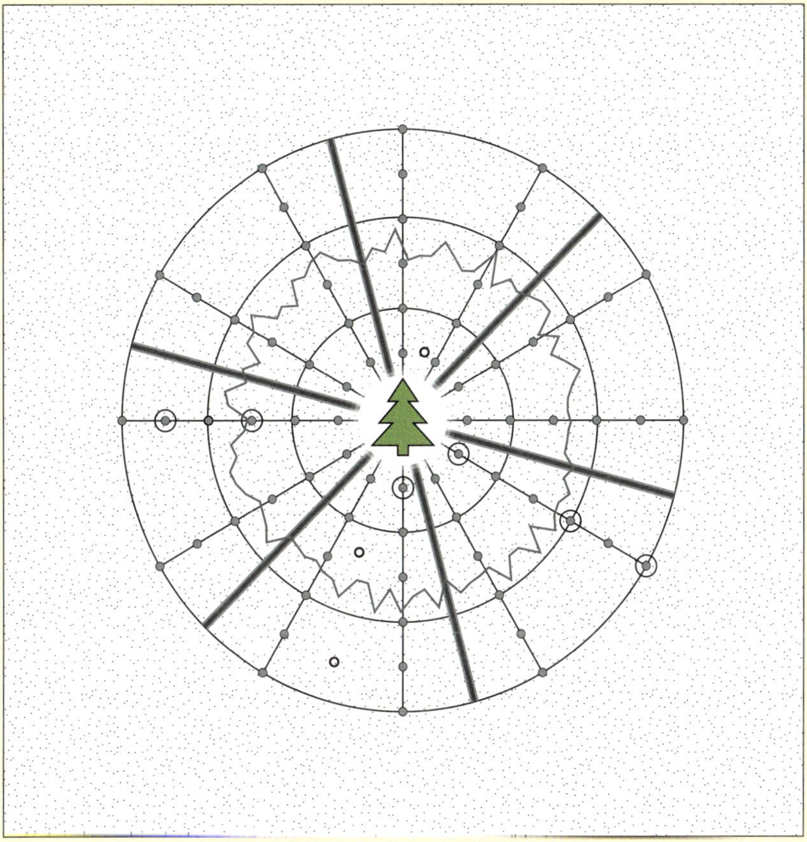

37°04’04.9”N 119°11’39.9”W

1 m

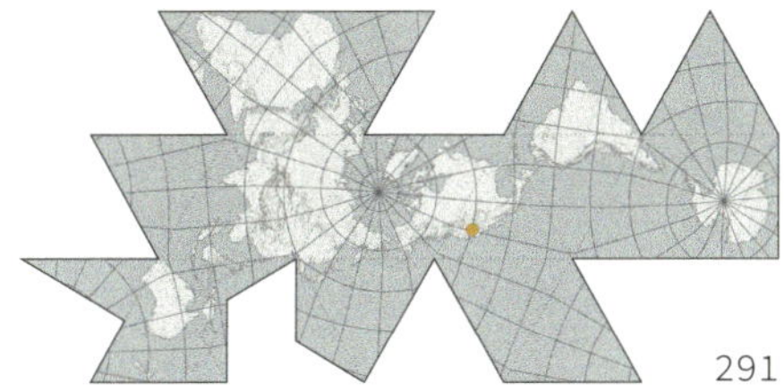

Terrestrial Metatron

Moulis, France

Look at a map of your city, your region, your country, or the entire planet and you will notice fragments of green space. Apart from domesticated animals and some vermin that can live in dense urban environments, most wild animals and plants—collectively referred to as biodiversity—exist within these green fragments, or 'habitat patches' as they are referred to by landscape ecologists. The long-term survival of the biodiversity in these patches is in part dependent on and shaped by the degree of connectivity between patches so that the gene pool can migrate over time, in response to different pressures and opportunities. This is especially important in a time of accelerated climate change.

It is the stated aim of the United Nations Convention on Biological Diversity, ratified by 196 nations, to create better connectivity between patches of habitat. Because most landscape is dominated by human uses, however, achieving said connectivity is no simple thing. Not only are the politics and economics of changing land use challenging, but also very little is known about how specific species behave under pressure and what they really need in terms of patch size and connectivity to not only survive, but thrive. To complicate matters, what might be good for one species might not be good for another, and in some cases connectivity can open vectors for invasive species and disease. In short, ecologists need to know much more about species migration so that this knowledge can be translated into the spatial planning of our cities, regions, nations, and ultimately the planet.

The Terrestrial Metatron at the Theoretical and Experimental Ecology Station in Moulis, France, is an experimental field established for exactly this purpose. The Metatron comprises 48 enclosures in which species' composition, temperature, light, and humidity can be controlled. Each enclosure is connected to others via small passages that can also be controlled. In this way the Metatron serves as a simulator of landscape conditions and how species interact with them. Since 2015, given the limitations of its size, experiments in the Metatron have predominantly focused on studying how butterflies and lizards move through the system, but many more species could be studied if a similar system was built at a larger scale. In essence, the Metatron is a learner's kit that helps scientists decide how best to reconstruct landscapes so they have good patches and the right forms of connectivity to sustain more biodiversity.

See Also: Yellowstone to Yukon Initiative (58), Banff Wildlife Crossings Project (64)

43°01’28.5”N 1°05’29.1”E

100 m

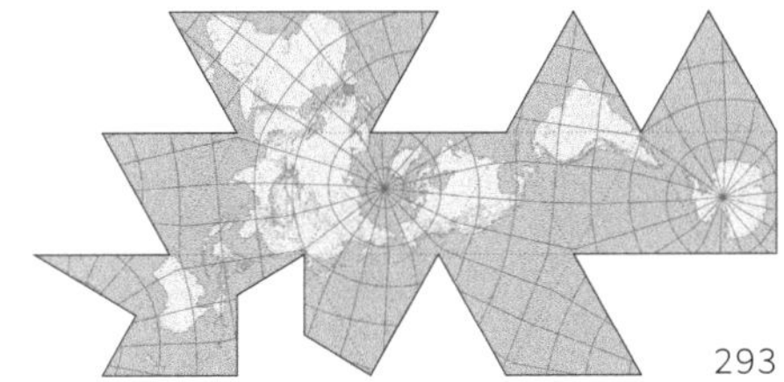

Wildlife Tags

International

For most of human history prior to the agricultural revolution, humans had to track animals and exhaust them before finally moving in for the kill. Today we track animals not to kill them, but to keep them alive. We seek to understand their migration patterns, their habits, and their responses to environmental change to conserve them from extinction. One of the keys to understanding and appreciating wild animals, particularly in an age of rapid climate change, is to know where, when, and why they move. Understanding these patterns can translate into land use decisions that better integrate the needs of wild animals with agriculture, industry, and urbanization.

Unless impeded by human infrastructure, all animals range over certain territory. These movements occur daily, seasonally, and over centuries. They take place locally, regionally, and in the case of birds and large marine life, at a planetary scale. While indigenous people know the movements of animals they depend on—and know how to conserve them—urban humans have very little knowledge of or sensitivity to the other species that are constantly moving around them and are impacted by their infrastructure.

Technology in the form of wildlife tags helps build this knowledge. The design of the lightweight tags generally consists of a solar battery, a waterproof casing, a radio transponder, and an antenna attached to an animal through gluing, clamping, or a band. The radio signals emitted by the tag can then be picked up by towers or hand-held receivers. One of the most sophisticated examples of wildlife tracking is the ICARUS (International Cooperation for Animal Research Using Space) initiative, which uses radio tags that call to a module on the International Space Station 400 kilometers above the surface of the earth.

Tracking systems can also use the animal as a carrier to detect and monitor environmental factors such as temperature and light, magnetic fields, oxygen levels, and other factors related to both terrestrial and marine environments. Where data from tracking can be most helpful is in relation to rewilding programs where animals are moved by humans from one habitat to another, or where animals are reinstated to their habitats after rehabilitation from injury, reintroduction from captivity, or released into the wild after being rescued from poachers. In the case of the latter some conservationists would argue that it is the poachers who should be tagged.

See Also: Yellowstone to Yukon Initiative (58), Griffith Park (182)

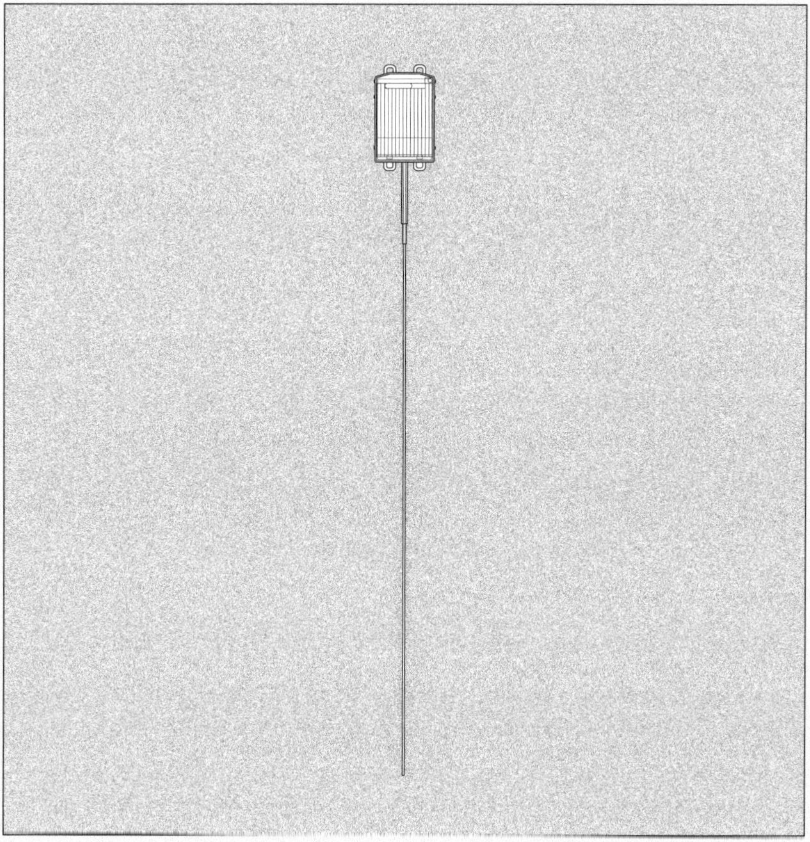

43°01’28.5”N 1°05’29.1”E

5 cm

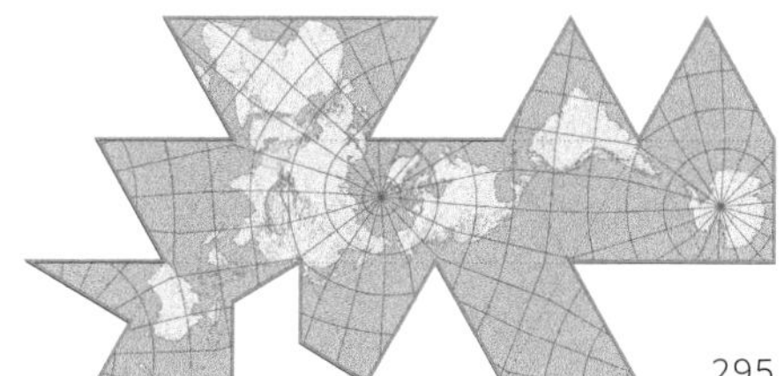

Roden Crater
Arizona, United States

Instead of making art objects, in 1966 James Turrell turned to light itself as the subject of his art. The way into Turrell's artistic oeuvre, should you wish to try it at home, is to look carefully at how a slither of light leaks into a room through a gap when it's darkened with curtains or blinds—the way it creates space, plays over surfaces, and dissipates. The interplay between controlled light and architectural volumes and how this can in turn affect our perception of space and time has preoccupied Turrell for his entire career. He has worked with these essential tools in galleries and specially constructed rooms the world over. His *magnum opus*, however, is the Roden Crater, an extinct cinder cone volcano located 75 kilometers from the town of Flagstaff in Arizona.

Turrell, a trained pilot as well as an artist, discovered the crater through aerial reconnaissance of the Southwest in 1974. With help from the DIA Art Foundation, he purchased the land three years later and has been developing it as a naked-eye observatory ever since. To his exact specifications, a series of tunnels, passages and chambers have been carved into the crater for the sole purpose of capturing and filtering particular sources of light. The various chambers align with and concentrate the light from the moon, the north star, and celestial events such as summer and winter solstices.

Turrell's mission is to curate a precise series of spatial relationships between the sensorial apparatus of the human body and cosmic radiation. As he explains it, he is not trying to overwhelm viewers with the sublime immensity of space, but to create a heightened level of intimacy between the two. Monumentalizing such alignments is hardly a new idea in the history of art and architecture, but to produce such spaces today without any ideological or religious baggage, certainly is.

In doing this, Turrell is not romancing mystical chambers of yore, nor is he vainly invoking the European Renaissance where the human eye is situated at the center of the universe. On the contrary, as memorably demonstrated by art critic Robert Hughes, who concluded his epic study of American art, *American Visions*, lying on his back in the crater, Turrell's architecture of the earth offers an oblique and profoundly disorienting kind of intimacy between self and world.

See Also: Garden of Cosmic Speculation (86), Spiral Jetty (258), Very Large Array (298)

35°25’32.7”N 111°15’32.0”W

1 km

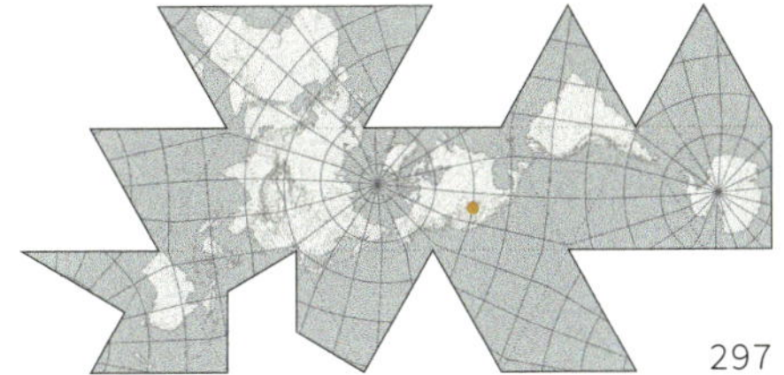

Very Large Array
New Mexico, United States

Located on the New Mexico Institute of Mining and Technology campus, the Very Large Array (VLA) comprises 27 radio telescopes (antennas), each 25 meters in diameter, arrayed along three 21-kilometer-long tracks forming a Y shape. The tracks enable the telescopes to be moved through a variety of observational configurations to optimize reception. The array's setting is crucial to its function. The landscape is arid, high-altitude desert surrounded by mountains and far from any cities. The mountains act as a protective boundary from the interference of radio waves, helping the VLA to listen for cosmic waves, which are billions of times fainter than broadcast radio waves. Also, because water molecules emit a similar signal to cosmic radiation, the antennae work best in arid environments with minimal humidity.

Since its construction in the 1970s, the VLA has been used for a range of important astronomical observations, but more recently the National Radio Astronomy Observatory has begun a collaboration with the SETI Institute (Search for Extraterrestrial Intelligence—a research non-profit founded by celebrity scientist Carl Sagan). A new system called the Commensal Open-Source Multimode Interferometer Cluster Search for Extraterrestrial Intelligence (COSMIC SETI) will be installed in the VLA to search for so-called 'technosignatures,' considered by SETI scientists to be sure signs of the existence of technologically advanced, extraterrestrial life.

Given the scale of the universe the odds are that there may well be life elsewhere. There is no guarantee, however, that it would be a form of intelligent life that uses technology in ways that our technology can recognize. And even if it did, the chances that the time of transmission would coincide with our time of reception in the universe's 14-billion-year time frame, is slim. That said, applying SETI's Drake Equation for calculating the odds of life similar to us existing in the universe, Director of the Hayden Planetarium Neil DeGrasse Tyson concludes there could be up to 100 radio-broadcasting civilizations just in our galaxy, and anything up to five billion beyond. We just can't hear them, yet.

See Also: Roden Crater (296), Voyager Spacecraft (306)

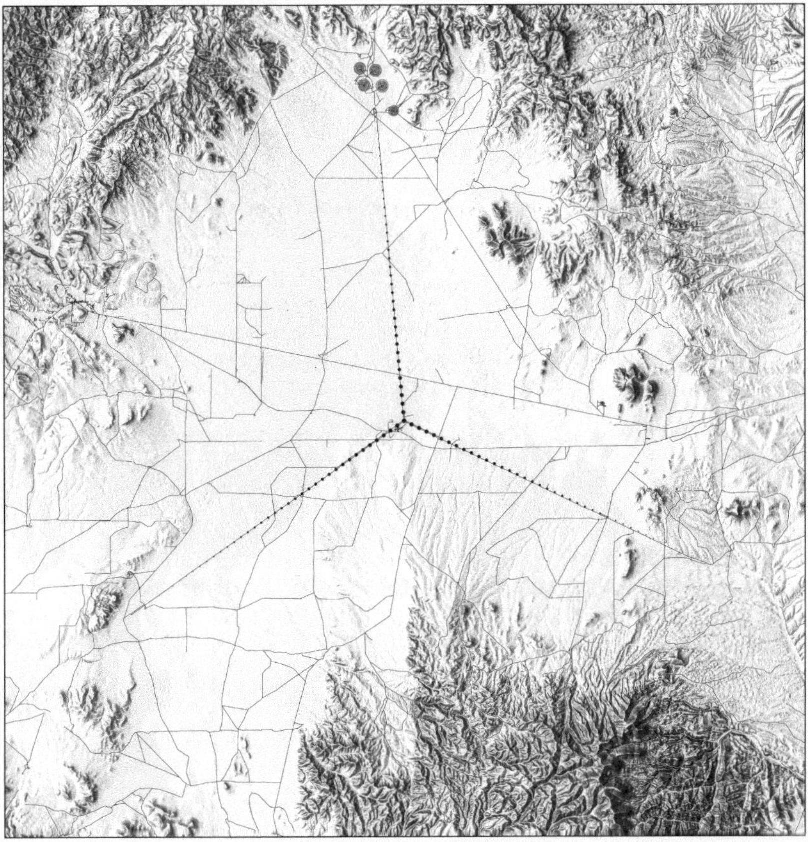

34°04’44.1”N 107°37’06.0”W

20 km

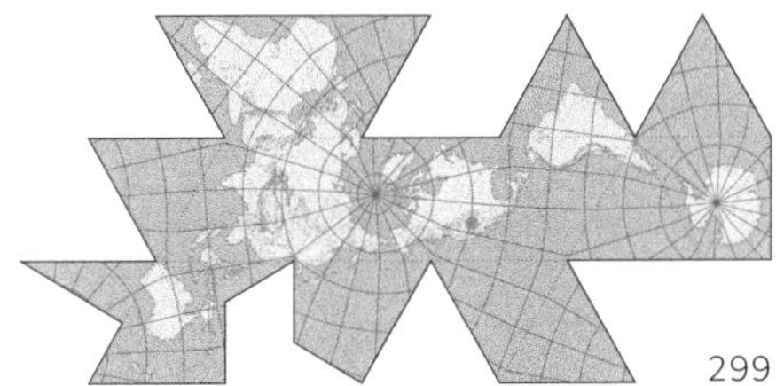

Landsat

Low Earth Orbit

It could be said that the most important discovery of the Apollo space missions in the 1960s was not the moon but the earth. The unprecedented view of the earth, known as 'the blue marble,' inspired a cultural revolution—one marked annually on April 22nd by Earth Day. It also inspired the United States Landsat program, the world's longest running program of methodically taking satellite images of the earth's surface.

Launched on July 23rd, 1972, Landsat 1 was the first earth-observing satellite to be placed in orbit with the express intent of monitoring the earth's changing surface. This of course sounds like global surveillance by a superpower, and in the hands of the military it is, but the Landsat images program also offers a full image of the earth's entire surface every 16 days as open-source information for anyone to use, for free.

Today more than 4,500 satellites orbit the earth and almost a quarter of them are for the purposes of looking back at the earth. The Landsat program is, however, particularly valuable because its historical imagery enables comparative analysis of how the earth has changed over the 50 years of its existence—a period of unprecedented human impact on the earth's ecosystem. When Landsat started in 1972 there were 3.9 billion people on earth, today there are 8 billion and counting.

Landsat data is gathered by detectors on the satellite that can sense a broader bandwidth of light than is otherwise visible to the naked eye. This data is transmitted to a receiving station on earth and converted into images, which can be studied to determine things such as plant health, surface temperature, fire and volcanic activity, snow and ice cover, soil and water quality, deforestation, agricultural expansion, desertification, and patterns of urbanization.

Due in no small part to images of the earth from outer space, humanity's sense of place is stretched from the local to the global and beyond. Landsat helps flesh out that which is in between and helps us make sense of our relationship to space and time, as well as the impacts we have on the ecosystem. It is important to recognize, however, that while Landsat images appear to lay the surface of the earth bare as incontrovertible evidence of our impacts, they only show effects, not causes. They show nothing of the complex cultural forces at work behind the spectral patterns they record; for that, you need to look around on the ground, with your own eyes.

See Also: The World (216), Magnetic Resonance Imaging (272)

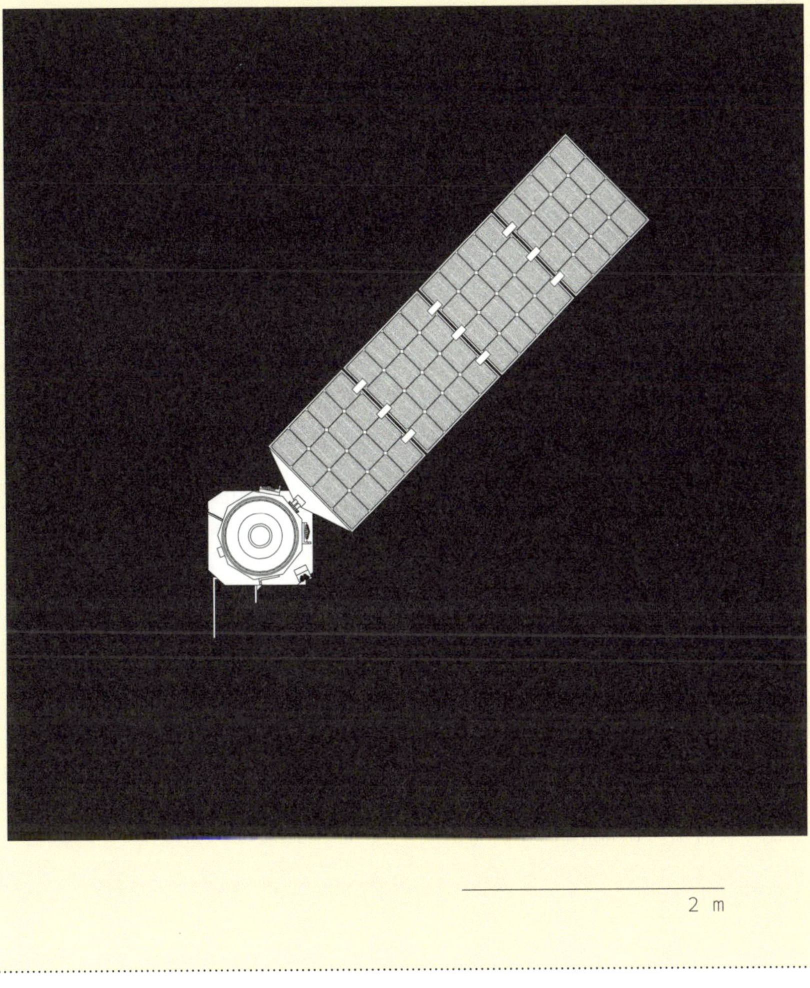

2 m

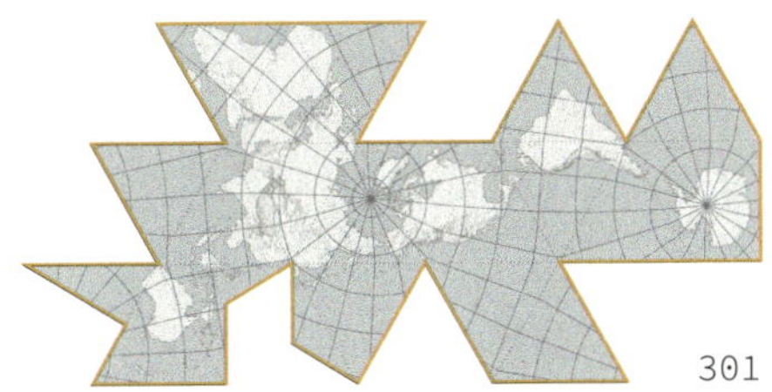

Space Garden
Low Earth Orbit

Traveling at close to 30,000 kilometers per hour, orbiting earth every 90 minutes, are two small gardens. These gardens are the size of suitcases embedded in the techno-labyrinth of the International Space Station (ISS). Rigged up to over 180 sensors and built-in cameras to transmit real-time telemetry back to NASA's Kennedy Space Center, environmental conditions in these gardens can be completely controlled so as to conduct experiments with plants in microgravity conditions. Originally known as the Lada system, after the Russian Goddess of the Spring, the gardens are now known as Advanced Plant Habitations using the PHARMER (Plant Habitat Avionics Real-time Manager in Express Rack) system.

For the history of gardens in space yet to be written, the first plants to have been jettisoned from the earth were single-cell green algae (chlorella) and the seeds of onions, peas, wheat, and corn onboard the satellite Sputnik 2 in 1957. The first terrarium containing a variety of plants was the 'Oasis' greenhouse on Salyut 1, the first space station launched by the USSR in 1971. In 1975, Salyut 4 took the honor of hosting the first vegetable garden in space and in 1982, on board Salyut 7, the first flower was cultivated inside its 'Phyton' growth chamber. The first space-farmers of note were Valery Ryumin of Salyut 6, who was renowned for his green thumb, and Valentin Lebedev who, during his 211 days on board Salyut 7, successfully grew peas, lettuce, tomatoes, coriander, and onions.

Just as life on earth was possibly catalyzed by the arrival of 'space pollen' some 4.5 billion years ago, many think now is the time to consciously relay the phenomenon of life to other barren planets. Elon Musk, for example, promises settlement on Mars by 2060 and the UAE's 'Mars 2117 Strategy' is a 100-year plan for more of the same. For humans to survive in space they will need to take parts of the earth with them, not least of all its plants. As they do on earth, plants in space will provide food, oxygen, and fuel. They will also sequester our carbon, clean our wastewater, and provide medicines.

That plants do all this work is remarkable, but also of interest to researchers is biophilia—the psychological benefits of growing and having contact with plants. In the homesick, claustrophobic world of space stations and outposts on barren planets, having a plant by your side will not only nourish your body, it might just keep you sane.

See Also: Biosphere II (126), Launch Complex 39 (174)

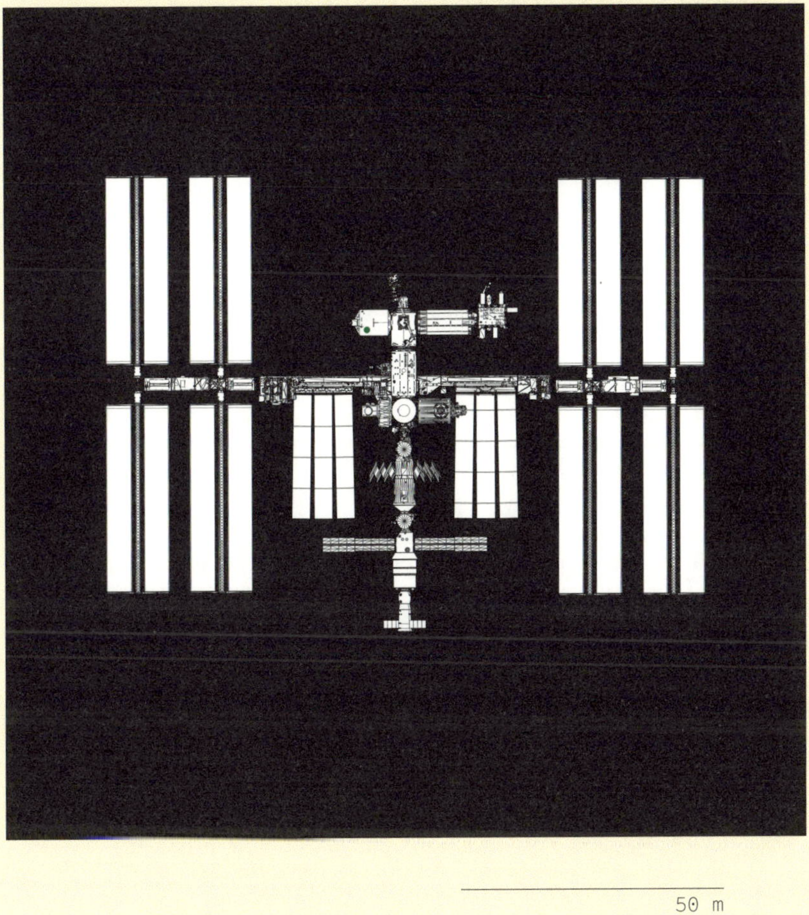

50 m

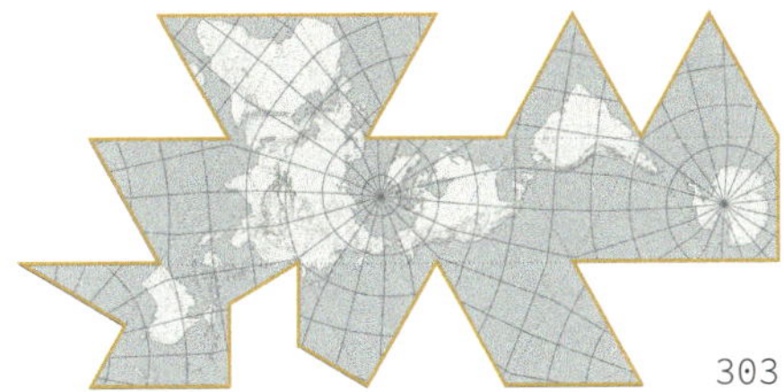

Perseverance Mars Rover

Jezero Crater, Mars

Having learned the basics of navigating rough terrain in the Mars Yard, a simulation of Martian landscape in the suburbs of Los Angeles, the first 'Rover' to be let loose on the red planet was 'Sojourner' on July 4th, 1997. Making Sojourner remotely operable on Mars was a technological breakthrough, but after a few weeks of inspecting some rocks with its one robotic eye, Sojourner refused to take any more instructions and is, as far as we know, permanently stalled in an area known as Ares Vallis.

In 2004, Sojourner was followed by its siblings 'Spirit' and 'Opportunity.' Both these rovers performed well for longer than expected, until the former became permanently bogged and the latter was, we think, swallowed whole by a ferocious Martian dust storm. These pioneers paved the way, so to speak, for 'Curiosity' in 2012. Curiosity is still operational and lauded for having identified organic molecules—a potential indicator of life—in the Martian regolith.

Curiosity has now been joined by 'Perseverance,' which boasts having the best set of eyes ever to see Mars firsthand and enough intelligence to learn from its mistakes. In other words, instead of just repeatedly pushing against say, a rock, Perseverance will go around it. It also has its own core sample drilling equipment, as well as a little helicopter that has already clocked 18 short flights. For those who dream of one day colonizing Mars, most important is that Perseverance also has an instrument for testing how oxygen could be manufactured in the otherwise asphyxiating Martian atmosphere.

The study area for Perseverance's field work is Jezero Crater, where it is now busy taking core samples. The samples Perseverance obtains are not only being tested immediately in its own on-board microlab, they are also being packaged by the robot for pick up by a future mission now in the planning, so that the samples can be returned to earth for more detailed analysis. In December 2021, scientists discovered from Perseverance's early samples that the bedrock of Jezero Crater is a volcanic rock that has interacted with water multiple times and also contains evidence of some organic molecules. These samples raise the question: Was there once life on Mars? Maybe. And will there yet be life on Mars? Maybe. Or perhaps, with Curiosity and Perseverance doggedly going about their work, there already is.

See Also: Biosphere II (126), Launch Complex 39 (174), Fendouzhe Deepwater Submersible (284)

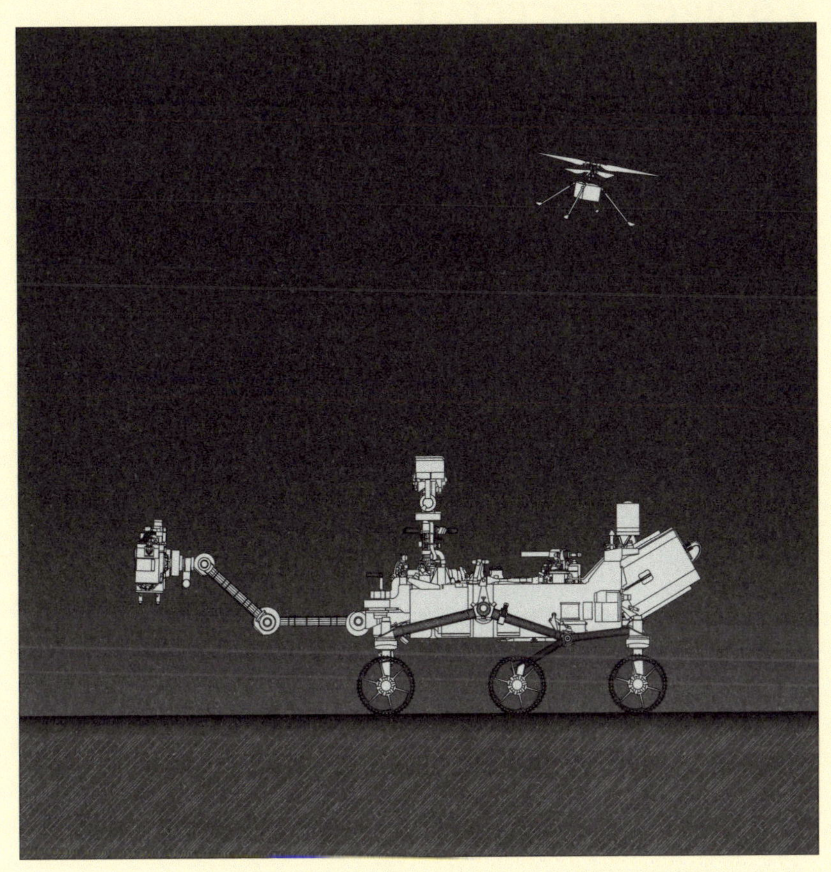

1 m

Voyager Spacecraft
Interstellar Space

NASA's Voyager program emerged from something most fitting to this book, called the Planetary Grand Tour. The Planetary Grand Tour involved sending two probes into space to take advantage of a propitious alignment of the outer planets that would give NASA much more bang for its exploratory buck. Voyager and Voyager 2 left earth in 1977 to get close-up images and conduct analyses of Jupiter, Saturn, Neptune, and Uranus. As well as the spectacular imagery of these planets they beamed back to earth, what most captures the public imagination is that the two Voyagers are continuing headlong into space with copies of the so-called Golden Record—a phonograph describing humanity's earthly presence in forms that we think an alien might understand.

We will lose contact with both Voyager and Voyager 2 very soon as they push on beyond our sun's gravitational bubble. Then, with a bit of luck, they will make it through the Oort cloud—a morass of comets and icy rubble—and, after about 40,000 years of dodging such obstacles, come into range of a few planets. Assuming they don't smash into those, then it should be pretty much plain sailing, into the void. Even if the capsules of the Voyagers are eventually blown away by cosmic dust storms, as is likely, the golden records themselves could continue to hurtle through space for a few billion years. By this time they will be distant memoirs of life on earth, because by that time the Sun will have exploded and incinerated the earth altogether.

Should an alien life form somehow pluck a 30-centimeter golden disc from the infinitude of space and then find a speck of the isotope uranium-238 encased on its surface, they should be able to backdate the postal date to 1977. Then, assuming they can comprehend the instructions engraved on its aluminum sleeve, they will be able to play the record. First, they will be greeted in 55 different languages, and then settle into an hour-and-a-half-long premiere of human culture. They will bear witness to humans eating pizza, making babies, dancing, shopping, and building things. They will marvel over leaves, snowflakes, dolphins, elephants, sunsets, and the Sydney Opera House. They will also hear music by Bach, Chuck Berry, and Australian Aborigines. They will hear crickets, dogs, birds, and finally, at the end of the record, they will hear the sound of a kiss goodbye.

See Also: Very Large Array (298)

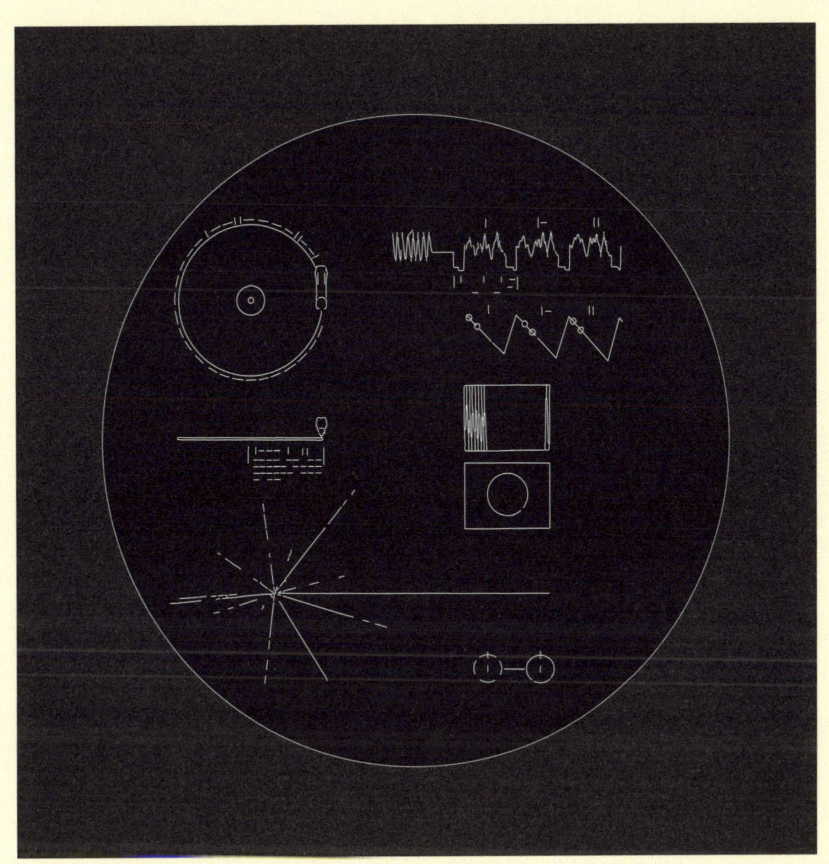

Acknowledgments

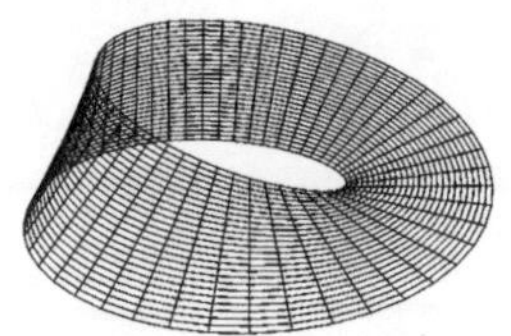

I would like to thank the students in my 2020 Culture of Nature class at the Weitzman School of Design at the University of Pennsylvania, who conducted some of the initial research and began the base plans of many of the places we visit on this tour. They are: Madeline Barnhard, Nicole Cheng, Jiajing Dai, Oscar Delgado, Yubing Ge, Audrey Genest, Zoe Goldman, Yuehui Gong, Bingtao Han, Shuyi Hao, Matthew Lake, Arisa Lohmeier, Olivia Loughrey, Daniel McGovern, Isobel Morrison, Aminah McNulty, Prakul Reddy Pottapu, Benjamin Regozin, Andrew Reichenbach, Priyanjali Sinha, Xiaomeng Sun, Qinyuan Tan, Zonghi Tang, Alexis Tedori, Florence Twu, Ari Vamos, Kelvin Vu, Qinhong Xu, Sujing Yi, Ling Zhang, Yining Zhang, and Dragana Zoric. Many thanks to LA+ Journal and Prakul Reddy Pottapu for the base image of the Great Pacific Trash Vortex.

Thank you also to my research assistants Aaron O'Neill and Alice Bell, and to my teaching assistants Rob Levinthal, Ian Dillon, Elliot Bullen, and Oliver Atwood, who assisted the students with their research and helped me reach the final list of destinations. Of this group I especially wish to acknowledge Oliver Atwood, who managed all the data and drafted the final collection of maps, plans, and images that illustrate this book. As is evident in the refinement of the drawings, Oliver brought great skill and precision to this task. Oliver, along with Tatum Hands and myself, was also instrumental in the design and layout of the book.

Thank you also to Henriette Mueller-Stahl of Birkhäuser for recognizing the value of this project and ensuring that it made it to press. Finally, as ever, I'm grateful to my editor and collaborator, Dr. Tatum Hands.

About the Author

Richard Weller is professor and former chair of landscape architecture and urbanism at the University of Pennsylvania, where he (together with Fritz Steiner) established the Ian L. McHarg Center for Urbanism and Ecology. He is co-founder (with Tatum Hands) and former creative director of *LA+ Interdisciplinary Journal of Landscape Architecture*, founding director (with Vladimir Sitta) of Australian design firm Room 4.1.3., and holds adjunct professorships at the University of Western Australia and the University of New South Wales. His work has been frequently awarded in international design competitions and exhibited internationally, including at the Guggenheim Museum in New York, the Venice and Rotterdam Biennales, the Museum of Contemporary Art in Sydney, the Isabella Stewart Gardner Museum in Boston, the MAXXI Gallery in Rome, the Canadian Design Museum in Toronto, and the Central Academy of Fine Arts in Beijing. His publications include *Room 4.1.3: Innovations in Landscape Architecture* (University of Pennsylvania Press, 2005), *Boomtown 2050: Scenarios for a Rapidly Growing City* (University of Western Australia Press, 2009), *Made in Australia: The Future of Australian Cities* (UWAP, 2013), *Transects* (ORO Editions, 2014), *Design with Nature Now* (Lincoln Institute of Land Policy, 2019), *Beautiful China: Reflections on Landscape Architecture in Contemporary China* (ORO Editions, 2020), *The Landscape Project* (AR+D Publishing, 2022), and *An Art of Instrumentality* (ORO Editions, 2023). 'The Atlas for the End of the World,' Weller's recent research work on biodiversity and cities, has been published in *National Geographic* and *Scientific American*, while his related research and design project to establish a 'World Park' is currently being considered for implementation by UNESCO.

Illustration Credits

Illustrations by Oliver Atwood